CHRISTIAN IDENTITY IN THE JEWISH AND GRAECO-ROMAN WORLD

Christian Identity in the Jewish and Graeco-Roman World

JUDITH M. LIEU

OXFORD
UNIVERSITY PRESS

OXFORD

UNIVERSITY PRESS

Great Clarendon Street, Oxford OX2 6DP

Oxford University Press is a department of the University of Oxford.
It furthers the University's objective of excellence in research, scholarship,
and education by publishing worldwide in

Oxford New York

Auckland Cape Town Dar es Salaam Hong Kong Karachi
Kuala Lumpur Madrid Melbourne Mexico City Nairobi
New Delhi Shanghai Taipei Toronto

With offices in

Argentina Austria Brazil Chile Czech Republic France Greece
Guatemala Hungary Italy Japan Poland Portugal Singapore
South Korea Switzerland Thailand Turkey Ukraine Vietnam

Oxford is a registered trade mark of Oxford University Press
in the UK and in certain other countries

Published in the United States
by Oxford University Press Inc., New York

© J. M. Lieu 2004

The moral rights of the author have been asserted
Database right Oxford University Press (maker)

First published 2004
First published in paperback 2006

British Library Cataloguing in Publication Data

Data available

Library of Congress Cataloging in Publication Data

Data available

Typeset in Imprint
by Regent Typesetting, London
Printed in Great Britain
on acid-free paper by
Biddles Ltd, King's Lynn, Norfolk

ISBN 0-19-926289-6   978-0-19-926289-2
ISBN 0-19-929142-x (Pbk.)   978-0-19-929142-7 (Pbk.)

1 3 5 7 9 10 8 6 4 2

PREFACE

THE seeds of this book were sown when I was asked to give a paper for a seminar on 'Identities in the Eastern Mediterranean in Antiquity' in honour of Fergus Millar, held at the Australian National University, Canberra (November 1997: the papers from the seminar were later published as *Mediterranean Archaeology* 11 (1998)). The challenge to reflect on my own specialism, early Christianity, in the company of historians of the ancient world, a challenge I had already encountered among my colleagues in the Department of Ancient History at Macquarie University, marked the beginning of an exciting journey from some relatively naive thoughts about identity to an awareness, if no less naive, of the complexities of the endeavour. I am grateful to initial respondents to that paper, those at the seminar and elsewhere, including, especially, Mark Brett (Melbourne) and Kath O'Connor (Sydney), for hints that were to prove very fruitful. Since then there have been many who, in response to papers on 'work in progress' or in conversation, have further stimulated my thinking; chief among these are colleagues and students in Ancient History at Macquarie University, and more recently those in Theology and Religious Studies at King's College London, and to them I also record my thanks. The anonymous readers for Oxford University Press also gave valuable advice. Yet this project also builds on my earlier interests, on the interaction between Jews, Christians, and their polytheistic neighbours, however we label them, both socially and in their representations of each other. I am fortunate in having had access to a range of good libraries in Sydney and London, without whose commitment to real books in a world of Information Systems and virtualia little of this could have been done. Particularly important have been the friends and colleagues outside the academic world whose interest and encouragement have confirmed me in my belief that seeking to understand Christian identity in the earliest centuries really does matter for today. Finally, as always, the mainstays of my life, Esther and Sam, have been my unfailing support.

J.M.L.

London
May 2003

CONTENTS

ABBREVIATIONS

AAR	American Academy of Religion
AGJU	Arbeiten zur Geschichte des antiken Judentums und des Urchristentums
AJA	*American Journal of Archaeology*
ANRW	*Aufstieg und Niedergang der römischen Welt*
ANZJS	*Australian and New Zealand Journal of Sociology*
BCNH	Bibliothèque Copte de Nag Hammadi
BETL	Bibliotheca ephemeridum theologicarum lovaniensium
BHTh	Beiträge zur historischen Theologie
BIS	Biblical Interpretation Series
BJRL	*Bulletin of the John Rylands University Library of Manchester*
BJS	Brown Judaic Studies
BZAW	Beiheft zur Zeitschrift für die alttestamentliche Wissenschaft
BZNW	Beiheft zur Zeitschrift für die neutestamentliche Wissenschaft
CBNT	Coniectanea Biblica. New Testament Series
CBQ	*Catholic Biblical Quarterly*
CRINT	Compendia rerum iudaicarum ad Novum Testamentum
CSCO	Corpus scriptorum christianorum orientalium
EH	Europäische Hochschulschriften
ET	English translation
FAT	Forschungen zum Alten Testament
GLAJJ	*Greek and Latin Authors on Jews and Judaism*, ed. M. Stern, 3 vols. (Jerusalem: Israel Academy of Sciences and Humanities, 1974–84)
GNB	Good News Bible
HdO	Handbuch der Orientalistik
HR	*History of Religions*
HTR	*Harvard Theological Review*
HUT	Hermeneutische Untersuchungen zur Theologie

ICC	International Critical Commentary
JbAC	*Jahrbuch für Antike und Christentum*
JBL	*Journal of Biblical Literature*
JECS	*Journal of Early Christian Studies*
JES	*Journal of Ecumenical Studies*
JFSR	*Journal for Feminist Studies in Religion*
JJS	*Journal of Jewish Studies*
JQR	*Jewish Quarterly Review*
JRA.SS	Journal of Roman Archaeology Supplement Series
JRH	*Journal of Religious History*
JRS	*Journal of Roman Studies*
JSJ	*Journal for the Study of Judaism in the Persian, Hellenistic and Roman Period*
JSNT	*Journal for the Study of the New Testament*
JSNT.SS	Journal for the Study of the New Testament Supplement Series
JSOT.SS	Journal for the Study of the Old Testament Supplement Series
JSP.SS	Journal for the Study of the Pseudepigrapha Supplement Series
JSS.M	Journal of Semitic Studies Monographs
JSSR	*Journal for the Scientific Study of Religion*
JTS	*Journal of Theological Studies*
LCL	Loeb Classical Library
LXX	Septuagint
MT	Masoretic Text
NCB	New Century Bible
NH	Nag Hammadi Codices
NHMS	Nag Hammadi and Manichaean Studies
NHS	Nag Hammadi Studies
NRSV	New Revised Standard Version
NTS	*New Testament Studies*
NT.S	Novum Testamentum Supplement
OECS	Oxford Early Christian Series
OECT	Oxford Early Christian Texts
OED	*Oxford English Dictionary*, 2nd edn. (Oxford: Clarendon Press, 1989)
OGIS	*Orientis Graeci Inscriptiones Selectae*, ed. W. Dittenberger, 2 vols. (Leipzig: Hirzel, 1905)

OTL	Old Testament Library
PEQ	*Palestine Exploration Quarterly*
PG	Patrologia Graeca
PL	Patrologia Latina
PMS	Patristic Monograph Series
PTS	Patristische Texte und Studien
RAC	*Reallexikon für Antike und Christentum*
Rech.Aug	*Recherches Augustiniennes*
REJ	*Revue des études juifs*
RevBib	*Revue biblique*
RevQ	*Revue de Qumran*
RSR	*Revue des sciences religieuses*
SBL	Society of Biblical Literature
SBL.MS	Society of Biblical Literature Monograph Series
SC	Sources chrétiennes
SHR	Studies in the History of Religions
SJLA	Studies in Judaism in Late Antiquity
SJOT	*Scandinavian Journal of the Old Testament*
S.JSJ	Supplements to Journal for the Study of Judaism
SNTS.MS	Society for New Testament Studies Monograph Series
SNTW	Studies in the New Testament and its World
SPB	Studia Post-Biblica
SR	*Studies in Religion/Sciences religieuses*
St.Phil.M.	Studia Philonica Monographs
SVTP	Studia in Veteris Testamenti pseudepigrapha
TAPA	*Transactions of the American Philological Association*
ThQ	*Theologische Quartalschrift*
TRE	*Theologische Realenzyklopädie*
TSAJ	Texte und Studien zum Antiken Judentum
TU	*Texte und Untersuchungen*
VC	*Vigiliae Christianae*
VC.S	Vigiliae Christianae Supplements
VT.S	Vetus Testamentum Supplements
WUNT	Wissenschaftliche Untersuchungen zum Neuen Testament
ZKG	*Zeitschrift für Kirchengeschichte*
ZNW	*Zeitschrift für die neutestamentliche Wissenschaft*
ZPE	*Zeitschrift für Papyrologie und Epigraphik*

I

Introduction: The Emergence of Christian Identity

'I AM A CHRISTIAN': WHAT AND HOW IS 'CHRISTIAN'?

In about the middle of the second century CE, Polycarp, bishop of the church in Smyrna, seals his own death warrant by acknowledging that he is a Christian. He has just had his offer to teach the interrogating proconsul about the nature of 'Christianity' ignored, and the public announcement of his confession provokes the outraged cries of 'the whole assembly of Gentiles and Jews living in Smyrna'.[1] Perhaps what is most striking about this brief scene is the way that the terms 'Christian' (χριστιανός) and 'Christianity' (χριστιανισμός) are used without comment or explanation. At what point in the century or more since the death of Jesus and the earliest preaching of his followers did this become possible? How would not only outsiders but also those who claimed the epithet 'Christian' have understood the label, and how did the sense of being a Christian emerge? Put in this form, and in relation to the scene just described, these may seem to be questions about an individual's allegiance, but they are more properly questions about groups; so it is that the cry of the audience is, 'This is the father of the Christians', an epithet that probably carries more of a political note than the familial one it

[1] *Mart. Poly.* 10. 1; 12. 1–2. On this scene and on the issues discussed in what follows see J. M. Lieu, *Image and Reality: The Jews in the World of the Christians in the Second Century* (Edinburgh: T&T Clark, 1996), 57–102; eadem, '"I am a Christian": Martyrdom and the Beginning of Christian Identity', in *Neither Jew nor Greek? Constructing Early Christianity* (Edinburgh: T&T Clark, 2002), 211–31. Parts of this chapter were given as the 2002 Manson Memorial Lecture at the University of Manchester.

sounds in modern ears. Indeed, the description of the waiting crowd as 'Gentiles and Jews' may be taken to imply that the Christians are to be seen as neither of these, a third grouping alongside them.[2]

This question concerning the emergence of Christians and of Christianity has been answered in a number of ways. A classic way, exemplified in numerous Histories of the Church, was to trace the development of distinctive structures—namely forms of ministry, of membership and discipline, of collective decision-making, and of worship and ritual—and also of distinctive patterns of belief, particularly as articulated through but not limited to creeds, as each of these evolved in dynamic relationship with the creative interpretation of the Jewish Scriptures and with the authority accorded to a growing new body of texts and tradition. We may leave until later the ways in which this could be presented, either more traditionally, as the unfolding of what was implicit or embryonic from the start, or more subversively, as the result of political processes and conflict. Yet it did provoke a very heated debate as to when and where the decisive move to 'the Church' took place: is it to be found only beyond the New Testament, or are its roots already to be seen there—a problem that at one stage was dubbed that of 'early catholicism'?[3]

More recently, as the Jewishness of Jesus and of his earliest followers has been taken more seriously, and as the rich variety of Judaism in the first century CE and beyond has become more inescapable, answers have related more to 'When did Christianity cease to be a Judaism?', or, perhaps better, 'When and why did Christianity and Rabbinic Judaism stop considering themselves, and recognizing the other, as belonging to the same religion?'[4] This, the question of the so-called parting of the ways, acknowledges that much of the thought of the New Testament can be construed as within Judaism, a situation into which Polycarp's experience as just described hardly still fits. Thus the emergence

---

[2] On Christians as the 'third race' see below, pp. 260–5.

[3] i.e. the emergence of structures deemed to frame access to the blessings of salvation and seen as present (only) in and through 'the church'; see below, Ch. 5, n. 93.

[4] G. Boccaccini, 'History of Judaism: Its Periods in Antiquity', in J. Neusner (ed.), *Judaism in Late Antiquity*, ii. *Historical Syntheses*, HdO I. 17 (Leiden: Brill, 1995), 285–308, 300, rejects the first form of the question in favour of the second.

of Christianity and of the sense of being a Christian has to be understood in relation to the separation between Judaism and Christianity, even if particular individuals, including Polycarp himself, had no personal Jewish background. This does not mean that the separation had been effected before the middle of the second century as once supposed; indeed, one result of the intensive work in the field has been to make it more rather than less difficult to assign a date to, or to speak unambiguously about, *the* separation, a problem to which we shall return.[5] The difficulty in determining what should count as evidence for the parting of the ways has led, for some interpreters, to equivocation and apology in the antithetical use of 'Judaism' and 'Christianity', as well as to the collapse of any usefulness being found in speaking of 'Jewish Christianity', for perhaps as long as the first four centuries CE.[6] None the less, the acknowledged ambiguities have done little to resolve the dilemma of how to speak of members of communities centred around faith in Jesus Christ in the first century: while allowing for due equivocation and qualification, the dominant tendency still remains—for convenience if not on principle—to refer to them as '(early, Pauline, . . .) *Christians'*.

One weakness in the description of the emergence of 'being a Christian' in the developmental terms described earlier, a weakness only partly attended to in the account of the separation from Judaism, is that Christianity appears as a self-contained phenomenon, subject, no doubt, to influence from the ideas of the time, and frequently engaged in resistance to them, and even ultimately victim of, or beneficiary of, external political movements, but still to be analysed as if fundamentally isolable and explicable in its own terms. There are here the seeds—or perhaps the fruit—of an essentialism that anyone with a theological commitment to Christianity may not be totally able to avoid.[7]

[5] The literature is extensive; see among others, J. D. G. Dunn, *The Partings of the Ways* (London: SCM, 1991); idem (ed.), *Jews and Christians: The Parting of the Ways AD 70 to 135*, WUNT 66 (Tübingen: Mohr, 1992); S. G. Wilson, *Related Strangers: Jews and Christians 70–170 C.E.* (Minneapolis, Minn.: Fortress, 1995).

[6] See the discussion by D. Boyarin, *Dying for God: Martyrdom and the Making of Christianity and Judaism* (Stanford, Calif.: Stanford University Press, 1999), 1–21; J. M. Lieu, ' "The Parting of the Ways": Theological Construct or Historical Reality?', in *Neither Jew nor Greek?*, 11–30.

[7] See below, pp. 21–3, 310–11.

Yet the movement that was to become Christianity cannot be understood except within the social, political, and ideological dynamics of the world of which its adherents were a part, the world of the eastern Mediterranean with its Hellenistic heritage and of the expanding Roman Empire, a world that can also be configured in its variety as 'worlds'.

This has been recognized by those who have sought to locate Christian groups within the social context of the time, teasing out how 'Christians' would have identified their belonging in relationship to other patterns of belonging in the ancient city, for example in relationship to the variety of voluntary associations (*collegia*, θίασοι) about which we know much more from inscriptions than from literary texts.[8] To do this is to put the emphasis on the local situation, and to leave less well mapped the emergence of a translocal identity. The same is often true when sociological models have been brought to bear: for example, the process by which sects are formed, break off from their parent body, and develop their own structures may be fruitfully applied to the changing relationship between emergent Christianity and its parent, Judaism; but if we are to engage properly in the encounter between theoretical model and social test-case this has proved better able to help us understand the particular, for example the Matthaean or the Johannine community, rather than the amorphous and generalized 'Judaism' or 'Christianity', which themselves await definition. Indeed, one consequence of this, and of other recent approaches, is that many have been much more confident about speaking of 'Pauline', 'Matthaean', or 'Johannine' Christianity in the first century than of 'early Christianity', leaving unresolved the question of when and how the sense emerged, however theoretical, of belonging to something that transcended the local.

This question is the more pressing because our texts resist their confinement to the local.[9] It is unsurprising that this is the case with the Gospels, whose genre hardly allows for explicit

---

[8] See e.g. J. Kloppenborg and S. G. Wilson (eds.), *Voluntary Associations in the Graeco-Roman World* (London: Routledge, 1996).

[9] Thus making possible the arguments of R. Bauckham (ed.), *The Gospels for all Christians: Rethinking the Gospel Audiences* (Grand Rapids, Mich.: Eerdmans, 1998), that they were not exclusively local in their purview.

local reference, but it is also the case with the locally engaged
letters: Paul's affirmation, 'There is not Jew nor Greek, there
is not slave nor free, there is not male and female; for you are
all one in Christ Jesus' (Gal. 3. 28), may, in context, be directed
very specifically to the situation in the churches to whom he is
writing, but its sentiments deliberately evoke and transform the
fundamental divisions of humankind. Indeed, what is so striking
about this affirmation, however Paul may have expected it to be
realized, is that at first reading it appears to undermine much of
what has been said so far about the uncertainties of the emergence of a Christian identity; it appears to assert such a distinct
identity already around the middle of the first century.

Two things undermine this apparent clarity. One is the way
that Paul immediately goes on to say, 'you are then the seed of
Abraham' (3. 29), drawing on the distinctive symbolic world
of Jewish identity. The other, more complex, is the history of
the interpretation of the verse, both in the early centuries and
in more recent times. More recently, the verse has been seen
as representing pre-eminently within the New Testament the
primordial vision that too often and too quickly was lost amidst
the pressures of social disrepute or of social conformity, and/or as
providing the measure of authenticity for any other articulation
of faith or practice.[10] Yet what was its original focus? It has been
variously defined as a baptismal formula, ritually relocating the
baptizand in a liminal process; as a Christological formula pointing to Christ as divine image; as an anticipation of an eschatological fulfilment; or as a return to the primordial unity. Given the
actual and perhaps inevitable continuation of both slave and free,
as well as of male and female, its facticity has been defined as the
ever-elusive 'spiritually' or 'before God', although there have
still been some who have claimed that it was an experienced reality 'in church', or, last and most usually least, that it proffered a
challenge for real social revolution.[11] Where, we may ask, in the
midst of all this uncertainty, would Polycarp or his detractors

---

[10] See e.g. E. Schüssler Fiorenza, *In Memory of Her: A Feminist Theological
Reconstruction of Christian Origins* (London: SCM, 1983), 205–41.

[11] The literature is vast: see H. D. Betz, *Galatians: A Commentary on Paul's
Letter to the Churches in Galatia*, Hermeneia (Philadelphia, Pa.: Fortress, 1979),
181–201; also W. Meeks, 'The Image of the Androgyne: Some Uses of a Symbol
in Earliest Christianity', *HR* 13 (1974), 165–208.

locate what it meant to claim to be a Christian in second-century Smyrna?

Our question is encouraged by the differing responses of early interpreters to Gal. 3. 28.[12] Unsurprisingly, the last clause, 'You are one in Christ Jesus', proves more quotable than the preceding elaboration, and we should also not be surprised to find a variety of strategies that blunt what modern readers see as the subversive potential particularly of the denial of the distinctions of free status and of gender.[13] This does not mean that early church writers were unaware of the plurality encompassed by the reception of the Gospel. It is for Clement of Alexandria a matter of pride that 'it is possible for one who follows our manner of life, even though illiterate (καὶ ἄνευ γραμμάτων), to practise philosophy, whether barbarian or Greek or slave or aged or child or woman'—although the disappearance of the normative 'male' and 'free', and of the perhaps no longer relevant 'Jew', is notable (*Strom.* IV. 8. 58). With a new, more international, awareness, but again with the marked absence of the Jews, Eusebius can claim that 'Before God is there neither barbarian nor Greek. For anyone who fears God is a wise man. Now are the Egyptians, Syrians, Scythians, Italians, Maurians, Persians, Indians, they all have become wise through the teaching of Christ' (*Theophan.* III. 79). Yet becoming 'wise' apparently leaves them as 'Egyptians, Syrians', etc. So, beyond this plurality, what were Christians? Is it no longer a case that 'there is neither . . . nor . . . because you are one', but, rather, that 'there are . . . and . . . yet you are one'?

[12] See further W. Schrage, 'Skizze eine Auslegungs- und Wirkungsgeschichte von Gal 3,28', in D. Aschenbrenner (ed.), *Der Dienst der ganzen Gemeinde Jesu Christi und das Problem der Herrschaft* (Gütersloh: Gütersloher Verlaghaus, 1999), 63–92.

[13] e.g. Ps.-Cyprian, *De Abusivis XII saeculi*, XII: there is 'no favouritism with God'; Clement of Alexandria, *Strom.* III. 13. 93: male represents temper and female desire, both to be overcome 'in Christ'; *Protrep.* XI. 112, Christ is undivided and so is 'neither barbarian nor Jew nor Greek, not male nor female'; Origen, *Cant. Com.* 3. 9 on 2. 6: both 'Bridegroom' and the church as 'Bride' transcend gender; *Tripartite Tractate* (NH I. 5) 132. 20–133. 6: 'from multiplicity to the final unity like the beginning where there is no male nor female, slave nor free, circumcised nor uncircumcised, angel nor man but Christ'. Mygdonia, heroine of the *Acts of Thomas*, hears of and longs to go as soon as possible to where 'there is neither day nor night, good nor evil, poor nor rich, male nor female, free nor slave' (§129)—conditions which, it would seem, belong irretrievably to all experience here.

This, however, is to look ahead, to a period when there was a growing interest in ethnography, namely in the variety of peoples, places, and practices, an interest that encouraged later Christian writers to project into the future or onto the level of the soul the New Testament vision of the dissolution of boundaries, and one that also meant that Christian responses to perceived present ethnic diversity were to remain ambiguous.[14] On the other hand, that ambiguity is arguably potential from the start: in what form can a cohesive Christian identity be articulated, and how does that identity subsist in relation to other structural identities? That is now, perhaps more than ever, a compelling question, and one to which we shall have to return again, but our concern here is with the earliest period, and with Polycarp's untroubled affirmation.

LITERARY CHRISTIANITY?

We have so far treated Polycarp's self-identification as a Christian as a paradigmatic moment, and yet we encounter it only in a text, in what is presented as a letter sent from the church at Smyrna to the church at Philomelium. Although purportedly written close to the events it describes, the letter is self-conscious and stylized, and, in the forms in which we now have it, probably has gone through a complex transmission history.[15] How far the account of Polycarp's hearing before the proconsul is likely to represent actual practice is a matter of dispute, and we have to treat it, first of all, as a literary representation.[16] That we are dealing with texts is important. Texts play a central part not just in the documentation of what it meant to be Christian, but in actually shaping Christianity. It is not just that non-literary or material remains

---

[14] W. Pohl, 'Telling the Difference: Signs of Ethnic Identity', in W. Pohl with H. Reimitz (eds.), *Strategies of Distinction: The Construction of Ethnic Communities, 300–800*, The Transformation of the Roman World, 2 (Leiden: Brill, 1998), 17–69, 25, 67, on the interpretation of the Tower of Babel as sign of disunity or as potential for unlimited diversity.

[15] It survives both as part of Eusebius, *HE* IV. 15, and in a separate manuscript tradition; on the questions of the tradition history see G. Buschmann, *Martyrium Polycarpi: Eine formkritische Studie*, BZNW 70 (Berlin: de Gruyter, 1994), 14–70.

[16] It is explored as such in the studies listed in n. 1.

are not available, or at least are not unambiguously identifiable, as evidence for Christianity in the first two centuries.[17] Rather, it was through her remarkable literary creativity and productivity that a multifaceted self-conscious identity was produced: in the words of Averil Cameron, 'But if ever there was a case of the construction of reality through text, such a case is provided by early Christianity'.[18]

As we shall see, such a claim does reflect a particular understanding of 'text' and of the nature of history or of the historian's task. Its value is in warning us against looking for some essential and abiding reality independent of the texts with which we must deal, and independent, too, of their creativity in how and what they represent; it is the textual construction of early Christianity that will form the central and controlling thread in what follows. Yet, there are preconceptions and deceptions inherent in such an approach of which we must be warned: first, it privileges literary sources and the elites who were responsible for them, and so we should be careful lest it blind us to the 'mute meanings transacted through the goods and practices, through icons and images, dispersed in the landscape of the everyday'.[19] Even in contexts where that 'everyday' landscape can be physically excavated, the sense of identity that may be constructed from material remains can sometimes only with difficulty, if at all, be correlated with that which emerges out of literary sources.[20] In the case of Judaism, for example, an identity constructed from the archaeological remains and one constructed from the literary texts frequently appear to bear little relationship to each other.[21]

---

[17] See G. F. Snyder, *Ante Pacem: Archaeological Evidence of Church Life before Constantine* (Macon, Ga.: Mercer University Press, 1985). Papyrological evidence also really begins only in the third century.

[18] A. Cameron, *Christianity and the Rhetoric of Empire: The Development of Christian Discourse*, Sather Classical Lectures 45 (Berkeley, Calif.: University of California Press, 1991), 21; see further in Ch. 2 at "Text and Community among 'the Christians'".

[19] J. and J. Comaroff, *Ethnography and the Historical Imagination* (Boulder, Colo.: Westview, 1992), 35. On this and what follows see below, especially Ch. 5; it should be noted that Cameron does also acknowledge the function of 'practice' in the building of the Christians' world (above, n. 18).

[20] See S. Jones, 'Discourses of Identity in the Interpretation of the Past', in P. Graves-Brown, S. Jones, C. Gamble (eds.), *Cultural Identity and Archaeology: The Construction of European Communities* (London: Routledge, 1996), 62–80.

Where the physical landscape cannot be excavated—as for earliest Christianity— different strategies of reading the texts, such as through attending to what is implicit, unremarked, or rejected, or by reading against the grain, can give voice to some of those 'mute meanings'; in these ways we can catch partial, but only partial, glimpses of a wider range of social experience than that directly represented by the texts. Indeed, even when we attend to the voice of the text, often that of a particular author, we may not always be confident of how far it is articulating an existing consensus, or how far it is engaged in construction, and only fully successful in that enterprise once it is internalized and authorized within the community. Literary texts, we shall argue, tend to be more exclusive than social experience; individuals and groups interact socially who textually are denied such intercourse. For whom, then, does Polycarp, the Polycarp of the literary *Martyrdom* that bears his name, speak?[22]

Indeed, there is a larger problem. Surely, might it not seem self-defeating to rely on literary texts to understand a world of highly restricted literacy? If we accept William Harris's by no means uncontested median figure of 10 per cent for the literacy rate in the Roman Empire, does a focus on texts not just silence but de-legitimate the majority 90 per cent?[23] This is a question to which we shall have to return in the next chapter, but for the moment it is evident that the issue is far more complex than such numbers might suggest. That there are different levels of literacy and different contexts in which it may be exercised is often noted, and it can be shown that, in a setting where literacy is a valued mode, as under the Empire, even the functionally illiterate may possess 'literate skills'.[24] To what extent the central role of 'the Book' among Jews and Christians would have led to a higher

---

[21] See A. T. Kraabel, 'The Roman Diaspora: Six Questionable Assumptions', *JJS* 33 (1982), 445–64; S. Schwartz, *Imperialism and Jewish Society, 200 B.C.E. to 640 C.E.* (Princeton, NJ: Princeton University Press, 2001), 119–29; also, below, p. 99 on boundaries.

[22] It is the independent Greek manuscript tradition (see n. 15 above) that identifies the 'letter' as the 'Martyrdom of the holy Polycarp . . .'.

[23] W. V. Harris, *Ancient Literacy* (Cambridge, Mass.: Harvard University Press, 1989); for discussion see M. Beard *et al.* (eds.), *Literacy in the Roman World*, JRA.SS 3 (Ann Arbor, Mich.: University of Michigan Press, 1991).

[24] See A. K. Bowman, 'Literacy in the Roman Empire: Mass and Mode', in Beard *et al.*, *Literacy*, 119–31.

level of such literate skills, if not also of literacy, is debated, and may be countered by suggestions that neither group could boast so many members of the male elites where literacy was concentrated.[25]

Yet, regardless of such variables, the problem of literacy equally encompasses the whole of the ancient world, and not just the Christians; despite this, and as we shall discover, studies of identity in antiquity have focused on texts, not only because it is these that survive, but out of a recognition of the constructive role of texts in that world, particularly that of the Roman Empire. Moreover, numerous references to reading as well as to writing demonstrate an assumption that a wide audience would have experienced Christian texts. It is the texts' own presupposition that they will shape their audiences' self-understanding, even if their authors must have taken for granted how few would actually *read* them.

However, even while acknowledging the cardinal position occupied by its literature in the making of Christianity, and in any understanding of it, we can but observe that the same literature also exemplifies the problem that we encountered earlier. We may label the *Martyrdom of Polycarp* 'Christian' because it is determined by the scene described above. Yet what, if anything, makes Paul's Letter to the Galatians Christian, if it was written at a time when, and by one to whom, as well as to those by whom the term was not known? To answer that the letter is determined by faith in Jesus Christ prejudges an exclusive understanding—

---

[25] R. L. Fox, 'Literacy and Power in Early Christianity', in A. K. Bowman and G. Woolf (eds.), *Literacy and Power in the Ancient World* (Cambridge: Cambridge University Press, 1994), 126–48 speaks of 'sacred literacy', and is more optimistic of a drive towards literacy among the early Christians; contrast K. Hopkins who concludes that 'by the end of the first century, all Christianity is likely to have included, at any one time, less than fifty adult men who could write [*sic*] or read biblical texts fluently' (*A World Full of Gods: Pagans, Jews and Christians in the Roman Empire* (London: Orion, 2000 (1999)), 85), but his calculations appear to treat Harris's inclusive 10% as referring to males only: see the more detailed argument in idem, 'Christian Number and Its Implications', *JECS* 6 (1998), 185–226. C. Hezser, *Jewish Literacy in Roman Palestine*, TSAJ 81 (Tübingen: Mohr, 2001), 496–504, argues for lower literacy rates in Palestine than elsewhere in the Empire, because of the predominance of a rural population, and because the emphasis on Torah could lead to less interest in other forms of literature.

exclusive of 'Jewish'—that is surely anachronistic. To answer in terms of its eventual acceptance as authoritative within Christian tradition is self-evidently proleptic and historically problematic.[26] In practice, neither answer will satisfy all the texts for which the epithet 'Christian' might be claimed: there are some that were never accepted as authoritative but to whose voice we should want to listen; there are others where 'determination by faith in Jesus Christ' has to be imaginatively presupposed. So we are led to ask how those texts that scholars—or some scholars sometimes—recognize as Christian do construct a sense of distinctive identity, and how did they do so for those who read them and who, in time, implicitly or explicitly, claimed for themselves and for their texts some such label.

With this we have come to the task before us: to explore, through the texts generated within the movement initiated in different ways by the life and death of Jesus of Nazareth, how they construct a distinctive identity. It is an identity that in the end we agree to label 'Christian', so long as we forswear further categories such as 'orthodox' or 'heretical'. But it will prove no less important to use any label with caution, for part of our quest is how such constructed identities are continuous with or differentiated from the various other vigorous forms of identity-making at the time.

THE CONSTRUCTION OF IDENTITY

Our discussion so far has been scattered liberally with the words 'identity' and even 'construction'. When speaking of a first- and second-century context, this is obviously an anachronism, and one that reflects the particular intellectual and ideological preoccupations of the contemporary world. It has become a commonplace to observe both that the term 'identity' is comparatively recent, and that, although as a significant concept it only really entered scholarly discourse in the 1950s, it has now become so ubiquitous there, as well as in the popular and

---

[26] What then are we to say of the books of the 'Old Testament', also recognized as authoritative in the Christian tradition? On this and related issues, see J. M. Lieu, 'The New Testament and Early Christian Identity', in *Neither Jew nor Greek?*, 191–209, and below, pp. 45–8 on 'crypto-Christian' texts.

political imaginations, that it risks trivialization[27]—an observation that will do nothing to stem the cascade of studies devoted to the subject, including the present one.

So, too, the inherent contradictions in the concept of identity are equally well charted. Conditioned by the word's putative etymology to indicate 'sameness', from its earliest application to the individual it has been recognized that it consists in bodies that are continually undergoing change and replacement.[28] Its application to defined groups is a more recent development, and one derivative from that earlier individual reference.[29] In what ways corporate identity remains *conceptually* dependent on notions of individual identity, and—a potentially different set of questions—how far the felt *senses* of corporate and/or of individual identity are separable, interdependent, or derivative one from the other, remain topics of heated debate.[30] This is a particularly important question when addressing the ancient world where, it is often argued, the individual's sense of the self cannot be compared to a post-Enlightenment concern for self-determination. However, if we are not presuming to inhabit the self-consciousness of a Polycarp, but are looking at the mechanisms of (implicit) labelling and so of identification of groups, this becomes a less pressing objection. To this end we may begin with a rudimentary definition of identity, that it involves ideas of boundedness, of sameness and difference, of continuity, perhaps of a degree of homogeneity, and of recognition by self and by others. Such a definition will certainly demand further discussion and refining, but that it can be applied to the past with which we are concerned is undeniable.

[27] J. Gillis, 'Memory and Identity: The History of a Relationship', in idem (ed.), *Commemorations: The Politics of National Identity* (Princeton, NJ: Princeton University Press, 1994), 3–24, 3.

[28] See *OED* s.v. for the dispute about etymology and for its appearance in the 16th century and application to the individual in the 17th; in the light of what follows note the inherent essentialism in the initial definition.

[29] The 2nd edn. of the *OED* still fails to include any form of group identity under its expanded entry.

[30] The dependence of concepts of group on the culturally specific individual identity is the basis of the critique of R. Handler, 'Is "Identity" a Useful Cross-cultural Concept?', in Gillis, *Commemorations*, 27–40; for the interrelationship of individual and of corporate identity, both under the rubric of 'social identity', see R. Jenkins, *Social Identity* (London: Routledge, 1996).

As applied to defined groups, 'identity' belongs within the same complex of ideas as 'nation/nationhood' and 'ethnicity', although the different configurations within which these terms can be related to each other are almost as numerous as their configurers. That each carries its own political capital in the modern world gives little impetus to resolving the conundrum. It may be easy on a common-sense level to distinguish between them: not all ethnic groups are constituted as nations, but, rather, 'ethnic' is often (mis)used of minorities within a nation-state; nations may not be, and perhaps rarely are, coterminous with ethnic groups; groups may claim an identity not at all based on ethnic similarity. Yet common sense, as well as reflection about the history of the last century, equally show how the language of one, for example of ethnic identity, can be used to substantiate another, for example independent national existence. The rudimentary list of components given earlier—ideas of boundedness, of sameness and difference, of continuity, of recognition by self and by others—might be applied to each of these concepts, and it is a feature of the scholarly literature that someone writing ostensibly about one, for example identity, appeals to previous work about another, for example nationalism.[31]

One reason for this overlapping or confusion of categories is that, although identity is often experienced or treated as an absolute and irreducible 'given', there has developed in recent decades a widespread consensus that it can better be understood and analysed as socially constructed. The essentialism inherent in the initial definition of identity lends itself to a primordialism according to which deeply rooted sentiments and ties predetermine other sets of relationships as non-negotiable; but this perception has been largely undermined by a myriad of attempts to define and to deconstruct the components and the processes in what is now seen as construction and its maintenance. Yet if this is true of identity, it is no less true of the apparently more tangible ethnicity, as also of another concept which is often brought into the same web of ideas and opacity, that of culture.[32] This

---

[31] So B. Anderson, *Imagined Communities: Reflections on the Origins and Spread of Nationalism*, rev. edn. (London: Verso, 1991 (1983)), is regularly cited by studies of ethnicity and of identity.

[32] See e.g. J. Friedman, 'Notes on Culture and Identity in Imperial Worlds', in P. Bilde, T. Engberg-Pedersen, L. Hannestad, J. Zahle (eds.), *Religion and*

'discovery' of their constructed nature has led to the regularly noted irony that claims to the actualities of nation-status, ethnicity, and identity increased in importance during the latter half of the twentieth century at the very time when the givenness of those concepts was being discredited.

Yet if constructionism, itself a Western construct, has passed into the category of the obvious,[33] there remains room for debate as to how to balance the tensions between subjectivity and choice, and objective framework, and as to how far the symbols of identity are primarily interest- or goal-driven, or how far they echo embedded impressions.[34]

Particularly important has been the insight that, while a core component in the sense, and certainly in the rhetoric, of identity—and regularly for 'identity' it is possible to read 'ethnicity' if not 'nationhood'—is stability, in practice identities are dynamic and subject to change. Thus, to recognize that identity is constructed is not to talk only about origins, but also about the mechanisms for managing change and claiming continuity, even, or especially, when these may be differently interpreted by different individuals who still recognize one another as belonging. In this way it also offers a way of understanding how actual variety and multiplicity, as well as even radical change, are contained by 'the symbolic construction and signification of a mask of similarity'.[35]

Religious Practice in the Seleucid Kingdom (Aarhus: Aarhus University Press, 1990), 14–39, 37, 'culture is about the practice of identity'; contrast J. Hall, *Hellenicity: Between Ethnicity and Culture* (Chicago, Ill.: University of Chicago Press, 2002), 17, who argues for ethnic and religious identities as specific but separate types of cultural identity.

[33] G. Schöpflin, *Nations, Identity, Power: The New Politics of Europe* (London: Hurst, 2000), 3, comments that the idea that the nation was invented or imagined 'does not make them any less real. For that matter all social phenomena are constructed, invented or imagined: class, gender, race, the lot.' On the self-destructive potential of constructionism see K. Gergen, 'Social Constructionist Inquiry: Context and Implications', in K. Gergen and K. Davis (eds.), *The Social Construction of the Person* (New York: Springer, 1985), 3–17.

[34] See E. Tonkin, *Narrating Our Pasts: The Social Construction of Oral History* (Cambridge: Cambridge University Press, 1992), 106–8; S. Jones, *The Archaeology of Ethnicity: Constructing Identities in the Past and Present* (London: Routledge, 1997), 13–14, 60–83.

[35] Jenkins, *Social Identity*, 105.

Yet similarity implies the possibility of difference, and, therefore, no less significant has been the recognition that the description of the self demands the description of the other; 'us' implies 'them'; the positive invites or presupposes the negative. With this, attention has focused particularly on the negative or destructive potential of identity-formation, the exercise of power in labelling and exclusion. How far is this intrinsic? how far does it have to be said with Regina Schwartz that 'acts of identity formation are themselves acts of violence'?[36] How far is it possible to find other strategies, other ways of relating to 'the other'? It is acknowledging identity as constructed that makes it possible to ask these questions, and imperative to do so in the contemporary world.[37] Yet, it is the very forcefulness of the rhetoric of 'the other' that at the same time invites us to explore how groups do in fact interact with others—what is meant by the often simplistically used phrases in the modern multi-anything world, 'to discover', 'to preserve', or 'to lose' one's identity.

Although we have noted the relatively recent emergence of the language of identity, and although one highly influential school of thought traces the origins of the idea of nations and of nationalism to the eighteenth century, albeit with earlier roots, there are good reasons for the application of the models of construction to the past. One such reason is that claims about past history and continuity are constitutive of nearly all articulations of identity: in his seminal study of nationalism, Benedict Anderson sees one of the foundational paradoxes of the idea of nations as their 'objective modernity versus their subjective antiquity'.[38] Thus history and archaeology have frequently been active or passive players in affirmations of identity, ethnicity, or nationhood,

[36] R. Schwartz, *The Curse of Cain: The Violent Legacy of Monotheism* (Chicago, Ill.: University of Chicago Press, 1997), 5.

[37] We shall return to this in the Conclusion; see also L. J. Silberstein, 'Others Within and Others Without: Rethinking Jewish Identity and Culture', in L. J. Silberstein and R. L. Cohn (eds.), *The Other in Jewish Thought and History* (New York: New York University Press, 1994), 1–34; H. Bhabha, 'Introduction: Narrating the Nation', in idem (ed.), *Nation and Narration* (London: Routledge, 1990), 1–7, and the other essays collected therein.

[38] Anderson, *Imagined Communities*, 4; Anderson presents the classic argument for the 18th-century origins. For a different view see A. Hastings, *The Construction of Nationhood: Ethnicity, Religion and Nationalism* (Cambridge: Cambridge University Press, 1997).

either when they have been supposed to supply the 'raw material' for subsequent constructions, or when they have been complicit in ordering their own material within constraints imposed by later concepts of the nature of particular identity or ethnicity.[39] In the face of this it is important to expose the different articulations or perspectives that the past may offer, not least the ways in which these challenge, or fail to conform to, subsequent models and expectations.

Another justification for applying the model to the past is that, whether or not the term 'ethnic' when used of antiquity is genuinely analogous with its modern reference, and certainly without indiscriminately legitimating claims made by contemporary groups to continuity with particular ethnic groups in antiquity,[40] we shall discover that ancient writers did use what can best be called 'ethnic categories' to describe others as well as themselves.[41] Moreover, as will become evident, the application of contemporary models of the construction of identity and of ethnicity have proved extremely creative in the analysis of the material remains, the society, and the literature of antiquity.[42] If this has not been applied extensively to early Christianity, it may be because the latter has been seen as different, the domain of theologians; but appearing as it does at a specific time and place, and undoubtedly generating a distinctive identity, early Christianity would seem to be ideal material for an analysis within the framework we have begun to outline.

Both discussion of the theoretical models of the construction of identity and applications of them to a wide variety of situations abound, and this initial survey is inevitably cursory. In the chapters to follow we shall be taking in turn particular influential

[39] See Jones, 'Discourses of Identity', and below, Ch. 4 n. 4.

[40] On the problem see e.g. J. H. C. Williams, *Beyond the Rubicon: Romans and Gauls in Republican Italy* (Oxford: Oxford University Press, 2001), 3–14, on the political implications of modern debate about the Celts in pre-Roman Europe. Pohl, 'Telling the Difference', represents an argument for continuities in a strong sense of ethnic identity.

[41] This offers an answer to Handler's potential critique, see n. 30 above.

[42] The bibliography is too extensive to be listed here and will emerge throughout the rest of this study. For a recent collection of essays and a substantial bibliography see I. Malkin (ed.), *Ancient Perceptions of Greek Ethnicity* (Cambridge, Mass.: Harvard University Press, 2001); the 'Introduction' by I. Malkin (1–28) echoes some of the issues discussed here.

models from recent debate in order to see how they may help us to trace in different texts the way a new Christian identity is being constructed; that is, the creation through literature of a sense of what to be 'a Christian' or what 'Christianity' means. No single model will be adopted here as definitive: the inevitable eclecticism, which ignores the often heated discussion between their separate advocates, may be justified by the fact that they are being used not prescriptively but heuristically, to generate a set of questions to be addressed to our literature.[43]

IDENTITY AND THE GRAECO-ROMAN WORLD

Awareness of sameness and of difference, of a shared past and agreed values, of continuities and of boundaries, whether physical or behavioural, were all present, either implicitly or explicitly, as Greeks and Romans viewed themselves and others. No doubt the same was true of other peoples, although their literary traces are generally more sparse.[44] Within the Greek world a sense of what differentiates 'us' from 'others' goes back very early, and the emergence of an 'ethnic identity' or of 'Greek self-definition' in the fifth century BCE has been fruitfully explored through the lens of the modern debate just discussed.[45] Yet it would not be surprising if such a sense became particularly pressing during the Hellenistic period, the late Republic, and the early Empire, as horizons extended, and as people needed to locate themselves within a wider world that could claim both unity and multiple difference. As we have seen, identity is to do with change and with the encounter with others, two major features of this period.

[43] I am encouraged in this eclecticism by M. Al-Rasheed, *Iraqi Assyrian Christians in London: The Construction of Ethnicity*, Mellen Studies in Sociology 21 (Lewiston, NY: Edward Mellen Press, 1998), who describes her approach as 'multi-variate' (p. xix). Cf. also T. H. Eriksen, *Ethnicity and Nationalism: Anthropological Perspectives* (London: Philo Press, 1993), 162, who emphasizes their heuristic function.

[44] That there were shared strategies of establishing an identity is well argued by E. Gruen, *Heritage and Hellenism: The Reinvention of Jewish Tradition* (Berkeley, Calif.: University of California Press, 1998).

[45] E. Hall, *Inventing the Barbarians: Greek Self-Definition through Tragedy* (Oxford: Clarendon, 1989); J. Hall, *Ethnic Identity in Greek Antiquity* (Cambridge: Cambridge University Press, 1997).

So, contemporary models have illumined the major players'—
Greeks', Romans', the elites'—construction both of themselves,
and also of the others who were drawn into their world or who
lived on its margins.[46] Moreover, the slippage between concepts
of ethnicity and of culture, or the difficulty of assigning these to
clearly separated categories, has also proved unavoidable in this
context.

Judaism was part of that same world: as is often noted, the term
usually so translated, ἰουδαϊσμός, first appears in the Maccabean
literature, which describes the Jews' most articulated encounter
with 'Hellenism'.[47] It is widely recognized that this marks a
distinctive new stage in the history of Israel, although one not
without roots in the period that precedes. There is a perhaps
unsurprising irony in that it is in this period, when it becomes
textually legitimate to speak of 'the Jews', that the rich diversity
of what 'Jews' did, thought, believed, and organized becomes
most visible, provoking a continuing debate as to what, if anything, constituted the core of Jewish identity. Even on the level
of texts, how are we to hold together a variety ranging from the
Scrolls of the Dead Sea, to the apocalyptic visions of the so-called
Pseudepigrapha, to the open ethos of a Philo, or to the earliest
strands of rabbinic literature?

The older debate on this, which fought over terms such as
'orthodoxy', 'orthopraxy', and 'normativity', both proved unproductive and retained a yearning for essentialism that failed to
engage with contemporary insights about identity as contextual-
ized and as contingent.[48] Instead, recognition of undeniable
diversity in observed characteristics has admitted a probable
equivalent diversity in the primary terms of self-definition. This

[46] e.g. E. Dench, *From Barbarians to New Men: Greek, Roman and Modern
Perceptions of Peoples of the Central Appennines* (Oxford: Clarendon, 1995);
Williams, *Beyond the Rubicon*; others will be cited during the course of this study.

[47] 2 Macc. 2. 21; 8. 1; 14. 38; also 4 Macc. 4. 26; the literature on this is extensive and will be referred to at various times in what follows. See, but also note
the term used in the title, S. Cohen, *The Beginnings of Jewishness: Boundaries,
Varieties, Uncertainties* (Berkeley, Calif.: University of California Press, 1999).

[48] For that debate see N. McEleney, 'Orthodoxy in Judaism of the First
Christian Century', *JSJ* 4 (1973), 19–42; D. Aune, 'Orthodoxy in First Century
Judaism? A Response to N. J. McEleney', *JSJ* 7 (1976), 1–10; L. Grabbe,
'Orthodoxy in First Century Judaism?', *JSJ* 8 (1977), 149–53; N. McEleney,
'Orthodoxy in Judaism of the First Christian Century', *JSJ* 9 (1978), 83–8.

is already true at a literary level, while we may suspect that at the levels of historical experience or of praxis the situation was both simpler and more complex: simpler in that groups whose literary self-definition may have been different did perhaps recognize each other as belonging to 'us' and not to 'the other'; more complex in that the radically alternative self-understandings of the 'Hellenists' of the Maccabean era, or of those sometimes labelled 'extreme allegorists' referred to by Philo, cannot now speak in their own voice. More recently, however, addressing some of these same concerns, now from within the identity debate, argument has turned to whether Jewish identity in the late Second Temple period should be defined as ethnic or as religious, or whether there was a movement between the two forms of identity—a distinction, analogous to what has already been said about culture, that probably proves a chimera.[49]

Against the tendency in some of these debates to treat Judaism as *sui generis*, it must be emphasized that in the late Second Temple period and beyond, Jewish self-definition was evolving within the wider context of the Graeco-Roman world. This would invite not just opposition but also assimilation or expropriation, both in the terms of self-understanding and in the strategies adopted. Neither 'opposition' nor 'assimilation' should be accorded any value-loading, nor assumed to lead necessarily to a clearer, to a separate, or to a weaker identity. None of these is invariably the case in modern multicultural contexts, while study of the actual texts of Hellenistic Judaism reveals a range of nuanced interactions with contemporary strategies and components of self-definition, even while maintaining the distinctive moments and symbols of her own particular story.[50] The diversity within Judaism extended into diversity in her interactions with the complexity of the wider world.

[49] For such a debate see Cohen, *Beginnings of Jewishness*, 5–8, 109–39; see the brief but perceptive comments by H. Lapin, 'Introduction: Locating Ethnicity and Religious Community in Later Roman Palestine', in idem (ed.), *Religious and Ethnic Communities in Later Roman Palestine*, Studies and Texts in Jewish History and Culture 5 (Bethesda, Md.: University Press of Maryland, 1998), 1–28.

[50] On the modern situation see W. Isajiw, 'Definitions of Identity', *Ethnicity* 1 (1974), 111–24; A. P. Cohen, *The Symbolic Construction of Community* (Chichester: Ellis Horwood, 1985), 36–7; on the Hellenistic-Jewish enterprise, E. Gruen, *Heritage and Hellenism*.

'Christian' identity-making was taking place in the same context. This requires emphasis, because early Christianity has sometimes been treated as non-comparable, and, as we have seen, has been described within a framework distinctive to it alone. That early Christianity was, in the words of Joshua Fishman, 'a de-ethnicizing movement' might seem to be established by Gal. 3. 28 and by the expansion of the church.[51] Guy Stroumsa goes even further: 'Since early Christianity did not form a culture of its own, and did not claim to represent an ethnical entity of any kind, the Christians had to invent new parameters according to which they could fashion their own identity.'[52] But we have already seen that such views may be an oversimplification. In the longer term, Christian missions have played a creative role in the articulation of local identities, and have even fostered group identities defined in terms of their specific Christian allegiance— Protestant, Catholic, Orthodox, or Arian have acquired a political or national tenor. '[T]he nation and nationalism', it has been suggested, 'are both . . . characteristically Christian things',[53] and it needs to be asked why that is.

More pertinently, as we shall discover in what follows, the Christian rhetoric of identity, even when making universalist claims, is articulated in the terms also used in Graeco-Roman ethnography and identity formulation.[54] In this, as in many other areas, early Christianity needs to be seen as implicated in, as well as contributing to, the dynamics of the world in which it was situated. We should look for continuities as well as for discontinuities between Greek, Roman, Jewish, and Christian

[51] J. Fishman, 'Language, Ethnicity and Racism', in idem, *Language and Ethnicity in Minority Sociolinguistic Perspective* (Clevedon: Multilingual Matters, 1989), 9–65, 51.

[52] G. Stroumsa, 'Philosophy of the Barbarians: On Early Christian Ethnological Representations', in H. Cancik, H. Lichtenberger, P. Schäfer (eds.), *Geschichte, Tradition, Reflexion: Festschrift für Martin Hengel zum 70. Geburtstag*, 3 vols. (Tübingen: Mohr, 1996), ii. 339–68, 341.

[53] Hastings, *Construction*, 186; see also Anderson, *Imagined Communities*, 12.

[54] So also D. M. Olster, 'Classical Ethnography and Early Christianity', in K. B. Free (ed.), *The Formulation of Christianity by Conflict through the Ages* (Lewiston, NY: Edward Mellen Press, 1995), 9–31; D. K. Buell, 'Rethinking the Relevance of Race for Early Christian Self-Definition', *HTR* 94 (2001), 449–76; eadem, 'Race and Universalism in Early Christianity', *JECS* 10 (2002), 429–68.

efforts to construct and to maintain an identity for themselves, in interaction with their past as well as with each other. Indeed, even to say this is to have to go on to acknowledge not only that there is not 'any universal meaning that can be attributed to terms such as "Roman", "Greek", "Christian", "barbarian"', Jew,[55] but also that these are not mutually exclusive categories, and so we can only expect to understand one term in its relations with the others.

THE UNIVERSAL AND THE LOCAL; CONSTRUCTION AND ESSENCE

Despite the strictures with which we started, it has proved impossible to proceed through this discussion without speaking of 'Christianity' as also of 'Judaism'. Whether this is justifiable, and what it means so to speak, are not only problems of the earliest historical period. The relationship between local, self-styled Christian communities with their own modes of expression, often inculturated within their own situation, and 'Christianity' per se, as not peculiar to time and place, has become in the modern period an urgent theological, historiographical, and ecclesio-political problem: the 'variety of senses of identity among Christians' still awaits but may not be patent of a solution.[56] A post-modern consciousness may not be desirous of a solution, and even in relation to the past we have become comfortable with speaking of diversity and even of '-isms'—as we have just seen in relation to Judaism*s*. Yet even to claim some continuity between these modern expressions of 'being Christian' and those of the first few centuries invites some analysis of Christian identity, for

[55] R. Miles, 'Introduction: Constructing Identities in Late Antiquity', in idem (ed.), *Constructing Identities in Late Antiquity* (London: Routledge, 1999), 1–15, 4; Miles does not add 'Jew'.

[56] G. R. Evans, 'Ecumenical Historical Method', *JES* 31 (1994), 93–110, 96; see also D. T. Irvin, 'From One Story to Many: An Ecumenical Reappraisal of Church History', *JES* 28 (1991), 537–54, 'Incarnationally, Christian histories do not displace the multiplicity of human histories but belong to them' (p. 554); J. S. Mbiti (ed.), *Confessing Christ in Different Cultures* (Bossey: Ecumenical Institute, 1977). The vigorous emergence of forms of theology and of biblical interpretation specific to particular, especially non-Western, situations is a *de facto* response to the dilemma. We shall return to this in the Conclusion.

identity is to do with experienced continuity amidst the constant change and decay.

For some, the question is much more theologically urgent: Ben Meyer probably speaks for what many instinctively feel when he asks, '[h]as the Church had a distinct and lasting identity?', and when he criticizes recent sociological analyses of early Christian communities for failing to explain how the diversity of early Christianity did not lead to schism.[57] Such a criticism, of course, ignores the histories of what came to be called 'orthodoxy' and 'heresy': since the work of Walter Bauer, the classic model of the original unity of 'the church', which was fissured in subsequent time only by schism (heresy), has been challenged by one of original diversity that achieved some form of unity (for some) only as the result of political processes.[58] Those processes and the mechanisms that accompanied them still require fuller explanation, and they certainly were not created *ex nihilo*. The apparent movement of texts and their reuse, exemplified by the relationship between the Synoptic Gospels, as well as the known movements of individuals such as Paul or Ignatius, cannot merely be seen as attempts to forge unity *de novo*, but at the very least betray some predisposition towards it. From very early, even texts which are locally conditioned convey a sense of the threads that connect them with others, perhaps particularly inspired by Paul's own self-understanding, and this means that the literary construction of Christianity's universal domain begins there also (for example, 1 Thess. 1. 6–10; Col. 1. 15–23).

How far was this different from what held the various Jewish communities together, or, indeed, even other new cults of the period?[59] How far can it be reconciled with the historian's justifi-

---

[57] B. Meyer, *Christus Faber: The Master Builder and the House of God* (Allison Park, Pa.: Pickwick Publications, 1992), 151; idem, *The Early Christians: Their World Mission and Self-Discovery* (Wilmington, Del.: Michael Glazier, 1986), 33–4.

[58] W. Bauer, *Orthodoxy and Heresy in Earliest Christianity* (ET. Philadelphia, Pa.: Fortress, 1971) = *Rechtglaubigkeit und Ketzerei im ältesten Christentum* (Tübingen: Mohr, 1934 (1965)).

[59] See M. Beard, J. North, S. Price (eds.), *Religions of Rome*, i. *A History* (Cambridge: Cambridge University Press, 1998), 245–9: 'clusters of ideas, people, rituals, sharing some common identity across time and place, but at the same time inevitably invested with different meanings in their different contexts' (p. 249).

able claim that there was no 'single church' in the first two centuries?[60] If we cannot start from an essentialized Christianity, it may be that a clearer delineation of the variety of constructions of identity will contribute to understanding how some such could be imagined, while also alerting us to the processes of exclusion and silencing that accompanied such an imagination.

THE CONSTRUCTION OF CHRISTIAN IDENTITY

In the chapters that follow we shall be taking different models of the construction of identity from contemporary analysis and using them to explore what is happening, and how, in the writings of those whom we label Greeks and Romans, Jews and Christians, as they articulated who 'they' were, often over against various 'others'.[61] The main focus of our attention will be on conventionally so-called 'Christian' texts, although to set them alongside these others is to suspend use of that label as an a priori signifier of difference—and we shall discover that this can lead to some very real problems when the texts themselves defy unequivocal categorization.[62] We shall concentrate on approximately the first hundred years following Paul's letters and the Gospels, the period when that label is most problematic but when the clearer contours of a later period are emerging—although we shall frequently look forward to texts from at least the following half-century.

There is an admitted but unavoidable contradiction in accepting even a broad classification of 'Christian' while also seeking to subvert its unity and differentness. Likewise, both the method, in adopting a variety of models, and the ad-hoc choice of texts to which they are applied, are deliberately eclectic or idiosyncratic:

---

[60] Hopkins, 'Christian Number', 207, 'The frequent claims that scattered Christian communities constituted a single church was not a description of reality in the first two centuries C.E., but a blatant yet forceful denial of reality.'

[61] Rabbinic texts will feature less frequently than perhaps they might, both because of the problems of their dating in relation to our time-scale, and because, while undoubtedly equally engaged in identity-construction, they do this in a characteristically solipsic manner: see S. Stern, *Jewish Identity in Early Rabbinic Writings*, AGJU 23 (Leiden: Brill, 1994).

[62] See below, pp. 45–8, 75–7.

any claim to comprehensiveness would not only be foolhardy but would also undermine the fundamental contentions adopted here that this is a period of open diversity and that the processes we are encountering are to be seen as construction, not completion. No doubt, even bringing these different readings together could be seen as such an undermining; but our model is that of a kaleidoscope through which we both see variety and also puzzle over the patterns of coherence that may be as much in our own minds as in the brightly coloured fragments that tantalize us.

Our gaze is directed to literary texts, with the ever-present possibility that we may be discerning the construction of their authors alone.[63] As we have seen, this is necessarily so, given that it is texts that survive from this period: other media would tell other stories. This means that we shall only occasionally venture to discern the social experiences behind the texts, not only from the need for some constraints on the task. The plethora of recent attempts to reconstruct from the texts the Pauline, Johannine, Matthaean, Thomasine, etc. communities, founded as they are on an assumption that we can work back from text to the distinctive community that generated it, have increasingly been recognized to rest on shaky foundations.[64] The constructive process is just as likely to be the reverse, at least in theory, although whether any text(s) did generate an actual community is not our primary concern. We should need also to be equally attuned to traces of disconfirming social experience, those who resisted or were resisted by the texts. On the other hand, we are not necessarily uncover-

---

[63] For recognition of the same problem see Stern, *Jewish Identity*, pp. xxix–xxxi, yet he still claims that this identity is 'dynamic, ever-resilient'.

[64] e.g. the reconstruction of the self-definition of 'Thomasine Christianity' from the *Gospel of Thomas* is hazardous in the extreme, particularly given the self-referentialism of the opening salvo which seems to source salvation within the text itself and its individualized reading: 'These are the hidden words which the living Jesus spoke, and Didymos Judas Thomas wrote. And he said, "Whoever falls upon the meaning of these words will not taste death".' Similarly, attempts to reconstruct communities behind the apocryphal Acts of the Apostles (e.g. S. L. Davies, *The Revolt of the Widows: The Social World of the Apocryphal Acts* (Carbondale, Ill.: S. Illinois University Press, 1980)) have given way to a recognition of their literary or rhetorical self-sufficiency (e.g. K. Cooper, *The Virgin and the Bride: Idealized Womanhood in Late Antiquity* (Cambridge, Mass.: Harvard University Press, 1996), 45–67). On Matthew and John see further below, pp. 87–8.

ing a self-conscious process of self-definition; we shall prescind
from determining whether, for example, Paul thought of himself
as establishing something separate. Our concern is the creative
role of most of these texts, as texts, in subsequent Christian discourse, whether or not they were 'rightly' understood, but it is
also the way that identity formation and maintenance may itself
be described as a discourse, in Bruce Lincoln's terms, a coherent
and sustaining sentiment which becomes effective as it is acted
upon.[65]

Perhaps inevitably, such a concern may seem to exercise a predisposition in favour of ideas over actions. This invites a clear
objection: recent work, particularly by those operating with
non-literary media, has emphasized the 'practice of identity', the
nexus of the shared symbolic domain, dispositions, behavioural
experiences and expectations, however these be understood to
co-operate.[66] However, if we are looking at ideas it will not be for
their conceptual content but for how they function, what they
'do': this is not a study of the 'theologies' of early Christian texts.
Conversely, we shall include an exploration not only of 'practice', but also of attitudes to gender and bodiliness, for identity
in its earliest definition is embodied; but we can do so only as
these are textually inscribed, and it may be that the relationship
between textual bodies and real bodies will ever elude us.

So all this does not mean that we can deal with texts from a
romanticist perspective, as if they floated free. Their embeddedness and social functions are paradigmatic; but these become alive
as we discover the way that texts construct readers and 'reality'
through acts of power, by silence and marginalization, as well
as by unarticulated assumptions, by the values and hierarchies
engendered, and by the authoritative voice claimed.

This will not be the last time that we have to tread a tight-rope

---

[65] See above, n. 18, and below, Ch. 2; B. Lincoln, *Discourse and the Construction
of Society: Comparative Studies in Myth, Ritual, and Classification* (New York:
Oxford University Press, 1989); U. Østergård, 'What is National and Ethnic
Identity?', in P. Bilde, T. Engberg-Pedersen, L. Hannestad, J. Zahle (eds.),
Ethnicity in Hellenistic Egypt (Aarhus: Aarhus University Press, 1992), 16–38.

[66] See below, Ch. 5, and the fundamental work of P. Bourdieu, *The Logic of
Practice* (ET. Cambridge: Polity, 1990), and the discussions in non-literary contexts by G. C. Bentley, 'Ethnicity and Practice', *Comparative Studies in Society
and History* 29 (1987), 24–51, 24–9; Jones, 'Discourses of Identity', 67–71.

of affirmation and its negation, of definition and the subverting of definition. To do so is perhaps intrinsic to the search for identity. What follows is a series of explorations. At their end we shall have to look for patterns of coherence and to reflect on their ever-present tendency to dissolution. We shall also have to return to the questions signalled so far: the relationship between texts and social experience; the appropriateness of terms such as 'Judaism' and 'Christianity', and the relationship between them; the various ways in which nascent Christian identity was both embedded within the multiplicity and hierarchy of identity constructions in the ancient world and yet distinctive from them, carrying the seeds of what could be seen as the creation of a radically new world. We shall not be able to describe or to explain the nature of Christianity and its expansion, but we should be prompted to reflect again on the search for its essence, the ever-elusive answer to the question, 'What is Christianity?'[67]

[67] A question taken from A. von Harnack, *What is Christianity?*, 3rd rev. edn. (ET. London: Williams & Norgate, 1904), and its German original, *Das Wesen des Christentums* (Leipzig: Hinrichs, 1900).

2

Text and Identity

That there is a relationship between identity and textuality should by now be evident: it is both the foundation of this study and the arena of its interrogation. In the chapters that follow we shall be exploring the various ways in which texts construct identity through their poetics. Here our focus is a narrower one: first, to introduce the ways in which early Christianity, like early Judaism, (re)produced itself through text-making; but, secondly, to ask how it is that texts acquire this pivotal role, so that they both shape and are shaped by communities' dynamic self-understanding. What are the ways in which texts function, but also can be manipulated, in the creation and maintenance of identity?

Averil Cameron, albeit discussing a period later than ours, has indicated very trenchantly the direction in which we shall go: 'But if ever there was a case of the construction of reality through text, such a case is provided by early Christianity . . . Christians built themselves a new world. They did so partly through practice—the evolution of a mode of living and a communal discipline that carefully distinguished them from their pagan and Jewish neighbours—and partly through a discourse that was itself constantly brought under control and disciplined'; and, again, 'As Christ "was" the Word, so Christianity *was* its discourse or discourses.'[1] What her account emphasizes is not only the way that Christian thought, behaviour, attitudes, values, and self-understanding were forged textually, but also the way that the multiple self-representations we encounter in the texts are themselves constructs, as is any representation. Yet, while we

[1] Cameron, *Christianity and the Rhetoric of Empire*, 21, 32; see above, Ch. 1 n. 18.

shall return to this description, it has to be set within a broader
context of the literary constructions of other contemporary
identity-making, Jewish and Graeco-Roman, as well as within a
wider account of the relationship between identity and texts.

TEXTS AND COMMUNITY IN THE ANCIENT WORLD

For the modern world, Benedict Anderson has accentuated the
essential role in the creation of 'imagined communities' that was
played by the invention of printing; this made it possible for a
new awareness of self and of others to be experienced quickly and
across great distances by those whose world was hitherto locally
highly circumscribed.[2] It generated new concepts of linearity
and simultaneity in time, enabling a sense of community with
those separated by time or by geography; yet, equally, it fixated
local distinctiveness over against a more universal heterogeneity.
Anderson's analysis refers specifically to the birth of the nation
state, and draws attention to the very different role of literature
in earlier, albeit literate, cultures.[3] To that extent the modern
experience cannot easily be transferred directly to the ancient;
yet there are obvious continuities in the ways in which access to
texts, and their broad dissemination, could generate senses of
community alternative to the locally constrained.

Yet even before the invention of printing, written traditions
could forge distinctive forms of community aware of their separation from the rest of the world. To understand the eleventh and
twelfth centuries Brian Stock developed the idea of 'textual communities', that is of groups formed around a text and its interpreters; although his analysis had rested on a contrast with the
role of orality and literacy in the immediately preceding period,
he later went on to argue for its relevance for interpreting both
Judaism and Christianity within the ancient world.[4] Others have

---

[2] Anderson, *Imagined Communities*, 37–46.

[3] See W. A. Graham, *Beyond the Written Word: Oral Aspects of Scripture in
the History of Religion* (Cambridge: Cambridge University Press, 1987).

[4] B. Stock, *The Implications of Literacy: Written Language and Models of
Interpretation in the Eleventh and Twelfth Centuries* (Princeton, NJ: Princeton
University Press, 1983); idem, *Listening for the Text: On the Uses of the Past*

adopted Stock's model and its application, finding the definition of a textual community that he offers particularly fruitful,
namely, that it is 'a group that arises somewhere in the interstices
between the imposition of the written word and the articulation
of a certain type of social organization. It is an interpretative community, but it is also a social entity.'[5] Here, textuality acquires
a formative precedence, both through the importance of the
foundational text and through the assumptions of a conceptual
framework that is determined by written traditions. This is in no
way undermined by the possibility that many of the group may
be illiterate, for, particularly when the text has been internalized, it can be 're-performed orally'.[6] This insight, we should
note, addresses usefully the concerns discussed earlier, in the
Introduction, about the validity of a textual focus in an age of
high illiteracy. It also coheres with other arguments that there is
no simple divide between the literate and the illiterate (sections
of) societies, but, instead, that orality functions in a variety of
ways through both, just as literacy itself cannot be measured on a
single scale, and just as texts are accessed by and experienced by
different groups in different ways, both written and oral.[7]

This has obvious implications when we turn to the ancient
world where we find both the importance of the written word
and low levels of literacy. Here, it has often been stressed, texts,
and specifically but not exclusively their production, bring us
pre-eminently into the world of the (male) elites; it was they who
not only wrote but who also largely controlled copying, transmission, access, and readings.[8] How far the texts can also take us
beyond that world then becomes a matter for debate; certainly,

(Baltimore, Md.: Johns Hopkins University Press, 1990), esp. 140–58, 'Textual
Communities: Judaism, Christianity, and the Definitional Problem'. On his
application of the model to Judaism and Christianity see further below, pp. 35,
60.

[5] Stock, 'Textual Communities', 150; the model is adopted e.g. by T.
Thatcher, 'Literacy, Textual Communities and Josephus' *Jewish War*', *JSJ* 19
(1998), 123–42; Fox, 'Literacy and Power in Early Christianity'.

[6] Stock, *Implications of Literacy*, 91.

[7] See Graham, *Beyond the Written Word*.

[8] On this see A. Bowman and G. Woolf, 'Literacy and Power in the Ancient
World', in eidem, *Literacy and Power*, 1–16; T. Habinek, *The Politics of Latin
Literature: Writing, Identity, and Empire in Ancient Rome* (Princeton, NJ:
Princeton University Press, 1998), 103–21.

we should not ignore the role of scribes, who exercised their own patterns of control and who act as a reminder that the authority to deal with the texts was not the exclusive prerogative of the social elites even in Graeco-Roman society, and even less in Jewish and Christian circles.[9] We may, none the less, reaffirm the concerns already voiced in the Introduction that to listen to texts may be to listen only to those who control them—although, after all, the construction and maintenance of identity has much to do with the interests of the elite, in any period. And yet, in his analysis of 'Discourse and the Construction of Society', Bruce Lincoln recognizes that the dominant discourse will be that of the dominant class but also argues that it will not be immune to subversion or to alternatives.[10] Similarly, David Potter acknowledges that in Rome 'historiography was the province of the dominant class': the world that was shaped by its account of past history was one that served their interests; yet he hesitates simply to describe 'Roman historiography as the discourse of the dominant', for, he claims, there were other voices, other sources of knowledge, and so there was the possibility of choice.[11] No doubt those other sources usually have less chance of survival unless they successfully modify or even replace those they challenged, but we should see that textuality is not simply the articulation of identity, for some or for all, but is also the field of its contestation.

This, then, has brought us to the role of literature in the world of Mediterranean antiquity. As we have just hinted, texts there, as in any age, construct a sense of 'who we are', even when they seem to be engaged in doing something quite different. We shall describe in later chapters how, at least from Herodotus, classical literature examines who 'we' are by describing the alien practices and nature of 'them', while Edith Hall has shown how the polarization of 'Greek *versus* barbarian' is explored in tragedy even before it becomes a concern of philosophical analysis.[12]

---

[9] See M. Goodman, 'Texts, Scribes and Power in Roman Judaea', in Bowman and Woolf, *Literacy and Power*, 99–100; K. Haines-Eitzen, *Guardians of Letters: Literacy, Power, and the Transmitters of Early Christian Literature* (New York: Oxford University Press, 2000).

[10] Lincoln, *Discourse and the Construction of Society*.

[11] David Potter, *Literary Texts and the Roman Historian* (London: Routledge, 1999), 152–5.

[12] See F. Hartog, *The Mirror of Herodotus: The Representation of the Other*

This does not make it a purely aesthetic exercise, for it emerged within a quite specific political context and, no doubt, excluded other constructions. It enabled the 'objectification of selfhood'—which Joshua Friedman has called the 'textualisation of identity'.[13] At the same time, we are also reminded of the element of performance that is integral to all ancient literature and to how it was experienced.

Another pivotal moment in the textual shaping of identity was undoubtedly the development of Latin literature in the second century BCE: the comparatively late date is itself remarkable. Thomas Habinek associates 'the invention of Latin literature with the survival strategies of the traditional Roman leadership in the wake of the Hannibalic invasion'.[14] Before long, not just language but also questions of style and subject matter would become weapons in a battle to establish difference, as well as to foster the interests of the elite. At the same time, the spread of the Roman Empire went hand in hand with the spread of text and of literacy, not only through the 'inscriptional habit', but also through the dissemination of literature: 'the Roman empire was an empire of the written word'.[15] Yet receptive acquiescence was not the only response: this literature could also inspire imitations that might conspire to undermine the colonizing master-narrative; subject peoples could construct alternative histories of origins—a Jew could imitate not only tragedy, but also even the revered prophecies of the Sibyl.[16]

Within this framework, the centrality of texts for Jewish self-understanding is not out of place within the Graeco-Roman world.[17] The *Letter of Aristeas* seeks to exploit this when it makes the translation of the Scriptures from Hebrew into Greek the

in the Writing of History (ET. Berkeley, Calif.: University of California Press, 1988); E. Hall, *Inventing the Barbarians*. See further, below, pp. 105–7.

[13] Friedman, 'Notes on Culture and Identity in Imperial Worlds', 38.

[14] Habinek, *Politics of Latin Literature*, 39.

[15] David Potter, *Prophets and Emperors: Divine Authority from Augustus to Theodosius* (Cambridge, Mass.: Harvard University Press, 1994), 95; Bowman, 'Literacy in the Roman Empire'.

[16] Cf. Gruen, *Heritage and Hellenism*; also below, p. 118; the Jewish examples are Ezekiel the Tragedian and the Jewish Sibyllines.

[17] Conversely, note how M. Beard, '*Ancient Literacy* and the Function of the Written Word in Roman Religion', in Beard *et al.*, *Literacy in the Roman World*, 35–58, challenges the assumption that writing was marginal in 'paganism'.

result of Ptolemy II Philadelphus's desire to have, if possible, all
the books in the world collected in his library, and, again, when
it underlines the awesomeness of the undertaking by examples
of literary presumption or carelessness from the Greek rhetorical tradition (*Aristeas* 9–11; 312–16).[18] Evidently, for *Aristeas*
at least, a specific language plays a less determinative role—
although whether it would have been equally sanguine about
translations into other tongues seems less certain.[19] Yet, if for
Aristeas the Jewish Scriptures can easily hold their own in a
world literature, it is self-evident that in the Second Temple
period there is much more than this to be said about the centrality of written text to the whole question of an internal Jewish
identity. It is not our task here to explore every aspect of the
uses and status of 'sacred literature' in Judaism, or indeed in the
Graeco-Roman world and eventually in Christianity;[20] all we can
do is sketch some of the different ways in which texts functioned
in marking identity.

  The presupposition of all that follows has to be the intensive
activity, whose precise contours are largely lost to us, that, out of
earlier sources and collections, led to the production of the texts
that were to form the Scriptures, reifying a particular 'memory'
of the past and interpretation for the future. Precisely how and
when this happened—for example, whether the earliest stages
can be traced at least to the monarchic period, or whether this
is a post-exilic enterprise—is a matter of heated debate.[21] The
former view might suggest that the texts emerged out of history
and experience, and subsequently, in particular circumstances,
creatively shaped Judaism in the late Second Temple period.
This would be the picture encouraged by 1 Maccabees where
destruction of the books of the law is the touchstone of the action
of the oppressor (1 Macc. 1. 45–57). The latter view would give

---

  [18] On the purpose of *Aristeas* see V. Tcherikover, 'The Ideology of the Letter
of Aristeas', *HTR* 51 (1958), 59–85.
  [19] See below, pp. 106–8, 110 on language.
  [20] See J. Sawyer, *Sacred Languages and Sacred Texts* (London: Routledge,
1999). On the Scriptures in Judaism see M. J. Mulder (ed.), *Mikra: Text,
Translation, Reading and Interpretation of the Hebrew Bible in Ancient Judaism
and Early Christianity*, CRINT 2. 1 (Assen: Van Gorcum, 1988).
  [21] T. Thompson, *The Bible in History: How Writers Create a Past* (London:
Jonathan Cape, 1999). On creating a past, see below, Ch. 3.

a much starker picture of a minority, through the production or redaction of particular texts, seizing the power to determine the controlling discourse and so to shape an identity that consciously excluded other memories and other groups.[22] A separate but ultimately related aspect, then, is the process by which these writings become elevated to 'Scripture', acquiring an authority that set them apart from other texts and ensured their role for future self-understanding. Interrelated again, although not identical, is the movement towards closure that begins to narrow the possibilities for further modification of these texts, and that, in time, will also result in the preventing of the addition of further texts.[23] To describe these as 'process' and as 'movement' deliberately hides the agencies behind them, as they are indeed largely hidden from us.

So, for example, the surprising pluriformity of text-forms witnessed by the biblical manuscripts found among the Dead Sea Scrolls suggests that there was as yet no standardization of the text, and no apparent concern about its lack, and, consequently, that the text was open to creative reunderstanding in a dialogical relationship with communal self-understanding in a specific context. It seems that this situation changes some time after the destruction of the Temple in 70 CE, when text-forms begin to appear that will remain much the same for another millennium.[24] Again, whatever the origins of the distinctive text-form of the Samaritan Pentateuch, it too enshrines a self-understanding that separates its readers from those of other Pentateuchs while also uniting them in the valorization of this particular body of literature. Yet, whereas among the Samaritans the Pentateuch alone gained defining authority, it would appear that among the Dead Sea sectarians *Jubilees* and the *Temple Scroll* were treated in much the same way as other Scriptures, while 'the prophets' may

---

[22] P. R. Davies, *Scribes and Schools: The Canonization of the Hebrew Scriptures* (London: SPCK, 1998), 3, 41–2.

[23] See S. Chapman, *The Law and the Prophets: A Study in Old Testament Canon Formation*, FAT 27 (Tübingen: Mohr, 2000).

[24] See E. Ulrich, 'The Community of Israel and the Composition of the Scripture', in C. Evans and S. Talmon (eds.), *The Quest for Context and Meaning: Studies in Biblical Intertextuality in Honor of James A. Sanders*, BIS 28 (Leiden: Brill, 1997), 327–42; idem, *The Dead Sea Scrolls and the Origins of the Bible* (Grand Rapids, Mich.: Eerdmans, 1999).

have included not only Daniel but also the Psalms. In these ways there is a dynamic and dialectical relationship between texts, the variety of levels on which they function, and the distinctive identity of these groups.

This creative interaction between Scriptures and community can be seen in other ways. For example, the language and style of the Scriptures may shape later writing, as when 1 Maccabees, which, as we shall see repeatedly, is presenting a particular understanding of Judaism within the political setting of Hasmonean rule, claims legitimacy by echoing the Deuteronomic History in both style and method.[25] In a similar way, Luke-Acts will in its early chapters recall both by style and by theme the narratives of barrenness and birth from Israel's early history. Other forms of re-presentation can be found in the various rewritings of the past through expansion, explanation, and modification that characterize the so-called inter-testamental literature, such as *Jubilees*, the *Testaments* of Abraham, of the Patriarchs, or of other revered figures of the past. While some of these may appear to be literary experimentation, we shall see through the chapters that follow how, although Scripture may appear to control, it also generates and legitimates new possibilities of self-understanding.

Its generative and legitimating functions also appear in the composition of commentary on and interpretation of those earlier texts; the Dead Sea Scrolls develop an idiosyncratic form of biblical commentary, the *pesher*, through which Scripture is shown to anticipate and so to confirm the community's own self-understanding. Where the experience of marginalization from actual power might seem to undermine certainty, an interpretation of Scripture that is available only by special divine revelation establishes an alternative identity, albeit one that is persuasive only to those already within: the eschatological interpretation of Habbakuk 2, which offers certain hope for the 'men of truth', is legitimated by understanding Hab. 2. 2 as referring to 'the Teacher of Righteousness, to whom God has disclosed all the mysteries of the words of his servants, the prophets' (1 QpHab 7. 3–5). Conflict over the interpretation of the text is the locus for conflicting claims to legitimate identity: on the same author-

---

[25] See S. Schwartz, 'Israel and the Nations Roundabout: 1 Maccabees and the Hasmonean Expansion', *JJS* 52 (1991), 16–38, 34.

ity Habbakuk is shown to anticipate the Wicked Priest, presumably a Jerusalem high priest, who betrayed the laws and opposed the Teacher of Righteousness, and whose final judgement is assured.[26] In this way the scriptural text could precipitate a number of groups with what they perceived as mutually exclusive self-definitions. At the same time, at least among the Scrolls, the generation of and exploration of meaning is a highly literate activity, producing new texts, themselves in need of reproduction, and so, as in Stock's 'textual communities', presupposing the authority of the interpreters and of the scribes.

The later rabbinic tradition is, of course, no less productive of texts, although using a very different set of styles and generic assumptions. Here, again, it appears that the community evolved through interpretation and reinterpretation, both of the text and of the interpretative tradition.[27] Indeed, so intense and encompassing is this activity and the world it produces that it has seemed to some modern readers almost impossible to speak of rabbinic Judaism except as a construct of the texts, and as having an uncertain relationship to actual social living: 'a cognitive commune . . . of the mind and imagination'.[28]

Yet the solipsism of rabbinic literature is countered by other contemporary new genres, sometimes through imitation of the genres of the Hellenistic world of the time, such as the *Sibylline Oracles*, the novelistic *Joseph and Aseneth*, or the work of Ezekiel the tragedian, in which 'indigenous' traditions and a cultural outlook shared with 'others' create a dialogue of self-understanding.[29] While writings such as these may have at least one eye focused on the outside Hellenistic world, most of the other literary strategies just listed can be construed as shaping the inner self-understanding of a smaller or a larger section of

[26] The anonymity of the 'Wicked Priest', who may be supposed to have had a number of 'incarnations', is an integral part of the method.
[27] See M. Halbertal, *People of the Book: Canon, Meaning, and Authority* (Cambridge, Mass.: Harvard University Press, 1997).
[28] J. Neusner, *A History of the Mishnaic Law of Purities*, Part 22. *The Mishnaic System of Uncleanness: Its Context and History*, SJLA 6 (Leiden: Brill, 1977), 268, 'The Mishnaic system of uncleanness is an intellectual construct located at the fringes of the villages where people lived, but isolated from what happened therein. The system reflects a cognitive commune, like the Essenes, but a commune of the mind and imagination, situated at the edges of the common consciousness.' [29] Cf. Gruen, *Heritage and Hellenism*.

the heterogeneous body we label Judaism. Thus, there is a very powerful argument that the rise of Jewish sectarianism from the mid-second century BCE, itself an intensification of and a response to the problem of identity, is directly attributable to the rise of literacy and its democratization.[30]

It is, then, the more striking that there is little to suggest that the Jesus movement was, in the person and circumstances of its founder, predicated upon the precise interpretation of the Jewish sacred literary texts.[31] None the less, if we take a bird's-eye view of the larger body of 'Christian' texts that we shall be exploring in this study, then the decisive impact of the Scriptures remains unmistakable. Frances Young, again focusing mainly on a later period, has traced the singular contribution of 'biblical exegesis', albeit in a dialectical relationship with contemporary Graeco-Roman strategies, to the 'formation of Christian culture'.[32] The salient point is not merely exegesis so much as the adoption of the alternative literary culture of the Jewish tradition in contra-distinction to the culture of the Graeco-Roman tradition with its Homeric roots. Rather than creating a distinction between scriptural source and Christian extrapolation, this means that, in the words of William Horbury, 'Jews and Christians shared a common sub-culture, the literary focus of which was the Jewish scriptures.'[33] However, sharing, we should remember, may not be co-operative, and one of the challenges of our exploration will be negotiating between a shared subculture and conflictual identity-claims. In what follows we shall attempt to mark some of the contours in this tripartite relationship, looking as much at the conflicting reliefs that appear as at those that are agreed.

[30] See A. Baumgarten, *The Flourishing of Jewish Sects in the Maccabean Era: An Interpretation*, S.JSJ 55 (Leiden: Brill, 1997), 114–36.

[31] This is well noted by Baumgarten, *Flourishing of Jewish Sects*, 127 n. 40.

[32] F. M. Young, *Biblical Exegesis and the Formation of Christian Culture* (Cambridge: Cambridge University Press, 1997), 49–75.

[33] W. Horbury, 'Jews and Christians on the Bible: Demarcation and Convergence (325–451)', in J. van Oort and U. Wickert (eds.), *Christliche Exegese zwischen Nicaea und Chalcedon* (Kampen: Kok Pharos, 1992), 72–103, 102. Cf. J. D. Levenson, *The Death and Resurrection of the Beloved Son: The Transformation of Child Sacrifice in Judaism and Christianity* (New Haven, Conn.: Yale University Press, 1993), who describes Judaism and Christianity as 'midrashic systems whose Scriptural base is the Hebrew Bible' and sees in this the grounds of their mutually exclusive identities (p. 232).

TEXT AND COMMUNITY AMONG 'THE CHRISTIANS'

As in the community of the Scrolls, so also for early Christianity, the construction of identity under the impact of a biblically shaped literary culture is by no means limited to biblical exegesis; for Christianity, especially as it spread in the Graeco-Roman world, the visible effect of that impact varies greatly, as measured by explicit quotation, implicit allusion, symbolism, or concept. If we return to Cameron's description of the early Christian 'construction of reality through text', we should also need to include within that text the adoption, the interpretation, and the expansion of received Scriptures, as well as the development of a new literary corpus, with its own (contested) claims to authority, which will itself generate further adoption and interpretation . . .

The Adoption and Interpretation of the Jewish Scriptures

Fundamentally, from the earliest Jesus traditions, from the letter of James, or from the letters of Paul, the Scriptures are the assumed starting point; 'it is written', γέγραπται, can be used repeatedly without justification, whereas explicit appeals to sources of authority from the Greek and Roman tradition are, at least before the time of the Apologists, remarkable for their rarity.[34] As we shall see, for *1 Clement* as for Paul, and for many others, Abraham, as a scripturally defined character who believed, is 'our father'. There are dissenting voices: Ignatius uses the talismanic 'it is written' to refuse to engage with any demand that he demonstrate that his reading of 'the Gospel' coheres with the Scriptures (*Philad.* 8. 2); neither the *Gospel of Thomas* nor Polycarp's *Letter to the Philippians* make any explicit scriptural appeal, but neither do they elevate alternative texts to their place. The greatest challenge in our period was to come from Marcion who assigned the Jewish Scriptures to another, lesser God; we know of him only from his adversaries, and can only tentatively reconstruct the themes of his 'Antitheses' from their polemics.[35] Certainly he casts a long shadow over subsequent constructions

[34] e.g. Titus 1. 12, Epimenides, 'a certain prophet of their own'.
[35] On the influence of Marcion see Lieu, *Image and Reality*, 261–70.

of the Jewish Scriptures as determinative of Christian identity, but he did not displace their pre-eminence.

Something that was to prove determinative was the adoption of the Septuagint as the primary form of the text.[36] In most of the writings that we shall explore the Hebrew text does not have a special place. Certainly, sometimes, as in the case of John or even Paul, it is difficult to decide whether some citations from Scripture are free translations, modifications, or are variant text-forms of the Septuagint;[37] this may reflect the continuing fluidity of the text, or the priority given to the needs of the immediate argument, and certainly suggests no conscious principle at work. Yet by the time we come to Justin Martyr in the middle of the second century, the situation is very different: in his *Dialogue with Trypho* he expends considerable energy in tackling the problem that the text-form he used in his proof-texts frequently diverged from that familiar to his Jewish interlocutors. At times, 'his' text was more favourable to the Christian argument, even containing words or passages absent—he claims excised—from the Jewish text (*Dial.* 71. 1–73. 4). Yet, he betrays his own vulnerability when he endeavours to base his arguments on the text acceptable to his opponents, and when he is forced to admit that the Scriptures are to be found in *their* synagogues (32. 2; 72. 3).[38] Paradigms of the dispute and of its significance would be the translation of the 'young woman' of Isaiah 7. 14 by 'virgin' (παρθένος), so crucial for Christian apologetic and identity, or the 'missing' words 'from the tree' in quotations of Ps. 96. 10 (LXX 95. 10), 'The Lord reigns.'[39]

---

[36] See M. Müller, *The First Bible of the Church: A Plea for the Septuagint*, JSOT.SS 206 (Sheffield: Sheffield Academic Press, 1996).

[37] e.g. on John, M. Menken, *Old Testament Quotations in the Fourth Gospel: Studies in Textual Form*, Contributions to Biblical Exegesis and Theology 15 (Kampen: Kok, 1996); on Paul, C. Stanley, *Paul and the Language of Scripture: Citation Technique in the Pauline Epistles and Contemporary Literature*, SNTS. MS 74 (Cambridge: Cambridge University Press, 1992); on 1 Peter, W. L. Schutter, *Hermeneutic and Composition in 1 Peter*, WUNT 2/30 (Tübingen: Mohr, 1989).

[38] On this see further Lieu, *Image and Reality*, 125–9. Augustine could still acknowledge the Jews as owners of 'the books' (*in Joh.* 35. 7): see R. Wilken, 'The Jews and Christian Polemics after Theodosius I *Cunctos Populos*', *HTR* 73 (1980), 451–71, 466–8.

[39] Justin, *Dial.* 43. 7; 73. 1; 84. 3; Irenaeus, *adv. Haer.* III. 21.

Hellenistic-Jewish authors such as *Aristeas* had already fought to promote the Septuagint translation of the Torah as no less authoritative than the Hebrew 'original'; before long, Christians would take over the legend of the origins of the translation, extending it to the prophets also, and in their retelling emphasizing its independent character as revelation (Justin, *Apol.* 31; Ps.-Justin, *Cohort.* 13. 1–5).⁴⁰ The text thus became a touchstone for 'difference': in a well-known debate with Jerome, Augustine claimed the Septuagint for the Christians, leaving the Hebrew for the Jews (*Civ. Dei* XVIII. 42–3).⁴¹ Although outside our brief, at some stage, when and where Greek continued to be used, the Jews produced alternative Greek versions, traditionally associated with Aquila, Theodotion, and Symmachus.⁴² When Irenaeus labels Theodotion and Aquila 'Jewish proselytes', and claims that the Ebionites follow them, he demonstrates both how the translation could become a symbol of boundary-drawing, and also how those boundaries might then be reapplied for internal differentiation (*adv. Haer.* III. 21).⁴³

In time the problem of text would be joined by that of canon. Already in the latter half of the second century Melito of Sardis reportedly went to the land 'where it happened' in response to a query about the identity of the books of 'the old covenant' (Eusebius, *HE* IV. 26. 14). Whether the authority Melito was looking for was Jewish or primitive Christian tradition is disputed, and the issue was by no means solved with him.⁴⁴ Yet with his quest we see a new stage in the need to establish a '(self-) definitive' form of the textual heritage, although one that does not seriously take shape until after our period.

However, of particular significance for our purposes is the interpretation of the Scriptures. Here there is no single model,

---

⁴⁰ See M. Müller, 'Graeca sive Hebraica Veritas? The Defence of the Septuagint in the Early Church', *SJOT* 1989/1 (1989), 103–24.

⁴¹ Müller, 'Graeca sive Hebraica', 118–22.

⁴² On the whole question see K. Treu, 'Die Bedeutung des Griechischen für die Juden im Römischen Reich', *Kairos* 15 (1973), 123–44, 138–44.

⁴³ On these patristic reports see A. Salvesen, *Symmachus on the Pentateuch*, JSS.M 15 (Manchester: University of Manchester Press, 1991), 283–97. On internal boundary-drawing see below, pp. 295–7.

⁴⁴ On Melito see Lieu, *Image and Reality*, 207–8; on the general problem see R. Beckwith, *The Old Testament Canon of the New Testament Church and its Background in Early Judaism* (London: SPCK, 1985).

and to summarize would be to misrepresent the range and variety, both of approaches and of scholarship.[45] Instead, we may
illustrate with five examples, to which countless more could be
added.

  1 Peter appears to presuppose a Gentile audience (1 Pet. 2.
10; 4. 3–4); of the various social and historical contexts that
have been proposed for the letter, few have found any reason to
argue in favour of one of conflict with 'the synagogue' or over
Jewish identity within the 'brotherhood' (5. 9). This may accord
with Pliny's failure to identify the Christian movement within
a Jewish framework in the provinces of Bythinia and Pontus,
the destination of 1 Peter (*Epist.* X. 96), even though his good
friend Tacitus was well aware of the Judaean connection of
'the Christians', and was hostile to the Jews. Yet 1 Peter's use
of scriptural allusions, frequently but not consistently septuagintal, is so deeply embedded within the text that it appears to
be second nature to the author; if they were inaccessible to the
audience, then the letter would lose much of its resonance.[46]
The prophetic reversal of Hosea (1. 6, 9; 2. 25) establishes them,
'once no people, now [as] people (λαός) of God', so that to them
can be applied the epithets scripturally ascribed by God to the
people at the identity-creating moment at Sinai (Exod. 19. 5–6),
'a chosen race, a royal priesthood, a holy nation, a people for a
possession' (1 Pet. 2. 9–10).[47] There is no hint that there were
others, also of 'the Dispersion' (1. 1), who claimed the same epithets and appealed to the same Scriptures. For this author, there
is no moment of discontinuity between the time of the prophets
and that of the audience who are experiencing that of which the
former spoke (1. 10–12). The Scriptures provide the vocabulary
of their identity, and we may conjecture that for those coming
from a Gentile background this invited a radical resocialization
or reacculturization; thus the women now find themselves part
of the story that looks back to the nameless 'holy women' of the

[45] See E. Ellis, 'Biblical Interpretation in the New Testament Church', in
Mulder, *Mikra*, 691–725; W. Horbury, 'Old Testament Interpretation in the
Writings of the Church Fathers', in Mulder, *Mikra*, 727–89.

[46] On 1 Peter's use of Scripture see Schutter, *Hermeneutic and Composition*.

[47] On this passage see J. H. Elliott, *The Elect and the Holy*, NT.S 12 (Leiden:
Brill, 1966); K. Snodgrass, '1 Peter ii.1–10: Its Formation and Literary
Affinities', *NTS* 24 (1977–8), 97–106.

past and pre-eminently to Sarah (3. 5–6). Yet when we ask about the textualization of identity and the construction of 'the other', it is remarkable that the only boundary being built is one that separates them from their own past as Gentiles, and so implicitly from those who still share and live within that past (1. 14–18; 2. 10). What remains particularly hard to envisage is how far, or in what ways, this textual or symbolic repositioning within a different literary culture and identity was socially articulated.[48]

The strategy of the Fourth Gospel, our second example, is completely different, and this cannot simply be ascribed to the gospel genre. Here it is almost impossible to separate the use of Scripture from the various oppositional patterns that structure this Gospel. Scripture and the ability to read and hear Scripture lie at the heart of the conflict, both at the narrative level of Jesus's ministry and of his encounter with 'the Jews', and at the hypothe- sized level of the encounter between 'the Johannine community' and 'the synagogue' which has become intrinsic to most recent interpretation of the Gospel (John 5. 39–40).[49] While some see a paradox between the recognition that John is the most Jewish of the Gospels, and the sustained antithesis with 'the Jews' that lies at the root of its indictment as a prime source of Christian anti- Judaism or anti-Semitism, these characteristics are but opposite sides of the same coin. Even within the Jewishness of John, which is exemplified by its scriptural shaping, there is an unresolved ambivalence as to whether Scripture does still remain founda- tional for the readers' (or for the 'community's') identity, particu- larly in the face of the deliberate embrace of an otherness, a new identity, 'born from above' and 'not of this world' (3. 3; 17. 16). This ambivalence is already there within the use of Scripture, for example in the careful simultaneous affirmation and denial of the appeal, 'He gave them bread from heaven to eat' (6. 31: Exod. 16. 4; Ps. 78. 24).[50] This chapter illustrates very well John's use of a 'scriptural screen';[51] beyond the explicit citation of Scripture,

---

[48] See further, pp. 230–1.

[49] See below, pp. 87–8.

[50] See the brief discussion and further bibliographical references in J. M. Lieu, 'Narrative Analysis and Scripture in John', in S. Moyise (ed.), *The Old Testament in the New Testament: Essays in Honour of J. L. North*, JSNT.SS 189 (Sheffield: Sheffield Academic Press, 2000), 144–63.

[51] The term and the idea is worked out carefully by B. Olsson, *Structure and*

the whole narrative of the chapter, including the comments by both the actors and the narrator, is projected upon or through the screen of the biblical narratives of the wilderness wanderings—the gift of manna, the murmuring of the people, the death of the first generation. Scripture provides the necessary means for reading the story of Jesus, but belief in Jesus is the only key to a true reading of Scripture.

Despite the numerous attempts to describe the history of 'the Johannine community', it remains totally unclear whether its initial readers were predominantly of Jewish or of Gentile background. In either case, this absorption into or of Scripture by the Gospel would have had very different implications and effects—the reconfiguration of a familiar narrative identity or the acquisition of a very new one. Yet, in contrast to 1 Peter, there are involved here very clear continuities and discontinuities, and, therefore, clearly marked boundaries. The narrative of the past loses its ultimacy; it can no longer be foundational, but neither is it reapplied without perceived hiatus; if the scriptural culture appears to shape the present, it is the present experience that exposes the true meaning of that past. It seems unlikely that the scriptural determination of the Johannine narrative is 'merely' a legacy of the earlier traditions of 'Jesus the Jew', or that it is adopted only for apologetic or for missionary purposes in a Jewish context. Yet it can hardly have been written without awareness that there were others who continued to claim these same narratives as part of their inscribed identity; that claim is declared invalid, their belief is redefined as unbelief (John 5. 47). No less important are the ways in which Jesus's word is finding a place alongside Scripture (2. 22), and that this is all within a self-consciously textual form of re-presentation, '*written* (γεγράπται) that you may believe' (20. 31).

By contrast, Justin's *Dialogue with Trypho* provides not only an example of the explicit encounter with an alternative reading of the text, but also, other than the uncertainly dated *Epistle of Barnabas*, the first surviving one. The argument from proof-texts has a well-established history before Justin, but with him it can no longer stand on its own; the selection and combination of texts must now be joined by their 'proper' interpretation. Justin knows that the Jewish teachers have their own explanation for 'messianic' passages such as Ps. 110 (LXX 109), but he asserts that the true meaning can only be given where hearts and ears are unblocked (*Dial.* 32. 6–33. 1); the community of the Dead Sea Scrolls adopted the same strategy through their characteristic *pesher* exegesis. It does not really matter for our purposes whether Justin is right about his claims regarding alternative Jewish exegesis, and whether there are also Jewish roots to his own interpretations, however they came to him. It is sufficient to note that all the evidence suggests a continuing interaction—borrowing, polemic, counter-argument—between Jewish and Christian exegesis of the Scriptures, however that was achieved. The model that is developed by Justin, however, is that Scripture does belong to the Christians and that it is they who have the necessary key to its interpretation; 'alternative' interpretations, those of the Jews, the apparent owners, are not in practice the subject of discussion or of investigation, but are unilaterally excluded, self-condemned.

Moreover, although presented as an oral encounter, this here takes a written form shaped by familiar literary conventions, the dialogue of the Greek philosophical and rhetorical tradition, and is, moreover, controlled by its author.[52] In these ways, it both presupposes an agreed foundation and a shared world-view— one in which these particular biblical texts matter, a point that not all in the Graeco-Roman world would concede—and also seeks to delegitimate 'the other' without whose texts and inter- pretation it cannot proceed.[53] Whether we decide for an external audience for the *Dialogue*, or for one of internal lack of confi- dence, the text constructs those who interpret the text correctly even if they are the paupers in its possession.

Another way of reading the text retells the story in a radical new direction, addressing perceived problems even while refus- ing to jettison it altogether. A good example of this would be the *Apocalypse of Adam* (NH V. 5) which traces through the story of Adam, of Noah and his sons, and of the destruction of Sodom (?),

---

[52] On the *Dialogue*'s literary roots see B. Voss, *Der Dialog in der frühchristli- chen Literatur* (Munich: W. Funk, 1970), 26–40.

[53] See Voss, *Der Dialog*, 325.

an alternative thread of insight and knowledge challenging that of the creator god whom the text might otherwise be thought to honour.[54] Other texts, such as the *Hypostasis of the Archons* (NH II. 4), achieve this through a much closer redaction, for example by having 'the rulers' forbid Adam to eat of the tree of the knowledge of good and evil, or determine to send the flood to destroy all creatures, only to be pre-empted by the superior power who warned Noah to make the ark.[55] While these texts are conventionally labelled 'gnostic', the tensions they address in claiming the Scriptures in a new context are those shared by each of our examples.

A different set of insights into the way that interpretation and identity are interwoven would emerge from taking a particular biblical text and exploring the tradition of its interpretation within Christian thought alongside Jewish exegesis of the same text. This has been done particularly fruitfully with the story of the 'Sacrifice of Isaac' (Gen. 22. 1–14), a richly creative text within our period. The way in which Isaac moves from being a relatively passive victim to becoming a willing participant, the development of the associations with Passover, and the concomitant theme of the redemptive efficacy of the blood shed (*sic*), the introduction of ideas of atonement and of a martyrological framework, these take their place within a fascinating dance between Jewish and Christian exegesis. Rather than ascribing priority to one or other tradition, it seems better to see these developments taking place in interaction, however that interaction may have been realized socially.[56] The differences may be intentionally polemical, such as the Christian emphasis that Isaac did not suffer (Melito, Fragment 9, l. 9).[57] However, they also reflect the different hermeneutical controls, such as the importance of typology within a Christian system—again the Christian 'story'

[54] On the *Apocalypse of Adam* (NH V. 5 (64. 1–85. 32)) see below, n. 63; for the possible reference to Sodom in Gen. 19, see 75. 9–15.

[55] II. 88. 24–32; 92. 4–14: the *Hypostasis of the Archons* is probably 3rd century.

[56] See Lieu, *Image and Reality*, 77–9; 225–7, and bibliography there cited; G. Stroumsa, 'Herméneutique Biblique et Identité: L'exemple d'Isaac', *RevBib* 99 (1992), 529–43; Levenson, *Death and Resurrection of the Beloved Son*.

[57] In S. G. Hall (ed.), *Melito of Sardis* On Pascha *and Fragments*, OECT (Oxford: Clarendon, 1979), 74–5.

provides both the interpretative key and the legitimation for the appropriation of the scriptural narrative. Even where the polemic is not explicit, and the exegesis is not used to draw boundaries against nor to invalidate the narrative of 'the other', the continuing and developing history of such a text is part of the exercise and reaffirmation of identity through appeal to a correct retelling of the scripturally enshrined past.

It is this that constitutes a thread through these five models. Scripture needs to be properly understood, and it is the certainties of the present that define correct understanding; yet Scripture is also perceived as an independent witness and source of self-understanding. But this is not always the case, and there are other texts, such as the *Gospel of Truth* (NH I. 3), or even the *Gospel of Thomas*, that construct an identity without reference to these earlier authorities, claiming, as we shall see, other avenues of legitimation.

The Expansion of the Scriptures

Yet alongside the self-conscious commenting on the Scriptures, now claimed as their own, we also find the production and the preservation, with or without redaction, of those expansions and reinterpretations of the scriptural past that we have already described as Jewish. Because many of these texts survived only within the Christian tradition, and because clearly distinguishing markers, such as references to Christ, sometimes appear to belong only to a redactional level, such texts embody the dislocation of any a priori exclusive classification, Jewish *or* Christian.[58] If we shall discover that elsewhere, on the whole, Christian textuality moves towards differentiation and the erection of boundaries, here the opposite may at first seem to be the case. It makes considerable difference for how we conceptualize the social realities and processes involved, whether *The Testaments of the Twelve Patriarchs*, *The Life of Adam and Eve*, and *3 Baruch* are Jewish texts, with some easily recognizable and extractable

---

[58] On the problem see the essays in *JSJ* 32 (2001), 367–444, on 'Christianization of Ancient Jewish Writings', and especially R. A. Kraft, 'Setting the Stage and Framing Some Questions', 371–95.

passages of Christian redaction, or whether they are, both in the form in which we now have them and in any earlier form recoverable by us, Christian texts, albeit drawing from earlier Jewish traditions; the same might be said of *Joseph and Aseneth* or of *The Lives of the Prophets*, both of which have been read either as first-century Jewish or as fourth-century Christian texts.[59]

On one level, undoubtedly these texts are Christian for they have survived through Christian transmission, and traces of their impact and function within Jewish tradition are rare or missing—although the same might be said of the Septuagint. Yet this makes the paucity, or in some cases the absence, of any distinctively Christian features—the usual grounds for identifying them as fundamentally Jewish—the more remarkable. One solution has been to label them 'crypto-Christian', but should this translate into envisaging crypto-Christians as those who preserved them?[60] Particularly when these texts are dated later rather than earlier, in what way can this denote a sense of shared identity with Judaism, the absence of boundaries? On the contrary, it can be represented as a statement of the absorption of Jewish past into Christian present, 'one of the strongest statements of an emergent Christian hegemony'.[61] It is, perhaps, a similar confidence that can put into the mouth of Isaiah a prophecy not simply of the descent and death of the Beloved, but even of the divisions and laxity that would weaken the church (*Asc. Isa.* 3. 13–31).[62]

[59] For a predominantly Christian reading of *The Testaments* see B. W. Hollander and M. de Jonge, *The Testaments of the Twelve Patriarchs: A Commentary*, SVTP 8 (Leiden: Brill, 1985), 82–5; of *Joseph and Aseneth* see R. Kraemer, *When Aseneth met Joseph: A Late Antique Tale of the Biblical Patriarch and His Wife, Reconsidered* (New York: Oxford University Press, 1998); of *The Lives of the Prophets* see D. Satran, *Biblical Prophets in Byzantine Palestine: Reassessing the Lives of the Prophets*, SVTP 11 (Leiden: Brill, 1995). On *3 Baruch*, see below, pp. 75–6; M. Eldridge, *Dying Adam with his Multiethnic Family: Understanding the* Greek Life of Adam and Eve, SVTP 16 (Leiden: Brill, 2001) makes a guarded decision for a Jewish origin (p. 264). See also M. Knibb, 'Christian Adoption and Transmission of Jewish Pseudepigrapha: The Case of *1 Enoch*', *JSJ* 32 (2001), 396–415, 396–400.

[60] For these as 'kryptochristliche Texte' see G. Kretschmar, 'Die Kirche aus Juden und Heiden', in J. van Amersfoort and J. van Oort (eds.), *Juden und Christen in der Antike* (Kampen: Kok, 1990), 9–43, 31–3.

[61] Satran, *Biblical Prophets*, 120.

[62] For the *Ascension of Isaiah* as a Christian text of the 2nd century see

A related but different question is posed by such texts as the *Apocalypse of Adam* (NH V. 5) which is often dated to the second century CE. This takes the form of a revelation from Adam to his son Seth, and involves a rewriting of the early chapters of Genesis, integral to which is the distinction between the eternal God and the god who created Adam and Eve. There are no explicitly Christian features, although the story moves towards the coming of the 'illuminator of knowledge' (76. 8). Here, a third label, 'gnostic', does nothing to solve the problem: is this text Jewish, despite its inversion of expected Jewish values, or Christian, despite the absence of any explicit markers? Both can be and have been argued.[63]

This will create a very real problem for us and for the present project: where is the identity constructed by these texts to be located? This is not just a question of asking whether we should assign the labels 'Jewish', 'Christian', 'Jewish-Christian', or even 'Jewish-and-Christian', never mind 'gnostic', but of asking whether the pattern of contours would change according to the wider set of texts or associations within which they were read. This dilemma will be reflected in the rest of this study. For the most part we shall read *The Testaments of the Twelve Patriarchs*, *Joseph and Aseneth*, and other similar texts, alongside those with which they seem to share patterns of self-understanding; because the explicitly Christian redaction often takes the form of doctrinal epithets or assertions this will figure less prominently. As a consequence we may seem to be showing how they work as Jewish

J. Knight, *The Ascension of Isaiah*, Guides to the Apocrypha and Pseudepigrapha (Sheffield: Sheffield Academic Press, 1995); as a Jewish core text (*The Martyrdom of Isaiah*) with later Christian expansion, M. Knibb, 'The Martyrdom of Isaiah', in M. de Jonge (ed.), *Outside the Old Testament*, Cambridge Commentaries on Writings of the Jewish and Christian World 200 BC to AD 200, 4 (Cambridge: Cambridge University Press, 1985), 178–92.

[63] See G. McRae (ed.), 'The Apocalypse of Adam, V,5:64.1–85.32', in D. Parrott (ed.), *Nag Hammadi Codices V,2–5 and VI with Papyrus Berolinensis 8502, 1 and 4*, NHS 11 (Leiden: Brill, 1979), 151–95, who regards it as Sethian but as reflecting the transition between Jewish and gnostic; he is followed by F. Morard (ed. and introd.), *L'Apocalypse d'Adam (NH V,5)*, BCNH 15 (Quebec: Presses de l'Université Laval, 1985), but challenged by G. M. Shellrude, 'The Apocalypse of Adam: Evidence for a Christian Gnostic Provenance', in M. Krause (ed.), *Gnosis and Gnosticism: Papers Read at the Eighth International Conference on Patristic Studies*, NHS 17 (Leiden: Brill, 1981), 82–91.

texts, although this may say more about the particular traditions and themes that we are isolating.[64] Yet, even so, what we shall have to recognize is that they not only can be, but were, read as Christian texts, challenging us imaginatively to reconstruct how reading and self-understanding informed each other.[65]

The Development of a New Literary Corpus

In these various ways the relationship between the production of new texts and the appeal to the authority of past texts is a tensive one. However, as we have seen, the same was no less true of the Dead Sea Scrolls, and in a different way of the Mishnah and later Talmuds. Yet the texts we shall now explore appear to operate in a quite different social context from either of those corpora, and to move in different directions of creativity.

As has been repeatedly noted, whatever conclusions we may reach about the social level of the members of the early Christian communities, particularly following the spread of the Gospel into the cities of the Roman East, Christianity is characterized, at least from our perspective, by the vibrancy and creativity of its literary productivity.[66] From the earliest evidences of this, among which must be Paul's letter to the church at Thessalonica, its authors saw their activity not as peripheral nor as transitory but as indispensable; 1 Thess. 5. 27 is remarkably solemn: 'I bind you by oath by the Lord that the letter be read to all the brethren.' Whether or not we subscribe to the argument that most of the early Christian writings had in view a primary audience in a specific locality and context,[67] both by authorial intent and by recipients' response 'Christian' texts were circulated, preserved, collected, and used as stimuli for the production of further writ-

[64] All would agree that the *Testaments* etc. use Jewish traditions, whether written or oral.

[65] How such texts as the *Apocalypse of Adam* were read is more difficult to determine given their apparent failure to generate a long tradition of reading and use, and given the uncertainties about the nature of the Nag Hammadi collection: see below, n. 83.

[66] In addition to our earlier discussions of the problem we should note that literacy is not one of the characteristics most noted by early Christianity's pagan opponents.

[67] See above, p. 4, and Bauckham, *The Gospels for All Christians*.

ing. Thus Ignatius sees himself as writing in 'apostolic character', assures the church at Ephesus that Paul mentions them in every letter, and organizes the exchange of various letters (Ignatius, *Trall.* praef.; *Eph.* 12. 2), while, within a generation of his death, his own letters were collected and exchanged as 'embracing faith and endurance and all building up which pertains to our Lord' (Polycarp, *Philipp.* 13. 2). Yet further in the future, in the fourth century, they would become the kernel of a new expanded edition of thirteen letters through which 'Ignatius' could address new needs.[68]

We may indeed see this as part of a contest for power, the primary survivors from which are the winners; notable are the number of texts that failed to survive even to the time of Eusebius, even though he had no doubt of their exemplary character.[69] For the moment, what we have to envisage is a base level of activity out of which there are generated various levels of suspension or crystallization, texts that are exchanged; texts that survive for more than a generation; texts that become significant for one or more areas or groups; texts that are explicitly contested, adopted by some, rejected by others; texts that are imitated, incorporated, or commented upon by subsequent authors; texts that are read on corporate, formal, liturgical occasions . . .

A particular feature of this literary contest is the different ways in which both Jesus and the Apostles become 'textualized'. We have already seen this happening in the Fourth Gospel; similarly, 'the living Jesus spoke the secret sayings . . . which Didymos Judas Thomas wrote down. And he said, "Whoever falls upon the meaning of these words will not taste death"' (*Gosp. Thom.* Praef.–1). When in the *First Apocalypse of James* (NH V. 3) Jesus reinterprets Scripture (26. 2–10), there is a triple layer of textualization: first, the unexplained 'Scripture' that previously had been explained only by 'one of limited understanding'; then,

---

[68] On the long recension of the Ignatian letters as reflecting the doctrinal conflicts of the 4th century see J. D. Smith, 'The Ignatian Long Recension and Christian Communities in Fourth Century Syrian Antioch', Th.D. thesis (Harvard, 1986).

[69] On this see F. Wisse, 'The Use of Early Christian Literature as Evidence for Inner Diversity and Conflict', in C. Hedrick and R. Hodgson (eds.), *Nag Hammadi, Gnosticism and Early Christianity* (Peabody, Mass.: Hendrickson, 1986), 177–90.

that of secret words of Jesus to James divulging the true meaning; and, thirdly, that of the revered James who describes the
experience and who, at the end of the narrative, then departs. In
a different text the same 'James' writes a letter as a 'secret book';
by describing a special revelation from the Saviour as the twelve
Apostles were setting their own memories 'in order in books', he
appears to presuppose other writings while he claims for 'his'—
namely, for the text we are reading—a special status: 'for apart
from the persons I have mentioned the Saviour did not give us a
revelation' (*Apocryphon of James* (NH I. 2) I. 8–2. 39; 16. 23–5).[70]
The *Gospel of Peter* similarly claims the first-person speech of 'I,
Simon Peter' (*Gosp. Peter* 60), while elsewhere 'Simon Peter'
warns against those who twist the letters of Paul as they do also
'the remaining writings' (2 Pet. 3. 15–16).

Here we move into the broader question of pseudonymity
which is such a widespread phenomenon among our texts. It
is probably not to be understood alongside the debates about
forged authorship in Greek and Roman literary circles, nor as
parallel to the 'production' of letters of long-dead philosophers;
even the creation of apocalypses and of testaments of the patriarchs of the earliest period of Israel's history does not work in
quite the same way, for 'Jesus' and 'the Apostles' rarely exploit
the predictive possibilities of hindsight to the same extent as do
those other texts.[71] Whether or not always polemically, Jesus and
the earliest Apostles can be regenerated textually to authorize
particular understandings of their teaching, and perhaps to deny
other understandings or structures.

Other strategies may be used to a similar end: the form of a
secret revelation, as given to 'James', already claims an exclusive and irrefutable authority. A similar self-reflexive strategy is
exercised by the *Shepherd of Hermas* when the mysterious lady

---

[70] See D. Rouleau, *L'Épître apocryphe de Jacques (NH 1,2)*, BCNH 18
(Quebec: Presses de l'Université Laval, 1987); the uncertainty regarding the
date of the *Apocryphon*—suggestions range from the 2nd to the 3rd century—
leaves it uncertain which other writings are presupposed here.

[71] On the problem of pseudonymity see D. Meade, *Pseudonymity and Canon:
An Investigation into the Relationship of Authorship and Authority in Jewish and
Earliest Christian Tradition* (Grand Rapids, Mich.: Eerdmans, 1987); there is
prediction in 2 Peter (as also in *Asc. Isa.*) but not with the same systematization
as in many Jewish apocalypses.

of his visions reads aloud from a book that Hermas at first fails to comprehend; given it to copy, still without understanding, he then receives a revelation as to its meaning, and he is instructed to give the book to the elders of the church (*Vis.* I. 2–4; II. 1–3).[72] The identity and status of the author is of no account—the revelations should have been given to those better than he (*Vis.* III. 4)—the text authenticates itself in its textuality. Indeed, since the lady it encodes is the church, church and text authenticate each other.

Although of the texts just cited only 2 Peter was eventually to make its way into the canon, such claims to authority provide the conceptual framework within which the latter was to emerge. Evidently we cannot think of the gradual linear emergence of an agreed body of texts alongside the existing recognized authority of the Jewish Scriptures, as has sometimes been pictured. Traditionally, accounts have started from the end of that process, the New Testament canon, and have found it is easy enough to look back and to trace how, when, and where its eventual constituents were cited and with what authority, as well as when and where the language of inspiration or of 'Scripture' come to be used of them.[73] A view from the beginning is less conducive to such a teleological account, which sets 'in' against 'out'. Instead, differing representations of the textual voice of Jesus and of his earliest followers clamour to be heard, whether it be as autonomous, or alongside and as the true meaning of the voice of the Jewish Scriptures.

The thrust of the development of what was to become the New Testament was that these texts should act as the primary hermeneutical key for the preservation and interpretation of the Jewish Scriptures.[74] Looking ahead beyond our period, we

[72] On this see P. C. Miller, *Dreams in Late Antiquity: Studies in the Imaginations of a Culture* (Princeton, NJ: Princeton University Press, 1994), 142; Haines-Eitzen, *Guardians of Literacy*, 5–6.
[73] For such 'histories of the canon', see B. F. Westcott, *A General Survey of the History of the Canon of the New Testament*, 7th edn. (London: Macmillan, 1896); B. M. Metzger, *The Canon of the New Testament: Its Origin, Development and Significance* (Oxford: Clarendon, 1987).
[74] G. Stroumsa, 'The Christian Hermeneutical Revolution and its Double Helix', in L. V. Rutgers *et al.* (eds.), *The Use of Sacred Books in the Ancient World* (Leuven: Peeters, 1998), 9–28, 13.

may cite Athanasius in his *39th Festal Letter*, which has become
one of the 'canonical texts' regarding the canon. Having listed
'the books which are canonized and handed down and believed
to be divine' of the Old Testament and of the New Testament,
he continues, 'In these books alone the teaching of piety is pro-
claimed. Let no-one add to them or subtract anything from
them. Concerning them the Lord put the Sadducees to shame by
saying, "You go astray because you do not know the Scriptures
[or their meaning]" [Matt. 22. 29], and he reproved the Jews,
"Search the Scriptures, for it is they which bear witness concerning me" [John 5. 39]': here the words of Jesus within the
New Testament are assumed to be self-referential and yet also to
encompass the Old Testament and its Christian location.[75] That
lies ahead, and both the difference from, but also the whispers of,
such a view may be heard at the beginning of the second century
when Ignatius apparently dismisses the independent authority
of the Jewish Scriptures, 'the archives': 'for me the archives are
Jesus Christ, the sacred archives his cross and death and resurrection, and faith through him' (*Philad.* 8. 2).[76]

Towards the end of our period, the first two centuries CE, the
bulk of what was to form Athanasius's canon appears to have
been recognized as of special status by many, although not all,
communities. Difficulties of dating mean that we cannot be sure
whether the polemical claims of other texts, for example of the
writings of 'James' or of 'Peter' quoted earlier, were mounting
a conscious challenge to this, or whether they simply reflect a
diversity that was soon to be forgotten or suppressed. Yet the
evidence of biblical manuscripts, of canon lists, and of usage
show that, for some, the inscribed authority of *The Teaching
of the Twelve Apostles* (*Didache*), of the letter of 'Paul' to the
Hebrews, or of *The Epistle of Barnabas* remained persuasive,
while the claims of antiquity gave a special place to *1 Clement* or
to the *Shepherd of Hermas*.[77] Ultimately, different concepts of
canonicity and so of the canon would emerge in different parts

---

[75] For a composite translation of all the surviving fragments see D. Brakke,
Athanasius and the Politics of Asceticism, OECS (Oxford: Clarendon, 1995),
326–32. A similar argument is often repeated by those who cite 2 Tim. 3. 16 to
assert the divine inspiration of their Scriptures, including 2 Timothy itself.

[76] See above, p. 37; on the translation and significance of 'archives', see Lieu,
Image and Reality, 37–9.   [77] See Metzger, *Canon*, 187–9, 310–11.

of the church, Ethiopic, Coptic, Western, and, later, Catholic and Protestant. Although long after our period, this is not the corruption of some prior pristine harmony but testimony to the ever-changing interrelationship between text and identity.[78]

Although within our period we do not have more than papyrus fragments of varying length, the evidence of the extent of variation in the later manuscript tradition suggests a similar diversity as intrinsic to Christian textuality. On this, as on every level, there is a danger in using texts as neutral quarries, without recognizing that even 'manuscripts themselves are part of the social matrix of antiquity'.[79] Textual variants cannot be ascribed to scribal error alone, but whether we think of the distinctive tradition of the Western text of Acts, or of the evidence of conscious reworking of the text in particular doctrinal or other interests, the text is both the product of and productive of distinctive identities.[80]

The production of texts therefore involves acts of power, of exclusion as well as of inclusion. Again, this has been traditionally explored from the perspective of 'histories of the canon': already Irenaeus can argue that 'since there are four zones of the world and four regions of the world, and the church is scattered over the whole earth and the Gospel is the pillar and foundation of the church', so there must needs be four Gospels (Irenaeus, *adv. Haer.* III. 11. 8). Tertullian dismissed the *Acts of Paul* as written in emulation of Paul by a presbyter in Asia, who duly lost his post on detection; Tertullian's problem with the *Acts* is, 'How could we believe that Paul should give to a female power to teach and baptise?' (*de Bapt.* 17). Tertullian had also rejected the appeal to Scripture by those *he* labelled heretics with the assertion that the crucial question is who has the right to possess the Scriptures, a question we have already heard Justin direct against the Jews (*de Praes. Haer.* 14. 10). According to Eusebius, Dionysius of

---

[78] See Lieu, 'New Testament and Christian Identity', 195–8.

[79] L. G. Blomquist, N. Bonneau, J. K. Coyle, 'Prolegomena to a Sociological Study of Early Christianity', *Social Compass* 39 (1992), 221–39, 230.

[80] This presupposes that we should not think of an original ur-text: see J. K. Elliott, *Essays and Studies in New Testament Textual Criticism*, Estudios de Filologia Neotestamentaria 3 (Cordoba: Ed. el Almendro, 1992), 17–43; B. Ehrman, *The Orthodox Corruption of Scripture: The Effect of Early Controversies on the Text of the New Testament* (New York: Oxford University Press, 1993); Haines-Eitzen, *Guardians of Literacy*.

Corinth composed 'catholic letters' for the churches, but complained of the 'apostles of the devil who filled them with tares' by omission and addition: 'it is not surprising then that some have even set about falsifying the Scriptures of the Lord (αἱ κυριακαὶ γραφαί)' (*HE* IV. 23. 1, 12). Again, to see where this might go we can look ahead to Athanasius in his *39th Festal Letter*, who here was following a well-established tradition: 'For truly the apocryphal books . . . are the beginning of discord . . . Therefore, it is even more fitting for us to reject such books, and let us command ourselves not to proclaim anything in them nor to speak anything in them with those who want to be instructed, even if there is a good word in them . . .'[81] In this way the canon becomes an instrument in the legitimation of structures and authority, and in the delegitimation of alternatives, 'even if there is a good word in them'; it draws boundaries by identifying what lies outside as well as by affirming what lies within.

Although here we have started with Athanasius, we should not see this as a single act by individual or by conciliar dictate: there is a canonical process stretching through the centuries before Athanasius and continuing in practice long after. Therefore it is much more difficult to demonstrate the inevitable exercise of authority and power within this process of exclusion—and as a consequence it has been easier for observers complicitly to see it as the unfolding of 'the mind of the church' or of what was implicit 'from the beginning'. Such a view favours an essentialist understanding of identity, and invites the historian to reinscribe a statically conceived crystallization in time. Yet, if identity is dynamic, and if the establishment of a dominant discourse is both contested and an act of power, those excluded also belong to the recovery of identity; so it is that the voices of the excluded or marginalized have been given a voice in recent reconstructions of Christian origins.[82]

---

[81] Brakke, *Athanasius*, 330–1, here following the Coptic text. On the context of Athanasius's letter as a strategy for excluding the Meletians and the Arian 'academic' model of authority, see D. Brakke, 'Canon Formation and Social Conflict in Fourth Century Egypt', *HTR* 87 (1994), 395–419.

[82] For the principle as developed within a feminist hermeneutic see E. Schüssler Fiorenza (ed.), *Searching the Scriptures*, i. *A Feminist Introduction*; ii. *A Feminist Commentary* (New York: Crossroad, 1993–4) which includes many other writings, but not those of the Old Testament.

Yet there is a danger, even while listening to the 'excluded other', of nevertheless conceding the identity ascribed to them either by future 'orthodoxy' or by later scholarship, a temptation encouraged both by a modern 'Apocryphal New Testament' or by the chance discovery of the fourth-century 'Nag Hammadi Library', misleadingly described as 'the sacred scriptures of the gnostic movement'.[83] It is Athanasius who fears lest 'a few of the simple . . . might begin to read other books, the so-called apocrypha, deceived by their having the same names as the genuine books', and who in this way creates the spectre of an alternative, imitative canon constituting an alternative, heretical identity.[84] His concern itself warns us against retrojecting the model to earlier centuries. It will be important in what follows not to think of canonical versus non-canonical, any more than of orthodox versus heretical, nor to think of particular texts as representing particular prior labelled positions. Diversity may be both tolerant and intolerant, and it is both the diversity and the (in)tolerance that we are exploring.

Finally, resisting any form of categorization is the vast flow of other literature that was the primary vehicle through which the central identity-bearing texts were actualized, but that neither claimed nor was accorded the authoritative status of the latter. Such actualization takes many forms, as we shall discover, but here we may note in particular the formative impact of these earlier texts, not only in inspiring imitation but also in the creation of a 'language'. The *Martyrdom of Polycarp*, which took

[83] J. K. Elliott (ed.), *The Apocryphal New Testament: A Collection of Apocryphal Christian Literature in English Translation* (Oxford: Clarendon, 1993). The Nag Hammadi description comes from the jacket-cover of J. Robinson (ed.), *The Nag Hammadi Library in English* (Leiden: Brill, 1977). For theories about the origins of the thirteen codices from Nag Hammadi, see S. Emmel, 'Religious Tradition, Textual Transmission and the Nag Hammadi Codices', in J. D. Turner and A. McGuire (eds.), *The Nag Hammadi Library after Fifty Years: Proceedings of the 1995 Society of Biblical Literature Commemoration*, NHMS 44 (Leiden: Brill, 1997), 34–43; M. A. Williams, 'Interpreting the Nag Hammadi Library as "Collection(s)" in the History of "Gnosticism(s)"', in L. Painchaud and A. Pasquier (eds.), *Les Textes de Nag Hammadi et le problème de leur classification: actes du colloque tenu à Quebec des 15 au 19 septembre 1993*, BCNH Études 3 (Quebec: Presses de l'Université Laval, 1995), 3–50.

[84] Athanasius identifies these heretical promulgators as Meletians: Brakke, *Athanasius*, 327, 332; idem, 'Canon Formation'.

place 'according to the Gospel' (*Mart. Poly.* 1. 1; 19. 1), is in part
a literary mimesis of the Passion narrative, probably from more
than one of the canonical Gospels—Polycarp enters the city on
a donkey, is encouraged by a voice from heaven, knows that he
must die, while his death is clamoured for by the crowds, including the Jews, and a certain Herod plays a key role.[85] Yet equally
striking is the way that this text is saturated with 'biblical' language: according to one estimate only thirty-six out of nearly
600 different words are not 'biblical Greek'; of these thirty-six,
eleven belong to the Hellenistic setting of the narrative, while
four reflect developing 'Christian' language of the second century (for example, 'Christianity' (χριστιανισμός)). Sometimes,
however, these 'biblical' words are used with a new meaning,
such as 'witness/martyr' (μάρτυς), while direct or explicit quotations are rare.[86] Again, we are observing the development of
a new literary culture and of a 'new' language, which mediate
between 'faith and the world'.

CHRISTIAN TEXTUALITY IN ITS CONTEXT

This new and yet not new literary culture—'not new' because of
its scriptural roots—brings us back to our earlier quotation from
Averil Cameron. Here we may note some further tensions in its
creation.

The various genres used by early Christian writers themselves
partake in and demonstrate the creation of a new cultural system, but one which none the less overlaps with and draws from
those already available within the Judaeo-Graeco-Roman world.
The dynamics of this have been much discussed: for example,
whether the Christian Gospels are a new, *sui generis*, genre, or
whether they belong to the tradition of the Graeco-Roman biography or novel, has often become the touchstone of theological
claims about the novelty or revelatory character of the Christian
Gospel.[87] A more nuanced view might see them as imitations,

[85] *Mart. Poly.* 5. 2–8. 2; 12. 2–3.
[86] M. L. Guillaumin, 'En marge du "Martyre de Polycarpe": le discernement des allusions scripturaires', in *Forma Futuri: Studi in honore del cardinale
Michele Pellegrino* (Turin: Battega d'Erasmo, 1975), 462–9, 464–5.
[87] R. Burridge, *What are the Gospels?*, SNTS.MS 70 (Cambridge: Cambridge

'outside of the canon of classical historiography, at times using its canons to make their own points', while some would argue for their reflective impact on the development of Graeco-Roman literary forms.[88] Similarly, the characteristic Christian letter, perhaps decisively shaped by Paul but imitated not only, as we have seen, by Ignatius but also by the first martyrdom accounts, has been illuminated by analyses of ancient epistolography, particularly in terms of its structure and conventions; however, this alone cannot account for the distinctive character not only of their origin, content, and length, but more importantly of their function.[89] The comparison of the Acts of the Apostles with contemporary conventional topoi, historiographic and novelistic, has been fruitful, yet in no way undermines recognition of the way it constructs an identity for its chief subject, while again drawing on the literary and conceptual traditions of the Jewish Scriptures.[90] While an ideology of martyrdom was not the creation of the early Christians, the development of a dedicated literature, the Acts of Martyrs, tells us as much about a new effort at world-building—interpreting experience for their readers but also productive of experience for those who share in them—as about the historical circumstances of persecution.[91]

On the other hand, as we have already seen, the Dialogue form, adopted in our period most creatively by Justin Martyr, draws on a specific philosophical tradition, even while using as the focus of the dialogue the alternative tradition of the Jewish Scriptures. Similarly, the Apology, which Christians adopted from the mid-second century on, belongs within a continuing

University Press, 1992); A. Dihle, 'The Gospels and Greek Biography', in P. Stühlmacher (ed.), *The Gospel and the Gospels* (ET. Grand Rapids, Mich.: Eerdmans, 1991), 361–86.

[88] For the first point, see Potter, *Literary Texts*, 145, 155; G. Bowersock, *Fiction as History, Nero to Julian* (Berkeley, Calif.: University of California Press, 1994), suggests the influence of the Gospels as a 'kind of narrative fiction in the form of history' on the literature of the period (p. 123).

[89] On letters see S. Stowers, *Letter Writing in Greco-Roman Antiquity* (Philadelphia: Westminster John Knox, 1986); for the martyr accounts as letters see *Mart. Poly.* and the letter of the Churches of Vienne and Lyons in Eusebius, *HE* V. 1. 3.

[90] See below, pp. 90–4.

[91] See Lieu, '"I am a Christian"', and below, pp. 200–02.

literary and political context within the early Empire that
had already been exploited by Jewish writers: when the latter
sought to present themselves as a people meriting the respect
and rights accorded to other political entities they presented
their Scriptures as their ancestral laws (πατρίοι νόμοι), adopting
categories familiar from the Greek world.[92] As we have seen, in
his *Apology* Justin rehearses the story of the Greek translation
of the prophets, developed earlier by *Aristeas*, because he too
believes that they will demonstrate that his claims about Christ
have not been invented (Justin, *Apol.* 30–1). As an apologist for
the Christians, Aristides is confident that should the Emperor
read their Scriptures he will find confirmed all the virtues claimed
(Aristides, *Apol.* 16. 5).[93] The Apologists joined the contemporary game of claiming antiquity and yet, by using Jewish texts as
their authority and norm, relativized the classical authorities of
their fellow players.[94] Admittedly, both *Dialogue* and Apologies
have prompted an unresolved debate as to whether outsiders or
only insiders would best read and make sense of them, yet for
their authors their texts did not put them outside the contemporary world but gave them a pre-eminent place within it. Whether
such convictions had any foundation is not our concern: in the
apologetic context Christian texts are constructed as persuasive
demonstration.[95]

All this and more could be expounded at length, and supported
by extensive bibliographies; some is explored in other chapters.
Those who read or heard such literature would find themselves
in a world at once both familiar and yet foreign. Frances Young

---

[92] See H. Kippenberg, 'Die jüdischen Überlieferungen als "patroi nomoi"',
in R. Faber and R. Schlesier (eds.), *Die Restauration der Götter: Antike Religion
und Neo-Paganismus* (Würzburg: Königshausen & Neumann, 1988), 45–60; see
further below, pp. 72, 224.

[93] Here I am assuming that the reference is in fact to the Jewish Scriptures,
although there could be a reference to distinctive Christian writings, especially in
the Greek version's 'the writings of the Christians' (αἱ γραφαὶ τῶν Χριστιανῶν).

[94] Young, *Biblical Exegesis*, 51–7, following A. Droge, *Homer or Moses? Early
Christian Interpretation of the History of Culture*, HUT 26 (Tübingen: Mohr,
1989); also M. Edwards, M. Goodman, S. Price, in association with C. Rowland
(eds.), *Apologetics in the Roman Empire: Pagans, Jews, and Christians* (Oxford:
Oxford University Press, 1999).

[95] On the question of genre and readership see Lieu, *Image and Reality*, 104–
9, 156–60.

argues that Justin was 'neither "Jew" nor "Greek" in terms of culture'—and he would be inconceivable without the precedents of both.[96] Yet she also denies that he was counter-cultural, here contrasting him with figures such as Marcion or Valentinus. This may be to reinscribe later boundaries between orthodoxy and heresy, and 'counter-cultural' may in some respects be more applicable to some literature, such as the Martyr Acts, than to others, such as the Apologies. Yet there is a sense in which these various genres, so different in presuppositions and style from the solipsic world-building of rabbinic literature, would locate early Christians both within the world of Graeco-Roman culture, in which Hellenistic Jewish literature had already claimed a place, and yet outside it.

Even the physical character of 'text' participates in this symbolic function: it has been suggested that it was only towards the end of the second century that Christians began to produce and to own manuscripts of the whole of the Old Testament; until then they were dependent on anthologies or on the Jewish possession of Scriptures. Yet there is also substantial evidence that the adoption of the codex form as opposed to the scroll was part of a search for differentiation, at least from the Jews on whom they depended.[97] Certainly, the codex enabled a very different role for the Scriptures by offering a greater ease of access, now available to a more diverse readership.[98]

This further illustrates how, as we have repeatedly seen, texts have a social function and cannot be understood apart from questions of literacy and of the structures of power.[99] Both manuscriptal variants and the delineation of authoritative texts have already testified to this. Here we should also emphasize how texts may articulate the exercise of power by their authors—a process

[96] Young, *Biblical Exegesis*, 68.

[97] For the first claim see O. Skarsaune, 'From Books to Testimonies: Remarks on the Transmission of the Old Testament in the Early Church', *Immanuel* 24/5 (1990), 207–19; for the second, I. M. Resnick, 'The Codex in Early Jewish and Christian Communities', *JRH* 17 (1992), 1–17; also Young, *Biblical Exegesis*, 10–16, 59, who sees this as a 'desacralizing'. However, see Habinek, *Politics of Latin Literature*, 117–21, for caution about attributing the codex to Christians and for a nuanced understanding of its functions.

[98] Habinek, *Politics of Latin Literature*, 117–21.

[99] See also H. Koester, 'Writings and the Spirit. Authority and Politics in Ancient Christianity', *HTR* 84 (1991), 353–72.

easily illustrated by Ignatius's use of letters to sustain and to extend his own conception of the church, and one frequently repeated by subsequent ecclesiastical letter-writers. Socially, too, the existence of texts provokes the need for authoritative interpreters of texts—a key feature of Stock's delineation of textual communities. The experience of Judaism from the mid-second century BCE demonstrates how the extension of the ability to interpret, or the emergence of different claimants to the right to interpret, could generate new groupings and self-identities.[100] Frederick Wisse has argued that many of the early Christian polemics, in practice, pivot around the authorization, or its lack, of the teacher, suggesting that the problem of orthocracy rather than that of orthodoxy best encapsulates this period.[101]

We might think here of the *Didache*'s convoluted attempts to maintain the authority of the itinerant prophet or teacher while also laying down rules of control, for example, against those who bring 'other teaching' or abuse the privilege accorded them; at the same time it seeks to mediate between these itinerants and the bishops and deacons appointed by the local communities themselves, 'for they also exercise the office of prophets and teachers' (*Did.* 11–13; 15). The reconstructed 'Preachings of Peter' (*Kerygmata Petrou*), which lies behind the Pseudo-Clementine literature, is prefaced by a letter of Peter to James: here strict rules of probation are enjoined before anyone is allowed to pass on Peter's teaching or to teach, 'for if we do not proceed in this way, our word of truth will be split into many opinions' (Ps.-Clem., *Hom.* Ep.P. 1. 2–2. 1). In a very different vein, Justin prefaces his *Dialogue* with a long narrative introduction in which he both establishes himself as a philosopher and claims, through the prophets, a more certain access to the truth than any philosopher could offer (*Dial.* 1–8); the account of his martyrdom will further present him as a teacher who claims no link to any communal organization (*Mart. Just.* 3). The texts participate in while they also reflect these criss-crossing lines of claim to authority and counter-claim, confuting any confidence we might have in capturing their embodiment in social practice.

We should therefore approach the question of text and reality

---

[100] See above, p. 35; Goodman, 'Texts, Scribes and Power'.
[101] Wisse, 'Use of Early Christian Literature'.

from a different perspective than from that which looks for the communal context of each writing. Texts construct a world; they do this out of the multiple worlds, including textual ones, that they and their authors and readers already inhabit and experience as 'reality'; that new world itself becomes part of subsequent 'reality' within and out of which new constructions may be made.[102] Yet this is not a self-generating system: constructions and worlds interact and clash with others, whether they are seen as congenial or as alien. It is this dynamic process that constitutes the field of our explorations in what follows, yet always at its edges will hover the elusive question of how, if at all, such textual knowledge becomes embodied, constructing Christians.

[102] See Lieu, *Image and Reality*, 11–13, for this process.

3

History, Memory, and the Invention of Tradition

Without continuity there can be no identity, and it is continuity over time, with all its inherent ambiguities of change and sameness, that offers the greatest challenges and the greatest rewards. Recent experience as well as numerous studies have shown that, although such a continuity, often popularly understood as 'history', may appear most secure as a given, it is notoriously open to challenge and to the needs of revision. The relationship between who we are and the past we tell is a reciprocal one and is rarely static: as John Gillis remarks, 'The core meaning of any individual or group identity, namely a sense of sameness over time and space, is sustained by remembering, and what is remembered is defined by the assumed identity.'[1] Thus, 'remembering' creates a history that provides a coherent continuity out of the discontinuities of all human experience; it not only explains the present but justifies it. Although it is often said that to discover the past is to understand how it created the present, no less important is the question, 'how did the present create the past?'[2] So, frequently, the actual historical facticity of the stories told of the past is not a major preoccupation for those who tell them, but only for the external scholarly observer; more important is how they shape the map on which present and future may also be plotted.[3]

For individuals this remembering is often expressed through one's 'story', a self-narrative that gives meaning to the present, although such stories can never be entirely separated from the norms and the expectations of the particular social context:

[1] Gillis, 'Memory and Identity', 3.
[2] So E. Tonkin, M. McDonald, M. Chapman, 'Introduction', in eidem (eds.), *History and Ethnicity* (London: Routledge, 1989), 1–21, 5.
[3] See Al-Rasheed, *Iraqi Assyrian Christians*, 102–35.

'one's sense of personal continuity is grounded in the continuity created in the self-narratives one generates, reinforced by the stability of one's social network and one's society and its institutions'.[4] In some contexts, of course, the individual's story will be inseparable from that of the group of which s/he is a member, and it is this interrelationship, however it may be analysed, that is constitutive of the vitality of the group.[5] In what follows we shall explore the dynamics of remembering in the creation and the maintenance of identity in the ancient, particularly the Jewish and Christian, world; although our focus may be on the corporate, the experience of individuals who claimed this identity can never be excluded from the imagination.

Few would dispute the paradigmatic role that 'remembering our story' has played in the Jewish and Christian traditions, in the maintenance of identity for the group and for those who claim membership of it, particularly within liturgy and theology. According to Deut. 26. 1–11, the Israelites on entering the land are to celebrate the Festival of First-Fruits with the words, 'A wandering Aramean was *my* father[6] . . . and the Egyptians oppressed *us* . . . And the LORD led *us* out of Egypt . . . and brought *us* to this place and gave *us* this land . . . And behold now *I* have brought the first-fruits of the soil which the LORD gave *me*.' Already the confession itself enshrines the alternation between individual and group which is part of the continuing identity of both. Yet, more significantly, the words will in fact be spoken by those who could not claim literal descent from the 'wandering Aramean' but who by incorporation would make this story their own—something the narrative context cannot by definition acknowledge, although the command to include 'the aliens who reside among you' (26. 11) perhaps both points to and denies this eventuality.[7] The 'memory' thus conspires to hide

---

[4] B. R. Slugoski and G. P. Ginsburg, 'Ego Identity and Explanatory Speech', in J. Shotter and K. Gergen (eds.), *Texts of Identity* (London: Sage, 1989), 36–55, 51, arguing against the theory that one's choices and decisions are prior in achieving identity to the explanatory speech that justifies them.

[5] For the interrelationship between, and the question of the relative priority of, individual and group, see R. Jenkins, *Social Identity*.

[6] So the MT, but the LXX's rewriting of this epithet as 'my father rejected Syria' ($\sigma\upsilon\rho\acute{\iota}\alpha\nu$ $\dot{\alpha}\pi\acute{\epsilon}\beta\alpha\lambda\epsilon\nu$ $\dot{o}$ $\pi\alpha\tau\acute{\eta}\rho$ $\mu o\upsilon$) illustrates the ever-present tendency to revision.

[7] Points to, because the problem of their presence in the land is acknowledged;

the complex origins of those who in the deuteronomic period
and later celebrated this festival, and, as contemporary debates
about the history of the earliest period demonstrate, conspires
successfully.[8]

However, when we begin to ask who is excluded here, we
notice the emptiness of the land given by the Lord; the other
peoples who, both at the narrative moment and later, inhabited
the land, and who in the narrative dynamic were to be driven
out (31. 3–6), are absent. Thus, the remembering of this tradition becomes paradigmatic for our purposes in another way, for
questions about the excluded have become unavoidable: neither
history nor memory is neutral; neither is 'given', prior to its use
and interpretation. If the discovery/recovery of history through
which identity is constructed involves a remembering, this is
necessarily selective and is driven by multiple needs and concerns. Inevitably, then, it also involves a forgetting, a forgetting
that is not an accidental amnesia but a deliberate 'not remembering', or perhaps a 'remembering otherwise'. This, as has been
shown in the modern world, is particularly important at times of
radical change or of new beginnings, when 'all profound changes
in consciousness, by their very nature, bring with them characteristic amnesia', the need to deny a different past.[9] In particular,
where change brings instability, or where the shape(s) of the new
identity are still open to negotiation, 'in a land without history
whoever supplies memory, shapes concepts, and interprets the
past will win the future'.[10] Yet what this means is that remember-

denies, because they remain 'aliens', recipients but not speakers. *m. Bikk.* 1. 4–5
denies the right of proselytes to say 'our fathers' but its view is rejected by the
Jerusalem Talmud, and the more liberal position became normative: see Cohen,
Beginnings of Jewishness, 308–40.

  [8] On Deuteronomy as an exilic attempt to 'construct Israel', see E. T.
Mullen, *Narrative History and Ethnic Boundaries*, Semeia Studies (Atlanta,
Ga.: Scholars Press, 1993).

  [9] Richard Esbenshade, 'Remembering to Forget: Memory, History, National
Identity in Postwar East-Central Europe', *Representations* 49 (1995), 72–96,
87; B. Anderson, *Imagined Communities*, 187–206 (204), with reference to the
French Revolution and the US War of Independence; see also Gillis, 'Memory
and Identity'. On the idea of 'purifying memory' see Evans, 'Ecumenical Historical Method', 104–5.

  [10] M. Stürmer, quoted by Esbenshade, 'Remembering to Forget', 75.

ing as well as forgetting—that is, the construction of the narrative of identity—are both acts of power and means of maintaining
power; if they include, they of necessity will also exclude.

Recognition of this has had widespread consequences: the
exclusion of the indigenous peoples and of the other victims from
the standard histories of the colonizers perpetuates the latter's
claims to power and to superiority; in response, the post-colonial
reinscribing of the former, of the excluded, in the memory of
all groups has profound consequences for politics as well as for
identity.[11] This may be most powerful where there are conflicting memories, collisions not only between those of victor and
marginalized, oppressor and oppressed, but also between different groups whose memory is one of oppression—so Richard
Esbenshade explores the collision at Auschwitz between 'competing senses of victimhood and martyrdom . . . in conflicting
Polish and Jewish memory'.[12]

Yet the endeavour for the sake of the present to give a voice
to those excluded, silenced, or marginalized from the formative
histories of the past has reached even further back: in the study of
late antiquity as well as of early Judaism and Christianity a feminist reconstruction has sought to develop a sophisticated hermeneutic that will not only write more boldly the traces left behind
by women, but that will also recover those lost without trace;[13]
the 'history of Israel' as told by modern as well as by ancient
authors has met a controversial and no less political challenge
from the perspective of the Palestinian peoples;[14] equally contro-

[11] e.g. the North American Indians or the slaves in the history of the
Americas, the place of the Aboriginal peoples and their massacre in 'Australian'
history, and the re-remembering of the recent as well as of the more distant
past in South Africa. For post-colonial readings of the Bible, see L. Donaldson
(ed.), *Postcolonialism and Scriptural Reading*, Semeia 75 (Atlanta, Ga.: Scholars
Press, 1996).

[12] Esbenshade, 'Remembering to Forget', 80.

[13] The literature is extensive: for significant contributions see R. Hawley and
B. Levick (eds.), *Women in Antiquity: New Assessments* (London: Routledge,
1995); A. Cameron and A. Kuhrt, *Images of Women in Antiquity*, rev. edn.
(London: Routledge, 1993 (1983)); J. Plaskow, *Standing again at Sinai: Judaism
from a Feminist Perspective* (San Francisco: HarperCollins, 1990); Schüssler
Fiorenza, *In Memory of Her*.

[14] K. Whitelam, *The Invention of Ancient Israel: The Silencing of Palestinian
History* (London: Routledge, 1996).

versially, Martin Bernal has challenged the modern consensus about the classical European heritage with an alternative account of 'the afroasiatic roots of classical civilisation'.[15]

As part of his project Bernal pays particular attention to the way that classical authors themselves explain, through legends of ancient journeys and colonization, the presence in Greek culture and religion of foreign names, unusual practices, and apparent parallels.[16] It is not our task here to engage with his methods or his conclusions; more important is the attention he draws to the way that Greek and later Roman writers used their sagas of the past, the stories of the gods but also of the adventures of the early heroes, to create an interlocking history in which both they themselves and also the other peoples whom they encounter have a place. 'Place' here is important, for we shall see that ideas of ethnicity or of kinship, combined with myth and history, shaped understandings of territory: geography and history belonged together through the people.[17] Within 'history', descent played the crucial role, and it was convoluted accounts of kinship that legitimated claims to a common identity among those who were to be recognized as Greeks.[18]

It is within this context that we should set Josephus's complaint against those who assume that the silence of Greek historians about the Jews means that the nation does not have a long history; his concern is not academic but has vital contemporary political significance (*c. Apion.* I. 1 (1–3)). Yet, as he goes on to show, and as other authors such as Tacitus demonstrate, it was not that there were no theories about Jewish origins, but, as Elias Bickerman explained long ago, that they always had to be fitted into the Greeks' own prehistory, shaped, as we have

[15] M. Bernal, *Black Athena: The Afroasiatic Roots of Classical Civilisation*, i. *The Fabrication of Ancient Greece 1785–1985* (London: Free Association Books, 1987).

[16] Bernal, *Black Athena*, i. 75–120.

[17] See below, Ch. 7; K. Clarke, *Between History and Geography: Hellenistic Constructions of the Roman World* (Oxford: Clarendon, 1999); R. Laurence, 'Territory, Ethnonyms and Geography: The Construction of Identity in Roman Italy', in R. Laurence and J. Berry (eds.), *Cultural Identity in the Roman Empire* (London: Routledge, 1998), 95–110.

[18] See Hall, *Hellenicity*, who thus counts kinship, together with territory and history, as the primary markers of an ethnic identity in the initial development of 'Hellenicity'.

just noted, by their own sagas.[19] For the other peoples, whose history, and hence whose identity, was thus constructed by the Greeks, the options were to mount a challenge with an alternative set of traditions, which might be equally imperialistic, or to accept the Greek version, or to adopt and to transform it to their own advantage. Erich Gruen has shown how Roman authors responded in this way, as, for example, when the foundation of the city by Aeneas after the Trojan war came to be set alongside the traditional story of Romulus and Remus.[20]

Josephus's endeavour to give a native account of Jewish origins for outsiders, however dense and impenetrable the modern reader might expect them to have found the *Antiquities*, was, therefore, engaging in a contemporary contest for respect and recognition. Unlike some other subject peoples, in the Jewish Scriptures he had the advantage of a long but highly idiosyncratic historiographical tradition, or at least a tradition that could be configured as historiographical.[21] The Scriptures thus provide both a model and a resource for subsequent rememberings.

SCRIPTURE AND REMEMBERING

We have already seen how the Scriptures of Israel are themselves the expression of, and the consequence of, a process by which a coherent remembering of a common past and of a shared experience of divine presence has been forged out of the inchoate multiple pasts, largely lost to us, of disparate peoples: 'when we read the Bible's narratives, are we looking at the means by which a culture and a tradition created continuity and coherence because of and out of the discontinuities of the people's experiences'.[22] Although these words belong to Thomas Thompson's contentions that biblical Israel exists only within a literary construct, and that no Bible as such existed in the Hellenistic period, the

---

[19] E. Bickerman, 'Origines Gentium', *Classical Philology* 47 (1952), 65–81. On Tacitus's account of Jewish origins (*Hist.* V. 2–5) see below, pp. 73–4.

[20] E. Gruen, *Culture and National Identity in Republican Rome* (Ithaca, NY: Cornell University Press, 1992), 6–52.

[21] See Potter, *Literary Texts*, 95–102, for Near Eastern records accessible in the Roman period.

[22] Thompson, *Bible in History*, 217.

conclusion is not tied to that particular argument;[23] debates have long raged in biblical scholarship as to the date of the patriarchal narratives, long—but how long?—after the events they purport to describe; as to whether only some among the subsequent 'twelve tribes' experienced the departure from Egypt; as to whether the deuteronomic picture of the judges as judging 'all Israel' (Judg. 2. 16–19) has been superimposed on disparate local traditions; or as to precisely who 'the people of the land' opposed by Ezra and Nehemiah were (Ezra 4. 4; 10. 11); each of these already presupposes that the surviving narratives are constructed to serve subsequent self-understanding.[24] In the last example, even to challenge the silence of the text as to the identity and position of those forcibly separated from their wives, and as to the fate of those women (Ezra 9–10; Neh. 13. 23–31), is to recognize the exercise of power and the silencing of other voices in this construction of a past.[25]

Our interest in what follows, however, will not be in how the scriptural foundational narratives already construct a particular narrative of self-understanding, but in the way that they provoke further retellings or re-rememberings in new settings. Such retelling of the past, and, increasingly, particularly of the patriarchal past, becomes a major characteristic of the literature of the late Second Temple period, both in the Land of Israel and in the Diaspora—although techniques and modes of presentation may vary considerably. The ways in which such retellings serve contemporary concerns, both sociopolitical and ideological, have been long recognized, and are well illustrated by *Jubilees*, usually dated to the second half of the second century BCE. Through a complex and nuanced rewriting of the relationship between Jacob and Esau as told in Gen. 25–36, *Jubilees* lays the ground for the contemporary Hasmonaean subjugation and incorporation of the Idumaeans (*Jub.* 19. 15–31; 24. 1–27. 12; 35–8); as in 1 Macc. 5. 65 and later authors, the latter are identified with bib-

---

[23] Thompson, *Bible in History*, 67, 254.

[24] On these various debates see J. H. Hayes and J. M. Miller (eds.), *Israelite and Judaean History*, Old Testament Library (London: SCM, 1977).

[25] D. L. Smith, 'Between Ezra and Isaiah: Exclusion, Transformation, and Inclusion of the "Foreigner" in Post-exilic Biblical Theology', in M. Brett (ed.), *Ethnicity and the Bible*, BIS 19 (Leiden: Brill, 1996), 116–42, 122–7.

lical Edom (24. 6).[26] Here, Esau is torn between his oath to love Jacob, as requested by Rebekah and as sworn to his father—an acknowledgement that they are brothers—and the plotting of his sons which drives him to treachery and earns him defeat and death (35. 18–38. 3). In this way, remapping the patterns and stories of kinship in the past legitimates current action or conditions.

This creative rewriting works to very different ends when 1 Macc. 12. 19–23 has the Spartans themselves acknowledge that 'a writing concerning the Spartans and the Jews' had been discovered demonstrating that they were brothers and of the family (γένος) of Abraham: here 1 Maccabees adopts a device which can be readily paralleled in earlier Greek appeals to discovered kinship for strategic purposes.[27] In a similar way, Josephus redacts the Genesis text (Gen. 21. 1–5; 25. 12–15) to identify the contemporary Arabs with the descendants of Ishmael, and to draw attention both to their practice of circumcision and to their common descent from Abraham (*Ant.* I. 12. 2–4 (214–21); II. 9. 3 (213)).[28] We have already seen how place belongs to the nexus of identity and history, and this means that such rewriting of the past can also serve to address the needs and problems of the land in the present.[29]

Pursuing another route to identity, *Jubilees* locates as pre-Mosaic, and so legitimates, festivals such as Shebuot by its com-

[26] On this and what follows see D. Mendels, *The Land of Israel as a Political Concept in Hasmonean Literature: Recourse to History in Second Century B.C. Claims to the Holy Land*, TSAJ 15 (Tübingen: Mohr, 1987), 75–82, who dates *Jubilees* to the period c.125 BCE on this basis. F. Millar, 'Hagar, Ishmael, Josephus and the Origins of Islam', *JJS* 44 (1993), 23–45, 31, notes the failure of any attempt to identify the Idumaeans with Ishmael the son of Ishmael in Gen. 25. 12–15 (LXX: MT דומה). B. Cresson, 'The Condemnation of Edom in Postexilic Judaism', in J. Efird (ed.), *The Use of the Old Testament in the New and Other Essays: Studies in Honor of William F. Stinespring* (Durham, NC: Duke University Press, 1972), 125–48, assumes that there is a historical continuity, but by the lacunae in his account testifies to the fact that this is a continuity of representation more than of demonstrable history; see J. R. Bartlett, 'Edomites and Idumaeans', *PEQ* 131 (1999), 102–14.
[27] e.g. Thucydides, *Hist.* I. 95. 1; VI. 76. 2; see below, p. 106, and J. Hall, *Ethnic Identity*, 34–8.
[28] On this see Millar, 'Hagar, Ishmael, Josephus', 30–1.
[29] See below, pp. 217–8; B. Halpern-Amaru, *Rewriting the Bible: Land and Covenant in Postbiblical Jewish Literature* (Valley Forge, Pa.: Trinity, 1994).

memoration of the flood (*Jub*. 6. 17–22), and Passover through its association with the (near) sacrifice of Isaac (17. 15–18. 18); moreover, it anticipates, and rules as illegitimate, rejection of the (solar) calendar and the consumption of blood from the time of and hence on the authority of their primeval inauguration (6. 32–8; 7. 26–33).[30] In this way, in response to the upheavals and the changes of status in the Hasmonaean period, '*Jubilees* proves again that people in the process of searching for a new identity desire to be placed, together with their laws and feasts, within a well-defined historical and social setting. The best place for these would be at the very beginning of the nation's history.'[31]

This redating and relocating of festivals and of practices presents something of a variation on the theme of 'the invention of tradition' as influentially described by Eric Hobsbawm and Terence Ranger.[32] Although that phrase, the title of their collection of essays, has come to serve almost as a truism of the creative remembering implicated in the discovery of a past such as acts as a thread through this chapter, Hobsbawm's own definitive essay applies it rather to 'a set of practices, normally governed by overtly or tacitly accepted rules and of a ritual or symbolic nature'; these 'seek to inculcate certain values and norms of behaviour by repetition, which automatically implies continuity with the past. In fact, where possible, they normally attempt to establish continuity with a suitable historic past.'[33] Hobsbawm describes such practices as serving, particularly in times of rapid change, to establish or to symbolize cohesion as well as to legitimate particular institutions and patterns of authority.[34] Given that invention need not mean 'making up out of nothing' but rather 'discovery' (*invenio*), such a description might well suit the representation and uses of circumcision and the food laws even before their 'reinvention' by *Jubilees*. Although these are biblically situated in the patriarchal and Mosaic periods, there is little evidence in

---

[30] Cf. also the anticipation of the avoidance of circumcision in the Hellenistic period in *Jub*. 15. 33–4.

[31] Mendels, *The Land of Israel*, 85.

[32] E. Hobsbawm and T. Ranger (eds.), *The Invention of Tradition* (Cambridge: Cambridge University Press, 1983).

[33] E. Hobsbawm, 'Introduction: Inventing Traditions', in Hobsbawm and Ranger, *Invention of Tradition*, 1–14, 1.

[34] Hobsbawm, 'Introduction', 9.

the biblical texts to demonstrate their continuing determinative status before their crucial role in the Maccabean revolt, or at least in its literary representation; this has plausibly often been taken to suggest that they attained that status only well into the Second Temple period. Yet other practices may have joined them to the same ends: the elevation of the *Shema*, in this case reflected not in *Jubilees* but in the New Testament Gospels (Mark 14. 29–30) as well as in later texts such as *m. Tamid*, 4. 3; 5. 1, may have been one such.[35]

The example of *Jubilees*, particularly in its primeval dating of the solar calendar, shows that such a remembering might serve the needs of a minority group, perhaps viewed as deviant by a more powerful majority, or even by an alternative minority; it would both legitimate their contested practice and offer an irrefutable polemic against those opponents. Very different, but at least as idiosyncratic if persuasive—and it is hardly the most patent of interpretations—would be Gideon Bohak's reading of *Joseph and Aseneth* as 'a fictional history which "foretells", and so justifies, the establishment of the Jewish temple at Heliopolis'.[36] It is hard to see how rememberings such as this would be effective for anyone except those already within the tradition—hence the considerable problems in interpreting them or in verifying any such interpretation. Yet different again is the *Damascus Document*'s description of God's visitation of Israel 390 years after Nebuchadnezzar's conquest, which thus wipes out all memory of the Return and of subsequent history (CD 1. 5–7). We move into a very different register when apocalyptic, from the perspective of the distant past, rewrites the past and anticipates the future in such a way as to redefine the meaning of the present, perhaps particularly for a beleaguered minority.[37]

[35] So A. Baumgarten, 'Invented Traditions of the Maccabean Era', in Cancik, Lichtenberger, Schäfer, *Geschichte, Tradition, Reflexion*, i. 197–210; Baumgarten notes that *Jub*. 20. 2 gives greater emphasis to Lev. 19. 18.

[36] G. Bohak, *Joseph and Aseneth and the Jewish Temple in Heliopolis*, Early Judaism and its Literature 10 (Atlanta, Ga.: Scholars Press, 1996), 102. *Joseph and Aseneth* rewrites the story of Joseph's marriage to the daughter of an Egyptian priest (Gen. 41. 45).

[37] So already Daniel, but more 'effectively' in the apocalypses attributed to a primeval worthy such as Enoch. On the problem of intention and audience, see L. L. Grabbe, 'The Social Setting of Early Jewish Apocalypticism', *JSP* 4 (1989), 27–47.

These uses of history seem very much to serve the internal needs of shaping identity through the creative remembering or forgetting of traditions that were shared either by all or by a broad, perhaps controlling, consensus; but 'Jewish' identity also had to be constructed within the competitive dynamics of the Hellenistic period where the prize went to whoever could demonstrate not only the antiquity of their civilization but also the debt to it of all other competitors. The claim to antiquity is easily illustrated by the importance of the term 'ancestral' (πατρίος) in the Maccabean and other contemporary literature, which betrays a new understanding of the significance of the past and of its traditions: implicitly used in contradistinction to the 'new' ways attributed to the 'Hellenizers', and to legitimate independence from them, it is itself indebted to Greek values.[38] Yet the pursuit for superiority demanded more imagination in the demonstration of priority: even *Jubilees* is not untouched by this pressure, as is shown by the inventions it ascribes to Noah, Cainan, and Abraham, namely the making of wine, the discovery of astrology, and the 'invention' of Hebrew (*Jub.* 7. 2; 8. 1–4; 12. 25–7). Other authors, particularly those writing in Greek, are even more committed to the enterprise: Artapanus, perhaps a near contemporary of *Jubilees*, ascribes to Abraham, Joseph, and Moses the distinction of having taught the Egyptians those skills that it had long been claimed had originated among the latter and had been taught by them to their successors, including the Greeks: astrology, measurements, and philosophy.[39] The biblical tradition, with its repeated sojourns in Egypt, provided a small hook on which to hang such an endeavour, but to be successfully executed a radical retelling of that tradition was needed, an exercise that seems as unproblematic to these authors as is the very different one undertaken by *Jubilees*.

The driving motivation behind Artapanus—and to him

---

[38] See above, p. 58 and below, p. 224; Kippenberg, 'Die jüdischen Überlieferungen'; M. Himmelfarb, 'Judaism and Hellenism in 2 Maccabees', *Poetics Today* 19 (1998), 19–40.

[39] Artapanus in Eusebius, *Praep. Evang.* IX. 18. 1; 23. 3; 27. 4; Moses even established the Egyptian religion! On Artapanus and this theme see Droge, *Homer or Moses*, 25–35; Gruen, *Heritage and Hellenism*; G. Sterling, *Historiography and Self-Definition: Josephus, Luke-Acts and Apologetic Historiography*, NT.S 64 (Leiden: Brill, 1992), 137–225.

we should add Eupolemus, Pseudo-Eupolemus, Cleodamus Malchus, and others—has been variously assessed:[40] was this a somewhat desperate attempt to shape an identity in a very different Hellenistic world, with very different values and status symbols, perhaps reflecting a discomfort with traditional self-representations? should it be described, perhaps pejoratively, as succumbing to the criteria of Hellenism? or was it, rather, merely an attempt to present Judaism in its most attractive guise to potential converts? Is it fundamentally antagonistic or conciliatory, asserting identity by the repudiation of inferior false claims, or seeking to demonstrate common ground and values? Erich Gruen has argued vigorously for an optimistic interpretation of these authors, as also of the various novelistic accounts of Jews successfully acting as counsellors in the courts of kings (Daniel, Esther), drawing attention at the same time to the frequent elements of humour to which sober scholarly analysis is so easily blind. He sees little evidence of antagonism, rather more of a self-definition against 'the other' not by opposition but by appropriation, facilitating a self-confident claim for cultural superiority.[41] Yet this too, as acknowledged by the subtitle of his monograph,[42] is another reinvention of Jewish tradition, another daring re-remembering of the past for the sake of the present. What remains unclear is how far it is primarily a literary exercise, how far we can see behind it the reshaping of the identity of the Jews of the Diaspora, now defined by being at home precisely because 'they got there first'.

The importance, however, of correctly establishing origins is unmistakable: as we have already noted, not all 'others' accepted the Jews' own account of their Egyptian sojourns, whether biblical or as rewritten by Artapanus or his colleagues; the alternative inimical retelling that would have the Jews expelled from Egypt as lepers was not just an exercise in scurrilous name-calling, it

[40] For these authors see C. R. Holladay, *Fragments from Hellenistic Jewish Authors*, i. *Historians* (Chico, Calif.: Scholars Press, 1983).

[41] Gruen, *Heritage and Hellenism*; also idem, 'Cultural Fictions and Cultural Identity', *TAPA* 123 (1993), 1–14; idem, 'Fact and Fiction: Jewish Legends in a Hellenistic Context', in P. Cartledge, P. Garnsey, E. Gruen (eds.), *Hellenistic Constructs: Essays in Culture, History and Historiography* (Berkeley, Calif.: University of California Press, 1997), 72–88.

[42] *Heritage and Hellenism: The Reinvention of Jewish Tradition.*

was a statement about the present.[43] The tradition of the Jews as having 'plundered' Egypt, a tradition with roots in their own accounts (Exod. 12. 36 LXX), needed careful explaining: their prosperity both was their due and was won without acts of vengeance (Philo, *Mos.* I. 25 (140–2)).[44] As reflections on the present, perhaps the greatest threat posed by negative tellings was how they might lead either to popular or to official retaliatory treatment—perhaps best exemplified by Apion's collation of such accounts when considered alongside his role in the action against the Jews of Alexandria under Flaccus; however, the threat to the credibility of their own internal self-presentation would be nearly as destructive. Josephus explicitly links Apion's scurrilous counter-narrative of the sojourn in and the exodus from Egypt to the contemporary disputes between Jews and Egyptians about the right to claim citizenship and the name 'Alexandrians' (*c. Apion.* II. 3 (28–32)); Tacitus's account, which accompanies his telling of the destruction of Jerusalem, claims that 'most authors agree' that the Jews were driven from Egypt 'to purify the kingdom' of a wasting plague because they were 'hated by the gods'—ideas that would provide an unequivocal commentary on the events that he is describing (Tacitus, *Hist.* V. 3. 1).

This makes it very difficult to draw a sharp line separating the rewriting of the past to serve present internal needs from that with a more overt apologetic purpose designed to shape the views of outsiders.[45] Josephus, when writing his *Antiquities* after the fall of Jerusalem, was perhaps engaged in a major work of apologetic historiography, aimed at 'making evident to those encountering the work concerning our race of the Jews that it is of the greatest antiquity and has kept its original character' (*c. Apion.* I. 1 (1)).[46] It would be difficult to pinpoint the precise effect of

---

[43] For this, see Manetho and Lysimachus in Josephus, *c. Apion.* I. 26 (225–52); 34 (304–11).

[44] The tradition continues both in Jewish writings and in Christian; see I. Levi, 'La Dispute entre les Égyptiens et les Juifs', *REJ* 63 (1912), 211–16; Lieu, *Image and Reality*, 247–9.

[45] See Sterling, *Historiography and Self-Definition*, 224, 'The fragments presuppose an international audience in which their cultural claims can be made . . . At the same time, the real audience were the authors' compatriots.' Compare the debates over and the different definitions of 'apologetics' in Edwards *et al.*, *Apologetics in the Roman Empire*.

[46] On this see Sterling, *Historiography and Self-Definition*, 226–310.

so vast and comprehensive a work on the realignment and maintenance of Jewish identity in those new circumstances; yet what
he must certainly be doing is denying that the present reality as
experienced by the Jewish people both in the Land of Israel and
in the Diaspora either demanded a negative rewriting of the past
or had brought to an end an identity that was built upon the past
and that could only by such a rewriting cross the bridge into the
future.

The irony here, of course, is that early Christian writers were
able to take Josephus and to use his tale to very different effect,
namely to construct a new, negative, identity for the Jews, and a
proud one for themselves: so Eusebius is content to cite Josephus,
'the most famous Jew of that time', for what happened 'to the
whole nation' forty years after their demand for Jesus's death,
while attributing those forty years' grace to the presence in
Jerusalem of James, the brother of Jesus, and others (Eusebius,
HE III. 7. 7–9; 9. 1–5). Yet this is to anticipate.

RE-REMEMBERING AND REWRITING

We have already seen how the texts that come to be associated
with early Christianity participate in the rewriting, remembering, and forgetting of scriptural history that was a feature of the
diverse Judaism of the period. The preservation by Christians not
just of the Scriptures in their Greek translation (the Septuagint)
but also of a range of other Jewish literature from the centuries
immediately prior to and indeed contemporary with their own
emergence, including those explored above, was itself an assert-
ive act of remembering. As we have seen, the fact that scholars are
often at a loss as to how to categorize such literature as 'Jewish' or
'Christian', and how to recognize Christian elements other than
the most obvious, for example Christological statements, testifies to the confident assumption of a continuity that presumably
was refracted through an interpretative lens.[47] *3 Baruch*, a text
where explicit Christian redaction is marginal but unmistakable,
illustrates both the problem—if the explicit redactional elements
are removed is the resultant text 'Jewish' or 'Christian'?—and

[47] On this see above, pp. 45–8.

the possibilities.[48] The narrative setting, Nebuchadnezzar's destruction of Jerusalem, and the opening theodical question as to why God allows the nations to say, 'Where is their God?' (1. 1–2), would be read differently, with a different expectation of resolution, among those for whom the dilemma of the defeat of 70 CE remained inexplicable than it would among those for whom the defeat was God's judgement for the rejection of Jesus. The final vision of the full baskets of flowers brought in by the angels, at least without the explicit redactional reference to 'the Church' (13. 4), leaves the reader to interpret its reference within their own context, 'Christian' mission or 'Jewish' hope of restoration.[49] That the vision is vouchsafed to Baruch, the contemporary of Jeremiah, authorizes all readers to claim the past he represents as part of their identity.

Another example is offered by 5 Ezra. This commences with God commanding Ezra to proclaim a long history of judgement against 'my people' which reaches its climax, 'Your house is desolate; I will drive you out as the wind drives straw . . . I will give your houses to a people that will come, who without having heard me will believe'; it then continues, 'and now father, look with pride and see the people coming from the east; to them I will give as leaders Abraham and Isaac, and Jacob, and Hosea', and the rest of the prophets (2 (4) Esdras 1. 33–5, 38–40). In a new image, the mother is ruined and widowed, and the people are to be 'blotted out from the earth, because they have despised my covenant'; but, shortly after this, the mother is invited to 'embrace her children' (2. 2–7, 15). The text constructs readers who will identify themselves with the coming people, and who will affirm the failure of 'Israel'; but it does so without identifying labels or, for the most part, without Christological reference,

[48] D. C. Harlow, The Greek Apocalypse of Baruch (3 Baruch) in Hellenistic Judaism and Early Christianity, SVTP 12 (Leiden: Brill, 1996), who shows how the text can be read as a Jewish text (pp. 109–62) and as a Christian text (pp. 163–205). He sees the lament form of the prologue as establishing the Jewish origin of the text while acknowledging that it can be read in a supersessionist way (pp. 88–96, 199–201).

[49] See Harlow, Greek Apocalypse of Baruch, 189–205; Harlow suggests that 16. 2, 'But since they angered me in their works, go and make them envious and provoked against a people that is no people, a people that has no understanding' (cf. Deut. 32. 12 LXX), is Christian redaction even though there are no explicit Christian terms therein (pp. 196–9).

but in almost seamless continuity with the prior tradition of the Ezra writings.[50]

It is this that has made it possible to argue that, even where such texts do not contain 'distinctively Christian' ideas or language, and even where they do not anticipate the discontinuity of the 'coming people', 'the Christian world view permeates the members of the Church to such an extent that their eyes see everything in the light of Christ's pivotal role in world history. This all-encompassing world view is capable of absorbing practically any concept, image and word.'[51] According to this view, texts that scholars may label 'Jewish' because they remain within the world of the Jewish patriarchs or of Israel's past could have been read by Christians as part of their own story. If this is true, it is at the same time no less true that such texts problematize labels such as 'Christian' and 'church'; readers are those who can be addressed by the patriarchs and prophets of Israel's past: they belong to one continuous history.[52]

It is characteristic here that the coming and the extension of the church in 5 *Ezra* are anticipated prophetically, and not by, for example, any narrative rewriting of the patriarchal stories to anticipate the subsequent inclusion of the Gentiles, nor by any attempt to claim for them a fictive descent from Abraham that might buttress their claim to a spiritual descent; there is no parallel to those Jewish sources that have Abraham and Sarah converting proselytes.[53] Although genealogies are common devices

[50] See T. Bergen, *Fifth Ezra: The Text, Origin and Early History*, Septuagint and Cognate Studies 25 (Atlanta, Ga.: Scholars Press, 1990); the reference to the young man identified as the Son of God in 2. 42–8 adds little.

[51] M. de Jonge and J. Trompf, *The Life of Adam and Eve and Related Literature*, Guides to the Apocrypha and Pseudepigrapha (Sheffield: Sheffield Academic Press, 1997), 68; I owe this reference to Michael Eldridge, a former research student at King's College London.

[52] See Kraft, 'Setting the Stage'. M. de Jonge, 'The Pre-Mosaic Servants of God in the Testaments of the Twelve Patriarchs and in the Writings of Justin and Irenaeus', *VC* 39 (1985), 157–70, cites the appeal to the patriarchs in Justin and Irenaeus as a way of understanding the purpose of the *Testaments of the Twelve Patriarchs*. This might suggest a framework within which the latter would be read, but the literary strategies are very different. See above, p. 46, on David Satran's argument that the *Lives of the Prophets* contains a confident claim to the past without the need for explicit Christianizing.

[53] In *Gen. Rabb.* 39. 14 in the name of R. Hunia on the basis of an exegesis

in legitimation and in claims of continuity, and are widely used as such in Scripture,[54] when Matthew and Luke introduce them into their Gospels they do not obviously intend to prepare the ground for a new reinterpretation of the line of descent. Even Luke's genealogy, reaching back as it does before Abraham to Adam, hints at but does not develop a universal potential.[55] On the contrary, a number of texts simply assume without comment that all believers may claim the scriptural 'descent' as their own. The Letter to the Hebrews betrays no difficulty in offering its audience, whose background in Judaism or in the Gentile world remains a topic of scholarly controversy, a history of faith reaching back to Abel, Abraham, and Moses as well as to more recent, probably Maccabean, martyrs, while also naming Jesus both founder and completor (Heb. 11. 1–12. 2). In a similar fashion, *1 Clement*, in this case clearly writing to those from a Gentile background, traces a history of jealousy, also starting with Cain and Abel, and including 'our father Jacob', alongside a history of humility shown by 'our fathers', namely Elijah, Ezekiel, Abraham, Moses, and David (*1 Clem.* 4; 62. 2 with reference to chs. 17–18).[56] Judith and Esther count as 'among us'; Jacob is equally the ancestor of the priests and Levites, and, 'according to the flesh', of the Lord Jesus, but also of a 'galaxy' of rulers, 'not through themselves or their deeds . . . but through [God's] will, and we ourselves called through his will in Christ Jesus' (*1 Clem.* 55. 2; 32. 2–4). In both Hebrews and *1 Clement* believers

of Gen. 12. 5 where Abraham brings to Canaan 'those whom they had made'; cf. *Gen. Rabb.* 53. 9; Millar, 'Hagar, Ishmael, Josephus', 39–44, recounts the inconsistency in Christian authors in exploiting Josephus's association of the Nabataean Arabs with Ishmael, and their consequent Abrahamic descent and practice of circumcision.

[54] M. D. Johnson, *The Purpose of the Biblical Genealogies*, SNTS.MS 8, 2nd edn. (Cambridge: Cambridge University Press, 1988); however, Hall, *Hellenicity*, 222–3, remarks on the comparative rarity of 'a properly "ethnic" basis of self-identification through genealogy' among Jews of the Hellenistic period.

[55] In fact, Luke reverses the pattern and ends with Adam, and this may have Christological as much as universal significance (Luke 3. 23–38). It is sometimes supposed that Matthew's inclusion of Tamar, Rahab, Ruth, and the wife of Uriah (Matt. 1. 3–6) contains a guarded hint of the role of the marginalized and foreign, but that they are women, anticipating the role of Mary, may be most important.   [56] Cf. also *1 Clem.* 31; 60. 4.

are drawn into a history which for the most part can only be described as 'scriptural', and to that extent as 'Jewish'; in what sense such a history constitutes for them a 'Christian' identity—a term that neither text uses—is to introduce alien and inappropriate categories.[57]

A narrative of continuity also appears in the reconstructed text behind the Pseudo-Clementine *Recognitions*, I. 27–71; here the 'history' is retold from Creation to Moses, and thence to the appearance of the prophet foretold by Moses (Deut. 18. 18), and then to the nations called to replace the unbelievers, 'so that the number that was shown to Abraham might be fulfilled' (*Rec.* I. 42. 1).[58] Reinforcing the continuity, the 'true prophet' had already appeared to Abraham and to Moses before his coming at the time for reformation (Syr.) or completion (Lat.) (I. 33. 1; 34. 4; 39. 1).[59] More than Hebrews or *1 Clement*, this text is aware that not all share the continuity; there are unbelieving Jews, but it is they who disrupt it, and not the other way around.

However, other writings pursue a different strategy through a radical retelling of the same past. Again with Gentile readers primarily in mind, Paul interpreted the chronological and sequential priority of Gen. 15. 6 over Gen. 17. 10 as a theological priority of faith over circumcision (Rom. 4. 9–12; Gal. 3. 6); he then had to explain the coming of the Law 430 years later as an introduction that did not nullify what preceded (Gal. 3. 17–18). Yet this is only minimally a re-remembering, relying as much on proof-texting as on retelling the past. More subversive is his reidentification of the narrative of Sarah and Hagar, where he totally inverts the Jewish story of descent from the child promised to Sarah and of the exclusion of Ishmael: the covenant from Sinai is now associated with Hagar, representing 'the present Jerusalem', in slavery with her children; the 'Jerusalem above' is free, and 'you are children of the promise according to Isaac' (Gal. 4. 24–8).[60] The

---

[57] *1 Clem.* 5. 1 turns from the ancients to more recent 'athletes' and proposes taking examples τῆς γενεᾶς ἡμῶν: this could be translated as 'of our generation', or as 'of our race'; since Peter and Paul, the examples given, were both Jews, if 'race' is intended it could only mean 'Christian'.

[58] See F. S. Jones, *An Ancient Jewish Christian Source on the History of Christianity*. PSEUDO-CLEMENTINE *RECOGNITIONS* 1.27–71, SBL Texts and Translations: Christian Apocrypha Series (Atlanta, Ga.: Scholars Press, 1995).

[59] Syr. ܪܓܬܐ; Lat. *impleo*.

[60] See further on this passage and the importance in it of 'place', below, p. 226.

same concern with descent—which, as we have seen, belongs to the rewriting of the past in Hellenistic thought—also leads him to redefine 'Israel' by implicitly rereading the nature of the election process that operated through the choice of Isaac (and not Ishmael), Jacob and not Esau (Rom. 9. 6–15). These interpretative moves prepared the way for similar ones by subsequent writers that belong as much to the history of exegesis of scriptural text as to the rewriting of the past.

No author attempts to create a continuous new genealogy that will have the Jews descended from either Ishmael or Esau, and the 'Christian' descent from Jacob is one that leap-frogs the intervening generations; none the less, the *Letter of Barnabas* can take the 'prophecy' of Gen. 25. 21–3 and say, 'You must understand who is Isaac and who is Rebecca and concerning whom it is shown that this people is greater than that' (*Barn.* 13. 3)—unlike Paul he now uses the language of two 'peoples' (λαός). Yet what of the subsequent scriptural history of Israel? For *Barnabas* this too needs rewriting: although Moses received the covenant in the form of the tablets of stone, the people immediately forfeited it when they turned to idolatry in the making of the golden calf (4. 7–8; 14. 1–3). Such a rewriting renders void all that follows in the biblical account; for *Barnabas* there is no chronological hiatus between their loss and 'our' reception of the covenant through the Lord (4. 8). We might then consider this a forgetting, yet it is not accompanied by an alternative remembering; *Barnabas* has little interest in a new continuity between Abraham (or Moses) and 'this people', not even a Pauline one of faith.[61]

Justin Martyr addresses the same 'history'; for him, too, the episode of the golden calf is determinative, initiating the characterization of the Jews by a history of idolatry that continues through to the story of Elijah and up to the present (*Dial.* 34. 8; 46. 6–7; 130. 4).[62] This forms but one thread within a more pervasive history of disbelief and disobedience: 'So you always . . . at that time sacrificing to the calf, and always appearing ungrateful,

---

[61] *Barn.* 5. 7 speaks of God fulfilling the promise to *the* (not 'our') fathers. However, note the Pauline-mediated 'quotation' of Gen. 17. 4–5 in *Barn.* 13. 6, 'What then does he say to Abraham, when he alone believed and was set down for righteousness? Behold, I have set you, Abraham, as father of Gentiles who believe through uncircumcision in God.'

[62] For this and what follows see Lieu, *Image and Reality*, 115–16, 145–7.

and murdering the righteous, and puffed up on account of race' (102. 6). In a long passage Justin traces the history from Exodus through to settlement and beyond as both prophetic of Jesus and as the story of their disbelief (131. 3–133. 1): 'and although these and all such glorious and marvellous things happened for you and were seen at different times, yet you are condemned by the prophets even for having sacrificed your own children to demons, and in addition to all this for having dared and still daring such things against Christ'. As in *5 Ezra* 1. 4–27, this becomes a reversal of the 'canonical' recital of Israel's history as one of God's saving acts for and through her—although *5 Ezra* plays the trump card, not available to Justin, of setting this as God's prophetic word given to Ezra. It is, of course, a 'biblical' history; there is no rewriting as in the retellings we explored above. Its effectiveness depends on its selectivity, most notably on the elimination of the themes of repentance, promise, and restoration. In as much as within Justin's *Dialogue* it is addressed to Trypho, and, behind him, to the Jewish people ('you') as implied readers, it is creating an alternative identity for them by ascription: its ultimate goal is 'now'. Yet, in so far as the actual audience of the *Dialogue*, as of *5 Ezra*, is almost certainly not Jews but Christians, it, like nearly all 'anti-Jewish' polemic, has a more immediate goal in shaping Christian identity.[63] By 'remembering otherwise' it frees the biblical story for an alternative Christian history. Contrary to some uses of the claim for common descent to foster alliance, here, as J. D. Levenson has noted, 'their appeal to their common root in Abraham ensures that Judaism and Christianity will be mutually exclusive'.[64]

Melito of Sardis achieves a similar end by a very different technique, typology. Although typology is used by earlier authors, including, as we have already seen, by Paul, Melito presents a more sustained and sequential pattern.[65] He weaves a rich pattern of contrast between type or model and truth, or between the temporality of the past and the final 'but now': 'The people was a type as a preliminary sketch . . . the church the repository of the

---

[63] On the audience of the *Dialogue* see Lieu, *Image and Reality*, 104–8.

[64] Levenson, *Death and Resurrection*, 219.

[65] See H. von Campenhausen, 'Die Enstehung der Heilsgeschichte: Der Aufbau des christlichen Geschichtsbildes in der Theologie des ersten und zweiten Jahrhunderts', *Saeculum* 21 (1970), 189–212, 202–4.

truth . . . the type is made void handing over the likeness to what is true by nature' (ll. 261–4, 273 (§§ 40, 43)); 'the narrow inheritance was precious but is worthless now because of the extensive grace' (ll. 292–3 (§45)).[66] So the Pascha becomes 'a mystery', the lengthy retelling of 'the words of scripture' a prelude to denying them any value except for those who listen to the 'structure of the mystery' (ll. 65–212, 301–2 (§§11–33, 46)). Without the shaping provided by the past, the 'present' would float anchorless; yet once the present has absorbed all meaning from the past, that past now becomes void, empty of any continuing power.

Yet more than this, in each of these authors the consequence has been to deny any alternative line of remembering. Israel's history of unfaithfulness can lead only to subsequent rejection; the memory of those who were faithful becomes an ever more finely drawn line, witnesses by word and suffering to Christ, denied to the Jews and offering no hope of further restoration. While such a negative remembering, and not-remembering of times of faithfulness and renewal, is a denial of the Jews' own claims to identity, it will also, although as yet hardly explicitly, rule out those of Jewish Christians.[67]

We encounter a similar process in Justin's interpretation of the recent experience of the Jews, and in the way that he relates this to the past. In the *Dialogue with Trypho*, the suffering and defeat of the Jews after the failure of Bar Kochba, and their consequent exclusion from Jerusalem, are linked directly back to the giving of circumcision to Abraham as 'a sign'—a phrase taken from Gen. 17. 10 but with the notable omission of the words 'of the covenant': 'a sign in order that you might be separated from the Gentiles and us, and that you alone might suffer what you now justly suffer . . .' (*Dial.* 16. 2–3). Here, the present shapes the meaning of the past, and the past can be remembered because, as now understood, it prepares for the present (23. 4; 92. 2); it no longer belongs to a history of election and promise but to one of separation for punishment.[68] This can be seen as an example of what has been called 'persuasive definition', the giving of a 'new conceptual meaning to a familiar word without substan-

---

[66] Following the line and paragraph numbering of Hall, *Melito of Sardis*.
[67] So Kretschmar, 'Kirche aus Juden und Heiden', 25.
[68] Lieu, *Image and Reality*, 118–19.

tially changing its meaning'.[69] As we have already seen, in time Christian authors were able to take Josephus's account of the destruction of Jerusalem, and, contrary to his own intention, to use it to add further evidence of God's rejection of the people.

Addressing the Romans, Justin does not merely interpret the fall of Jerusalem as the fulfilment of prophecy, but chooses a passage purportedly spoken by the people themselves: Isa. 64. 10–12, 'Zion has become a desert . . . and you have greatly humbled *us*', becomes no longer a lament but an act of self-condemnation. At the same time, he asserts that this is something the conquerors themselves 'know very well' (*Apol.* 47). Justin also is emphatic that the Jews' suffering cannot be interpreted in martyrological terms as is that of the Christians, although his protests suggest that they did so interpret it (*Dial.* 110. 5–6).[70] It is not simply *what* is remembered but *how* it is remembered that is both sustained by and defines identity; in this case conflicting perceptions of identity are inseparable from conflicting modes of remembering. Once again, the 'you' of Justin's address, ostensibly to the Jews, serves by default to free the broader sweep of 'biblical' history for the Christians. As for *Barnabas*, so for Justin, what might appear to be a shared remembering need not lead to a shared contemporary identity. Unlike *Barnabas*, Justin struggles both to respond to the realities of contemporary Jewish presence and possession of the Scriptures, and of the other signs of their worship of God, and at the same time to maintain for Christians the claim to be 'Israel' (*Dial.* 123. 9).

This, indeed, was the dilemma with which Christians struggled: how to claim the continuity with the past without admitting the Jews' own claim, which would entail losing a sense of separate identity. From the middle of the second century, particularly within the Apologists, the issue becomes explicit as the Christians faced the outside world. The philosopher Celsus, who wrote in his *True Word* a refutation of Christianity perhaps not long after Justin's own work, was well aware of this dilemma.[71]

---

[69] J. S. Vos, 'Legem statuimus: Rhetorische Aspeckte der Gesetzesdebatte zwischen Juden und Christen', in van Amersfoort and van Oort, *Juden und Christen*, 44–60, 45–6.   [70] See Lieu, *Image and Reality*, 122.

[71] Droge, *Homer or Moses*, 72–7, argues that Celsus may have been aware of and be responding to Justin's *Apology*; see also H. Chadwick (trans. and ed.), *Origen* Contra Celsum (Cambridge: Cambridge University Press, 1953).

On the one hand, he charges the Christians with apostasizing from the Jews, and for added effect puts the charge in the mouth of a textual 'Jew': 'His Jew then says to believers from the Jewish people, "Quite recently, when we punished this fellow who cheated you, you abandoned the law of your fathers"' (Origen, *c. Cels.* II. 4). On the other hand, aware of the Christian claim to this 'descent' and history, Celsus repeats many of the standard denigrations of the Jews—Moses' disreputable character and his deceit of the people, the latter's lowly origins as runaway slaves, and their subsequent ignominious history (IV. 31–5; V. 41–53). Yet the Christian response was not to declare a lack of any interest in this competitive enterprise on the grounds that they were not a particular people or race; instead they adopt the Jewish tradition of demonstrating patriarchal and Mosaic antiquity while also developing their own variations on it.[72] In various ways, Justin, Tatian, and Theophilus of Antioch argue for the temporal priority of Moses over the vaunted Greek originators of civilization; in time the tradition will be continued and receive definitive form in Eusebius's *Preparation for the Gospel* which seeks to demonstrate by exhaustive citation of his—not always harmonious—predecessors 'that the writings of Moses and the prophets were more ancient than those of the Greeks' (*Praep. Evang.* X. 14. 1).[73]

As Arthur Droge has shown, Christian writers, like their Jewish predecessors, were often drawing, sometimes by direct interaction, on the view already found in Greek writers that Greek civilization was derivative from, and even a corruption of, 'barbarian wisdom'. Christianity, through its appropriation of Moses, thus claimed to be representing, even restoring, the most ancient and original of truths. Yet there are differences of nuance, with significant effect for the identity constructed. Theophilus, whose 'Jewishness' has often been noted, demonstrates antiquity by a careful 'whole chronology' which runs from Creation to the flood, to Abraham, to Isaac, to Moses (and Joshua), to David (and Solomon), to the Babylonian exile (and Cyrus), and thence to the death of the Emperor Aurelius Verus (Theophilus, *Autolyc.*

---

[72] See Droge, *Homer or Moses*, who shows how the tradition is continued in later writers; also Olster, 'Classical Ethnography and Early Christianity'; and below, pp. 260–2 on 'race'.

[73] Droge, *Homer or Moses*, 189–90.

III. 22–9).[74] Here, there is no place for Jesus, either as saving figure, nor as fulfilment of the prophets. Instead, 'the characteristics of the prophets and the gospels are in agreement with the righteousness spoken of by the law because all those who were inspired spoke with the one spirit of God', and it is 'the holy word' as well as the 'Gospel voice' that is his authority (III. 12). Tatian, however, who also never names Jesus, appeals to Moses as 'originator of every barbarian wisdom'; he invokes the 'barbarian writings' without explicitly identifying these as the *Jewish* Scriptures (*Orat.* 31. 1; 29. 1).[75] Such approaches prepare for a universal history, drawing on Hellenistic writers such as Diodorus Siculus, which will encompass all known knowledge.[76] Justin presents a different form of this ecumenical vision when he draws into his history of 'those who live with the Word' not only Abraham but also Socrates, and when he not only claims them as his past but brings them into the present: 'those who lived and live with the Word are Christians' (*Apol.* 46. 3–4).

On one level, all this contributes to the apologetic refutation of the repeated charge that Christianity was 'new', a serious flaw from the perspective of a culture that valued antiquity, one of the few saving graces that 'pagan' writers conceded to the Jews.[77] So 'Diognetus' wishes to know, among other things, 'why this race or practice has entered life as new now and not earlier' (*Diog.* 1), although the answer he is given never seriously addresses this question other than by demonstrating the vacuity of the pagan

[74] On Theophilus see R. M. Grant, *Greek Apologists of the Second Century* (Philadelphia: Westminster, 1988), 165–74; idem, *Theophilus of Antioch,* ad Autolycum, OECT (Oxford: Clarendon, 1970).

[75] On Tatian see Droge, *Homer or Moses,* 82–101; W. Petersen, *Tatian's Diatesseron: Its Creation, Dissemination, Significance and History in Scholarship,* VC.S 25 (Leiden: Brill, 1994). On 'barbarians' see below, pp. 292–3.

[76] See R. Mortley, 'The Hellenistic Foundation of Ecclesiastical Historiography', in G. Clarke with B. Croke, R. Mortley, A. Emmett Nobbs (eds.), *Reading the Past in Late Antiquity* (Ruschcutters Bay: Australian National University Press, 1990), 225–50, who says, 'the world was made one, not in Christ but in hellenistic historiography' (248).

[77] Tacitus, *Annal.* XV. 44, emphasizes the death of its founder in the time of Tiberius; Suetonius, *Nero,* 16. 2; Origen, *c. Cels.* III. 5, 'a revolt against the community led to the introduction of new ideas'; Tatian, *Orat.* 35. 2; cf. A. Stötzel, 'Warum Christus so spät erschien—das apologetische Argumentation des frühen Christentums', *ZKG* 92 (1981), 147–60.

and Jewish alternatives, and by marvelling at God's patience until the present.

Part of the dilemma was that newness had long been part of Christian self-understanding, not least through its claim to the 'new covenant' of Jer. 31. 31 (see 1 Cor. 11. 25)—although this was understood eschatologically rather than temporally. Melito is unusual among the Apologists in turning this to a virtue when he dates the origins of the Christian religion to the birth of the Empire under Augustus, and thereby, rather than writing a history of the church, demands a rewriting of the history of the Empire, whose success is now 'shown' to be dependent on it (as quoted by Eusebius, *HE* IV. 26. 7). Aristides, too, in his account of the 'races' of humankind, stresses the distant mythical figures from whom the barbarians, Greeks, and Jews trace 'the origin of their race', while finding no problem in stating that 'the Christians trace the origin of their religion from Jesus Christ'.[78]

Yet, barring these exceptions, the argument from antiquity remains a fundamental weapon in the armoury of Christian apologetic, as it also had been from a much earlier date for the Jews. However, apologetic, the justification of oneself in the face of the doubts of 'the other', also builds up the group's own sense of identity, securing it against alternative constructions. In this way, Christian claims to antiquity, their 'demonstration' of the Jewish history of obduracy and so of discontinuity, and, we must add, their refutation of internal suggestions that Christianity was indeed 'new', such as that offered by Marcion, are inextricably interdependent (Justin, *Apol.* 58).[79]

REMEMBERING JESUS

So far it has been the re-remembering of a scriptural history that has shaped the new identity of this new people; and for many of our writers this is the primary history. Yet what of that history that, following Aristides, most modern accounts would see as in some—if in a disputed—sense the origins of Christianity, that of

---

[78] On this see below, pp. 260–1.

[79] See D. P. Efroymson, 'The Patristic Connection', in A. T. Davies (ed.), *Antisemitism and the Foundations of Christianity* (New York: Paulist Press, 1979), 98–117, 108–10.

its founder, Jesus of Nazareth? Tatian's other claim to fame is of having composed a Diatesseron, a harmony of the four Gospels; one advantage that such an enterprise would offer would be that of presenting a single narrative of Jesus, a narrative that could provide a single identity for its users. By contrast, contemporary scholarship has become accustomed to treating the extant Gospels as each providing a distinct legitimation for their own time through the story of Jesus. Redaction criticism assumed that the final shaping of the individual Gospels reflected the concerns both of their distinctive audiences and of the communities for whom they wrote. More specifically, it has been argued that the Fourth Gospel provides, through the narrated experiences of Jesus and of those who responded to him, a mirror account of the readers' own recent history, particularly of exclusion from 'the synagogue' (John 9. 22).[80] Similarly, Matthew's Gospel has been seen as a response to 'the Matthaean community's' own tension-filled relations with their Jewish neighbours and their claim to constitute 'Israel', while also their extension of the preaching of the Gospel 'to all nations' (Matt. 28. 19).[81] Within this reading, the Gospels represent distinctive 'rememberings' of the Jesus story that maintain a reciprocal dialectic between the telling of the past and the needs of the present; in this way they have been seen as each constituting the '"charter myth" of the foundation of the group'.[82] However, matters are not so straightforward, for what the Gospels fail to do is to trace any explicit continuity between the story they tell and the communities they supposedly represent, so that these 'communities' necessarily remain constructions of the scholars as much as, if not more than, of the texts they read. Only Jesus's foray into Samaria in

---

[80] See J. L. Martyn, *History and Theology in the Fourth Gospel*, 2nd edn. (New York: Abingdon, 1979); R. E. Brown, *The Community of the Beloved Disciple* (London: Chapman, 1979).

[81] Although opinions are divided as to the degree of split between 'church and synagogue' in Matthew; see A. Saldarini, *Matthew's Christian-Jewish Community* (Chicago, Ill.: University of Chicago Press, 1994); D. Sim, *The Gospel of Matthew and Christian Judaism* (Edinburgh: T&T Clark, 1998); G. N. Stanton, *A Gospel for a New People: Studies in Matthew* (Edinburgh: T&T Clark, 1992).

[82] So L. M. Wills, *The Quest of the Historical Gospel: Mark, John and the Origins of the Gospel Genre* (New York: Routledge, 1997), 179.

John 4, contrary to the traditions of his avoidance of that area in the Synoptics (Matt. 10. 5; Luke 17. 11), may reflect the retro-jection of subsequent territorial concerns into the earlier history such as we have found in the Jewish tradition.[83] For this reason it is not obvious quite how the Gospels fit into an exploration of the construction of Christian identity through the remembering of the past; although as soon as this is said, it has to be admitted that in practice they have often been so used, for example when the polemic against the 'scribes and pharisees, hypocrites' (Matt. 23) has become part of Christian constructions of the Jews, and, in a form of reverse imaging, of themselves.

Yet, in so far as recent study has emphasized the diversity that lies behind the superficially common shape of the canonical Gospels, it offers a reminder that from the very beginning we are experiencing multiple constructions of identity through texts, and not just one expression of a single prior given identity; to cast the net wider is to discover yet more diversity and to reinforce the reminder.[84] So, for example, the *Gospel of Thomas* does not root the origins of the Christian conviction in the death and resurrection of Jesus, but can be read as implying groups shaped by and intent on realizing a new vision of social life legitimated by the 'sage-like' teaching of Jesus.[85] Other texts, by grounding their authority in secret revelations of Jesus, effectively render devoid of significance any public traditions of his life and teaching.[86]

Yet perhaps more striking is the relative rarity with which Jesus traditions are used outside the Gospels, canonical and non-canonical, to establish or to reinforce Christian identity. That Paul considered the coming of Jesus, and particularly his death and resurrection, as the foundation of his Gospel is not to be

[83] For the argument that John 4 reflects the extension of the Johannine com-munity see Brown, *Community*, 35–6; some have seen here the self-legitimation of the 'Hellenists' who, according to Acts 8, were actually responsible for this extension: see O. Cullmann, *The Johannine Circle* (ET. London: SCM, 1975), 39–56.

[84] So R. Cameron, 'Alternative Beginnings—Different Ends: Eusebius, Thomas, and the Construction of Christian Origins', in L. Bormann, K. del Tredici, A. Standhartinger (eds.), *Religious Propaganda and Missionary Competition in the New Testament World: Essays Honoring D. Georgi*, NT.S 74 (Leiden: Brill, 1994), 501–25.

[85] So Cameron, 'Alternative Beginnings', 518–25.

[86] See above, pp. 49–50.

denied, nor that he knew and valued at least some Jesus traditions, even if the extent and significance of these is disputed. Yet
the dispute is possible precisely because, with the possible exception of 1 Cor. 11. 23–6, Paul does not use Jesus traditions as foundational; they do not provide a history. This is a phenomenon
that is to continue into the second century; both the Apostolic
Fathers and the Apologists are striking for their relative lack of
interest in the life of Jesus, so that it is more by default than by
triumphant demonstration that we can trace the extent and the
influence of Jesus traditions in this period. So, for example, some
time around the turn of the first two centuries, the *Didache* challenges its readers/hearers to choose the way of life instead of the
way of death; the 'way of life' includes, without either explicit
scriptural or dominical appeal, elements of Torah, sometimes
expanded, alongside new moral rules—'if someone strikes you
on the right cheek turn to him also the other' alongside 'commit no murder, adultery, sodomy, fornication, no theft' (*Did.*
1. 4; 2. 2). This has been presented as the development of a new
and differentiated world-view, in particular set over against that
of pre-70 Judaism (*Did.* 1–5),[87] although such a judgement may
wrongly construct the latter as a unitary phenomenon; yet what
is equally remarkable is that this distinctive morality, although
at times bearing some relationship to synoptic Jesus traditions, is
never legitimated through ascription to Jesus.[88] Narrative traditions about Jesus are equally elusive, although, reinforcing the
lacunae in our knowledge, Melito takes for granted such details
as Jesus's birth from Mary, his healing of lepers and a withered
hand, his raisings of the dead, and even Pilate's washing of his
hands, and he constructs from them a story of Israel's wilful
unbelief.[89]

---

[87] So C. N. Jefford, *The Sayings of Jesus in the Teachings of the Twelve Apostles*,
VC.S 11 (Leiden: Brill, 1989), 98–118.

[88] *Did.* 4. 13 'See that you do not neglect the commandments of the Lord, but
keep them just as you received them' echoes Deut. 4. 2 and so does not undermine this conclusion.

[89] Melito, *Peri Pascha* ll. 495, 508–11, 548, 676 (§§71–92).

HISTORY AND FIDELITY

The exception to this lack of interest in a continuity from Jesus
to the later church is Luke's decision to continue his Gospel
with a second volume, the Acts of the Apostles. Whatever his
intentions when he wrote his first volume, the opening verses
of the second (Acts 1. 1–2) clearly signal a continuity between
'what Jesus *began* to do and teach' as already described, and the
birth and spread of the church 'in Jerusalem, in all Judea and
Samaria, and to the ends of the earth' (1. 8) that is to come.[90] It
is a continuity that is expressed not only through the prologue of
Acts but also through the constant retelling of the 'Jesus story'
in the speeches (10. 36–43), as well as through mimetic themes:
the signs and wonders done by the apostles, Peter's raising of
Tabitha, Stephen's dying vision and words, all recall that earlier
story (3. 1–10; 9. 36–43; 7. 58–60).

Despite the detection of other genre traits in Acts, such as those
of the novel or of the biography, it is most persistently and best
seen as in some sense apologetic, although the intended audience
and specific focus of such an apology remain matters of debate.[91]
In a number of ways Acts does make sense as responding to the
distinctive circumstances of the end of the first century—the
passing of the first generation of believers and apostles; the need
to come to terms with and to make some sort of self-presentation
to the wider social and political world; the experience of an
increasingly predominantly Gentile church and the consequent
struggle to understand the place of the Jews; the pressure to deal
with a heritage of tensions over that very development as well
as with alternative responses to the church's relationship with
the past and with an anticipated future. In the 'remembering' of
Acts Paul no longer wrestles, as he does in his letters, with the
extreme tension between his conviction that the Gospel embraced
Gentile believers without any demands of adherence to Jewish

---

[90] On the need to translate ἤρξατο in 1. 1 explicitly as 'began' (contra NRSV)
see C. K. Barrett, *A Critical and Exegetical Commentary on the Acts of the
Apostles*, ICC, 2 vols. (Edinburgh: T&T Clark, 1994–9), i. 66–7.

[91] See the nicely nuanced and careful assessment by L. Alexander, 'The Acts
of the Apostles as an Apologetic Text', in Edwards *et al.*, *Apologetics*, 15–44; on
the problem of 'apologies', see above, p. 58.

Torah, and his need to preserve some unity with the 'apostles before him', for whom Torah continued to figure in their determination to preserve a unity between believers of Jewish and of Gentile birth, and between present and past acts of God (Gal. 1. 15–2. 14). Instead, the apostles act in this instance 'with one accord' (ὁμοθυμαδόν, Acts 15. 25) as they do so often in other situations (1. 14; 2. 46; 4. 24; 5. 12). Indeed, contrary to Paul's classification of Peter as responsible for the circumcision (Gal. 2. 7), the extension of the Gospel to Gentiles is accomplished by Peter himself when he goes to Cornelius (Acts 10), just as he had earlier embraced Philip's preaching in Samaria (8. 14–25). In both chapters, the work of the Spirit and the intervention of an angel (8. 26, 39; 10. 3, 19, 44) lift this history above the vagaries of human choices, and, in both style and mode, insinuate a longer continuity with a much older biblical history. These latter characteristics, which could be more extensively illustrated (see e.g. 16. 6–10), militate against seeing Acts as a history of the church; there is no interest in structures or organization, although it is hard to imagine that there were none such when Luke was writing.[92] It is true that, in the manner of the testamentary patriarchs of Jewish texts, Paul, anticipating false teaching and schism to come, urges the elders of the church at Ephesus to shepherd the church of which they are 'overseers' (ἐπίσκοποι) (20. 18–35); but this is but a brief forward glimpse and only minimally offers a blueprint for the future.

The picture in Acts is still a long way from that of *1 Clement* 42–4, according to which God commissioned Jesus, Jesus commissioned the Apostles, and the Apostles the bishops and deacons to follow them, making provision, too, for the continuity of this process—which was in any case 'not new but written from long ages before . . . "I will establish their bishops in righteousness, and their deacons in faith"' (*1 Clement* 42. 5, citing Isa. 60. 17).[93] Moreover, while it is undoubtedly the intention of Acts to trace the spread promised in 1. 8 'to the ends of the earth', symbolized

---

[92] This argues against H. Cancik, 'The History of Culture, Religion and Institutions in Ancient Historiography: Philological Observations Concerning Luke's History', *JBL* 116 (1997), 673–95, who sees Acts as the history of an institution.

[93] This is probably based on the LXX, 'I will give your rulers in peace and your overseers in righteousness.'

by its centre, Rome, where the story concludes 'with all boldness and without hindrance' (Acts 28. 31), the narrative as told does not justify any particular organizational relationship between the various churches, nor does it even very obviously celebrate the foundation-charter of any particular community.[94]

Certainly, Acts provides its readers with a history, and a history that, especially in the words and acts of the apostles, is exemplary. Presumably, through the models of preaching and behaviour, including both the idealized picture of the early church's harmony and the negative models of Ananias and Sapphira and of Simon Magus (2. 42–7; 5. 1–11; 8. 18–24), it offers a form of 'remembering' that would exclude some potential developments while also legitimating what may have been a compromise between the earlier conflicting perceptions of the nature of the church. Going beyond this, Gregory Sterling has suggested that there are significant parallels between Josephus's *Antiquities* and Luke-Acts that intimate a significance for the latter beyond the internal tensions of the church: both authors are engaged in apologetic historiography, the writing of one's own history in order to enable self-definition in changed conditions by a minority group within the wider culture. Josephus had to address the position of Judaism in the aftermath of the failure of the revolt and the fall of Jerusalem in 70 CE, and in face of its negative press under Domitian; he demonstrates an unbroken continuity reaching back into antiquity, a steadfastness of opinion and behaviour, together with a well-documented record of foreign, particularly Roman, support; in this light, the Jews, although scattered, are 'a race' (γένος), and one worthy of admiration and with a rightful place in the Hellenistic world.[95] So, too, according to Sterling, as the church faced a new stage it needed a way of understanding and defining itself through an account of its past; this involved

[94] Paradigmatic here is the story of Cornelius (10) which is sometimes supposed to have recorded the founding of the church at Caesarea (cf. Barrett, *Acts*, i. 496), but which nowhere refers to anything subsequent upon the baptism of Cornelius's household, and which sits uncomfortably alongside the separate tradition of Philip's sojourn there (8. 40; 21. 8–9).

[95] G. E. Sterling, *Historiography and Self-Definition*; Sterling claims both an external (Greek and Roman) and an internal audience for the *Antiquities*: 'For Josephus the issue is not Judaism or Hellenism, but Judaism in Hellenism. He recasts Jewish history in these terms hoping to reconcile both Greeks to Jews and Jews to Greeks' (p. 308). See above, p. 74.

setting it within the world, that of the Graeco-Roman Empire, as well as within its past, that of Judaism, but it also meant giving it its own history, 'the *traditio apostolica*'.[96] Similarly, Marianne Bonz has suggested that Luke-Acts 'creates an imaginative and schematized historical story in order to provide a memorable and definitive interpretation of the underlying meaning of Christian history'.[97]

Luke betrays an important aspect of this self-understanding in the 'biblicisms' (often Septuagintalisms) of style and language that we have already noted. For the reader sensitive to the echoes, that means for the inside reader who knows her Scriptures, or at least is familiar with their story, the narrative of Jesus from his birth, and of the church, shares much with and runs in continuity with that of Israel in the past. On the other side, there are sufficient ambiguities in Luke-Acts' treatment of the Jewish people to leave interpreters taking opposite positions as to whether he is solidly 'anti-Jewish' or whether the continuity he traces from Jerusalem in Luke 1 to Jerusalem in Acts 1, and thence to Rome in Acts 28, means that God's people are not irrevocably excluded.[98] Stephen's retrospective of Israel's history in Acts 7. 2–53, and Jesus's anticipation of the future in Luke 19. 27, 41–4; 21. 20–4, particularly if these equally express the mind of the author—and we may be more confident of this in Jesus's case than in Stephen's—present a gloomy picture, but they may not be enough to constitute an alternative remembering of and on behalf of Israel.[99]

Yet almost as important as the achievement of Acts are the two facts that its immediate impact seems to have been slight, and that there was apparently no further attempt to write a Christian history until Eusebius some 250 years later.[100] Despite the way in

[96] Sterling, *Historiography and Self-Definition*, 388.

[97] M. P. Bonz, *The Past as Legacy: Luke-Acts and Ancient Epic* (Minneapolis, Minn.: Fortress, 2000), 13.

[98] For opposing positions see J. T. Sanders, *The Jews in Luke-Acts* (London: SCM, 1987) and J. Jervell, *Luke and the People of God* (Minneapolis, Minn.: Augsburg, 1972).

[99] Although a certain amount hangs on whether 'until the times of the Gentiles are fulfilled' in Luke 21. 24 anticipates a restoration beyond. If Luke is drawing on a source for Stephen's speech we may be less confident of ascribing its views to him, although presumably he cannot have entirely disagreed.

[100] See von Campenhausen, 'Enstehung der Heilsgeschichte'; Cameron,

which the narrative of Acts eventually came to shape subsequent Christian remembering and rewriting of its past, allusions to Acts are few and uncertain until the latter half of the second century. This may be because until then the church did not know 'what to do with it'; it came into its own particularly in response to Marcion's divorce between Jesus and Israel's past history, and between Paul and the other apostles (Irenaeus, *adv. Haer.* III. 12–14).[101] Thus Acts served to establish that the church was not going to trace its history only from the appearance of Jesus, as Marcion would have it. This determination carried with it both the reaffirmation of the Christian appropriation of Israel's history, and the consequent retelling of Israel's history as one of judgement, which we have traced above. More important for Christian identity, then, was this prior history that found its climax in Jesus than any subsequent one that took its start from him.[102]

However, other constructions of the past, and so of the present, do appear in texts that later were to be marginalized. The account from Creation to the apostolic 'present' in Ps. Clement, *Recognitions* 1. 27–71, does challenge Acts through its description of the 'certain hostile person' who disrupts James's converting speech to the Jews, stirs up a fierce persecution, and even attempts the murder of James; apparently this is a mask for Paul himself and so creates a very different self-understanding for those who locate themselves in this story.[103] F. Stanley Jones dates this text to the end of the second century, and by then we find that the challenge of alternative readings of the Christian story, and so of alternative constructions of identity, did lead to other partial reconstructions of history. Already at the end of the first century, as we have seen, *1 Clement* 42–4 asserts a succession history that will legitimate one set of claimants to presbyteral authority over others. At a later stage Polycrates will

'Alternative Beginnings', 501–11. G. F. Chesnut, *The First Christian Histories*, 2nd edn. (Macon, Ga.: Mercer University Press, 1986), sees Eusebius as the first of such histories and does not list Acts or Luke in the index.

[101] On the eventual pre-eminence of Acts' view see Cameron, 'Alternative Beginnings'. On its early history see Barrett, *Acts*, i. 30–48 (the quotation comes from p. 48), and ii. pp. lxiii–lxx.

[102] von Campenhausen, 'Enstehung der Heilsgeschichte', 210.

[103] Ps.-Clement, *Rec.* I. 70–1; see above, n. 58.

claim Philip and his daughters, John of Ephesus, Polycarp and Thraseas, Sagaris and Melito, and a succession of prophets and martyrs, in defence of the quartodeciman Easter practice of Asia Minor (Eusebius, *HE* V. 24. 1–7); in turn other churches will 'discover' a continuous tradition through their bishops back to apostolic security.[104]

This assertion of fidelity to an idealized and normative past as opposed to the possibility of new developments was reinforced in the rejection of Montanism which is repeatedly denigrated for its 'novelties'—despite their own claim to stand in a succession reaching back through the unknown Ammia to the prophetic daughters of Philip.[105] Claim and refutation meant revisiting the past, and out of the process would arise the theme of the earliest church as an unsullied virgin, the standard and ideal by which all subsequent developments would be measured and to which the church would ever seek to return.[106] So, too, Hermas's vision of the tower whose lower layers of square, white, well-cut stones contrast with subsequent layers, where some are rejected while others need shaping, creates for the present a sense of inadequacy, caught between a glorious past and the hope for completion in the future (*Vis.* III. 2–8). A similar lachrymose story of decline and of corrupt desire for power in the *Ascension of Isaiah* perhaps gives meaning to marginalized prophetic groups: they are the 'few here or there' ignored by the violence of the elders (*Asc. Isa.* 3. 19–31).[107]

A different construction of history is achieved through the later writings associated with the Apostles. Although pseudonymity could be seen as an alternative strategy to 'history', the Pastoral Epistles arguably present a picture of Paul to a later generation; here as author he legitimates a structure of bishops and/or elders, and deacons, and a carefully controlled list of widows; narrative details offer biographical verisimilitude (2 Tim. 4. 9–15). But a

---

[104] See Eusebius, *HE* IV. 5. 1, although he admits he has no written dates but has 'gathered from the documents' the list he provides for Jerusalem; Bauer, *Orthodoxy and Heresy*, 45, 63–4, 114–17.

[105] Hippolytus, *Refut.* VIII. 19. 2; Eusebius, *HE* V. 16. 4, 7, 10; 17. 3 (quoting an anonymous writer of the 2nd century).

[106] Cf. R. Wilken, *The Myth of Christian Beginnings* (Garden City, NY: Doubleday, 1971), 43–4, 71–3, quoting Eusebius, *HE* III. 32. 7–8; IV. 22. 4–6.

[107] See Knight, *Ascension of Isaiah*, 31–8.

competing picture of Paul is offered by the *Acts of Paul*, particularly, as has often been argued, by the possibly self-contained section dealing with Paul and Thecla. This is closer to novel than to history, and it is notoriously difficult to judge its function and its intention. Some have seen in Thecla's self-baptism and growing self-determination the foundation narrative of groups of women who, whether in fact or fantasy, sought the authority of the past to pursue an ascetic lifestyle, and perhaps the freedom to preach and baptize as did their heroine. Certainly, Tertullian's blustering reproach that Paul would never give such authority witnesses to the power of the past to shape the present, as too does its more recent adoption by those with feminist commitments.[108]

In different ways these discovered histories serve both to legitimate and to draw boundaries, no longer against Judaism but against competing claimants to a common identity. At the same time, these rejected rivals are given a history of their own. Writing 'in their own image', the heresiologists describe the succession from Simon Magus, but also that from other heresiarchs, including Dositheus and Valentinus (Hegesippus in Eusebius, *HE* IV. 22. 5–6). It is a model that the surviving texts associated by recent scholars with these figures and their schools fail to adopt for themselves.[109] Instead, some of these so-called gnostic texts offer an alternative history: remembering takes on a new significance through its corollary in the gnostic theme of forgetfulness. The complex myths of a cosmic fall offer enlightenment because they enable the gnostic to 'remember' their true origin; it is a remembering that necessarily separates the gnostic from her peers who do not remember and who remain sunk in forgetfulness.[110] These highly idiosyncratic histories, each different although sharing common themes, would, presumably, offer a highly individualized history that finds its climax in each individual who claims it. To that extent it is a denial of the themes explored in this chapter, for it offers no continuity beyond, yet it

[108] See Davies, *Revolt of the Widows*; S. E. McGinn, 'The Acts of Thecla', in Schüssler Fiorenza, *Searching the Scriptures*, ii. 800–28; also above, Ch. 1, n. 64; p. 53.

[109] See the attempts to associate various texts from Nag Hammadi with groups 'known' from Irenaeus: Robinson, *Nag Hammadi Library*.

[110] e.g. *Tripartite Tractate*, 81. 30–83. 5.

belongs no less here as a reminder of alternative models that we shall meet more forcefully in other contexts. On the other hand, when one such remembering is given to Shem, the son of Noah, who is instructed to 'rejoice greatly over [his] race (γενεα)' we return again to the beginning of our quest.[111] The irony here is that the 'remembering' of the Genesis origins in such texts often creates a radical rupture, that between the creator god and the almighty God, source of all true knowledge.

'Without that historical continuity any answer to the identity question can only be invented rather than discovered.'[112] We may at the end of this exploration question the antithesis between invention and discovery. Yet although we have traced different constructions of historical continuity, what sort of identity has been 'discovered'? Traditionally, answers have been given in terms of adjectives such as 'gnostic', as has just been done, or 'Jewish-Christian' of the Pseudo-Clementine source quoted earlier,[113] or, simply, 'Christian'. Such labels are unhelpful if they mask both differences and similarities: the same history can be used differently by different claimants, while different histories may be reconciled with each other in a single text or author. The ever-present challenge of the Jewish Scriptures was felt by all, but its effects were as diverse as the texts that survive. Yet the historical setting of the wider world increasingly demanded recognition, as too, with the passage of time, did an internal history whose patterns achieved continuity only in retrospect. What has remained a constant in different settings is the continual engagement with the need to trace a thread from the past to the experienced realities of the present, both through coherence and through rupture, resulting in stories that are never stable, and never closed.

---

[111] *The Paraphrase of Shem* (NH VII. 1) 26. 1; as with the other Nag Hammadi texts, dating is difficult, and a cautious dating would put the *Paraphrase* outside our period in the early 3rd century. Where Greek loanwords are used in the Coptic they are given in Greek script. Cf. also the *Apocalypse of Adam*, probably to be dated to the 2nd century but difficult to characterize.

[112] D. Novak, *The Election of Israel: The Idea of the Chosen People* (Cambridge: Cambridge University Press, 1995), 2.

[113] Jones, *Ancient Jewish Christian Source*.

4

Boundaries

If identity implies a sameness constituted by continuity—the 'remembering' just explored—it also demands difference, and between the two stands a boundary. Thus boundedness is integral to the idea of identity, for it is boundaries that both enclose those who share what is common and exclude those who belong outside, that both ensure continuity and coherence, and safeguard against contamination or invasion—or so it seems. It is part of the seduction of identity that the encircling boundary appears both given and immutable, when it is neither. Any interpretation of identity that prioritizes aspects of territory or kinship is prone to seeing boundaries as objective and even primordial; those that emphasize human organization, interaction, and construction will necessarily have a greater sense of the contingency of the boundaries even while acknowledging their indispensability.[1]

The language of boundary is, of course, the language of metaphor, and it is important to remember this. Even in its literal application it arguably reflects the contemporary preoccupations of the modern nation-state, whereas an earlier age would be more concerned with frontiers;[2] frontiers, particularly in antiquity, did not represent fixed lines so much as zones of influence or areas of control.[3] Then, as now, they lay themselves open to mockery at

---

[1] See esp. F. Barth (ed.), *Ethnic Groups and Boundaries: The Organization of Cultural Difference* (Oslo: Universitet Forlaget Bergen; London: G. Allen & Unwin, 1969); also R. Jenkins, *Social Identity*, 90–103.

[2] So A. Giddens, *The Consequences of Modernity* (Cambridge: Polity, 1990), 14.

[3] See A. Rouselle, 'Présentation', in eadem (ed.), *Frontières terrestres, Frontières célestes dans l'antiquité* (Paris: Presses Université de Perpignan, 1995), 7–16, 9–10, who cites Seneca as follows. Seneca is, however, referring to the insignificance of the earth to the mind as it roams the heavenly spheres. For the issues see also C. Whittaker, *Frontiers of the Roman Empire: A Social and Economic Study* (Baltimore, Md.: Johns Hopkins University Press, 1994).

human conceit: *O quam ridiculi sunt mortalium termini* (Seneca, *Quaest. Nat.* I. praef. 9). Archaeologists, too, have increasingly rejected the human conceit that would seek to discover a fixed correlation between known group identities, 'typical' cultural artefacts, and marked geographical regions, as if they occupied the same, and only the same, territory.[4] This refusal has been particularly important in the study of 'ancient Israel', as scholars have distanced themselves from the endeavour to identify particular artefacts or styles as Israelite in contrast to Canaanite, and on that basis to establish the separate existence, culture, and territory of Israel from an early stage.[5] The dissolution of such material boundaries—or the exposure of their fallaciousness—has forced radical new attempts to understand the process of boundary-making in the construction of Israel's identity both in the past and by those with contemporary concerns.[6]

One consequence of the metaphor of boundary can be the tendency to see it as fixed and stable, again a conceit perhaps most natural to inhabitants of an island state. Such a view encourages the supposition that identities also remain constant over time and space, and, indeed, perhaps one function of boundaries is precisely to foster such an imagination. In practice the boundaries that mark identity are always subject to change—to be 'British' or 'Australian' at the beginning of the twenty-first century may be very different from what it was in the 1950s, or even at the beginning of the twentieth century. This is because while boundaries persist, they are the result of human negotiation and interaction; they imply selection and the giving of value amidst the experience of difference, and so, perhaps, they are better seen as 'temporary check points rather than concrete walls'.[7] In

---

[4] See esp. Jones, 'Discourses of Identity'; eadem, *Archaeology of Ethnicity*; Dench, *From Barbarians to New Men*, 186–98.

[5] See further W. Dever, 'Archaeology and the Emergence of Israel', in J. Bartlett (ed.), *Archaeology and Biblical Interpretation* (London: Routledge, 1997), 20–50; N. A. Silberman and D. Small (eds.), *The Archaeology of Israel: Constructing the Past, Interpreting the Present*, JSOT.SS 237 (Sheffield: Sheffield Academic Press, 1997).

[6] See pp. 63–5; also K. L. Sparks, *Ethnicity and Identity in Ancient Israel: Prolegomena to the Study of Ethnic Sentiments and their Expression in the Hebrew Bible* (Winona Lake, Ind.: Eisenbrauns, 1998).

[7] R. Jenkins, *Social Identity*, 99.

the same way, boundaries may appear to be rigid: 'By turning names into things we create false models of reality. By endowing nations, societies or cultures with the qualities of internally homogenous and externally bounded objects, we create a model of the world as a global pool hall in which entities spin off each other like so many hard and round billiard balls.'[8]

In practice, however, as the check-point analogy should remind us, they are permeable and may also be contested. At the most basic level boundaries permit, and indeed encourage, interaction, while providing rules for it; they are not merely defensive but also allow for trade. Again the model of frontier may be helpful here. Yet beyond, and indeed because of, this, they also allow some degree of 'crossing the boundary', and such crossing may in turn result in their redefinition or redrawing.

Most of the work on which these introductory explorations have drawn has been addressed to ethnic groups; as developed by Frederick Barth its value has been to suggest a distinction between culture, which may be more extensive than the particular group, and at the same time less internally differentiated, and ethnicity, whereby particular 'differences' acquire boundary-marking significance.[9] This distinction, which also gives the lie to the assumption that identity demands homogeneity, will prove valuable in exploring both Judaism and Christianity, provoking questions both as to whether a shared culture points to a shared identity, but also as to how cultural change need not undermine the identity of the unit that carries that culture.[10] Yet it is also clear that the analysis of boundaries in the construction of identity need not be restricted to ethnic groups, particularly since it is the symbolic rather than the material markers that are of most importance.

However, it is the application of such an analysis to ethnic

---

[8] E. Wolff, *Europe and the People without History* (Berkeley, Calif.: University of California Press, 1982), 6, as cited by S. Jones and P. Graves-Brown, 'Introduction: Archaeology and Cultural Identity in Europe', in Graves-Brown, Jones, Gamble, *Cultural Identity and Archaeology*, 1–24, 4.

[9] See Barth, *Ethnic Groups*, 9–15; however, not all accept this contrast, see above, Ch. 1 n. 32.

[10] See above, Ch. 2 nn. 32–3 on their sharing of a common subculture; Barth's emphasis on the persistence of boundaries despite change in the 'cultural stuff that it encloses' (*Ethnic Groups*, 15) has clear consequences for the question of Hellenization.

groups in diaspora contexts—both as minorities and as sustaining
a translocal identity—that is particularly insightful for our purposes. Here, the 'other' whose existence necessitates the boundaries—and of whom more later—is much closer, all around, and
perhaps more both to be feared and to be emulated.[11] As minorities in a dominant culture, such diasporic groups are commonly
perceived as static, committed to preserving a received heritage
of difference; in practice, they may exercise a variety of potential strategies for the maintenance of identity. On the one hand,
identity may persist despite the fading of traditional culture,
suggesting the recognition by selves and by others of new boundaries of difference and of belonging; in other cases, minorities
may come to represent 'cultures of resistance' when a specific
contemporary situation intersects with historical processes.[12]
Even so, resistance implies interaction and not isolation, and the
same is true of evidences of minority culture.[13] Neither can it be
assumed that assimilation is a natural, ultimately inevitable (and
desirable) goal, with attendant difficulties for those who fail to
adapt, for contemporary experience has proved otherwise. This
is true particularly when the dominant culture itself is recognized
as not necessarily homogenous; moreover, there may be different
levels and contexts of belonging as well as of separation.[14] Yet
such groups are having continually to present and re-present
themselves in the shifting circumstances of their total situation,
to themselves as well as to outsiders.[15] The lines between inside
and outside are in practice ever shifting, and necessarily 'stress
interconnection as much as distinction'.[16]

[11] On 'the other' see below, Ch. 9; on Diaspora and ideas of space, see pp.
220–5.
[12] For the former see Isajiw, 'Definitions of Identity', 120–2; for the latter,
E. Vasta, 'Multiculturalism and Ethnic Identity: The Relationship between
Racism and Resistance', *ANZJS* 29 (1993), 209–25.
[13] So P. S. Wells, *The Barbarians Speak: How the Conquered Peoples Shaped
Roman Europe* (Princeton, NJ: Princeton University Press, 1999), 168–70.
[14] See G. de Vos and L. Romanucci-Ross, 'Introduction', in eidem (eds.),
Ethnic Identity, Cultural Continuities and Change, 2nd edn. (Chicago, Ill.:
University of Chicago, 1982), pp. ix–xvii, xii.
[15] See S. Hall, 'Cultural Identity and Diaspora', in J. Rutherford (ed.),
Identity: Community, Culture, Difference (London: Lawrence Wishart, 1990).
222–37.
[16] See M. Keith and S. Pile, 'Introduction: Part 1 The Politics of Place . . .',

Yet there is another side to this: for minority experience has also underlined the power relations implicit in the maintenance of boundaries. Where assimilation is easy, the group itself may generate sanctions sustaining separation, and these may relate to very specific aspects of the adoption of the behaviour of the majority—a curious example might be the Greek hats of 2 Macc. 4. 12.[17] On the other hand, discrimination from outside may inhibit if not prevent transgression of the boundaries, and these may be drawn differently by those outside than by those within. Although generally some coherence between the two seems necessary, as also between the 'being seen' and the 'seeing oneself' which constitute identity, this is not always the case. Anticipating the next stage in our argument, the Roman literary description and categorization of those outside her boundaries cannot be directly correlated with the archaeological data concerning those groups; yet the categorization by others, particularly by the more powerful, clearly does impact on the way that groups understand themselves.[18]

Finally, viewed from the perspective of a diaspora identity that crosses geographical boundaries, new elements emerge. Here shared territory and boundaries reveal their truly metaphorical character; recent studies have resisted the temptation to speak of what unites in essentialist terms, for example as 'the Black experience'—the formative case study—while affirming the connections and the unifying elements within 'an imagined geography'.[19]

What all this has emphasized is that, despite the comfortable feel of changelessness behind the idea of boundaries, as equally behind that of the sameness of identity, we have to speak of process, of a dynamic that sometimes, but for a while, may appear to achieve closure. It is a process that is generated by the inter-

in eidem (eds.), *Place and the Politics of Identity* (London: Routledge, 1993), 1–21, 18.

[17] On specific sanctions being generated in particular contexts as concrete boundary maintenance see G. de Vos, 'Ethnic Pluralism: Conflict and Accommodation', in de Vos and Romanucci-Ross, *Ethnic Identity*, 5–41.

[18] See pp. 239–40 below; Wells, *The Barbarians Speak*, 109–21.

[19] Keith and Pile, 'The Politics of Place . . .', 17–18; also P. Gilroy, 'Diaspora and the Detours of Identity', in K. Woodward (ed.), *Identity and Difference* (Milton Keynes: Open University, 1997), 299–343. See below, p. 212.

action of individuals and that does not simply act as a constraint upon them. Thus boundaries are not 'given' but are produced and reproduced. Yet, as throughout this study, what we catch sight of is these boundaries as experienced and as represented in texts—from outside as well as from within—leading us to ask what patterns of relationship there might be between these literary representations of self-perception and rhetoric, and the boundaries of social experience. It is the multidirectional dynamic that is perhaps most difficult to capture from the past and to commit to writing in the present.

As will have become clear, the issue of boundaries is far from bounded, and will offer routes into, or display overlaps with, a number of other questions. To think of boundaries is to think of 'the other', while in many early Christian texts it is specifically to think of 'the world' which constitutes the other side, yet both these representations demand separate discussion. Further, despite efforts to distinguish the role of boundary maintenance in the construction of identity from any specific or cultural 'content', this is far from straightforward in practice, and 'practice' will also occupy a chapter of its own.

It is also the case that within the study of the early church, boundaries have been analysed in a number of other connections. Perhaps closest to our concerns here, the role of boundaries in sectarian formation and in the differentiation of sect from 'church' or from 'world' has been much discussed. This has been particularly fruitful in the analysis of specific Jewish or Christian groups, such as the communities of the Dead Sea Scrolls or of the Fourth Gospel, both in their relationship with 'formative' or 'mainstream Judaism' and in their self-identity against 'the world': somewhat simplistically, firm and high boundaries, vigorously rhetorically maintained, are seen as synonymous with a strong sectarian consciousness.[20] In that context it is the fact of boundaries more than their nature that is determinative, but it

---

[20] Here B. Wilson, *Patterns of Sectarianism* (London: Heinemann, 1967) has been particularly influential; see S. Barton, 'Early Christianity and the Sociology of the Sect', in F. Watson (ed.), *The Open Text: New Directions for Biblical Studies* (London: SCM, 1993), 140–62; Stanton, *Community*, 85–107; R. Scroggs, 'The Earliest Christian Communities as Sectarian Movement', in J. Neusner (ed.), *Christianity, Judaism, and Other Greco-Roman Cults: Studies for Morton Smith at Sixty*, 4 vols. SJLA 12 (Leiden: Brill, 1975), ii. 1–23.

may also be useful to remember that boundaries are not the sole
prerogative of, and therefore not determinative for, sects.

   Also fruitful has been the exploration of the interrelationship
between boundaries in the different worlds that people inhabit.
Mary Douglas influentially emphasized the coherence between
the human body and the body politic: concern about the integrity of the boundaries of the one may articulate a similar concern
about those of the other. The need to observe sacred boundaries,
variously articulated, but in Judaism particularly through food
and purity laws and the structuring of the Temple, correlates
with the importance laid on well-defined and well-protected
social boundaries.[21] With a different focus, Jack Lightstone has
argued for a similar correlation between the relatively permeable
sociocultural boundaries of Jewish diaspora communities and the
permeability of sacred boundaries in their system, for example
in the way that mediation between human and divine could be
exercised through holy men, through the cult of the dead, and
through the growing sacredness of synagogues.[22] Without necessarily subscribing to either interpretation or historical reconstruction, such studies are suggestive of how we should look for
an overall coherence in any symbolic universe, within which
identity plays a constitutive role.

BOUNDARIES IN THE GRAECO-ROMAN WORLD

Although with Douglas and Lightstone we have already strayed
towards boundaries in Judaism, their construction within the
Greek and Roman worlds demands our attention first. Here the
most foundational and enduring boundary is that between Greek
and barbarian: 'with those of other races, with barbarians there
is and will be for all Greeks an eternal war'—so Livy, echoing
earlier words of Plato.[23] A generation before Plato, Thucydides

   [21] M. Douglas, 'The Abominations of Leviticus', in eadem, *Purity and
Danger*, 2nd edn. (London: Routledge, 1978), 41–57.
   [22] J. Lightstone, *Society, the Sacred and Scripture in Ancient Judaism*, Studies
in Christianity and Judaism, 3 (Waterloo, Ont.: Wilfred Laurier University
Press, 1988), esp. 45–58.
   [23] Livy, *Hist*. XXXI. 29. 15, 'Cum alienigenis, cum barbaris aeternum
omnibus Graecis bellum ist et eritque': Livy puts these words in the mouth of

had recognized the changed circumstances of his day when he commented that Homer does not describe the Greek contingent at Troy as a whole as 'Hellenes', and that 'neither did he speak of barbarians, because "Hellenes", as it seems to me, had not yet been distinguished under one name in opposition' (*Hist.* I. 3); for Thucydides the sense of unity now achieved had priority over that of alterity, a sequence that some would want to reverse. Edith Hall has argued that it was the experience of the Persian wars—the context of Thucydides' work—that, by demanding concerted action by the Greeks, gave a new impetus to an existing sense of shared identity and so provoked the development, which we find deployed in fifth-century tragedy, of the model of the barbarian as the antithesis of the Greek.[24] In addition there was an internal political context at Athens, that of the development of the idea of the *polis* and of democracy, which gained further credit from the stereotyped depiction of the barbarian as 'anti-Greeks against whom Hellenic culture and character were defined'.[25]

The multidimensional characterization and its, at times, quasi-mythic quality make the 'barbarian' the archetypal 'other', as shall be explored later, and yet the primary boundary markers between Greek and barbarian remain surprisingly constant over a long period of time—and are even reproduced in modern analyses of identity.[26] In the first century BCE Dionysius of Halicarnassus talks about the ease with which those who live 'among the barbarians' or 'in barbarian climes' (ἐν βαρβάροις) forget 'Greekness' (τό Ἑλληνικόν), namely language, customs, gods, and laws 'by which Greek nature most differs from barbarian' (ᾧ μάλιστα διαλλάσσει φύσις Ἑλλὰς βαρβάρου) (*Ant. Rom.* I. 89). This is little different from the words that Herodotus had put in the mouths of the Athenians protesting 'the Greekness' that they

the Macedonians addressing the Aetolian league against the Romans. Cf. Plato, *Repub.* V. 470C, το μὲν Ἑλληνικὸν γένος αὐτὸ αὑτῷ οἰκεῖον εἶναι καὶ ξυγγενές, τῷ δὲ βαρβαρικῷ ὀθνεῖόν τε καὶ ἀλλότριον.

[24] E. Hall, *Inventing the Barbarians*; on the model of the barbarian, see below, pp. 271–9.

[25] Ibid. 51; see J. Hall, *Hellenicity*, 7–9, for the argument that there is here a shift from an ethnic to a cultural emphasis.

[26] Those that we shall discuss in what follows are much the same as those analysed by Al-Rasheed, *Iraqi Assyrian Christians*.

shared with the Lacedaemonians and that prohibited any alliance with the Persians—common blood, language, temples and sacrifices, and customs: 'τὸ Ἑλληνικὸν ἐὸν ὅμαιμόν τε καὶ ὁμόγλωσσον καὶ Θεῶν ἱδρύματά τε κοινὰ καὶ θυσίαι ἤθεά τε ὁμότροπα' (Hist. VIII. 144).[27] What is missing from Dionysius is kinship, which still takes first place in Herodotus; as a theme, often achieved through fictive reconstruction, kinship recurs frequently in contexts of common action in defence or aggression, as well as being a standard feature of classical ethnography.[28] Yet, as important are what we might call the more cultural markers—the gods, or, since many would have argued that even the barbarians worshipped the same gods under other names, the way, as Herodotus would have it, in which they were worshipped;[29] and customs, combined for Dionysius with law, ideas which were to provoke other writers to a potentially endless yet implicitly coherent evocation of Hellenic order and justice.

However, of these criteria, it is language that takes pride of place, as witnessed both by the putative etymology of 'barbarian', and by the predominantly linguistic sense of the denominative verbs, βαρβαρίζειν and ἑλληνίζειν.[30] Demonstrating the triumph of language over descent, Thucydides can describe how the people of Argos in Amphilocia learned Greek ('were hellenised in language') from the neighbouring Ambraciots who moved into their city, 'while the rest of the Amphilocians were barbarians' (Hist. II. 68). Among a host of examples we may think of Apollonius

---

[27] Herodotus is constructing an idealized unity that never really existed. See further J. M. Lieu, '"Impregnable Ramparts and Walls of Iron": Boundary and Identity in Early "Judaism" and "Christianity"', NTS 48 (2002), 297–313; some of the ideas explored in that article are reworked here.

[28] For examples see J. Hall, Ethnic Identity in Greek Antiquity, 34–8; Dench, From Barbarians to New Men, 183–4. See further above, pp. 68–9 on 'history'.

[29] E. Hall, Inventing the Barbarians, 181–4.

[30] See M. Casewitz, 'Hellenismos: Formation et function des verbes en ΙΖΩ et de leurs dérivés', in S. Said (ed.), Ἑλληνισμός. Quelques jalons pour une histoire de l'identité grecque, Actes du Colloque de Strasbourg 25–27 octobre 1989 (Leiden: Brill, 1991), 9–16, 'Ἑλληνίζω implique d'abord, dès ses premiers emplois, une opposition entre les Barbares et les Grecs, et cette opposition est d'ordre linguistique' (14); however, J. Hall, Hellenicity, 112–16, questions whether βαρβάρος was originally a linguistic term, and notes that the Greek dialects may not have been mutually intelligible.

of Tyana's meeting with King Phrastes in India; although by his own admission seeming to be 'a barbarian by fate', he reveals his true character by his ability to speak Greek and to be a philosopher amidst his barbarian court.[31] From a different perspective, Koen Goudriaan has argued from Ptolemaic papyri that what made a Greek Greek, and an Egyptian Egyptian, was not class, status, profession, descent, or even immigrant status, nor, before Roman rule, juridical or legal position, but language—although in urban centres behaviour might also determine whether other Greeks would accept as Greek a newcomer from the countryside.[32]

In this case what is noticeable is that, when under Roman rule the categories of Greek and Egyptian became of both fiscal and juridical significance, new tensions arose, and the need to find new modes of maintaining the boundaries became urgent. This is all too clearly evidenced by the conflicts involving the Jewish community in Alexandria under Flaccus's governorship where the Jews joined the competition over boundary drawing; where language would no longer suffice for Josephus to exclude Apion or for the latter to exclude the Jews, other criteria were called into play, worship of the gods against the Jews, descent against Apion (Josephus, *c. Apion.* II. 6 (65–70); cf. Philo, *Leg.* 26 (166)).

Here, the different lines drawn both from within and from without serve to underline the contested nature of boundaries. Yet the children of a Greek who, according to Goudriaan, in the Ptolemaic period might be classified on linguistic grounds as Egyptian, and vice versa, together with Thucydides' Amphilocian Argives mentioned above, also demonstrate how it is part of the nature of a boundary to be crossed. As we shall see, there are differences as well as continuities between the Roman and the Greek construction of boundaries, and of their maintenance; yet awareness of their permeability remains. In Tacitus's description of Britain, those closest to influence adopt Roman practice—although this is something that Tacitus regrets, for Roman

---

[31] Philostratus, *Life of Apollonius*, II. 24–41, 27; he was also accustomed to exercise 'after the Greek manner'. Evidence of the otherness of the barbarians is seen in how this 'barbarian' refers to those who threaten his boundaries as 'the barbarians' (II. 26).

[32] K. Goudriaan, *Ethnicity in Ptolemaic Egypt* (Amsterdam: Gieben, 1988), esp. 90–4, 117–19.

humanitas is in truth for them an element of slavery (*Agric.* 21).[33]
Such crossing of boundaries is fraught with ambivalence: from
a Greek perspective, there is a world of difference between a
barbarian (becoming) Greek (μιξέλλην) and a Greek (becoming)
barbarian (μιξοβάρβαρος).[34]

In these ways boundaries become transitional, loci of negotiation and interaction, something that a purely oppositional model
may not adequately encompass. As has been frequently pointed
out in recent study, this is particularly important when thinking about Hellenization, which should no longer be thought of
as a one-way invasive takeover of a passive victim, but in much
more nuanced and multidimensional terms: when plotted on the
territorial landscape, there may be movement in both directions
and for various purposes; when considered in terms of symbolic
boundaries, it is important to ask how the construction of continuity and of discontinuity is understood by those who map
them; when understood in terms of culture or practice, it is the
interpretation and use of these that are more significant than the
mere fact of new styles—a topic for a later chapter.[35]

BOUNDARIES IN THE JEWISH WORLD

It was in this context that the Jews also had to negotiate their
boundaries as they found themselves a part of an expanded
Hellenistic world, while looking back to the earlier patterns enshrined within their traditions. In narrative terms this emerges
so powerfully within the Maccabean literature that the boundary that 1, 2, 3, and 4 Maccabees inscribe around 'Judaism', a
term first appearing in 2 Maccabees, has long been reinscribed as
archetypal—Hebraism versus Hellenism, a supposedly immutable boundary of mythic proportions whose shadow still reaches

[33] Significantly, Tacitus's example is language: 'qui modo linguam Romanam
abnuebant eloquentiam concupiscerent'; as we shall see, the barbarian can also
offer a model of a purity unsullied by modern decline, below p. 278.
[34] See M. Dubuisson, 'Remarques sur le vocabulaire grec d'acculturation',
Revue belge de philologie et d'histoire 60 (1982), 5–32.
[35] See Dench, *From Barbarians to New Men*, 219; Jones, *Archaeology of
Ethnicity*, 24–5, 36; K. Goudriaan, 'Ethnical Strategies in Graeco-Roman
Egypt', in Bilde *et al.*, *Ethnicity in Hellenistic Egypt*, 74–99, 95; below, Ch. 5.

to the present.[36] Yet, that the term 'Judaism', ἰουδαϊσμός, appears only in Greek, and not just as a Greek formulation but in literature that is confidently Greek in outlook and in self-presentation, only serves to demonstrate the selectivity and interpretation of any boundary drawing.[37] The tension is illustrated by 4 Macc. 18. 5 when it describes how Antiochus IV finally gave up and left Jerusalem because 'he was in no way able to compel the Jerusalemites *to become foreign* (ἀλλοφυλεῖν) and to desert their ancestral practices': here, the terminology of 'foreignness' and of 'ancestral practices', τὰ πατρία ἔθη, is Hellenistic, but, as a more detailed analysis would show, through narrative example each of the texts echoes past experience as it gives shape to what that might mean, albeit with different emphases even while claiming to speak with incontrovertible authority.[38] More recently, that not just diaspora but also Palestinian Judaism was Hellenized has become a *shibboleth*, but this has not really provided the key either to describing the peculiar identity of each, nor to plotting the boundary as the various texts draw it.

Certainly, the claim to a long continuity of separateness and of boundaries, and so of identity, is a common one within 'Jewish' texts. Yet the claim probably has been too readily accepted by some more recent historians, both as unambiguously representing 'how it was', and also as largely univocal. It is now widely agreed that those markers most familiar from the inter-testamental period were probably of recent post-exilic construction—namely Abrahamic descent, male circumcision, sabbath, calendar, laws restricting what might be eaten and with whom, or indeed who might be married, and, perhaps, purity; yet they are still too often presented as the uncontested social and self-determining boundary markers of Judaism.[39] Once we

[36] See the special number of *Poetics Today*, 19/1–2 (1998) entitled 'Hellenism and Hebraism Reconsidered: The Poetics of Cultural Influence and Exchange, I–II', and particularly the Introduction by D. Stern, pp. 1–17; also T. Rajak, 'Jews and Greeks: The Invention and Exploitation of Polarities in the Nineteenth Century', in M. Wyke and M. Biddiss (eds.), *The Uses and Abuses of Antiquity* (Bern: P. Lang, 1999), 57–77.

[37] Ἰουδαϊσμός appears in 2 Macc. 2. 21; 8. 1; 14. 38 and 4 Macc. 4. 26; both texts are literary models of Greek dress clothing a confident Jewishness.

[38] See further below, pp. 282–3, and J. M. Lieu, 'Not Hellenes but Philistines? The Maccabees and Josephus defining the "Other"', *JJS* 53 (2002), 243–63.

[39] On their more recent origin, see above, pp. 70–1.

acknowledge that the construction of boundaries frequently constitutes a fictional claim for continuity, and that it masks the exercise of power through both inclusion and exclusion, we may find such assumptions less certain: instead we should be alert to the variety of shapes that these boundaries actually take and to the different ways in which they are reinforced—as will become clear in what follows. Indeed, even the conceptualized kinship traced back through Jacob and Isaac to Abraham, and predicated on God's promise to Abraham and God's separation of a people through him—'You chose the seed of Abraham before all nations' (*Ps. Sol.* 9. 9)—which was presupposed by our last chapter is less stable than we may at first suppose.[40]

So, for example, the *Letter of Aristeas* famously declares that 'our lawgiver . . . fenced us round with impregnable ramparts and walls of iron, that we might not mingle at all with any of the other nations, but remain pure in body and soul . . . worshipping the one Almighty God'; this encompassing boundary is immediately illustrated by the laws of purity as determining 'food and drink and touch and hearing and seeing' (139, 142).[41] Yet, these words are spoken in calm and polite explanation for a supposedly Gentile audience, and they are immediately subverted: special dining arrangements are made for the Jews, not because they are unusually fastidious, but in accordance with the purported norm of deference to the distinctive customs of eating, drinking, and reclining of all visitors to the royal court (182). Similarly, while admitting that the translation of the Scriptures into Greek was 'contrary to nature' (44), *Aristeas* nevertheless gives that translation both human and divine support of the highest order, and celebrates the inclusion of the Scriptures in the library of Ptolemy Philadelphus, presumably symbolically at home among 'all the books in the world' (9). In sharp contrast with this, in *Jubilees* Hebrew is the language of creation (*Jub.* 12. 27),[42] and

---

[40] See above, Ch. 3 n. 53.

[41] διὰ βρωτῶν καὶ ποτῶν καὶ ἀφῶν καὶ ἀκοῆς καὶ ὁράσεως; cf. Lieu, '"Impregnable Ramparts"'.

[42] Although many have denied that language was a boundary marker for Jews, F. Millar, *The Roman Near East, 31BC–AD337* (Cambridge, Mass.: Harvard University Press, 1993), 521, 319–36 points out that Aramaic survived among Jews within the Roman Empire more than did other native languages. On the politics of Hebrew see S. Schwartz, 'Language, Power and Identity in Ancient Palestine', *Past and Present*, 148 (1995), 3–47.

the theme of separation is urged with more consciously divisive consequences: Abraham blesses Jacob—neither of whom are mentioned in *Aristeas*—counselling him, 'Separate from the nations, and do not eat with them. Do not act according to their deeds, and do not become their companion; for their works are unclean, and all their ways are a pollution and an abomination and detestable' (22. 16).[43]

These two examples also illustrate how, while such boundary markers have important social consequences, their textual function for the creation of an image of internal identity is no less significant. So, in a further example, although food laws undoubtedly did function to maintain social separation, in 4 Maccabees their real importance is a *textual* one, as a powerful symbol of personal and national purity. Although 4 Maccabees interprets Antiochus IV's decrees as an attempt to enforce the renunciation (ἐξομνύσθαι) of Judaism, it is the 'eating of defiling food' that defines such renunciation, almost to the exclusion of all else (4 Macc. 4. 26). For 4 Maccabees the problem is not that the food is 'unclean' (ἀκάθαρτος = טמא), the term used in *Aristeas* who here follows the language of the Septuagint, but that it is defiling, for which the author coins a new and expressive term, 'defiled eating' (μιαροφαγία):[44] Eleazer retorts to Antiochus's attempts to get him to taste 'this excellent meat', 'You shall not defile (μιαίνω) my honourable mouth now old nor the vigour of a law-abiding life . . . the fathers will receive me pure (ἁγνός)' (5. 36–7). If we were to extend our analysis to other texts, we would find yet other ways of constructing this 'common' boundary.[45]

In *Jubilees*, however, the rhetoric of separation belongs not to food but particularly to sabbath, calendar, and circumcision. Tracing each of these distinguishing marks back into Creation itself, *Jubilees* none the less anticipates their flouting, which will be a source of 'abomination . . . pollution, uncleanness and destruction' (*Jub.* 6. 34–8; 15. 33; 23. 17–19).[46] Anchoring the

---

[43] Cf. 4Q219 (= 4QJub^d) II. 24, 28 (= *Jub.* 21. 23) where the Hebrew terms are חבל, תועבה.

[44] ἀκάθαρτος: *Aristeas* 128–9, 147, 166, 169; ctr. μιαρός: 4 Macc. 4. 26; 9. 15, 17, 32; 10. 18; 11. 4; μιαροφαγ- 5. 3, 19, 25, 27; 6. 19; 7. 6; 8. 1, 2, 12, 29; 11. 16, 25; 13. 2 (cf. 9. 9A).

[45] See Lieu, '"Impregnable Ramparts"', 305–7.

[46] Although circumcision only appears with Abraham, the angels of pres-

sabbath in the Creation narrative, God declares 'I will separate for myself a people from among all peoples, and these shall keep the sabbath day' (2. 19, 31–2); the distinctive ordering of the 364-day year is 'lest they forget the feasts of the covenant and walk according to the feasts of the Gentiles' (6. 35).[47] Elsewhere, the Gentiles are, by definition, 'uncircumcised', and the male who is not circumcised on the eighth day but behaves 'like the Gentiles' is to be 'removed and rooted out of the land' (15. 26, 34); in this case, circumcision takes priority over descent, for it is also required of foreign slaves born or purchased (15. 12, following Gen. 17. 12)—showing how this is a matter of corporate and not just of individual identity. Yet the Gentiles are also those 'who uncover themselves', something that, consequent upon God's clothing of Adam and Eve, is proscribed for 'all those who know the judgement of the law' (*Jub.* 3. 31).

Here we may suspect that it is the boundary that determines who are Gentiles or that constructs them, namely as those who fail to observe these demands. It is within this framework that we should read the particularly uncompromising polemic against 'intermarriage': a father who gives his daughter or his sister to a Gentile is to be stoned, while the woman is to be burnt—a combined application of Lev. 18. 21; 20. 2, the penalty for giving a child to Molech, and of Lev. 21. 9, concerning the promiscuous daughter of a priest: 'Israel will not be free from this uncleanness if it has a wife of the daughters of the Gentiles, or has given any of its daughters to a man who is of any of the Gentiles' (*Jub.* 30. 14). The roots of this perspective lie in the Ezra tradition (Ezra 9–10) where such marriages mean that 'the holy seed has mingled (ערב√) itself with the peoples of the land', peoples who are defined by their practice of 'abominations' (תועבה) (9. 1–2); yet we are bound to ask, who was the prohibited 'Gentile' of *Jubilees*?[48]

---

ence and the angels of holiness keep the sabbath and are circumcised (*Jub.* 2. 18; 15. 27). *Jub.* 3. 8–15 traces the laws of uncleanness following childbirth to the creation of Eve; see above, pp. 70–1.

[47] J. C. Vanderkam (trans.), *The Book of Jubilees*, CSCO 511. Script. Aeth. 88 (Louvain: Peeters, 1989), 43, n. on 6. 35 compares 4QpHos[a] 2.16 במועדי הגואים; he suggests that *Jub.* 6. 33 may see the use of the wrong calendar as leading to the years being 'confused' (rather than 'moved').

[48] On Ezra see C. Hayes, 'Intermarriage and Impurity in Ancient Jewish Sources', *HTR* 92 (1999), 3–36; H. Zlotnick-Sivan, 'The Silent Women of

Given that *Jubilees* is usually dated to the Maccabean period,
it is noteworthy that it is completely silent regarding any of the
food laws other than the consumption of blood (*Jub.* 6. 9–13).[49]
For the author or community of this text diet did not belong to
the boundary markers: was it not contested or was it negotiable?
This ambiguity illustrates well that we can never conclude that
what is ignored in any of these texts was not observed: boundaries imply situationally determined selection from practices.
Further, as we have seen, for *Jubilees* the boundaries are drawn
not only against those whom we would recognize as Gentiles,
particularly represented by the Seleucids, but both against those
more open to them, traditionally the Hellenizers, and equally, if
not more so, against the majority holders of power in Jerusalem,
who, among other things, did not observe the 364-day solar calendar.[50] It was in this 'sectarian' context that appeals to circumcision, festivals, and sabbath gained particular rhetorical power.

We should not be surprised, then, that the sense of boundary is
developed particularly vigorously in the Dead Sea Scrolls. Here
the language of boundary and the consequent sense of separation
is characteristically focused: 'they are to be segregated (בדל√)
from within the dwelling of the men of sin to walk to the desert'
(1QS 8. 13). This is not simply a statement about the physical
withdrawal of the community, for the texts themselves claim
applicability to 'all their places of residence', requiring only a
quorum of ten (1QS 6. 1–2, 6); rather, it establishes a symbolic
boundary that is no less tangible. Repeating the language traditionally directed against the Gentiles, 4QMMT declares that
'we have separated ourselves (פרש√) from the rest of the people
and . . . we avoid mingling (ערב√) in these affairs and associating

Yehud: Notes on Ezra 9–10', *JJS* 51 (2000), 3–18. On Ezra as the background to
Jubilees here see E. Schwarz, *Identität durch Abgrenzung: Abgrenzungsprozesse
in Israel im 2. vorchristlichen Jahrhundert und ihre traditionsgeschichtlichen
Voraussetzungen*, EH XXIII/162 (Frankfurt am Main: P. Lang, 1982), 63–81;
see also B. Halpern-Amaru, *The Empowerment of Women in the* Book of Jubilees,
S.JSJ 60 (Leiden: Brill, 1999). D. Suter, 'Fallen Angel, Fallen Priest: The
Problem of Family Purity in *1 Enoch*', *HUCA* 50 (1979), 115–35, traces the
concern in 1 Enoch. See below, pp. 120–1 on the theme in other texts.

[49] *Jub.* 22. 16, 'eat not with them', cited earlier, refers to association, and not
to food in particular.

[50] See Schwarz, *Identität*, 125–6.

with them in these things'; for its part, the *Damascus Document*, pertinently for this discussion, condemns those who 'removed the boundary with which the very first had marked their inheritance'.[51] Here, the language of separation and of abstinence provides the necessary antithesis to that of cohesion and unity: each is to 'seek the peace of his brother . . . and to keep apart (בדל√) from every uncleanness (טמא√) . . . without anyone defiling (שקץ√) his holy spirit' (CD 6. 14–7. 7). The boundary markers that preserve this separation are interpretation of the Law, purity regulations expressed stringently in meals, and distinctive (פרוש: CD 6. 18, 20) observance of sabbath and of calendar.

Surprisingly, idolatry, traditionally the mark of the Gentile, is not reconfigured in any significant way in these texts, nor, unlike the other markers, is it used very extensively to characterize those who now most immediately stand outside the boundary.[52] Circumcision, too, can become a boundary marker only through reinterpretation; members are those who have 'circumcised the foreskin of their inclination (יצר) and of their stiff neck' (1QS 5. 5), but the metaphor is notably rare.[53] Kinship also has to be redefined with the result that it no longer functions directly as a boundary marker: Abraham has no place, although there will be written on the banner that leads the sons of light in the eschatological war, 'People of God and the name of Israel and of Aaron and the names of the twelve tribes of Israel according to their genealogies' (1QM 3. 13–14); however, whom this includes and excludes, and why, remains unclear. Instead, correct and insightful exegesis—evidently an internal boundary marker—does become a keystone. Yet the most pervasive and

[51] 4QMMT 92–3 = 4Q397 frags. 7–8, ll. 7–8; CD 1. 16; 5. 20; 19. 15–16, where the reference to Hos 5. 10 is made explicit.

[52] On Gentiles and idolatry see below, p. 118; 1QH 11. 14–19 does describe the hymnist's opponents as looking for God 'among the idols'. Otherwise, the new entrant must have turned aside from 'the idols of his heart' (1QS 2. 11); detestation of 'the uncleanness of idolatry' is just one among a number of characteristics of the spirit of truth in 1QS 4. 2–7.

[53] R. le Déaut, 'Le Thème de la circoncision du cœur (Dt. XXX 6; Jér. IV 4) dans les versions anciennes (LXX et Targum) et à Qumran', in J. Emerton (ed.), *Congress Volume Vienna 1980*, VT.S 32 (Leiden: Brill, 1981), 178–205, 190–8, cites only 1QS 5. 5; CD 16. 6; 1QpHab. 2. 3; 4Q184 and 4Q177; in most cases the metaphor is to 'circumcise the heart'. Cf. also 1QH 2. 7, 18, 'uncircumcised lips'.

deeply etched line along which the boundary is drawn is purity:
the one who does not enter the Community cannot be cleansed
by any acts of atonement or by any amount of water, but 'defiled,
defiled (טמא) shall he be all the days he spurns the decrees of
God'; membership signifies eventually to be allowed to share in
'the pure [food]' of the Community, while infringement of any
rule, not just the ritual, earns separation from the Community
and from its 'purity' (1QS 2. 25–3. 6; 6–9).[54] Yet while this might
be seen as an intensification of concerns in the wider community,
the 'others' thus excluded are primarily those who saw themselves, and were widely seen, as Jewish. Purity and commen-
sality, it has been suggested, were equally determinative for the
Pharisees.[55] Competing claims to the maintenance of boundaries
may address internal dynamics among minority groups as much
as the actual relations of the wider community beyond.

It is in this framework that we may turn to the *Testaments of
the Twelve Patriarchs*, which, as we have already seen, exemplify
the problem of Jewish definition.[56] Unlike *Aristeas*, they are self-
evidently interested in the line of Abraham; like *Aristeas*, and
also 4 Maccabees, they display no interest in circumcision nor
in the sabbath.[57] Yet, while the boundary with the Gentiles is
important, here it is policed pre-eminently by marriage and sexual liaisons: Joseph avoids the food sent by Potiphar's wife not
out of dietary observance but because he knew that she had mixed
it with aphrodisiacal enchantments (*T. Jos.* 6). The language of
pollution is again important, but here it is constituted by sexual

[54] On the primacy of purity for the self-understanding of the Community
see F. G. Martinez, 'The Problem of Purity: The Qumran Solution', in F. G.
Martinez and J. T. Barrera (eds.), *The People of the Dead Sea Scrolls: Their
Writings, Beliefs and Practices* (ET. Leiden: Brill, 1995), 139–57.

[55] In so far as anything confidently can be said about the Pharisees: see
A. Baumgarten, 'Graeco-Roman Voluntary Associations and Ancient Jewish
Sects', in M. Goodman (ed.), *Jews in a Graeco-Roman World* (Oxford:
Clarendon, 1998), 93–111, 102–5. Also J. Neusner, *The Idea of Purity in Ancient
Judaism*, SJLA 1 (Leiden: Brill, 1973), 110–19.

[56] Above, pp. 45–8.

[57] Circumcision appears only in passing at 4 Macc. 4. 25; contra its importance in 1 Macc. 1. 15, 60–1; 2. 46; 2 Macc. 6. 10. It is not mentioned in *Aristeas*,
and only in relation to the story in Gen. 34 at *T. Levi* 6. 3, 6, in the *Testaments*.
Similarly, sabbath does not appear in the *Testaments*, in *Aristeas*, nor in 4 Macc.,
in contrast to its importance in 1 and 2 Macc.

unchastity and by out-marriage, a preoccupation that we have already noted in *Jubilees*: 'Beware of the spirit of fornication . . . Take to thyself a wife without blemish or pollution (βεβηλωμένην) . . . and not of the race of foreigners (ἀλλοφυλοί) or of Gentiles' (*T. Levi* 9. 9–10). Again, the actual possibility of renegotiating this boundary is recognized, albeit condemned: 'you shall take the daughters of Gentiles as wives, purifying them with an unlawful purification (καθαρίζοντας αὐτὰς καθαρισμῷ παρανόμῳ)' (*T. Levi* 14. 6); although here a specifically priestly concern, it is not restricted to the priestly line (compare *T. Jud.* 23. 2). Sexual impurity in general is allied with idolatry: 'for a pit unto the soul is the sin of fornication, separating it from God and bringing it near to idols' (*T. Reub.* 4. 6).

A similar combination of out-marriage and idolatry is important for *Joseph and Aseneth* where Joseph refuses 'to kiss a strange woman who will bless with her mouth dead and dumb idols and eat from their table bread of strangulation . . . for this is an abomination (βδέλυγμα) before the Lord God' (*Jos. & Asen.* 8. 6–7). Despite the emphasis on Joseph's separate table (7. 1), this does not seem to be a reference to Jewish dietary laws, and the happy couple later eat with her parents without authorial comment (20. 8): since the alternative is 'bread of life and cup of blessing', it seems rather to be a case of food over which a blessing has been offered to God as opposed to that implicated in the worship of idols.[58] However, for this text, Aseneth can become an acceptable wife once she has forsworn her idols and recognized 'the Lord God of Heaven . . . the God of the Hebrews': her foreignness as such is not a problem, perhaps in reaction against those who would have followed Ezra, *Jubilees*, or the *Testaments*. The difference is not between a soft and a hard position but between two contrasting perceptions of the boundary, and so of identity; it is a contrast that does not follow the boundary between Judaism and Christianity as traditionally conceived.

Also from Egypt, Philo offers a different perspective on the

---

[58] Cf. *Jos. & Asen.* 8. 9; 15. 5; 16. 16; 19. 5; 21. 13–14, 21. For blessing God before eating as characteristically Jewish, see *Sib. IV*, ll. 25–6, and its importance in the Dead Sea Scrolls (1QS 6. 5–6). ἀγχόνη ('strangulation') is not used in the LXX; Philo does refer to strangling as 'an unclean death' for both animals and humans (*Aet.* 5 (20); *Mut.* 8 (62)), but its use here with ἄρτος makes an explicit reference to meat less likely.

boundary policed by marriage and descent. He unashamedly acknowledges the 'mingled multitude' (עֵרֶב√) of the Exodus (Exod. 12. 38); probably reflecting mixed marriage as a pressing issue in Alexandrian Judaism, it is a 'bastard' (νόθος) crowd that accompanies the Hebrews from Egypt, including children of Egyptian women and Hebrew fathers (*Mos.* I. 27 (147)).[59] Also present are those who had joined them, impressed by the evidences of divine favour or punishment: such 'proselytes' (ἐπηλύται) figure significantly in Philo's thought, and all that he asks of them is that they 'acknowledge the sovereignty of one, not of many', on which basis they are then to be treated as 'dearest friends and closest kin' (*Virt.* 33 (179)). Abraham, who rejected his father's beliefs, like the foreign wives of the patriarchal narratives together with their children, are examples to be held against those who trust in ancestral virtue rather than in a sound and secure life (*Virt.* 39–41 (211–26)). Philo considers, too, that Moses rightly valued the kinship that bound the Hebrews and Edom together, despite the latter's abandonment of their common 'ancestral practices and earlier communal life' (*Mos.* I. 43 (241–2)).[60] Yet he reserves dire threats against those 'who neglect the laws of piety and righteousness and are seduced by polytheistic opinions . . . and have forgotten the teaching of their race and fathers', and even more dire ones against those who have so subverted them to 'destroy their ancestral practices' (*Praem.* 28 (162); 29 (169–70)). Such practices are for him the boundaries whose removal Deut. 19. 14 forbids, although his concern alerts us to competing attempts to redraw them; most famous among these would be 'the allegorists' whom he condemns, but does not exclude, for their disregard of the physical in their enthusiasm for the allegorical significance of calendar, circumcision, and sabbath (*Spec. Leg.* IV. 28 (149); *Migr. Abr.* 16 (80–93)).

From an observer's perspective we may plot such constructions on a register of assimilation and/or acculturation;[61] yet for the participants they are ways of redrawing or redefining the

---

[59] See A. Mendelson, *Philo's Jewish Identity*, BJS 161 (Atlanta, Ga.: Scholars Press, 1988), 71–4, on intermarriage. However, for a more cautious view see *Migr. Abr.* 29 (158).

[60] On attitudes to Edom see above, pp. 68–9.

[61] So J. Barclay, *The Jews in the Mediterranean Diaspora* (Edinburgh: T&T Clark, 1996).

boundaries, perhaps as much concerned with continuities—'we still value circumcision'—as with their dissolution. Yet if with Philo we are sometimes left wondering just how negotiable the boundaries may be,[62] the one immutable one is that against idolatry, whose contravention he feels deservedly merits death (*Spec. Leg.* I. 10 (56–8); 58 (315–16)). In his uncompromising contrast between biblical truth and Greek myths Philo draws this boundary, even while speaking the language and idiom of a Greek mind.[63]

Idolatry is pervasively the fixed point of the boundary and the primary hallmark of the Gentiles as 'other', evidenced by the numerous mocking accounts of the making and worship of idols from stone or wood. Witnessing again to the dextrous manipulation of boundaries, it is the Jewish Sibyl who adopts a Gentile persona in order to lament the Greeks 'who offer vain gifts to the dead and sacrifice to idols', and to presage the 'holy race of God-fearing men' to whom alone God has given understanding in that 'they do not give themselves to vain deceits nor honour the works of men's hands . . . idols of dead gods of wood and stone' (*Sib. III*, ll. 545–89). Yet, for the Sibyl, what also distinguishes 'the holy race' or 'sons of the great God' who live around 'the temple' (ll. 573, 702) is that 'they do not hold unholy intercourse with boys as do the Phoenicians, Egyptians, and Latins, and spacious Hellas, and many nations of other men'—in fact everyone else (ll. 596–600). However, despite the rhetoric, such a boundary would include many non-Jews—indeed, perhaps this is precisely its function, through an appeal to what John Collins has called

---

[62] Mendelson, *Philo's Jewish Identity* uses the two headings, 'orthodoxy' and 'orthopraxy', under the latter listing circumcision, sabbath, festivals, dietary laws, and intermarriage. His discussion of dietary laws (pp. 67–71) shows that Philo valorized those willing to die for them (*Flacc.* 11 (96); *Legat.* 44 (361)) but not that he presented them as a boundary; on festivals (pp. 62–7) he suggests that Philo was stricter about the Day of Atonement than about Passover. Another example would be his attitude to the sabbath, a term that appears infrequently in his writings (8 times) because he prefers the symbolism of the seventh day; yet he cites with approval the death penalty enacted against one who broke the sabbath law (*Spec. Leg.* II. 45 (250)).

[63] On his attitude to Greek myths see M. Niehoff, 'Philo's Views on Paganism', in G. N. Stanton and G. Stroumsa (eds.), *Tolerance and Intolerance in Early Judaism and Christianity* (Cambridge: Cambridge University Press, 1998), 135–58.

'the common ethic'.[64] Here we could also call to witness the many Hellenistic Jewish texts that are silent about circumcision, and even about diet, calendar, or sabbath, while in no way denying Jewish particularity.

Even more openly, the *Testament of Abraham* eulogizes the 'pious, entirely holy, righteous, and hospitable Abraham' for welcoming 'everyone . . . friends and strangers, neighbours and passers-by' (*T. Abr.* 1. 2); yet the text's concern is with the future judgement of 'sinners' for failings that include murder, theft, and sexual immorality, but, significantly, not idolatry (10. 1–15). God's choice of Abraham is vigorously affirmed (1. 5–7), but there is no hint that this produces a division between his descendants and the nations, nor that either one or the other are characteristically sinful. Drawing boundaries in this way would allow sympathetic outsiders to feel themselves insiders—and we need not ask whether their males would be required to undergo circumcision in order to be considered Jews, for to do so is to introduce terms and concepts that do not belong to the identity being constructed: at this point the division between 'Jewish' and 'non-Jewish' is ours, not that of the texts. This does not mean that these texts, and others adopting a similar strategy, betray a diluted or indistinct sense of Jewishness: membership of the community may have been secured in other ways, including Abrahamic descent however constructed, and we cannot tell whether this produced a consensual boundary that needed no reinforcement; however, other patterns of identity, including those based on behaviour, are here deemed ultimately more significant, perhaps both on the stage of divine judgement and on that of social co-operation.

What we have discovered, then, is vigorous reinforcement of the immutability of the boundaries, together with multiple attempts to redraw them or to negotiate them, sometimes in the same texts. Reinforcement is achieved by the totalizing and powerful language of pollution that we have found in a number of texts, describing both 'the nations' and their effect on Israel: for example, in *2 Baruch*'s vision of alternate torrents of black and bright waters, the fifth black waters are 'the works which

---

[64] J. Collins, *Between Athens and Jerusalem: Jewish Identity in the Hellenistic Diaspora* (New York: Crossroad, 1983), 137–74.

the Amorites worked . . . and the mingling of their pollution' (*2 Bar*. 60. 1).[65] The pervasive language of pollution should not be reduced to the much-debated question as to whether and when Gentiles were perceived as a source of impurity; it belongs rather to the rhetoric of boundary drawing, and while it may have contributed to such views, it says much more about the creation of 'the other' as a reverse mirror of the self. Tacitus, similarly, could recount the fear that Nero's introduction of Greek-style games would corrupt the youth into degeneracy and pollute even the nobles (*Ann*. XIV. 20).[66] Equally potent has been the threat of 'mingling', a transgression of the boundaries: 'you will be mixed with the abominations of the Gentiles' (*T. Judah*, 23. 2). Yet, again, although it could be so construed, this is not a mark of *Jewish* particularism—we find the same antipathy to mixing with the barbarian in Greek sources.[67]

By contrast, and at the same time, boundaries become the place for negotiation and movement. Already in the Hebrew Bible, the 'alien' (גר), although as such not an Israelite, may be treated as an insider (for example, Lev. 18. 26; 22. 18), and there are even traces of such an attitude within the community of the Scrolls.[68] The Septuagint sought to formalize this through the translation of גר, where possible, as προσήλυτος, a new coinage indicating a new sense of boundary as something where entry (and exit) could be marked. So, in a fresh twist to the concern about 'mingling' that it shares, *2 Baruch* draws a clear division between those 'who withdrew and mingled themselves (ܐܬܚܠܛܘ) with the seed of the mixed (ܡܥܪܒܐ) peoples' and 'those who before knew not but then knew life and mingled (ܐܬܚܠܛܘ) with the seed of the people[s] which

---

[65] 'Pollution', ܛܘܠܫܐ, is the term used in the Syriac of Dan. 11. 31 (= שקץ); for this in the Dead Sea Scrolls, see above, pp. 113–15.

[66] See further below, p. 285. See also Hayes, 'Intermarriage and Impurity', who argues for the priority of the moral idea of pollution; S. Stern, *Jewish Identity*, 52–3.

[67] See M. Casewitz, 'Le Vocabulaire du mélange démographique: Mixo-barbares et Mixhellènes', in V. Fromentin and S. Gotteland (eds.), *Origenes Gentium*, Ausonius Publications 7 (Paris: de Boccard, 2001), 41–7; also above, n. 34.

[68] See C. van Houten, *The Alien in Israelite Law*, JSOT.SS 107 (Sheffield: Sheffield Academic Press, 1991); Sparks, *Ethnicity and Identity*, 239–41; K. Berthelot, 'La Notion de גר dans les Textes de Qumrân', *RevQ* 19 (1999), 171–216.

had separated (ܪܬܒ) itself' (*2 Bar.* 42. 4–5).[69] Baruch is perplexed: 'will the last times receive them? Or perhaps their time will be weighed and as the scale inclines they will be judged?' (41). As we have already seen in Philo, both proselytes and apostates challenge any conception of the boundaries as rigid, and create a tension with halakhic definition precisely because these are two different ways of addressing a common problem.[70]

Yet even where there is no crossing, strategies are needed in order to deal with the connectedness that boundaries establish. *m. Ab. Z.* 3. 6 considers the problem of a Jew whose home shares a wall with a pagan shrine: what is he to do should it collapse?[71] Here the boundary is shared, a point of contact, albeit troublesome. The social implications of such a scenario, if possible in Israel how much more so in the Diaspora, may give us pause for thought, but it is the literary construction that interests us here. Yet this is not an isolated example: while the Mishnah reflects second- and third-century perceptions, the *Damascus Document* already had counselled against staying near Gentiles or asking a foreigner to fulfil a commission on the sabbath, implying that even for this supposedly isolationist community both were otherwise conceivable—depending on whom *we* identify as Gentile here. The prohibition in both the *Damascus Document* and in the Mishnah against selling them something that might be used for sacrifice leaves open a range of other possible dealings (CD 11. 2, 14–15; 12. 8–9; *m. Ab. Z.* 1. 5). The symbolic significance of the Mishnaic example above is the more impressive: the solution— to rebuild at a minimum distance of 4 cubits—in effect creates a neutral space where interaction is possible, and the category of 'other' is suspended; the decision that the wall belongs half to each acknowledges the reality of contiguity created by any

---

[69] For ܣܒܪ cf. *2 Baruch* 58. 1; 60. 1 (cited above); also 27. 23; 70. 6 of disorder. 'Mixed peoples' may be taken from Jer. 25. 20, 24 (although the Syriac does not so understand the obscure Hebrew הערב at that point); at Exod. 12. 38 the Syriac follows the Hebrew (ܥܪܒ).

[70] On the ambiguities and the halakhic issues see Cohen, *Beginnings of Jewishness*, 157–62; L. Schiffman, *Who was a Jew? Rabbinic and Halakhic Perspectives on the Jewish–Christian Schism* (Hoboken, NJ: KTAV, 1985).

[71] I owe this example and reflection on it to M. Halbertal, 'Co-existing with the Enemy: Jews and Pagans in the Mishnah', in Stanton and Stroumsa, *Tolerance and Intolerance*, 159–72.

boundary. An analogous temporal space is created by the injunction not to buy or sell from a Gentile three days either side of one of their festivals (*m. Ab. Z.* 1. 2). So, more generally, rabbinic literature creates a distinction between Gentile as 'foreign', with whom dealings are necessary, and Gentile as idolater with whom they are to be avoided at all costs.[72] Thus, once again, it is idolatry that forms the most tangible boundary, but we may not always be able to determine exactly who stood on either side of that boundary: the frontiers may have been peopled by those whom we and whom they themselves, but not the rabbis, might see as Jews.[73]

These last examples have already brought us into the uncertain territory of the textual construction of social example—how far do these really reflect the shifting boundaries of social experience? And should we go on to search for the much-debated 'God-fearers', those Gentiles who, whether or not an identifiable category across a range of epigraphic and documentary texts, also in one way or another straddled or even crossed the boundary?[74] True, not all of these 'became Jews';[75] our dilemma, and the scholarly debates, arise when we look for precision where the indeterminacy and even the no man's land of frontiers, with its characteristically diasporic shifting lines of interconnection and separation, may serve us better.

Yet this would be to leave our textual ground, and so, instead, we may ask how the boundary was perceived or drawn from the other side, by those whom the Jews labelled 'Gentiles'. It has too often been easy to be rather simplistic about this: assuming that male circumcision, dietary laws, and sabbath were what Jews

---

[72] See G. Porton, *GOYIM: Gentiles and Israelites in Mishnah–Tosefta*, BJS 155 (Atlanta, Ga.: Scholars Press, 1988), 287–8; Stern, *Jewish Identity*, 195–7. See below, pp. 281–2.

[73] See M. Goodman's suggestion that behind the 'Gentile' of rabbinic discourse may stand non-rabbinically halakhic Jews, in 'Identity and Authority in Ancient Judaism', *Judaism* 39 (1990), 192–201, 193–4.

[74] See the chapter entitled 'Crossing the Boundary and Becoming a Jew', in Cohen, *Beginnings of Jewishness*, 140–74; B. Wander, *Gottesfürchtige und Sympathisanten*, WUNT 104 (Tübingen: Mohr, 1998), 229: 'Das Proprium der ganzen heidnischen Bewegung zum Judentum hinbesteht aber doch gerade dahin, daß es nach der Quellenlage eine Vielzahl sich "überschneidenender" Sympathieerweise geben kann, die wieder terminologisch noch phänomenologisch eindeutig zu erfassen sind.' [75] See Cohen, above, n. 74.

saw as keeping themselves separate, it has been natural to focus on pagan comments, usually derogatory, about these Jewish practices, and then to remark on this coherence between inside and outside tracings of the boundary, both as grounds for the supposedly relatively stable conceptions of Jewishness, and as mutually reinforcing the latter's objectivity. Yet the boundaries that Greek and Roman authors erect reflect as much about themselves as about those whom they thus isolate. Tacitus's much-quoted account illustrates this well: his vehement assertion that 'among the Jews all things are profane that we hold sacred; on the other hand, they regard as permissible what to us seems immoral' is a powerful statement of immutable boundaries, but one that, as we shall see, is no less a statement about the Rome of the time: it serves his historiographical interests and his Roman ideals. Moreover, he is concerned only with the Jews ultimately defeated by Titus; in the Diaspora he has no interest.[76]

This is not to deny that outsiders looking in were particularly conscious of Jewish 'peculiarities' regarding food, sabbath, and circumcision, so that the 'sabbath of the circumcised' could become a by-word of 'superstition' (Persius, *Sat.* 5. 184; compare Horace, *Sat.* I. 9. 68–70), or so that even Philo could represent Gaius as asking 'Why do you refuse to eat pork?'—although that Philo pens these words is too often forgotten (*Leg.* 45 (361)).[77] Jewish separatism, too, becomes proverbial—although, warned by what we have read of Tacitus, this should often be heard more as the inability of the observer to accommodate a non-conformity that could not readily be assimilated or be described in terms of Greek or Roman ideas and cults of the gods. So, already, Hecataeus, according to Diodorus Siculus, asserted that 'he [Moses] established sacrifices and ways of life far removed from those of other nations; because of their own expulsion he introduced a manner of life both unsocial and hostile to strangers' (*Bibl. Hist.* XL. 3. 5). Once established, Jewish 'misanthropy' was easily repeated, but may speak more for Greek and later Roman intolerance and stereotypes of barbarians.[78]

[76] See below, pp. 276–7.

[77] Pagan accounts of the Jews are readily available in *GLAJJ*, and have been widely discussed; see P. Schäfer, *Judeophobia: Attitudes towards the Jews in the Ancient World* (Cambridge, Mass.: Harvard University Press, 1997).

[78] See below, pp. 272–8.

Most of these authors are writing about the 'Jews' of Judaea, an ethnographical oddity who resisted total absorption into either the Hellenistic or the Roman Empire, and the record of whose resistance survives. For them sabbath and circumcision are the peculiar practices that require aetiological explanation by recourse to earlier history or myth in the same way as do the names or practices of other peoples. How far these observers saw Jewish communities in the Diaspora in similar terms remains beyond our knowledge, particularly before the influx of slaves into Rome following Titus's victory. It is in that new context that Juvenal can famously describe the son who exceeds his father's awe of sabbath and abstention from pork, by 'laying aside his foreskin . . . despising Roman laws . . . and learning . . . not to show the way except to one who practises the same rites' (*Sat.* 14. 96–106). What troubles Juvenal, as it does Tacitus (*Hist.* V. 5), is the undermining of patriotism: it is Roman values that are threatened, and the polemic serves most to underscore those values—which in Juvenal's view had been subverted not by the Jews but by poor parenting.

That Jewish communities in the Diaspora needed protection for their observance of sabbath and, on occasion, of food laws, and that in times of conflict opponents might target precisely these practices, is true; but it is significant that our evidence for this comes from Jewish sources, and so we have little way of knowing whether other ethnic groups were similarly treated.[79] Yet without such possibilities of comparison it is difficult to decide whether we should use such evidence to speak of the boundaries thus constituted and recognized, or whether it does not rather represent strategies of negotiation rendering harmless the divisive potential of differentness—and the answer need not be the same in every place nor at every time. Neither can we know who was included by these provisions, and how: were the 'Israelites who worship on Mt Gerizim' who are known from inscriptions from Delos covered by the proconsular directive on behalf of

---

[79] See the records collected by Josephus, *Ant.* XIV. 10. 1–26 (185–267); XVI. 6. 1–7 (160–73); Philo, *Leg.* 40 (311–18). On occasion the Jews can claim that they were exempt from restrictions imposed on other groups (*Ant.* XIV. 10. 8 (213–16); Philo, *Leg.* 40 (316)), but this implies that in other respects, and when such restrictions lapsed, they resembled these groups.

'the Jews in Delos' (Josephus, *Ant*. XIV. 10. 14 (231–3)).[80] That question reminds us, too, that in collecting and recording these decrees—and possibly in ignoring other less favourable ones—Josephus is constructing his own markers, not so much for these communities as for his own times. By contrast, we would expect that the (non-)worship of other deities, de facto through their material representation, would provide one of the most enduring components of the boundary: so, according to Josephus, it was an erstwhile Jew who at Antioch suggested that Jews be exposed by being invited to sacrifice 'as the rule (νόμος) is for the Greeks' (*BJ* VII. 3. 3 (50)). Our problem is that our ignorance is far greater as to how this boundary was negotiated in the daily practicalities of city life for much of the time.

Thus the apparent coherence between pagan perceptions of the boundary function of circumcision, sabbath, and food, and the use of these practices in 'Jewish' sources may be misleading. They function differently, perhaps for different groups and at different times, and may not indicate the same actual behaviour, and certainly not the same understanding of that behaviour. Attention to them may also serve to hide differences: on the Jewish side, as symbols, sabbath, circumcision, and the rest can hardly be understood apart from the ideas of Law and covenant and of God's own separation by choice of this people (Lev. 20. 22–6).[81] Such themes are passed over in silence by outsiders; they know nothing of 'a covenant', neither, for the most part, do they know anything of the role of the sacred writings of the Jews.

The picture drawn thus far is necessarily indeterminate. We have traced, on the one hand, a continuity in the boundaries, and hence a continuity of self-identity, even when the bearers of that identity are changing—such as the community (communities?) of the Scrolls at the various stages of its history—or when different groups might claim the same territory. On the other hand, discontinuities in emphasis and configuration allow for the emergence of the new within the framework of what precedes.[82]

---

[80] On the Samaritans at Delos see L. M. White, 'The Delos Synagogue Revisited: Recent Fieldwork in the Graeco-Roman Diaspora', *HTR* 80 (1987), 133–60, esp. 141–7.

[81] See Schwarz, *Identität*, 74–81.

[82] See, however, E. J. Christiansen, 'The Consciousness of Belonging to God's Covenant and What it Entails According to the Damascus Document and the

We should, then, read with some caution Josephus's eirenic description of the 'three philosophies' alongside his assertion of a 'remarkable harmony' (*BJ* II. 8. 2–14 (119–66); *c. Apion.* II. 19 (179–81)). True, we can speak of 'the Jews', and even to some extent of 'Judaism', in the late Second Temple period, although the variety in the selection of symbolic markers that constitutes boundary-making has led some to speak of Judaism*s*. But whereas Tacitus's claim that the 'whole people were called Germans' was not to be realized in the region he is describing for another thousand years,[83] whether he could more successfully have made an analogous claim about the Jews of Judaea, Antioch, Alexandria, Rome, and elsewhere remains a question more easily asked than answered. At any rate, as we have seen, he did not, and this is significant. Many of the texts, both 'Jewish' and 'pagan', that we have, or could have, included do not use the term 'Jew/s', and many have a fairly parochial focus: not until the early third century can Cassius Dio say that 'Jews (ἰουδαῖοι) is also applied to others, even foreigners, who follow their laws' (*Hist. Rom.* XXXVII. 17. 8). It is the modern scholar who identifies both Persius's 'circumcised sabbath' (*Sat.* 5. 184) and the *Songs of the Sabbath Sacrifice* (4Q400–5) as 'Jewish', a term neither text knows. Whether the adherents of one would have recognized the other is another question.

BOUNDARIES IN PAUL AND HIS SUCCESSORS

It is within this framework that what was to become Christianity emerges as yet another variation. Certainly, when it comes to many of the earlier texts anything that can be said needs to be intuited; yet this should by now be no surprise in what may also be considered 'Jewish' texts written or surviving in Greek. 1 Thess. 1. 9 may be particularly explicit in characterizing believers as

Community Rule', in F. H. Cryer and T. L. Thompson (eds.), *Qumran between the Old and New Testaments*, JSOT.SS 290 (Sheffield: Sheffield Academic Press, 1998), 69–97, who sees in 1QS through the use of the term *yahad* 'a radical breach with the First Testament and its covenant identity' (p. 97).

[83] *Germ.* 2; so M. Hutton in *Tacitus Dialogus*, trans. W. Peterson, Agricola. Germania, trans. M. Hutton, LCC (London: Heinemann, 1970 (1914)), 132–3 nn. 2, 4.

having 'turned to God from idols', a clear instance of crossing a boundary, but it is difficult to think that any early Christian—or Jewish—text would have significantly dissented. Again, this becomes a stable and enduring boundary, yet one that none the less provokes some contention. Paul, in discussing food sacrificed to idols in 1 Cor. 8; 10. 14–33, attempts to explore the room for negotiation along that boundary, but he chooses his vocabulary and his path with utmost finesse, and his efforts probably would not have been impossible within a Jewish community.[84] While it is not surprising that many of his immediate peers and followers, like many more recent commentators, failed to be persuaded by him on this particular issue, as is already shown by Rev. 2. 14, 20, the realities of social life in the Graeco-Roman society would, as they did for other Jews, demand careful articulation of how, when, and where this particular boundary was to be policed.

Abrahamic descent also constitutes a further highly significant boundary for Paul, even if it is one that needs radical redefinition away from that of blood kinship (Rom. 4). Here, too, continuity outweighs difference, although once again subsequent authors prefer to ignore the challenge of negotiating these, even while claiming the same heritage of memory and of history.[85] However, where Paul has been seen as doing most to challenge and so to rewrite the boundaries has been over the observance of sabbath, dietary code, and male circumcision.[86] These observances, it has been argued, are 'the works of the law' ($\check{\epsilon}\rho\gamma\alpha$ $\nu\acute{o}\mu\sigma\upsilon$) whose efficacy for 'justification' Paul denies (Rom. 3. 20, 27–8; Gal. 2. 16; 3. 2, 10); what he is rejecting is their use to draw a socially articulated boundary, namely to define membership and to exclude all others. Understood in this way, Paul can be absolved of identifying Torah per se as 'works', and so of undermining it as divine gift, or indeed of supposing—wrongly, as has been demonstrated from a range of contemporary Jewish texts—that the successful observance of Torah was seen as a guarantee of salvation.

---

[84] In the 'more liberal' ch. 8 Paul avoids the language of 'worship' ($\epsilon\check{\iota}\delta\omega\lambda o-\lambda\alpha\tau\rho$-).   [85] See above, pp. 78–81.

[86] On this and what follows see especially the work of J. D. G. Dunn, e.g. in 'Works of the Law and the Curse of the Law (Galatians 3.10–14)', *NTS* 31 (1985), 523–42; Dunn was developing the definitive study of E. P. Sanders, *Paul and Palestinian Judaism: A Comparison of Patterns of Religion* (London: SCM, 1977).

While this social rather than theological interpretation of Paul means that he is neither wilfully ignorant of, nor deliberately misrepresenting, Jewish understanding of Torah, the consequences for the construction of identity are no less radical: the boundary line drawn is being erased.

The problem here, both with Paul and with his modern interpreters, is that if this is indeed how his argument is to be understood, then the line that he wishes to erase is one that he himself has first drawn. It is Paul who so elevates male circumcision that it alone can become a metonym for a Jew, or even for the Jewish people (Gal. 2. 7–9, 12; Rom. 4. 12; Col. 4. 11; taken up by Acts 10. 45; 11. 2; Titus 1. 10). This is not the rabbinic near-identification of (blood of) circumcision and (of) covenant, terms that Paul does not use in close association;[87] rather, as Eph. 2. 11 recognizes in reverse (namely, by adding 'so-called' to both 'uncircumcision' and 'circumcision'), he comes close to adopting an outsider's view—like that of Persius.[88] The fixation on circumcision, whether or not inspired by others, as Paul himself suggests (Gal. 6. 12–13; cf. Acts 15. 1)—and we only have his word for this—contrasts with its relative infrequency in a range of other Jewish texts. If this fixation is inspired by the focus on the boundary with total outsiders ('uncircumcised' Gentiles), we may contrast the silence in other Hellenistic Jewish texts that prefer to emphasize what is shared; instead, the closer analogy, albeit reversed, would be with the more sectarian polemic of *Jubilees*.

This contrast with Hellenistic Jewish writings highlights how little Paul attempts a strategy similar to them: for all the multiple contacts between Paul and the Graeco-Roman literary and social conventions of his day, he sees few grounds for negotiation. The analogy with *Jubilees* draws attention to Paul's attempt, not wholly worked through, to affirm a spiritualized signification of circumcision against that 'in flesh (ἐν σαρκί)' (Rom. 2. 28–9; Col. 2. 11; cf. Eph. 2. 11); to this attempt belong also Gal. 6. 16 and Rom. 9. 16 (and possibly 11. 26) where Paul seeks a redefinition of 'Israel' as opposed to that 'according to flesh' (1 Cor. 10. 18).

[87] Covenant language is separated from circumcision in Romans and Galatians. Cf. J. Marcus, 'The Circumcision and the Uncircumcision in Rome', *NTS* 35 (1989), 67–81.
[88] *Sat.* 5. 184.

Some post-Pauline writers, perhaps less rather than more sensitive to the potential social conflicts, take this much further: 'at that time you were alienated from the polity of Israel, foreigners when it comes to the covenants of promise . . . but now you who were far off have become near' (Eph. 2. 12–13). Similarly, for 1 Peter, without justification or comment, '[you] once no people are now the people of God' (1 Pet. 2. 10). Much later, Justin Martyr will assert, 'we . . . are called and are Jacob and Israel . . .' (*Dial.* 123. 9).[89] Here, we have to speak of a continuity of boundaries, and so of identity claimed, despite a radically changed content.

Very different is Paul's approach to matters either of diet or of the observation of any particular day, which he refuses to treat as matters of boundary negotiation (Rom. 14); this is not the striking silence of the *Testament of Abraham*, still less the allegorization of Philo and his peers, but a deliberate denial of any who would so position them.[90] In Rom. 14, in contrast to the discussion of circumcision, these concerns are distanced from any consideration of Law, still less of covenant or of divine purpose, and become *adiaphora*, matters of choice; in Gal. 2, in contrast to the pages of scholarly analysis of 'table-fellowship', they are put into a subordinate position by the ambiguous references to 'eating together' and to 'living in Gentile' or 'in Jewish fashion' (Gal. 2. 12, 14), serving entirely to further the primary Law/circumcision conundrum. Certainly, in both contexts the struggle is over what we might call 'Jewish' identity, but once again it is Paul who determines the line along which the boundaries are to be contested—the continuity he claims is on his own terms.

By contrast, as we have seen, this 'apostle to the Gentiles' makes no attempt to create a continuity with any Gentile identity, which, as in other Jewish sources, is constructed by negation: idolatry takes its place, and not even first place, alongside various forms of heterosexual and homosexual 'immorality', which belong beyond negotiation to 'the other': 'and these things some of you were, *but* you have been made holy' (1 Cor. 6. 11;

---

[89] See further above, pp. 40, 83, and Lieu, *Image and Reality*, 136.

[90] Cf. J. Barclay, ' "Do We Undermine the Law?": A Study of Romans 14.1–15.6', in J. D. G. Dunn (ed.), *Paul and the Mosaic Law: The Third Durham–Tübingen Research Symposium on Earliest Christianity and Judaism (Durham, September, 1994)*, WUNT 89 (Tübingen: Mohr), 287–308.

cf. 12. 2, 'when you were Gentiles (ἔθνη)'). Similarly, 1 Peter, putting its focus on other excesses, can tell its Gentile readers that 'the time that is now past is sufficient for working the purpose of the Gentiles' (1 Pet. 4. 3). This becomes a familiar topos as Gentile converts discover a boundary both against their past and against their peers, constructed for the most part not by any other more specific social or cultural practices but by catalogues of vices familiar from other Jewish rhetoric (cf. Col. 1. 21–2). These boundaries become mythicized by the language of the division between flesh and spirit, darkness and light, and, most pervasively, against 'the world' (Gal. 5. 16–26; 2 Cor. 6. 14; cf. 1 Pet. 2. 11).[91]

The primary symbol of crossing the boundary, baptism, also becomes heavily invested with the imagery of non-negotiability: 'such of us as have been baptized into Christ Jesus, have been baptized into his death; we have been buried with him through baptism into death' (Rom. 6. 3–4).[92] In post-Pauline writings this mythicizing is such as to leave behind the dilemmas of socio-cultural embodiment that troubled Paul (Eph. 2. 1–5; 4. 17–19; 5. 8–13). Giving an impression of impermeability, does this process in fact betray the search for new ways of discovering identity in an unstable world?

While much of this language could be interpreted in a highly individualized sense, Paul thinks primarily in corporate terms. Echoing the concerns of other Jewish writers, he would clearly prefer that marriage, if needs must, be between believers (1 Cor. 7. 39, 'in the Lord'), and that legal cases be tried within the community (6. 1–6); yet he considers an unbelieving partner 'sanctified' by the believing, as too are children (7. 14), and he is more concerned about inappropriate association with insiders whose behaviour flouts the boundaries than with those whom he calls 'outsiders', with whom association is inevitable (5. 9–13). All this leads to considerable ambiguity and instability in Paul's construction of the boundaries, and it is no surprise that some within the communities he founded drew conclusions that he

---

[91] On 'the Gentiles' see below, pp. 286–9, and on 'the world', p. 294.

[92] On the importance of baptism as a boundary marker see E. J. Christiansen, *The Covenant in Judaism and Paul: A Study of Ritual Boundaries as Identity Markers*, AGJU 27 (Leiden: Brill, 1995).

would then disown (1 Cor. 8).[93] His response is to develop to a very high degree the language of mutuality that embraces not only Jew and Gentile, but also any complexity of relationships (1 Cor. 12. 13; Gal. 3. 28); moreover, he develops a range of models to express this mutuality and boundedness, models of body, kinship, family, or household, which challenge the received models of 'people' or of 'Israel'. Thus, the very high value placed on internal cohesion, which we shall explore elsewhere,[94] is not a correlate of clearly defined boundaries, as is sometimes supposed, but of the reverse.

Having said all this is probably to appear to have ignored the most fundamental of boundaries, that of faith in Jesus Christ— although here it becomes particularly difficult to separate discussion of boundaries from that of shared practice. Thus 'outsiders' are also 'unbelievers' (ἄπιστοι), although, since this epithet appears only in the Corinthian correspondence, it probably refers only to Gentile outsiders.[95] For Paul it is surely right to say that identity is fundamentally Christocentric, and that from this stems all else; circumcision cannot act as a boundary marker, not because it is wrongly perceived to earn salvation, nor because it keeps people out, but because it does not point to this central focus of identity.[96] Yet the reason why analysis cannot rest here is twofold: on the one hand, 'faith in Jesus Christ' begged—and begs—further definition and exegesis, as the examples of 1 John and, later, Ignatius will demonstrate; on the other, for Paul at least, to speak of faith in Christ was first of all to speak of God and of God's purposes, known through promise and prophecy, in continuity and not through disjunction. Hence his, and our, dilemma: what are the social and experiential correlates of such a conviction?

Paul's letters allow us to pay particularly close attention to one attempt to respond to that dilemma and to define these new communities as part of a single greater whole, although even here

[93] See W. Meeks, *The First Urban Christians: The Social World of the Apostle Paul* (New Haven, Conn.: Yale University Press, 1983), 117–25, 159–62; G. Theissen, *The Social Setting of Pauline Christianity* (ET. Edinburgh: T&T Clark, 1982), 121–74.
[94] See pp. 165–9.
[95] 1 Cor. 6. 6; 7. 12–15; 10. 27; 14. 22–3; 2 Cor. 6. 14–15 (4. 4).
[96] So rightly Christiansen, *Covenant in Judaism and Paul*, 272–320.

the picture changes from letter to letter, and between author and those to whom he wrote. We can imagine that for those outside, 'both Jew and Gentile', this ambiguity was replicated. How could his communities not have earned the same opprobrium from pagan observers as did other Jewish ones, and how could they not have provoked both the same anguished attempts to achieve clarity as challenged Philo and his peers, and also, perhaps, a certain sympathy from others (non-Jesus-believing Jews) who were more like-minded?

VARIETY AND NEGOTIATION

If even here we have to speak of variety, other early communities and texts need not have drawn the boundaries in the same place. As we have already seen, 1 Peter agrees in marking the separation against the dissolute behaviour of the Gentiles, which also belongs to its readers' own past, and in claiming the scripturally determined identity of the 'holy nation', but seems unaware of the Pauline dilemmas of circumcision and other observance. In this, the letter shares much with other Hellenistic Jewish texts and leaves us at a loss as to its social implementation, but it also implies that, for whatever reason, the boundaries with other forms of Judaism are not a matter of dispute. Matthew, on the other hand, is no less aware that the real outsider who stands beyond the boundary is the Gentile (Matt. 5. 46–7; 18. 17), but, by coining a new term, ἐθνικός, he hints at the need for redefinition now that there are also Gentiles, ἔθνη, within.[97] Those with whom the boundaries are contested are 'the hypocrites', a label that precludes any identity not based on caricature, the boundaries being the familiar Jewish ones of praxis (5. 17–20; 6. 1–6, 16–18; 23. 1–2, 16–23), but not of sabbath, diet, or circumcision, whose (non-)observance can only remain a matter of speculation.[98] In the *Didache*, distinction from 'the hypocrites' is main-

---

[97] The curious link with 'tax-collector' probably, however, betrays a continuity with other Jewish constructions of the outsider.

[98] It remains unclear whether Matt. 24. 20 implies that sabbath was observed in the Matthean community. Although sabbath observance is a matter of dispute in all the Gospels, and thus inherent in the Jesus traditions, it is difficult

tained by the days of fasting—Wednesday and Friday in place of Monday and Thursday—and by the wording of prayer (*Did*. 8), thus affirming both practices (along with first-fruits and tithing, 13) as normative, and leaving us even more at a loss as to how to define those, living on both sides of the boundary, whom the text refuses to further specify.[99] By contrast, in the *Gospel of Thomas*, when the disciples ask as to the continuing meaning of fasting, sabbath, and circumcision (27, 53), there is no hint that there are real conflicts over practice: here, perhaps, the markers are retained only because they have become fixed within the rhetoric of reinterpretation.

This sort of ambiguity could be repeated in other texts commonly dubbed 'early Christian', reinforcing the tendentious use of the label, at least if it be supposed to exclude 'Jewish'. The pervasive rejection of the ways of the Gentiles, epitomized by idolatry and by a range of other 'vices' of sexual and intemperate behaviour, and the continuity of boundaries of election, Abrahamic heritage, and 'holiness', as well as of the aniconic worship of one creator God, all belong here. Yet what is equally striking is the avoidance of drawing the boundaries along more tangible social and cultural lines, so that it will take another century or more before attendance at theatre, baths, or processions, or participation in various professions, will become explicit points of conflict.[100] Similarly, despite Rom. 2. 21–2, it will be close to another century before the boundary of idolatry and other vices will be drawn against the Jews as well as against the Gentiles, when Justin can contrast 'we', who have given up the worship of idols, with 'you', who, despite Moses, are exposed as idolaters by Scripture itself (*Dial*. 46. 6–7; 130. 4).[101]

At the same time, as we move into the second century some authors will begin to discover that the boundary with 'the Gentiles' also provides room for both negotiation and connectedness. This will be particularly the task of the Apologists, who, like Jewish authors before them, find in the thought of Greek

to draw certain conclusions for the communities behind them, while the silence about circumcision is even more impenetrable.

[99] See p. 162, below. It is often assumed that 'the hypocrites' are 'the Jews', but which ones, and what renders the author non-Jewish?

[100] As they do for Tertullian, Clement of Alexandria, etc.

[101] See Lieu, *Image and Reality*, 115–16.

philosophy more to join than to separate them. Justin Martyr's solution is to dub Socrates and Heracleitos 'who lived with the *logos*' 'Christians before Christ' (*Apol.* 46. 3); here, however, the temporal distance saves him from having to consider social contiguity: it seems unlikely that he would recognize a Socrates among his 'pagan' contemporaries. Yet even before Justin, Clement of Rome acknowledges, 'even among the Gentiles', examples of those willing to sacrifice themselves 'in order through their blood to rescue their citizens' (*1 Clem.* 55. 1).

Clement illustrates well the problem of discerning boundaries even as we begin to expect a greater self-awareness. As we have seen, he recognizes no discontinuity between a Jewish past and his own present;[102] yet, the Gentile world, too, is close, both through the transparency of creation (20; 25–6), and through exempla of human nobility: it is through birth and not conversion that God has brought 'us' from the grave and darkness (38. 3)—the language of alienation that *1 Clement* has inherited from 1 Peter has lost any clear social expression that it might have had (*1 Clem.* Praef.).[103] Yet this is not a correlate of a spiritualized identity that is oblivious to all social realities: Clement is aware of the sins of intemperance to be fled (30. 1), of the foolish and untutored who will mock (39. 1), and of the impious and lawless who may persecute the righteous (45. 4). But his real burden is that these are to be found not outside but within, generating the dissension that threatens the community: the person who recognizes him- or herself to be the source of division is urged to depart, to go away—to effect a new boundary (54. 2).[104] Clement's solution to this dissension, the high regard for order in worship and ministry, and the prioritizing of mutuality (40; 21; 62), is no less a response to the difficulties of discerning more visible cultural boundaries.

Just how different, different constructions of the boundaries, and so of identity, might be within a close period of time is illustrated by the contrast with Ignatius. Ignatius, too, gives high priority to order in worship and ministry as the non-negotiable

---

[102] See above, pp. 78–9.

[103] Cf. 1 Pet. 1. 1, 17; 2. 11 and see pp. 232–3.

[104] Such a one is assured that 'every place will receive him' (54. 3) but who—believers or unbelievers—is thus intended is unclear, and the following examples of leaders willing to face death are less comforting.

precondition of unity, and sees the spectre of dissension, here provoked by doctrinal, especially Christological, disagreement, wherever he looks. But he achieves this in a way diametrically opposed to that espoused by Clement. As we shall see, Ignatius is the first to coin the term 'Christianism', creating a new opposition to 'Judaism' which is totally non-negotiable—in his rhetoric, if not in the practice of the churches.[105] To the boundary that separates them belong 'sabbathizing' and circumcision (*Magn.* 8. 1; 9. 1; 10. 3; *Philad.* 6. 1); these, in contrast to Paul's anguished debates, it would appear are devoid of any scriptural or theological significance, and how far they represent actual practice, how far they have become slogans, remains unclear and perhaps unimportant—although antithetical to the former is 'living according to the Lord's (*either* day *or* life) on (*or* by) which our life also rose'. The prophets demand no analysis nor any redefinition of boundaries, for they belong firmly on *this* side with 'us' (*Magn.* 8. 2; *Philad.* 9). Although we might consider that at numerous points Ignatius still betrays the Jewishness of his Christianism, there is no sense that he is consciously or implicitly engaged in exploring or redrawing boundaries inherited from that past.

This does not prevent Ignatius from using oppositional language derived from Judaism: 'the one who is within the altar is clean, the one who is outside of the altar is not clean' (*Trall.* 7. 2)—although here propinquity determines state and not vice versa; but it is unlikely that he is aware of the powerful forces associated with the imagery, or of earlier contests about the boundaries of pure and impure. More important, he is using the language to effect boundaries within by imaginatively locating them outside. He harnesses to this endeavour a range of oppositions, the carnal against the spiritual, incorruptibility against the loss of life; outside stands not just 'the world', but its prince, Satan (*Eph.* 8; 17). Exhortations to exclusion and to avoidance conspire to reinforce a division and to prohibit commerce across it (*Eph.* 5; 7; *Smyrn.* 7). Despite the incompatibility between God and the world, each with its own 'mark' and destiny (*Magn.* 5), 'ordinary outsiders' are less threatening, marked certainly by error and animosity, but for whom prayer and hope of better things is possible (*Eph.*

---

[105] On this and what follows see below, pp. 251–2, and Lieu, *Image and Reality*, 29–35.

10).[106] Ignatius evidently faces a situation where boundaries have been drawn more expansively than he can accept. How they have been drawn is less evident: presumably, despite his charges of denial (*Magn.* 9. 1), by some form of confession of Christ, and also, because of his silence, by a rejection of idolatry and by acceptance of the one God. However, specific patterns of worship and of communal life, and, above all, of acknowledgement of monarchical governance, have not been treated as determinative—and it is this which provokes his uncompromising intervention. For Ignatius there is an indissoluble link between belief and structure: to be positioned or to position oneself outside the one is to be set outside the other. However isolated his voice may have been in his own time, it was to gain in strength, and to point the way for the future. 'Order' will now, at least in his construction and under its subsequent influence, not only be definitive for unity but also, by centrifugal force, determine how, where, and by whom the boundary line is to be drawn—the acts of power involved have been unmasked.

Ignatius has catapulted us into the territorial defences of faith in Jesus; here, surely, as we have already acknowledged, is the most stable, enduring, and non-negotiable boundary. So, Paul's antithesis to the boundary of works of the law is that of faith in Christ (Gal. 2. 15–16),[107] and he can see some correlation between 'being led astray to dumb idols' and crying 'Accursed be Jesus', both belonging on the other side of the dividing line from the Spirit-led affirmation, 'Jesus is Lord' (1 Cor. 12. 2–3). Baptism, the symbolic moment of crossing, was, it must be assumed, inextricably linked with the confession of Jesus as Christ or as Son of God (Acts 8. 12). Confession of Jesus is already seen in the Gospel narratives as the ultimate choice facing would-be followers (Matt. 10. 32; Luke 12. 8); in time this would become experientially and rhetorically fixed in the later martyrological tradition.[108] So, already, Revelation harnesses the dichotomies of the apocalyptic tradition to the faithful confession of Jesus even in the face of death, and, by projecting from here an ultimate division between the blessedness of the saints and the destruction of

---

[106] See below, pp. 290–1, 295–6.

[107] This surely remains true even if πίστις Χριστοῦ is translated 'the faith(fulness) of Christ'.

[108] See below, pp. 251–7, and Lieu, '"I am a Christian"'.

'the peoples and multitudes and nations and tongues' (Rev. 17. 15), seeks to effect an impermeable 'virtual' boundary around the churches to whom he writes.

Yet this boundary is no less contested than the others that we have investigated. In Revelation the appeal to eschatologically founded certainties may, of course, bear witness to their actual fissility.[109] Faced with those whom he wishes to exclude, but who are undoubtedly within the churches, the author does not, probably cannot, charge them with a failure to confess or with false confession; instead he has to appeal to scripturally hallowed models of the dissolution of identity, namely eating food sacrificed to idols and 'fornication' (Rev. 2. 14, 20–3). If we are to take these accusations seriously, then, there were presumably those who sanctioned a more open association with 'outsiders'.[110] Christological confession could not mediate here, but neither, apparently, could the voice of authority enforce boundaries and impose an exclusion, which is instead left to an eschatological threat.

Elsewhere, Christology becomes the touchstone of belonging, most explicitly in the Johannine letters: 1 John's 'they went out from us, but they were not of us; if they had been of us they would have remained with us' (1 John 2. 19) is an attempt to assert that stable 'virtual' boundaries had always been in place, despite the contradictory evidence of recent experience. The apparent simplicity of the boundary drawn, 'Jesus is the Christ' or 'Son of God' (2. 22; 5. 5), is deceptive; this is the 'original' ('from the beginning', 2. 24) primitive confession, but how is it intended? As a bulwark against Jews—but how could they have ever appeared to have been 'of us'—or, by implicit reinterpretation, against those who do not interpret that multivalent confession in the way our author does?[111] The vigour with which the author constructs the

---

[109] So recent scholarship on Revelation has tended to move away from locating it within formal external persecution, towards localized pressures and internal conflicts: see A. Y. Collins, *Crisis and Catharsis: The Power of the Apocalypse* (Philadelphia, Pa.: Westminster, 1984).

[110] Even so, 'fornication' is probably a scriptural model of 'unfaithfulness' pictured as sexual promiscuity; Paul would have disagreed, and 'Jezebel' (2. 20) may be a 'Paulinist', see p. 127 above.

[111] This is the majority view among scholars, although there is neither space nor reason here to discuss just what this 'wrong' interpretation was.

boundary, again by reworking eschatological traditions (2. 18, 22), and by the dualism not only of light and darkness but even of God and the devil (3. 8–10), probably conversely testifies to the difficulties in drawing it along more patent lines either of behaviour or of creed. There are attempts at credal redefinition (4. 2–3; 5. 6–10), but their obscurity underlines the problem with which the author wrestles. 2 and 3 John, which labour under a different intrinsic obscurity, offer their own testimony to the attempt to appeal to tradition and to authority to sustain boundaries whose real fragility was becoming all too clear.[112]

Yet here we have moved to a fundamentally different view of the territory. Despite the Fourth Gospel's concern with 'the Jews', and despite the antithesis with 'the world' throughout the Johannine tradition, there is no careful definition of the boundaries with (other) Judaism, at least in the letters, nor with the predominantly Gentile 'outside' in which these texts and their putative community are usually located: 'Johannine Christianity' does not explicitly define itself over against 'the other', either of Jewish or of Gentile culture and practice.[113] Instead, its incipient concern with the articulation of belief, which, as we have seen, is developed particularly vehemently by Ignatius, foreshadows a characteristic sense of boundary that will run as a fault-line through subsequent history.

This is not without precedent in earlier Jewish writings, where, as already described, *Jubilees* can probably treat as Gentiles outside the boundary those who, no doubt, would have positioned themselves within, but who did not share that text's interpretation of calendar; likewise, *m. San.* 10. 1 can proleptically exclude (from a share in the world to come) those who reject more recent sectarian credal norms.[114] Paul's vehemence is against those who proclaim 'another Gospel' (Gal. 1. 8), while his imitator fears those who will turn aside to foolish words (1 Tim. 1. 6). 2 Peter anticipates false teachers and their probable success (2 Pet. 2. 1–4), and so the story will continue. It is customary to argue that these 'opponents' come from within, as we have just seen of

---

[112] See J. M. Lieu, *The Second and Third Epistles of John: History and Background*, SNTW (Edinburgh: T&T Clark, 1986), 148–65.

[113] The anomalous 1 John 5. 21, 'Little children, keep yourselves from idols' demonstrates rather than undermines this.

[114] i.e. who claim that there is no resurrection from the dead in Torah.

1 John, but the rhetoric of boundaries denies them that status except by deceit and insinuation; the same rhetoric prescinds from any more articulate account. The power of the text resides more in mystification than in demonstration and argument; with this we shall move into the stereotyped world of 'the other'.[115] It is as if the drawing of boundaries has become endemic, a self-justifying and self-perpetuating exercise, which itself constructs identity while retaining the power to bestow it on whom it chooses.

Even more solipsist is the claim to revelation or exclusive knowledge. Such claims by definition conjure a self-legitimating enclave, but one whose defences, unless reinforced by more tangible practices, are more likely to be derided than infiltrated by those outside. So the community of the Dead Sea Scrolls claimed the exclusive interpretative authority vouchsafed to the Teacher of Righteousness or to the sons of Zadok (1QS 5. 8–10): for them it was this that effectively set them apart from others who shared the same Scriptures, practices, and covenantal framework.[116] Significantly, Josephus, who chooses to ignore this claim, also ignores their separatist self-understanding.[117] To some extent, all those who identified themselves by faith in Jesus also claimed possession of a new revelation from God: to them 'has been given the mystery' which leaves others 'outside' (Mark 4. 11). For Paul, what separates him from his life in Judaism is God's apocalyptic intervention (Gal. 1. 15–16): this is not a mystical experience that enhances but does not structurally alter his sense of self and destiny, but something that compels him, and those whom he converts, to discover new bonds of identity. Ephesians characteristically develops this much further, piling up the vocabulary of insight, mystery, knowledge, and revelation to set its readers apart from 'humankind in other generations' (Eph. 1. 3–10, 17–18; 3. 3–5). As 'mystery', this knowledge is, of course, particularly in outsiders' eyes, intangible; hence its rhetorical evocation works rather for those inside, for whom it might also substitute for more tangible barriers. Once again, the characteristic emphasis on 'knowing' in the Johannine tradition correlates

---

[115] Hence subsequent commentators' perplexity as to the target of such polemic; see below, pp. 295–7.   [116] See above, pp. 34–5.

[117] Assuming the near-identity of the community with Josephus's Essenes; see below, Ch. 8 n. 39.

with its lack of explicit concern about distinctive behavioural or structural patterns (John 8. 31–2; 17. 3, 6–8; 14. 5–9).

The examples of the Dead Sea Scrolls and of the Johannine literature may suggest that this prioritizing of the seemingly impalpable confines of 'knowledge' perversely serves to engender a higher sense of separateness. How far this was necessarily always socially realized is more problematic. The literature that subsequent scholarship has come to dub 'gnostic' is particularly shaped by this claim to revealed knowledge available only to the few, but we may be wrong to imagine a separate identity lurking behind each text. The *Apocryphon of James* is predicated on the contrast between what the Saviour revealed to Peter and James, and what was vouchsafed to the rest of the twelve; in what could be taken as an aetiology of dispersion and diversity, the latter react with anger and are sent 'each one to a different place' (NH I. 16. 2–11).[118] However, another text claims to be precisely the revelation given to one of those just excluded, Thomas, although by leaving meaning to the interpretation and seeking of the reader (*Gosp. Thom.* 2–3), this 'Gospel' effectively deconstructs itself, leaving little scope for community. Here Jesus resolutely refuses to answer questions about prayer, charity (contrast Matthew), or diet (*Gosp. Thom.* 6), perhaps again implicitly refusing to inscribe any more structural boundaries. Adopting a different tactic, the *Gospel of Mary* first ascribes to Mary additional revelations, but then has Levi (or all the disciples) going out to preach because Jesus had instructed them not to lay down any rules or to promulgate any laws (*Gosp. Mary* (BG 8502) 10. 7–17. 8; 18. 6–21). Despite the heresiologists' constructions of numerous 'gnostic' groups, it seems difficult to distil from such texts as these either one or a number of sectarian identities.[119] Whether, and how, these texts function to establish or to reinforce boundaries remains highly uncertain, although if dateable to the second century they need to be set contrastively alongside the structural self-consciousness of Ignatius. In that context, too, they provoke us to ask how far the boundaries of true and false belief that he sought to erect were perceived by others, particularly the 'others' thus created.

---

[118] On this see above, Ch. 2 n. 70.
[119] So Wisse, 'Use of Early Christian Literature'.

Within the territory that we have mapped so far three boundaries have emerged, that drawn in terms of the scriptural heritage, as much with as against Judaism, that drawn against but
also among those who for the most part continue to be labelled
'Gentiles' (or, later, 'Greeks'), and that which is most contested,
both by, with, and against 'those within'. There is a fragility
about each of these boundaries that demands buttressing by
rhetoric where praxis fails. We should not, of course, expect
every text to be a microcosm of the whole map, and the contrasting constructions of the different texts need not always represent
incompatible identities. However, as the multiple prepositions
demonstrate, not only are these boundaries themselves inherently labile, but they also shift, both in relation to and independently of each other, generating multiple possible constructions
of identity. We cannot, therefore, simply say, as has often been
done, that in the second century 'the church' had to wage war on
three fronts, against the Jews, against the 'pagans', and against
heresy, as witnessed by the writings so labelled of Apollinarius,
Justin, or Miltiades;[120] this model wrongly presupposes that both
the church and these fronts were stable and clearly demarcated.
Instead, these are the frontiers under both construction and
contention, at times rather more a potentially well-populated,
perhaps transient, no-man's land, where movement and connectedness is at least as common as separation.

So, for example, we could explore and seek to map along the
first of these, the boundary with 'the Jews', Justin's invention of
the idea of a 'second circumcision' which he claims for 'us' (*Dial.*
114. 4); Barnabas's more extensive allegorization of scapegoat,
dietary laws, and circumcision (*Barn.* 7–10) in order to assert
that 'we proclaim the commandments having understood them
rightly' (10. 12); the *Apocalypse of Adam*'s (NH V. 5) exalta-
tion of Adam over the 'God of the powers' who created him
(64. 1–19); or the attempts by subsequent writers to retain the
whole of Scripture while contesting both the right of those they
labelled 'the Jews' to interpret it, and the interpretation itself.
At each point we would find both distancing and connection,

---

[120] Although this was a view, adding a fourth front, the state, that I repeated
in *Image and Reality*, 156–7, following E. Osborn, *Justin Martyr*, BHT 47
(Tübingen: Mohr, 1973), 1.

trade—perhaps even in the materialia such as scriptural texts as well as in ideas—and its prohibition, rhetoric or rule belying practice, improbable alliances, and family feuds. Nor is the map ever completed: ideas or individuals ruled outside the boundary at one period might be comfortably at home in another; while the language of rule acknowledges the exercise of power that is involved.

A similar sketch could be drawn of the other frontiers, even within the first two centuries, and much more so in subsequent ones. That cannot be the task here; it is perhaps the confluence of these boundaries that is more significant than precisely how and where they are drawn at any one moment. This means that who or what is included or excluded is not fixed, the continuing activity is the constant.

FROM THE OTHER SIDE OF THE BOUNDARY

To set this in relief we may also ask how, and how far, the lines of demarcation were drawn from the other side on these fronts. If the label 'Christian' was first coined as a term of derision or of denigration, it suggests that allegiance to Christ was for outsiders their distinguishing mark; but this is quickly, perhaps from the beginning, elaborated by suspicion of specified and unspecified crimes, by the label of 'superstition', and by charges of the rejection of social virtue and of loyalty.[121] So, for Tacitus, the Christians targeted by Nero are 'a class hated for their abominations' (*Ann.* XV. 44); we may wish to give this as much—or as little—credence as we have given similar pagan caricatures of the Jews, for it shares the same hostility to separateness, to perceived self-erected boundaries within the common life. Clearly, pagans neither recognized in themselves the catalogues of vices by which Christians turned them into 'the other', nor marvelled at the palisade of virtues that excluded them. Ironically, both sides conspire to assert a boundary of separation whose social tangibility we are forced to question: Christian authors vehemently distance themselves from pagan dissoluteness, pagan opponents denounce Christian isolation; but the real dilemma

---

[121] See below, pp. 250–1.

was that neither was true.[122] As we shall see, in other settings writers can affirm that Christians were to be found almost anywhere and everywhere.[123]

More tangible, surely, was Christian avoidance of idolatry, particularly expressed through their refusal to participate in the imperial cult. The primitive affirmation 'Jesus is Lord' could be taken as a direct counterblast to the acclamation of Caesar; yet it is only sporadically in persecution that this becomes defining, and only for some: how did their neighbours view Christians in the intervening periods? More fundamental from a pagan perspective were not the ideological disputes about the nature of the gods nor of their representations, but stubbornness and non-cooperation—something Christian apologists denied.[124] This meant, of course, that the credal distinctions, which for some Christians were cardinal to any affirmation of identity, were indiscernible to an external construction: those believers inspired by the construction of Christianity advocated by Marcion or Montanus were not distinguished from their internal opponents by the crowds or by the officials who urged their arrest and condemnation (*Mart. Poly.* 4; Eusebius, *HE* IV. 15. 46). Yet, beyond the world of persecution and its literary construction stand the epigraphic and archaeological evidence of ideas of the gods or of death held in common across boundaries, which suggest a shared identity between those we wish to label pagans, Jews, *or* Christians, a shared identity that our texts seek to deny.[125]

How far pagan observers recognized a boundary between Christians and Jews is much more difficult to determine. The allusiveness of Tacitus's acknowledgement of the Judaean origins of the Christians, and the silence of Pliny, despite his invocation of the incense test already used at Antioch against the Jews, resist any confident conclusion as to how either would have answered our question.[126] With a different focus of interest, and

[122] See J. W. Hargis, *Against the Christians: The Rise of Early Anti-Christian Polemic* (New York: P. Lang, 1999).

[123] See below, pp. 234–6.

[124] So already, Pliny, *Epist.* X. 96, 'pertinaciam certe et inflexibilem obstinationem'.

[125] See further, Lieu, 'Parting of the Ways', 28–9; below, Ch. 5 nn. 87–8.

[126] Tacitus, *Annal.* XV. 44; Pliny, *Epist.* X. 96.

so with different identifying criteria, Galen, towards the end of the second century, famously derided the unifying irrationality of 'the school' or 'followers of Moses and Christ' (*Puls. Diff.* 2. 4; 3. 3). Contemporaneously, Celsus is sensitive to the anomalies involved, and exploits them to his own advantage by denouncing the Christians' apostasy from the Jews as well as the scriptural and Mosaic contumacy that they share; but the few other pagan observers add little.[127]

Equally difficult is recovering how other Jews may have drawn the boundary. Here attention has tended to focus on the rabbis in Palestine, particularly through the long debate as to whether they instigated specific measures against Christians, and how they identified them, notably through the *birkat-hamminim* or so-called 'Benediction of the Heretics'.[128] The debate itself, and the impossibility of recovering whether, and when, those whom we, or they themselves, would call 'Christians' hide behind the *minim* of rabbinic sources, and whether in any given context these might be Christians of Jewish descent or of Gentile birth and practice, demonstrate that here we are in the world of the self defined by the archetypal 'other'. Equally opaque is any sense that in rabbinic eyes Christians could or should be distinguished from pagans—it is often observed that rabbinic sources barely reflect the transition of Rome and the Empire from pagan to Christian.[129] To some extent this opacity is a function of the solipsism of the rabbinic world-view, at least as expressed through the texts. Yet it also serves as a reminder that from *some* perspectives what bound Gentiles together in their otherness was greater than that which differentiated some of them or brought them closer to the observing Jews.

This may not always have been the case, and whether this perception would have been replicated in every diaspora community largely remains lost to us. The oft-cited examples of those in Origen's Sunday audience who appealed to what they had learned on the sabbath in the synagogue, or of the targets of John Chrysostom's ire who, or whose wives, found particular inspira-

---

[127] On Celsus see above, Ch. 3 n. 71; Lucian's description of the Christians of Palestine in terms that sound 'Jewish' is equally difficult to interpret (*Mort. Peregr.* 11).

[128] See Lieu, 'Parting of the Ways', 25–6.

[129] See Stern, *Jewish Identity*, 27–8.

tion or pleasure in the 'theatricalities' and holiness of the synagogue, are evidence that not everyone drew the lines of hostilities in the same place.[130] A focus on practice will reveal others who failed to see the boundaries where our ecclesiastical and rabbinic authors were so concerned to erect them.[131] How, too, should we define those in the synagogue who offered refuge to members of Pionius, bishop of Smyrna's, flock in time of persecution, as well as those who accepted it (*Mart. Pion.* 13), if we at the same time recall Justin's confidence that Jesus and his followers were the subject of cursing in the synagogues?[132] We should not be perplexed by the apparent incompatibilities between such attitudes, nor suppose that one set disproves the other, for they represent different possibilities in different places and at different times: shifting and contested boundaries, with patterns of connectedness as well as of separation. At the same time they are mediated through texts with their own agendas that might distort the questions and the answers that we seek.

The *Epistle to Diognetus* asserts that 'Christians are not distinguished from the rest of humankind by land, tongue or customs' (*Diog.* 5. 1)—a claim that, in so far as it is true, could also be made of the Jews—and then struggles through the rest of the letter both to affirm and to deny difference.[133] We have already quoted Guy Stroumsa's argument that 'since early Christianity did not form a culture of its own, and did not claim to represent an ethnical entity of any kind, the Christians had to invent new parameters according to which they could fashion their own identity'.[134] Yet this might seem to suggest that Christianity and Christians could exist prior to and independently of their fashioning of parameters, an impossible position. Instead, what has become clear is that the historian—and so, likewise, I would suggest, the theologian—looking back, cannot define who were the early Christians, or what was Christianity, by adopting one set of clear boundaries. The effort of drawing boundaries is a

---

[130] Origen, *Hom. in Lev.* V. 8; Chrysostom, *Hom. adv. Iud.* I. 5.

[131] See below, pp. 174–7.

[132] *Dial.* 16. 14; 47. 4; 93. 4; 95. 4; 96. 2; 108. 3; 133. 2; 137. 2; see Lieu, *Image and Reality*, 130–6.

[133] See further below, pp. 234–5.

[134] G. Stroumsa, 'Philosophy of the Barbarians', 341, quoted above Ch. 1 at n. 52.

common one, and the fronts on which they are drawn, in our definition, repeated; the lines inscribed and the territory enclosed is contested. This has necessarily been the longest chapter, for many of the other models of identity refer back to some degree to the idea of boundaries. Yet, this means that to discover the lability of the boundaries that we have sought to trace is to be reminded of the elusiveness of the identity that they are designed to encircle.

5

The Grammar of Practice

In Philo's account of the *Life of Moses*, Moses rebukes the two tribes who wanted to settle down in Transjordan before the nation as a whole had secured its territory on entry to the land: 'You are all entitled to equal honour, you are one race, you have the same fathers, one house, you have the same customs, a community of laws, and an infinite number of other things, every one of which binds your kindred closer together, and cements your mutual good will' (*Mos.* I. 59 (324)).[1] It would be difficult to think of a clearer affirmation of shared identity, predicated both on subjective experience and on objective reality, prior to any sense of the 'difference' evoked when Moses goes on to remind them of the destruction of 'our enemies', the previous inhabitants of the land. The objective reality of a shared and exclusive culture, practice, and set of myths may at first glance, as it has conventionally in earlier study, seem to provide the prior foundation of separate identity.[2] Yet, as we have seen, this has become ever more difficult to maintain, as the historically contingent social processes involved in the construction of all identity have been increasingly recognized. None the less it remains important to affirm the subjective sense of familiarity, and the way that individuals and

[1] These are the tribes of Gad and Reuben in Joshua 1, here transferred to Moses. Compare the quotation from Herodotus, *Hist.* VIII. 144, Ch. 4 at n. 27; see also Josephus, *Ant.* V. 1. 25 [97] on the same occasion, below, p. 222.

[2] So still A. D. Smith's definition of 'ethnie' as 'named human populations with shared ancestry, myths, histories and cultures, having an association with a specific territory and a sense of solidarity', in 'Structure and Persistence of *ethnie*' (extract) in M. Guibernau and J. Rex (eds.), *The Ethnicity Reader: Nationalism. Multiculturalism. Migration* (Cambridge: Polity Press, 1997), 27–33, 27; (originally published in *The Ethnic Origin of Nations* (Oxford: Blackwell, 1986)).

groups act on this as independent, at least in their experience, of any sense of differentness from others. Looked at from this perspective, identity and its construction can be analysed from within; but how can a shared subjectivity be understood in its historical contingency and without mystification?

One approach is to explore how communities create, and are created by, 'a mask of similarity' that is articulated in symbols, in practice, and in patterns of interpretation; often lying below the conscious level, and so compatible with a diversity of actual views and practice, individuals are none the less socialized into such shared patterns.[3] In exploring this, students of the New Testament and of the early church have been particularly influenced by Berger and Luckmann's sociology of knowledge, and by their emphasis on a 'social universe' of meaning that, often unconsciously, shapes perception and behaviour.[4] However, for our purposes this approach may put the accent too firmly on ways of knowing or on an epistemology, and it may suggest that there is greater coherence than is actually discernible. An alternative framework was suggested by Leander Keck in his programmatic study of the ethos of the early Christians; here he defined 'ethos' as 'a Gestaltic term, gathering up into itself the practices and habits, assumptions, problems, values and hopes of a community's style'.[5] It is symptomatic of the way that scholarship shifts that, although Keck's advocacy of the need to understand that ethos was not widely adopted at the time, it now resonates with the concerns we are taking up.

Keck traced his own intellectual genealogy back to the social historians of the Chicago school of the early twentieth century rather than to more recent theorists. However, more influential in other disciplines, including the study of antiquity, has been Pierre Bourdieu's concept of 'habitus' or 'dispositions', the apparently ingrained patterns of interpretation and understanding that shape the way people articulate their experience and determine their responses and their actions. These dispositions are inculcated in us within a social context, often, but not necessarily, that

---

[3] See Jenkins, *Social Identity*, 104–18.

[4] P. Berger and T. Luckman, *The Social Construction of Reality: A Treatise in the Sociology of Knowledge* (Harmondsworth: Penguin, 1967).

[5] L. E. Keck, 'On the Ethos of Early Christians', *JAAR* 42 (1974), 435–52, 440.

into which we are born and brought up; they are implicit rather than explicit, with the result that the responses that they generate are rarely premeditated, yet they are necessarily also constrained by the specific historical contexts in which they are expressed.[6] Inevitably, this is a dynamic, for such habitus is a social process that both shapes shared practices and perceptions and is shaped by them as they evolve. Moreover, the possibilities of change and resistance suggest that this is not as coercive as it might sound: many would want to maintain the reality of individual choices that make possible discontinuity within society.[7]

Although generally more widely applied, this 'theory of practice' raises particularly pertinent questions when applied to an understanding of newly (re-)emergent groups; here an important area of debate has been whether the dominant symbols of identity are primarily interest- or goal-driven, or whether they articulate existing deep-rooted commonalties and sentiment.[8] Both views have their proponents, and perhaps most helpful is a mediating model that envisages a dialectic between subconscious dispositions, themselves generated by social conditions and by inculcation within a group, and the articulations that follow; this allows both for the felt sense of sameness and continuity, and for the fact of change as new conditions make new dispositions or patterns of understanding possible or desirable.[9] Useful also for our purposes is A. P. Cohen's insight that community is not so much 'an *in*tegrating mechanism' as an '*agg*regating device': that it is the triumph of the common language of shared symbols and practices over the different meanings that individuals may give to these.[10] This gives pride of place to subjectivity over against attempts at a purely external structural analysis, and it

---

[6] See e.g. P. Bourdieu, *The Logic of Practice*; idem, *Language and Symbolic Power*, ed. and introd. J. B. Thompson (ET. Cambridge: Polity, 1991). For discussion and adoption of the model see G. C. Bentley, 'Ethnicity and Practice'; Jones, *Archaeology of Ethnicity*; eadem, 'Identities in Practice: Towards an Archaeological Perspective on Jewish Identity in Antiquity', in S. Jones and S. Pearce (eds.), *Jewish Local Patriotism and Self-Identification in the Graeco-Roman Period*, JSP.SS 31 (Sheffield: Sheffield Academic Press, 1998), 29–49; Tonkin, *Narrating Our Pasts*, 106–8.

[7] So Tonkin, *Narrating Our Pasts*, 106.

[8] On this divide, see above, pp. 11–15.

[9] See Bentley, 'Ethnicity and Practice', 24–9; Jones, 'Discourses of Identity', 67–71.   [10] Cohen, *Symbolic Construction of Community*, 20–1.

circumvents any suggestion that community and individuality, or community and diversity of interpretation, are incompatible with each other.

PRACTICE AND MEANING AMONG GREEKS AND JEWS

In our earlier discussion of boundaries in the self-presentation of Greeks, Romans, and Jews it has already proved impossible to avoid speaking both of perceptions or values and of practices. But while in that context it was the sense of differentness, and therefore the need to maintain boundaries, that had to take priority, here our concern must be how these ingrained dispositions are structured and reproduced; how practice and meaning are experienced as shared, and so are objectified. Furthermore, groups that share with each other similar boundary markers that differentiate them from one dominant 'other' may themselves be constituted by very different internal sense-structures of this kind.

In this way we might explore Herodotus's account of Greekness, not so much in terms of the boundaries it erects, but as an objectification of a way of being and of shared symbolic resources; as such, Greekness, as we have seen, continued apparently unchanging for centuries, while in practice undergoing significant changes, and being differently perceived by those who claimed its virtues. In the second century CE Apollonius of Tyana could tell the Ionians that they do not deserve to be called Hellenes because they have abandoned the 'symbols of their ancestors', namely customs, laws, language, and life (βίος ἴδιος);[11] here, we may see a sense of true Greekness as 'a socially constructed style, one strand in a skein of valorized concepts (civilization, intelligence, manliness) which could not be disentangled meaningfully'.[12] Yet since these deep sentiments have to be played out in particular social contexts, we may be able to plot

---

[11] *Epist.* 71: τα τῶν προγόνων σύμβολα.

[12] T. Whitmarsh, ' "Greece is the World": Exile and Identity in the Second Sophistic', in S. Goldhill (ed.), *Being Greek under Rome: Cultural Identity, the Second Sophistic and the Development of Empire* (Cambridge: Cambridge University Press, 2001), 269–305, 273.

within this model the different negotiations between inherited values and the context of the Hellenistic world in which those values had to be expressed: the 'problem' of Hellenism.[13] A different form of the negotiation and articulation of such 'structuring structures' might be found in the Roman ideology of affirming its own mores, even while claiming to spread Greek *humanitas* to the world, again as constructed through its literature.[14]

Some of these themes of the wider Graeco-Roman context are explored elsewhere; instead, here we shall focus on how this provides a useful perspective from which to consider the problem of Judaism in the late Second Temple period. A vigorous debate has been conducted around the tension between, and the opposing claims to primacy for, on the one hand, conviction or belief, and, on the other, practice; frequently this debate has all too easily become enmeshed in a conflict between orthodoxy and orthopraxy as the constitutive framework for understanding Judaism.[15] Advocates of the practice-centred model reject a focus on orthodoxy on the grounds that this is a peculiarly Christian concept, alien to the Jewish tradition and nowhere found within it, for example as expressed by creed, conciliar decision, or the anathematization of heresy. From this perspective it is practice that constitutes a common Judaism, conventionally the centrality of sabbath and festivals, of male circumcision, of laws of diet and of purity, but also the varied means of acknowledging the centrality of Temple and of sacrifice.[16] Even so, it is widely agreed that the ortho- of the preferred orthopraxy may wrongly suggest patterns of centralized control that in fact did not exist in this period.

[13] Here G. C. Bentley's case-study, in 'Ethnicity and Practice', of an educated Maranao woman's attempt to reconcile her 'habitual dispositions' and the structures in which she had to live and feel at home offers valuable insights.

[14] See G. Woolf, 'Becoming Roman, Staying Greek: Culture, Identity and the Civilizing Process in the Roman East', *Proceedings of the Cambridge Philological Society* 40 (1994), 116–43; on the role of literature in this, Habinek, *Politics of Latin Literature*. For 'structured structures predisposed to function as structuring structures', see Bourdieu, *Logic of Practice*, 53.

[15] See above, Ch. 1 n. 48; also A. Mendelson's analysis of Philo's minimal definition of Jewish identity in terms of orthodoxy and orthopraxy in *Philo's Jewish Identity*, 29–75, and above, pp. 116–18.

[16] For 'common Judaism' see E. P. Sanders, *Judaism: Practice and Belief 63 BCE–66 CE* (London: SCM, 1992).

For the other side in the debate, practices presuppose faith convictions concerning their significance; the phenomenon of conversion into Judaism, peculiar within the ancient world before Christianity, presupposes ideological principles of exclusivity; and—for our purposes most significant—only commonly held tenets of belief could provide an overarching unity that would embrace the varied manifestations of Judaism in this period. Behind the specific shared practices, so it is argued, lies the world-view that sustains them. Yet attempts to define this unity, while also acknowledging the empirical variety, have proved rather more problematic.[17]

Philo affirms as

the two most necessary principles: first, that the same being was the father and creator of the world, and likewise the lawgiver of truth; secondly, that the man who adhered to these laws, and clung closely to a connection with and obedience to nature, would live in a manner corresponding to the arrangement of the universe, with a perfect harmony and union between his words and his actions, and between his actions and his words. (*Mos.* II. 8 (48)).

Josephus's much quoted analysis of the Jewish 'theocracy' strikes a similar note, 'ascribing the authority and power to God, and persuading all the people to have a regard to him as the author of all the good things . . .' (*c. Apion.* II. 16 (165–6)). Yet both these formulations sound somewhat colourless and inclined to a philosophical framework to which only a minority may have consciously subscribed. Indeed, the fact that both authors are engaged in apologetic perhaps renders them unreliable witnesses for the actual generative dynamics of contemporary Jewish thought and practice.[18] The external, and much later, scholarly observer might specify monotheism; a linear history as the vehicle of a divine purpose characterized by a moral goal; individual responsibility within a communal or covenantal framework; the world as divine creation and as the sphere of human activity but not as the ultimate realm of divine intention and

---

[17] See above, n. 15.

[18] See A. J. Droge, 'Josephus between Greeks and Barbarians', in L. Feldman and J. Levison (eds.), *Josephus' Contra Apionem: Studies in its Character and Context with a Latin Concordance to the Portion Missing in Greek*, AGJU 34 (Leiden: Brill, 1996), 115–42.

resolution; the separation of a people called to a particular knowledge of, and to conscious response to, the one God and on behalf of the rest of humankind; and a shared narrative of the past. Yet even this catalogue would be subject to a myriad of qualifications imposed by the diverse silences, the varied emphases, and the elastic potential of the texts themselves.

Bourdieu's understanding of habitus provides one way forward towards resolving a debate that is too easily shipwrecked on problems of definition, for it allows for the truth of the former (practice) position while acknowledging the need to address the demands of the latter (belief). Rejecting a binary oppositional hierarchy between thought and practice, it speaks instead of the 'embodied history, internalised as a second nature and so forgotten as a history', which generates subsequent thoughts as well as actions.[19] Such a definition also encourages a sense of the dynamism and interaction between practice, perception, and response that a more static, credal model fails to accommodate. So, already moving in this direction, David Aune, in his contribution to the orthodoxy-versus-orthopraxy debate, speaks of a 'complex religious and cultural reality construction'.[20] In the nature of things, this generative system—symbolic universe or habitus—is not available for description, except through the perceptions and actions it produces; neither need we expect these to be monochrome, for, given the diversity in its production, there will also be diversity in its potential.[21]

It is important that here we are not speaking of self-conscious boundaries; these are not necessarily beliefs or practices that were deliberately manipulated to separate Jews from the others, nor are they constraints that actively incorporated people in, or excluded them from, membership. Instead, from this perspective we need not focus on Judaism as exclusive and isolationist, but on its inner structure and pattern, and on its subjectivity.[22]

---

[19] The quotation is from Bourdieu, *Logic of Practice*, 56.

[20] Aune, 'Orthodoxy', 6.

[21] Bourdieu, *Logic of Practice*, 55, 'As an acquired system of generative schemes, the *habitus* makes possible the free production of all the thoughts, perceptions and actions inherent in the particular conditions of its production— and only those.' If the final words sound over coercive, we should note that some interpreters have wanted to make more allowance for the role of human choice: see n. 7 above.

[22] So Wander, *Gottesfürchtige und Sympathisanten*, 20 n. 19, who rejects

Advocates of 'multiple Judaisms' in the Second Temple period have tended to assume that divergent interpretations—which can be objectively mapped in the texts of the period—create (or presuppose) divergent communities or identities.[23] Yet within this model it becomes clear that the sense of shared symbols can allow people to ignore the inevitable diversity of meaning that they may portend: 'Like the deep structures of generative grammars, the schemes and dispositions constituting the habitus produce an infinite variety of surface expressions, but all these expressions can be comprehended by those competent in the underlying code.'[24]

It is only when this sense of what is shared is lost or becomes outweighed by competing shared worlds or by the awareness of difference, that common identity is threatened.[25] For an understanding of first-century Judaism it is, therefore, important to observe how this is happening in some of the texts from the Dead Sea; here we find a condemnation of any who fail not only to live according to the Law but also to listen to the Teacher's voice (for example, 1QpHab. 2. 1–10): as the traitors of the last days and the objects of God's eschatological wrath it is hard to see how they could have been felt to share the same symbolic world, although to the external observer all were equally 'competent in the underlying code'. Yet, even then, we need not suppose that all members of the 'wider' community experienced the tension expressed in this denunciation in the same way; neither did all, not even a majority of people, live at the level of intensity voiced in texts such as these. In sharp contrast, J. Z. Smith has directed our attention to the symbols and the values expressed in Jewish inscriptions, specifically epitaphs, from the Diaspora: here 'piety' and a set of values predicated on the law can be recognized by all as a mark of honour, without the need to provide

the language of identity because of its frequent misuse: 'Hier wird nicht ein sich-selbst-abschießendes und ausschließendes Judentum skizziert, sondern ein Wesenszug und eine Grundstruktur ernst genommen.' For an emphasis on Jewish identity as subjectively physical, see Stern, *Jewish Identity*, 51–81.

[23] For example, J. Neusner, W. S. Green, E. Frerichs (eds.), *Judaisms and their Messiahs at the Turn of the Christian Era* (Cambridge: Cambridge University Press, 1987).

[24] Bentley, 'Ethnicity and Practice', 29; see also below at n. 51.

[25] So Cohen, *Symbolic Construction of Community*.

precise definitions or measurement of what it is to be a 'lover of the law' ($\phi\iota\lambda\acute{o}\nu o\mu os$).[26] Symbols, whether it be menorah or shofar, or a representation of the sacrifice of Isaac on a synagogue floor, may evoke instant recognition and a sense of familiarity without waiting for a disquisition on their precise theological meaning. On the other hand, 'instinctive' attitudes to the Gentiles, such as avoidance of their products, may have anticipated textual formulations about their impurity.[27] Here, as throughout, the generative power of the complex pattern of symbols within the Scriptures energizes both cohesion and difference.

Moreover, if by adopting this approach we can begin to explore the common convictions and underlying ethos shared by different and separated Yahweh-worshippers, we can also recognize those points at which some of them may have experienced a shared identity with those of their neighbours whom we would expect to be considered 'outsiders'. It is of the nature of the complexity of the elements comprising Bourdieu's habitus that it becomes multidimensional; individuals or subgroups may discover different identities when different elements surface in different contexts.[28] So, for example, between inscriptions ostensibly set up by Jews and those set up by Gentiles in parts of Asia Minor we find continuities not just of language and of terminology, but also of attitudes to mediation between the human and the divine, to the need for penitence, and to patterns of piety; these, as we have seen more than once, suggest that shared identities may have been more strongly *felt*—and 'felt' is the operative word here—than separated ones.[29] On the other hand, symbols

---

[26] J. Z. Smith, 'Fences and Neighbours: Some Contours of Early Judaism', in W. S. Green (ed.), *Approaches to Ancient Judaism II*, BJS 9 (Chico, Calif.: Scholars Press, 1980), 1–26; for such epithets, see P. W. van der Horst, *Ancient Jewish Epitaphs: An Introductory Survey of a Millennium of Jewish Funerary Epigraphy (300BCE–700CE)* (Kampen: Kok Pharos, 1991), 65–8.

[27] See M. Goodman, 'Kosher Olive Oil in Antiquity', in P. R. Davies and R. T. White (eds.), *A Tribute to Geza Vermes: Essays on Jewish and Christian Literature and History*, JSOT.SS 100 (Sheffield: Sheffield Academic Press, 1990), 227–45.

[28] So Bentley, 'Ethnicity and Practice', 35.

[29] So P. Herz, 'Einleitung', in P. Herz and J. Kobes (eds.), *Ethnische und religiöse Minderheiten in Kleinasien von der hellenistischen Antike bis in das byzantinische Mittelalter* (Wiesbaden: Harassowitz, 1998), pp. xiii–xx, xiv–xv, 'Gab es einen religiösen Grundkonsens an Werten oder Glaubensinhalten, die

or practices are not simply the sum of the details that may be described by the external observer. The common 'symbol' of the ritual slaughter of an animal in a space designated as dedicated to the deity self-evidently did not promote in the Jews of antiquity a sense of shared identity with their various neighbours. Whether or not Herod's Temple may have come close architecturally to many another public building in the ancient world, it did not dissuade Jews from destroying 'pagan' altars and temples, even if such action became a matter of contention because of the consequences it might provoke. These symbols function not in the way that they may be phenomenologically described but in the way that they are experienced and offer a language for meaning.

'HAVE THAT UNDERSTANDING WHICH YOU HAVE . . .'

Such ambiguities as these serve only to underline the difficulties we face when trying to understand the formative experience of a shared world by those who saw themselves, or whom we might label, as 'Christians'. In this case we are not speaking of ingrained patterns of perception and practice that, either by birth or by integration, are inculcated into individuals, but of the generation of a new and distinctive set of such patterns through and within the experiences and the responses of individuals. It would still be a long time before the majority of believers would proudly trace their own convictions to their earliest upbringing and to their parents.[30] Many may have been converted to one aspect of the Christian message and way of life, be it the awesome God as judge, or the persuasive power of exorcism;[31] they may then have come only slowly, if at all, to understand the fuller impli-

über die eigentlichen Kulte oder Religionen hinausreichten und eine allgemeine Verbindlichkeit für sich beanspruchten?' See also p. 122 above.

[30] Although Justin, *Apol.* 15. 6 talks of 60- and 70-year-olds who have lived in chastity as disciples of Christ from childhood. Cf. also Polycarp's claim that he had served Christ for 86 years, *Mart. Poly.* 9. 3; and in *Mart. Just.* A. 4. 5–7, two of the martyrs claim that they 'received being a Christian' (παραλαμβάνειν χριστιανὸς εἶναι) from their parents.

[31] Cf. R. MacMullen, 'Two Types of Conversion to Early Christianity', *VC* 37 (1983), 174–92.

cations of their new commitment, and throughout our period levels of understanding must have varied greatly, especially in the absence of a formal catechumenate.[32] The Philippian jailer who responds to an earthquake with the question, 'What must I do to be saved?', and is then immediately baptized (Acts 16. 25–34), presents a colourful and compelling dramatic character, but a highly problematic model of self-conscious Christian identity, and one that is simultaneously challenged by the unasked-for baptism of his household.

Instead, we are forced to begin with literary texts that consciously seek to inculcate appropriate attitudes but that simultaneously recognize that their audience, who already feel themselves to share an identity, do not fully hold these. Here, most of all, the texts are manipulative, offering for their readers, including ourselves, a set of dispositions as if these were determinative, when in fact they cannot have been so; they seek to persuade us of an authentic common life, the deviation from which—a deviation they de facto acknowledge—has to be seen as a falling away or failure. Thus the texts attempt to seduce us either into a utopian quasi-essentialism that ignores both the variables of social and historical context, and the actual experience and roles of the individuals and groups involved, or into a paradigm of ideal versus contingent manifestation that sets up a tension between the one and the other.

Reminiscent of this dilemma, a structure commonly discerned in early Christian texts is that of indicative and imperative: 'become what you are'. The indicative of the—in modern jargon —'Christ event', especially as embodied in the incorporation of individuals within the community, is, through the imperative, to be actualized in their lives through their obedient response: 'If then you have been raised with Christ, seek the things that are above . . . For you have died and your life is hid with Christ in God . . . Put to death, therefore, what is earthly in you' (Col. 3. 1–5). Theoretically, then, we might suppose that the underlying convictions and outlook that shape the subsequent behaviour of

---

[32] A catechumenate is first clearly presupposed by Hippolytus, *Apostolic Tradition*; cf., however, *Did.* 7. 1, and also Justin's description of the 60- and 70-year-olds as 'having been discipled to Christ' (n. 30); Hopkins, 'Christian Number', 221, argues for the importance of 'simple capsules of Christian belief statements' for incorporating new recruits.

Christians and that determine their common identity are those expressed through the indicative side of the equation, 'the Christ event' and their incorporation within it: so Paul, again, addresses disunity in his congregation, 'Have this mind in you (*imperative*), which [you have/was] in Christ Jesus (*indicative*)' (Phil. 2. 5). Elsewhere, the Pauline 'in Christ' (ἐν Χριστῷ) formula and its derivatives serve a similar end of urging a manifest identity of practice predicated on a distinctive and shared pattern of experience and interpretative conviction. This may, indeed, lead to practice continuous with the wider society, such as obedience to parents (Eph. 6. 1), as well as to that divergent from it, such as restricted marriage (1 Cor. 7. 39); it may even inspire opposing patterns of self-understanding, as is reflected by 1 Cor. 4. 8–13; none the less, such different results pale into insignificance compared with the shared motivating force.[33] Following this pattern, it has become common to analyse Pauline, and, more generally, New Testament, 'ethics' in terms of their extrapolation from the theological principles, particularly those founded on an interpretation of the life, death, and resurrection of Jesus Christ.[34]

However, while in such texts we may be witnessing an attempt to provide an inchoate group with the structures that will generate identity, to focus all our attention on doctrinal principles may prove to be at once both too exclusive and too indeterminate. Indeed, even on theological grounds, the relationship, and the possibility of a separation, between the two poles of indicative and imperative, faith conviction and behaviour, will provide the material for vigorous controversy throughout the subsequent centuries, as they do already within the earliest texts: 'What is the advantage if someone says they have faith but does not have deeds: can their faith save them?' represents one pole; 'Everyone born of God does not do sin . . . and cannot sin, because they have been born of God', the other (Jas. 2. 14; 1 John 3. 9). Not only is identity here contested, but both the possibility of confronting, and the need to confront, such contestation become integral to the generation of identity. Moreover, to equate Bourdieu's 'dispositions', which undergird cohesive interpretations of and

---

[33] 'Pauline' here means Pauline tradition; the uncertainty of the reading ἐν κυρίῳ in Eph. 6. 1 makes the point in a different way.

[34] See e.g. W. Schrage, *The Ethics of the New Testament* (ET. Edinburgh: T&T Clark, 1988), 167–72.

responses to experience, with theological convictions or affirmations may be to have to choose between the inclusivity of 1 Cor. 12. 3, 'no-one can say Jesus is Lord except by the Holy Spirit', and the exclusivity of the increasingly detailed doctrinal formulations of the fourth and fifth centuries with their attendant anathemas; alternatively, it is to identify changing Christian identity with the process from the supposed inclusivity to exclusivity, and, in so doing, to reinscribe the power of those who issued such directives.

Perhaps it is better to recognize that in any society there is an interplay between ideal standards and actual behaviour, but that the latter is not necessarily to be seen simply as a falling away from the former. Individuals and groups consciously 'define, manipulate, interpret, ignore, violate, and, ultimately, reproduce' the acknowledged codes of law and ethics, both in their social practice and in the construction of underlying implicit social norms. As ever, rules, practice, and explanatory discourse are interconnected within actual socio-historical contexts.[35]

Certainly, the vast majority of Christian texts assume that there is a distinctive way of being to which members should aspire.[36] As we have seen, the Jesus-narrative or myth frequently provides one of the generative structures of such a way of being. However, this might function quite differently for those addressed by different texts, even, for example, by the *Gospel of Thomas* as opposed to the Gospel of Matthew. The Jesus of Matthew's Gospel departs, leaving 'everything I have commanded you' as a prescription both for the disciples and for future generations—presumably an internal reference to the text it concludes (Matt. 28. 20). The Thomasine Jesus avoids prescription—or so we may suppose: when his disciples seek his presence he retorts, 'There is a light within a person of light and it shines on the whole world. If it does not shine it is dark' (*Gosp. Thom.* 24). Yet beyond the narrative Gospels, the Jesus story is slow to become a symbol of the character of the common life except through the symbols of commemoration that it generates; the paucity of direct appeals to

---

[35] For this see D. Cohen, *Law, Sexuality, and Society: The Enforcement of Morals in Classical Athens* (Cambridge: Cambridge University Press, 1991), 18–24, 23; Cohen draws on Bourdieu's work.

[36] For a different approach to all that follows see J. I. McDonald, *The Crucible of Christian Morality* (London: Routledge, 1998).

stories about Jesus in early texts continues to provoke surprise.[37]
On the other hand, what Justin Martyr labels 'living according
to the noble suggestions of Christ' (κατὰ τὰς τοῦ Χριστοῦ καλὰς
ὑποθημοσύνας βιώσαντες) (*Apol.* 14. 3) does, as we shall see, slowly
begin to provide a template for behaviour, even if with an eclecticism that may surprise the modern reader.

More pervasive, and perhaps more problematic for many early
converts, would be the acquisition of the template of the Jewish
Scriptures, in time to be provided with the interpretative, but no
more self-explanatory, lens of a new kernel of writings. Those
with no prior experience must have found the style of argument,
the pattern of models and examples, and the appeal to the authority of those Scriptures, painfully difficult to absorb. If in Rom. 9–
11 Paul is seeking to provide readers from a Gentile background
with a framework for understanding themselves and their Jewish
compatriots, we can well imagine them wondering why the passages of Scripture or the arguments used here were determinative rather than some others; what was there to authenticate *this*
as an evocation of their common identity? In a different way,
1 Clement is startling for its total absorption of Old Testament
narrative as providing the means for readers to understand their
own present, and for the way it presents this without apology or
explanation to a Gentile audience.[38]

As we have seen elsewhere, these Scriptures would have provided a shared narrative of the past, a framework, and a language
for speaking of the one God, but also a pattern of living. Yet all
this was fraught with ambiguity: the same narrative when equally
claimed by 'others' who were deemed outsiders (the 'Jews')
could generate an awareness of a common identity with them;
but more commonly it became a divisive double narrative, of
sin and judgement, on the one hand, for 'them', and of hope and
salvation, on the other, for 'us'. Typology, allegory, or simply
creative exegesis meant that the framework and language could
be respoken so as to reveal not-previously-anticipated shared
symbols or divisive walls. The 'common' pattern of living was
both normative—such as honour of parents—and suspended—
such as male circumcision or purity observation; suspended, that
is, by some, although here we are challenged by our ignorance of

[37] See above, pp. 88–9.   [38] See above, pp. 78–9.

how, for example, the *Testaments of the Twelve Patriarchs* were read by those Christian circles who preserved them. Given such inherent contradiction, it is of little surprise that contradiction should characterize what emerged, sometimes in identities that held on to the one or to the other side, sometimes in an unresolved tension. Within such a scenario we might plot Jewish Christians on one side, as those who experienced continuity and a shared experience; a Marcion on the other, as one for whom discontinuity was determinative; a Justin Martyr in the tension between the two. All these share a common generating system; they may be seen at one and the same time as having a common identity with, and as also being sharply separated from, each other. Similarly, some so-called Jewish Christians would experience a common set of 'structuring structures' with their non-Jesus-believing Jewish neighbours, generating a similar range of potentially contrasting consequences.

This pattern can be expanded from conscious responses to the Scriptures to the broader set of perceptions and values that they and their legacy of the late Second Temple period generated. Here it might be interesting to explore the use of biblical narratives and motifs in art by those labelled Jews or Christians by their modern interpreters, or in settings usually identified with one or the other.[39] From a different perspective, interpretations of, and ways of telling, martyrdom by both Jews and Christians sufficiently express a common pattern of ordering and valuing as to make it possible to deduce 'the close contact and impossibility of drawing sharp and absolute distinctions between these communities or their discourses throughout this period'.[40] Yet, at the same time, these narrative interpretations also generate self-consciously bounded and differentiated self-constructions of identity.[41]

This tension between continuity, and the creation of difference within it, on a scriptural base can be sensed already in early Christian writings. A common set of structures, recourse to a common interpretative schema, is denied as evidence of a

[39] See J. Elsner, *Imperial Rome and Christian Triumph: The Art of the Roman Empire AD 100–450*, Oxford History of Art (Oxford: Oxford University Press, 1998), 213–21.

[40] D. Boyarin, *Dying for God*, 117.

[41] Lieu, ' "I am a Christian" '.

common identity: 'when you give alms do not [. . . do . . .] like the hypocrites' (Matt. 6. 2); 'let not your fasts be with the hypocrites, for they fast on the second and fifth day; you are to fast on the fourth day and on the day of preparation' (*Did.* 8. 1);[42] or, alongside other contemporary values, 'when you hold a meal or banquet, do not invite your friends or family . . .' [as was the social norm] (Luke 14. 12). Yet this determined 'othering' by the texts surely reflects the more real ambiguities both of felt experience and as seen by the external observer.

Yet, as we have already noted, the external observer cannot be our primary measure, and superficially similar symbols may function either without any reference or in deliberate antithesis to each other. The latter, a logic of antithesis, perhaps follows from the ambiguity just described. So, early Christian writers recognize and determinedly reimagine symbols apparently common to themselves and to those deemed outsiders: Christian baptism may be a reconceived circumcision (Col. 2. 11–13), but this could prove a hazardous equation, while it was even more necessary to differentiate it from any apparently similar ritual associated with the pagan mysteries.[43] Similarly, Justin Martyr asserts that the use of bread and water in Mithraic mysteries has to be ascribed to imitation of the Christian eucharist by 'the wicked demons', perhaps suggesting alternative interpretations that gave positive value to the similarity (*Apol.* 66. 4). At the same time, Christians celebrated their own 'Pascha', but the weight of the symbolic narrative that shaped it had to ensure that it offered no route to a sense of common celebration with the Passover/Pascha of the Jews: Melito of Sardis's apparent evocation of Jewish Passover traditions in his paschal homily (*Peri Pascha*) is evidence of just how confident he feels of using similarity in order to differentiate.[44] Despite his confident tone, in inner Christian controversy the charge of Judaizing continued to be a powerful argument against those who favoured a 'historical' dating of the Easter festival to coincide with the Jewish Passover.[45]

---

[42] Note the use of the Jewish counting of the week.

[43] For the contemporary debate see A. J. Wedderburn, *Baptism and Resurrection*, WUNT 44 (Tübingen: Mohr, 1987).

[44] On Melito's *Peri Pascha* see Lieu, *Image and Reality*, 199–240.

[45] On this charge see ibid. 232–3.

Much has been made of how the symbolic rituals of baptism and eucharist would have functioned to create a sense of shared identity within, and of separation from, a 'world' that belonged both to the past and to the outside—again it becomes impossible to separate the exploration of boundaries from that which binds together those within them.[46] That is certainly true in the Pauline literature, where the interpretation of baptism as a dying and rising effects a total break from any previous or external existence and set of relationships, and where the eschatological interpretation of the shared meal prohibits by divine sanction any failure in absolute allegiance (Rom. 6. 3–11; 1 Cor. 11. 23–32).[47] The practice of naked baptism would, no doubt, have reinforced powerfully this sense of discontinuity with past relationships. Hermas's deep anxiety about the possibility of repentance beyond baptism also betrays the impact with which it was embedded in the consciousness, at least of some and as an ideal (Hermas, *Mand.* IV. 3).

No less striking, even in the early period, is the range of other possible interpretations that these symbols could generate. Meals particularly, in the ancient world as in most societies, generate and sustain community, while potentially bearing multiple, and multiple layers of, meanings. In their rejection as well as in their mimicry of the conventions of society, they both claim and construct a place within 'the world'. The Greek symposium tradition offered a subversive force from within society, while various forms of vegetarianism sharply reject a social order founded on the normative sacrifice of meat.[48] Similarly, Andrew McGowan has argued that traditions in early Christianity that emphasize the liturgical use of water rather than of wine, and which also reject meat eating, should indeed be seen as expressions of their proponents' broader, often differentiating, self-positioning in

---

[46] See Meeks, *First Urban Christians*, 150–62; G. Theissen, *The Religion of the Earliest Churches: Creating a Symbolic World* (Minneapolis, Minn.: Fortress, 1999), 121–38. However, here we are not simply pursuing an anthropological understanding of the religious function of ritual as reinforcing base symbols.

[47] See Meeks as cited in n. 46.

[48] On the symposium see O. Murray (ed.), *Sympotica: A Symposium on the Symposium* (Oxford: Clarendon, 1990); on vegetarianism in the Roman Empire see A. McGowan, *Ascetic Eucharists: Food and Drink in Early Christian Ritual Meals*, OECS (Oxford: Clarendon, 1999), 69–79.

relationship to society, to its institutions, and to its structures—
'in each case . . . a space for the construction of a different community self-definition was involved'.[49] Even here, however, he
detects considerable differences between the various groups that
advocated similar practices. So too, remarkably, the *Didache* sees
the broken bread as a symbol not of the death of Jesus but of
the gathering of the scattered church (*Did.* 9–10); for Ignatius it
is quite differently conceived, as 'the medicine of immortality'
(Ignatius, *Eph.* 20. 2); in startling contrast, Agathonice describes
the martyrdom that she has just recognized as her vocation as
'a glorious repast prepared for me', which would surely radically redefine for readers their own experience of the communal
meal.[50] How far should we posit differentiated social identities
on the basis of differentiated interpretations? Although this has
been the trend in recent years, it might be better to recognize
that one function of common symbols is to allow for a variety
of unarticulated interpretations, and also to take more seriously
the fact that 'contradiction, conflict, and ambivalence are fundamental characteristics of normative systems and of the social
practices in which they are instantiated'.[51]

'TRAINING IN THE CHRISTIAN DISCIPLINE'

Perhaps more consistent through a wide range of texts, long
before Attalus can be described as 'trained in the Christian discipline' (ἐν τῇ χριστιανῇ συντάξει γεγυμνασμένος), or Clement of
Alexandria will coin the phrase 'the life called Christian' (τὸν βίον
τὸν χριστιανὸν καλούμενον),[52] is the assumption of a common set
of formative values. For Justin Martyr, as for other authors, it is
this that marks the sharpest boundary against the past and the
rest of society:[53]

Those who preferred means of raising money and possessions more
than anything, now bring what they have together and share it with

---

[49] McGowan, *Ascetic Eucharists*, 276.
[50] *Mart. Carp.* A. 42.
[51] Cohen, *Law, Sexuality, and Society*, 31; on this in Judaism, see above,
pp. 153–4 and n. 24.
[52] Eusebius, *HE* V. 1. 43; Clement, *Paed.* II. 1. 1.
[53] On behaviour as a boundary see above, pp. 132–3.

anyone in need. Those who hated and murdered each other and never had common meals with those who were not of the same race on account of customs, now after the appearance of Christ have become those who live their lives together. (*Apol.* 14. 2–3)

The language of commonalty and mutuality here is particularly striking, although the topos is found already in Acts as part of the representation of the earliest community (e.g. Acts 2. 42–7).

Text after text reiterates that members are bound by an obligation to each other, and by an obligation that is not predicated on the patterns of euergetism or reciprocity that were common in the contemporary world: 'owe no-one anything, except to love one another' (Rom. 13. 8).[54] It has become a truism, and as such properly liable to falsification, to say that the early Christians took and refashioned the concept of *agape* (ἀγαπή), 'love', as their cardinal virtue. Yet if we need not, for the moment, search for uniqueness, the pervasiveness of the verb, its derivatives, and its semantic field in early Christian literature is undeniable. The mutual support implied, often with very practical expression, is an assumed norm, even if it needs continual reiteration—and, we may suspect, continually encounters misunderstanding. It is this, so the texts presuppose, that holds individual communities together even when they are constituted by those who would normally feel no such obligation to each other, rich and poor, master and slave.[55] The Apologist Aristides gives expression to this in his definition of 'the race of the Christians': they love their neighbour, show compassion to both widows and orphans, offer hospitality to the stranger, burial to the pauper who dies, and sustenance to those imprisoned for faith or in want (*Apol.* 15. 7–9). Yet, even more, this sense of mutual obligation holds separate communities together, manifested in the collection made by various Pauline communities for the church in Jerusalem, by the ease with which Ignatius can move through Asia Minor in constant receipt of personal support, and by the hospitality

---

[54] See P. Veyne, *Bread and Circuses: Historical Sociology and Political Pluralism*, abridged and introduced by O. Murray (ET. London: Allen Lane, 1990), 19–34.

[55] On the norms of euergetism and reciprocity in the ancient world, and on Paul as challenging that norm, see G. W. Peterman, *Paul's Gift from Philippi: Conventions of Gift-exchange and Christian Giving*, SNTS.MS 92 (Cambridge: Cambridge University Press, 1997).

whose virtue is celebrated by text after text, and whose openness to abuse is no less acknowledged (Heb. 13. 2; 1 Pet. 4. 9; *Did.* 11–12).[56]

One of the symbols that serve to undergird this search for mutuality is the ideology of the formation of a family. This emerges early: already Paul envisages his own evangelistic work through the image of childbirth (1 Cor. 4. 15; Gal. 4. 19), and urges them to 'work what is good towards all, especially towards those who belong to the household of faith' (Gal. 6. 10); not only his fellow workers, but also his readers are 'brethren'.[57] The latter convention is widespread, not only in direct address and in the exhortation, drawing on Lev. 19. 18, to love one's brother, but as an appellative where looser English translations are wont to substitute 'believer' or 'Christian': 'If a brother has an unbelieving wife . . . the unbelieving wife is sanctified by the brother . . . If the unbeliever separates, let them separate. The brother or sister is not bound in such circumstances' (1 Cor. 7. 12–15).[58]

1 Peter both urges his readers 'to love the brotherhood (ἀδελφότης)', and also speaks of the sufferings experienced by their 'brotherhood in the world' (1 Pet. 2. 17; 5. 9). It has been argued that in 1 Peter this familial image belongs with the depiction of the community as a household (οἶκος: rather than a house (1 Pet. 2. 5)), and that here the church was providing a 'home for the homeless';[59] a further step would make this the interpretative key to the letter, and even subsume within it the household codes (2. 18–19; 3. 1–7), so that, rather than being conformist, they contribute to an alternative structure that subversively mirrors the wider society—although this is probably to invest the image with more than it can sustain.[60] None the less, the household metaphor must have been more than a metaphor, for to some

[56] It does not matter here that Paul may have given the collection a highly distinctive interpretation. On hospitality in the early church see Lieu, *Second and Third Epistles of John*, 125–35.

[57] In modern translations ἀδελφοί is rendered as 'brothers and sisters', but this may accord Paul an inclusive gaze that he did not possess.

[58] So e.g. the *NRSV* opts for 'believer' (which bypasses the problem of inclusive language) while the *Good News Bible* prefers 'Christian man/woman'.

[59] J. H. Elliott, *A Home for the Homeless: A Sociological Exegesis of 1 PETER: Its Situation and Strategy* (London: SCM, 1981).

[60] So, rightly, D. Balch, *Let Wives be Submissive: The Domestic Code in 1 Peter*, SBL.MS 26 (Atlanta, Ga.: Scholars Press, 1981); see below, at n. 67.

extent it must have intersected with the actual structuring of the early communities on the basis of households of those converted, and of their houses, where perforce they met.[61]

It is all too easy to project from this a rosy and a cosy picture of homeliness, into which the lonely, the oppressed, and the dehumanized were warmly welcomed. This is to misrepresent the ancient household or family, which was as hierarchical as the state of which it was a microcosm: 'It is essential that a bishop organize his own household properly . . . for if someone does not know how to be in charge of his own house, how can he be responsible for the church of God?' (1 Tim. 3. 4–5).[62] Yet the symbol of the community as family is one that pervades the literature. Thus Aristides, whose examples of communal support were cited earlier, affirms 'for they call each other brethren not in fleshly terms but in spiritual', and asserts, as if this were worthy of special note, that if one of their slaves or freedmen became Christian 'they call them brethren without discrimination' (*Apol.* 15. 6–7).[63] When Athenagoras hastens to assert that such familial affection has nothing physical about it, and that any abuse of the ritual kiss brings the direst penalty, he betrays the creative power of a metaphor of self-understanding that could become actualized through ritual (*Leg.* 32. 3).[64] Almost as pervasive is the sense that this is an alternative family, membership of which may, and indeed sometimes inevitably will, entail the sundering of any natural family ties (Mark 3. 31–5; 10. 29–30; *Gosp.Thom.* 6; 101).[65] This takes narrative form in the *Martyrdom of Polycarp* where those who betrayed him were his household members (*Mart. Poly.* 6. 2), and it feeds into a pattern of expectation that redirects loyalty to the new community.[66]

---

[61] On this see H.-J. Klauck, *Hausgemeinde und Hauskirche im frühen Christentum*, Stuttgarter Bibelstudien 103 (Stuttgart: Katholisches Bibelwerk, 1981).

[62] For the argument against a rosy egalitarian view of the early church as family, see H. Moxnes, 'What is Family? Problems in Constructing Early Christian Families', in idem (ed.), *Early Christian Families: Family as Social Reality and Metaphor* (London: Routledge, 1997), 13–41.

[63] It is difficult to avoid the masculine here.

[64] On this see M. Penn, 'Performing Family: Ritual Kissing and the Construction of Early Christian Kinship', *JECS* 10 (2002), 151–74.

[65] On this theme see S. Barton, *Discipleship and Family Ties in Mark and Matthew*, SNTS.MS 80 (Cambridge: Cambridge University Press, 1994).

[66] Cf. Tertullian, *Apol.* 7. 3, where among 'our enemies' are 'by nature itself

Again we find ourselves facing something of a problem. Clearly, many of these texts are both idealistic and prescriptive, and it would be wrong to be seduced into taking them as descriptive. The importance of meeting together is betrayed by exhortations to do so more assiduously. The virtues that are celebrated need reiterating precisely when they may be lacking, and there are warnings enough and more against pride, abuse of power, neglect of the needy: 'and many will exchange the glory of the garments of the saints for the garment of the covetous' (*Asc. Isa.* 3. 25). So, the *Shepherd of Hermas* feels compelled to warn the leaders of the church against being like poisoners, and urges them to mutual discipline and peace (*Vis.* III. 9. 7, 10). For Hermas the church is an aged lady, in near mortal decline, given over to indifference and conformity with the world (*Vis.* III. 11). Yet we should not simply reproduce his picture of a falling away from an initial ideal, for his was the lived experience of many of the Christian community which we are here seeking to understand, and the actual practice of those involved would need to be seen within their own interpretative frameworks, if we but knew them.

Moreover, there are other patterns of behaviour that are encouraged which some may feel sit uncomfortably with the ideals of mutual support and forbearance. We have warned against over-idealizing 'the family', and the so-called 'household codes', which urge upon wives, children, and slaves due submission (Col. 3. 18–4. 1; Eph. 5. 22–6. 9; 1 Pet. 2. 18–3. 7), suggest that for some mutuality was sharply conditioned by other unquestioned norms about the necessary structuring of any society.[67] As numerous recent studies have noted, subsequent authors' comments on women serve only to reinforce this sense of accommodation; an older scholarship assumed that such views represent a decline and a tendency to assimilate to the (non-Christian) mores of the contemporary world, but this reconstruction is supported

our very own servants'; in turn, this intersects with Graeco-Roman fears of the 'barbarian within', in the person of the slaves of the family; cf. below, Ch. 9 n. 31.

[67] On these see Balch, *Let Wives be Submissive*; for the tension created regarding family relationships by the eschatological understandings, see K. Coyle, 'Empire and Eschaton: The Early Church and the Question of Domestic Relationships', *Église et Théologie* 12 (1981), 35–94.

neither by the demonstrable diversity of that world, where women could achieve a measure of independence, nor by careful analysis of the texts themselves, which suggest that an inherent ambivalence was there from the earliest period.[68]

Moreover, 'mutuality' can serve a number of constructions of community: exhortations to love for one another may also lead naturally into injunctions to avoid division, and this in Ignatius is, in turn, to be manifested in 'unity with', namely in submission to, the bishop (Ignatius, *Magn.* 2. 1; 7. 1). Justin virtuously contrasts the love with which Christians respond to their persecutors with the hatred that others display towards them, but he does so in a text that is not without some vitriol itself, and plays its own part in the developing Christian denigration of the Jews (*Dial.* 133. 6). Much earlier, 2 John saw no contradiction in celebrating the command of mutual love while threatening dire condemnation on those who even associated with any potential visitor who did not 'bear this teaching' (2 John 5, 9–11).[69]

For all this, however much we may wish to qualify the actual working out of the idea, particularly in contrast to modern conceptions of egalitarianism, the image of a common life, and of a set of values predicated on mutual support, must surely be an inalienable element in the shared symbols that shaped early Christian identity: it is, after all, their symbolic potential more than their practical realization that is our interest. Moreover, a somewhat cynical observer, Lucian of Samosata, could assume that his satirical sketch of the Christians rushing to support the imprisoned charlatan, Proteus Peregrinus, would find a believing and an amused audience (*Mort. Peregr.* 12–14).

---

[68] For the 'decline' construction see B. Witherington, *Women in the Earliest Churches*, SNTS.MS 58 (Cambridge: Cambridge University Press, 1988), 212, 'It is relatively clear, however, that in the period between AD 80–325 there is justification for seeing an increasingly non-Christian patriarchal orientation taking over the Church'; for caution about the earliest period, see L. Fatum, 'Image of God and Glory of Man: Women in the Pauline Congregation', in K. Börreson (ed.), *Image of God and Gender Models in the Judaeo-Christian Tradition* (Oslo: Solum Forlag, 1991), 56–135.

[69] On the situation, see Lieu, *Second and Third Epistles*, 95–8, 145–9.

THE AMBIGUITIES OF THE NEW

As we have begun to see, bound up with the sense of new family is the exclusion of the old; implicit in the celebration of mutual love and obligation is the assumption that others do not so behave. In these ways, common mundane symbols become potentially symbols of alienation, and will feed into the problematizing of 'the world' that we shall explore elsewhere. Nowhere else is this ambivalence more sharply expressed than in the symbolic weight assigned to the body, which also becomes so central in developing Christian self-consciousness as to demand separate treatment.[70] Even in a single author such as Paul, and indeed within a single letter such as 1 Corinthians, the body-image can carry a range of different symbolic freight—as an image of unity and reciprocity, but also as one of subordination; as making present the physical experience of Jesus Christ, and so also of his death as mediated and experienced; as grounds for a deep concern about what believers do with their bodies, and so about sexuality (1 Cor. 6. 13–20; 11. 3–8, 27–30; 12. 12–27; 15. 35–44). There are articulated here interwoven threads that will produce a kaleidoscope of perceptions and fixations in subsequent discourse; they reinforce the intrinsically embodied character of the symbolic world of the Christians, as well as the inherent sense of perplexity about such embodiment.[71]

Conjoined with this is a no less embedded ambiguity about 'history'.[72] Different texts articulate this ambiguity in profoundly different ways, but widespread is the conviction of living within a temporal framework whose main referents are fundamentally alien to those of other more conventional time systems. Whether or not with a firm foundation in Jesus's own preaching of the Kingdom, substantial elements of the movements generated by his life and death interpreted those events within the framework of Jewish eschatological expectation: there 'something as decisive happened in the midst of history as had happened in

---

[70] See Ch. 6.
[71] See D. B. Martin, *The Corinthian Body* (New Haven, Conn.: Yale University Press, 1995).
[72] See Coyle, 'Empire and Eschaton'.

primal times and would happen in the end-time'.[73] This conviction not only shaped the way that the Jesus story was told, but
also determined the understanding of present existence: for 1
John both the darkness and the world are passing away, and life
must be lived within that certainty (2. 8, 17); for the author of
the *Didache* the moment of the Lord's coming is ever uncertain
and ever imminent, so that a moment's inattention might undo
'all the years of your faith' (*Did.* 16. 2). The exhortatory power
of such a conviction is self-evident, as too is the potential impact
of a more realized sense of the presence of the future—'we know
that we have passed from death to life' (1 John 3. 14). What was it
like to live with such a sense of assurance or of urgency, and how
far did this experience engender a pattern of interpreting events
that would bind those who shared it together and separate them
from the uninitiated?: 'How much more shall God raise up on
the day of judgement those who believe in him and are chosen of
him, for whose sake he made the world . . . And this shall come
at the day of judgement upon those who have fallen away from
faith in God and have committed sin . . .' (*Apoc. Pet.* 4–5). This
is not just a distinctive view of the pattern of history, but also of
one's own place within it, and of the place of others, expressed in
the vivid images of punishment at which modern readers baulk.
Alongside the confidence, it also might generate the fear of sin
and guilt that so troubles Hermas. To recapture such a way of
interpreting experience, we have only imagination to guide us,
enlivened by 'parallels' in subsequent millennial sects, many of
them derivative from at least the literature of early Christianity.[74]
Yet, perhaps the story of the sudden paralysis of Rufina when a
clairvoyant Peter recognizes her unworthiness for the eucharist,
like the earlier story of Ananias and Sapphira (*Act. Pet.* 2; Acts
5. 1–11), captures, at least novelistically, the sense of the ever-
imminent divine watchfulness and judgement.

Yet again, the range of different interpretations possible even
on the basis of a common foundation can hardly be ignored. A

[73] In the fluent formulation of G. Theissen, *Religion of the Earliest Churches*,
287. On the 'apocalyptic Jesus' or 'Jesus movement' see B. Ehrman, *Jesus:
Apocalyptic Prophet of the New Millennium* (New York: Oxford University
Press, 1999).
[74] See J. Gager, *Kingdom and Community: The Social World of Early
Christianity* (Englewood Cliffs, NJ: Prentice-Hall, 1975), 19–65.

shared 'two ways tradition', perhaps going back to a common source, is used in fundamentally different ways by the *Didache* and by *Barnabas*: in *Barnabas* the government of the Two Ways by 'the light-bearing angels of God and the angels of Satan' sets the ethical exhortation under the shadow of a judgement (*Barn.* 18; 19. 10). This last is absent from the parallel section of the *Didache*, producing the ironic consequence that it is *Barnabas*, otherwise notable for its anti-Jewish polemic, that appears to share the ethos of the *Manual of Discipline* where those who walk in the spirit of deceit are set for eternal damnation (1QS 4. 9–14).[75]

An older scholarship, founded on the scoffers' demand, 'Where is the promise of his coming?' (2 Pet. 3. 3–4), and on the expectation of how 'it must have been', proffered theories of a crisis at the turn of the first century forced by the 'delay of the parousia'. Such theories have proved hard to sustain in the face of the continuity of imminent eschatological expectation in texts and movements of the second century. None the less, the *Shepherd of Hermas*, notoriously difficult to date, does struggle with 'the weakness of the people and the cunning of the devil' during the passage of time, and so offers a final 'second' repentance (Hermas, *Mand.* IV. 3): here sin and its seduction is all around, and if Hermas is to be grateful that he has been shown the tribulation before its coming in order to avoid its worst, so too must be his readers (*Sim.* VII. 5). A movement such as Montanism, the 'New Prophecy', apparently driven by a sense of the geographical as well as of the temporal imminence of the new Jerusalem, is particularly intriguing; arising in the second half of the second century, does it represent the continuity and survival of earlier Christian forms of intense expectation in the Phrygian region of its origin, or is it a new phenomenon, perhaps owing as much to indigenous or to other earlier traditions in its homeland?[76] The attraction of Montanism for Tertullian in North Africa possibly tells us only about the contradictions within that individual's character, but

[75] See J. Kloppenborg, 'The Transformation of Moral Exhortation in *Didache* 1–5', in C. Jefford (ed.), *The* Didache *in Context*, NT.S 77 (Leiden: Brill, 1995), 88–109.

[76] The thorough study of the movement by C. Trevett, *Montanism: Gender, Authority and the New Prophecy* (Cambridge: Cambridge University Press, 1996) assumes a Christian trajectory.

the presence of a similar ideology in the account of the *Passion of Perpetua* does indicate how congenial the interpretative framework provided by such intense eschatological expectation was in the face of persecution: this is the time of the 'latter deeds', 'in accordance with the pre-eminence of the grace promised in the last age of the world'; so Perpetua sees her fight as not with the beasts but with the Devil, while for Saturus it is the gateway into the promises of eschatological bliss (*Pass. Perpet.* 1. 3; 10. 14; 11).[77] Yet, already by that date (*c*.204 CE), accounts of the martyrdom of Polycarp at Smyrna or of a number of believers at Lyons had testified to the power of an eschatologically determined symbolic universe, and had ensured at least one form of its reappropriation in the narrative world of the Martyr Acts: 'for with all his strength the adversary launched upon us, foreshadowing already his coming that shall soon be' (*HE* V. 1. 5).[78]

This is, however, but an illustration of the multivalent potential of a shared set of symbols: much earlier, 1 John interpreted schism as the manifestation of the antichrists (1 John 2. 18–19), while the prophet John re-envisioned contemporary history as shaped by 'the mark of the beast' (Rev. 13). Not long after, the *Apocalypse of Peter* retold Mark 13, purportedly for the sake of those whom Peter and his fellow apostles would install in the church; it anticipates a resurgence in Israel, the coming of a deceiver, the false Christ, and the threat of martyrdom (*Apoc. Pet.* 2).[79] Each of these bear literary testimony to a tension between what was held in common and the way in which its various forms of expression might sharply divide.

Yet this ambiguity about the place of the present could take other forms. The certainty of future judgement serves as a carrot-and-stick only at the end of Aristides' more reasoned attempt to put forward the evident virtues of the Christian way: 'All who did not know God may come to them and receive incorruptible words, which are eternal and everlasting. For they may thus avoid

---

[77] The *Passion of Perpetua* is often described as Montanist, although there is nothing exclusively Montanist about it.

[78] On this see Lieu, ' "I am a Christian" ', and below, pp. 294–5.

[79] For this as a reference to Bar Kochba, see R. Bauckham, 'Jews and Jewish Christians in the Land of Israel at the Time of the Bar Kochba War, with special reference to the *Apocalypse of Peter*', in Stanton and Stroumsa, *Tolerance and Intolerance*, 228–38.

the terrible judgement that shall come through Jesus Christ on the whole human race' (Aristides, *Apol.* 16. 8). Aristides, however, is producing apologetic for an outside audience, and it is in the same mood that Melito of Sardis could argue more optimistically that the age of the church was coterminous with that of the Empire.[80] This seems a world away from the *Gospel of Thomas*'s description of the Kingdom as 'inside of you and outside of you', and its claim that the repose of the dead that they long for has already come, unrecognized (*Gosp. Thom.* 3; 51).

For all its multiformity, all this might suggest that the early Christians perceived their world in a profoundly radical way, and that this would generate a sharply distinctive sense of who they were. Certainly, this is how many presented themselves, describing in detail how their lifestyle distinguishes Christians from the rest: 'those who once rejoiced in sexual immorality now welcome only restraint, those who used magical arts, now entrust themselves to the good and unbegotten God' (Justin, *Apol.* 14. 2; cf. 27. 1). In practice they may have been far less distinctive than they claimed, and they certainly did not win the plaudits for moral superiority that we might have expected from such a self-presentation. It is striking here that Aristides' account of the Christian lifestyle summarized earlier does not differ greatly from the virtues ascribed to the Jews, even in his own telling, so that some have suggested that he may have drawn from, or at least belong to the same tradition as, Hellenistic Jewish Apologia, which sought to defend or to promote themselves through 'a common ethic'.[81] 'Love of brethren', φιλαδελφία, was also a virtue celebrated on Jewish epitaphs.[82] Here again we encounter the ambiguities of continuity, and so of commonalty, with a contemporary Jewish heritage. There is a similar continuity in the *Didache*, although here perhaps a more self-conscious one: in an account of 'the way belonging to life', the proscriptions of the Decalogue are expanded without comment to include 'magic, sorcery, abortion, infanticide', while the use of omens or witchcraft is identified with idolatry. At the same time, the *Didache*

---

[80] See above, p. 86.
[81] See above, Ch. 4 at n. 64. Also Lieu, *Image and Reality*, 172–5. Unlike some authors, such as Justin, there are few if any echoes of the teaching of the Gospels in Aristides.
[82] van der Horst, *Jewish Epitaphs*, 162.

also urges humility alongside frequent recourse to the company of the saints and to confession 'in the assembly' (ἐκκλησία); woven in with all this are unmarked echoes of the sayings of the Jesus tradition—'learn to be meek, for the meek are to inherit the earth'. These perhaps also serve to generate a new separate identity, even while allowing scholars to label the document 'Jewish'(-Christian') (*Did.* 2–4).[83]

Some authors even acknowledge their participation in the shared values of pagan society, while also trying to differentiate themselves from them: according to the writer to Diognetus, 'Christians are not distinguished from the rest of humankind by territory, language or customs . . . They obey the ordained laws, and in their own lives surpass the laws' (*Diog.* 5. 1, 10). Tertullian struggles to affirm how Christians share every aspect of life with their neighbours, filling every social institution, 'and only leave the temples to you' (Tertullian, *Apol.* 37. 4; 42).[84] This, clearly, is not a stark either/or: some accommodation is necessary in order to be able also to recognize differentness; a delicate negotiation is demanded between sustaining a claim to secure a place within society and firmly asserting an independent identity. Further, in these cases this is the stuff of apologetics, directed to the outsider.

When we turn to social practice, recent study has tended to emphasize how Christian groups did share some of the same communal dynamics as those that inspired not only Jewish synagogues but also the various 'associations' that were endemic in Graeco-Roman society; many of these were also designed to enable patterns of mutual experience and support, and some had their own defining codes of behaviour.[85] Concerns about self-mastery and an anxiety about the body have been seen as

[83] See C. N. Jefford, *The Sayings of Jesus*, 98–118. If, as seems probable, *Did.* 1. 3b–2. 1 is redactional, we may be able to trace a progressive differentiation through the later inclusion of 'Jesus material'.

[84] See W. Wischmeyer, 'A Christian? What's That? On the Difficulty of Managing Christian Diversity in Late Antiquity', in M. F. Wiles and E. Y. Yarnold, with the assistance of P. M. Parvis (eds.), *Studia Patristica 34: Papers Presented at the 13th International Conference of Patristic Studies held in Oxford 1999* (Leuven: Peeters, 2001), 270–81.

[85] See further Kloppenborg and Wilson, *Voluntary Associations*; McDonald, *Crucible of Christian Morality*, 150–61.

a common trait in the early Empire, in which Christians participated as well as to which they contributed from a distinctive direction.[86] Once again in Asia Minor, Christian dedications frequently reflect the same shared perceptions and piety as their Jewish and pagan neighbours—a trend towards monotheism, a search for mediation between the human and the divine, expressions of penitence and patterns of piety.[87] Although too late for our purposes, Richard Rothaus describes the cultic votive practices in the mid-fifth to sixth centuries at the Fountain of Lamps in Corinth where 'Christians and pagans could leave votives in nearly identical ritual. For this reason the terms pagan and Christian seem of little use here';[88] a similar observation could probably be made at numerous times and places where worshippers, whether or not they conceived of their deity/ies in what we would expect to be contrasting terms, none the less observed common practices. And, of course, there were numerous occasions in the future when Christians would affirm an identity with their non-Christian neighbours perhaps in conflict with others, Christian as well as not.[89] This will provoke the question as to whether we should describe these multiple identities in hierarchical or in conflictual terms.

Perhaps, then, we should not be surprised that when Christoph Markschies came to describe the 'structures of earliest Christianity' he found himself drawing for the most part on texts from the fourth century; he even suggests that for Antioch the first 'reliable information' we have about daily life comes from the sermons of John Chrysostom—and these, of course, show all too clearly the gap between homiletic ideal and pragmatic experience.[90] He also stresses the need to be conscious of the considerable variety between different regions, and even within a single region, for example, between town and country.[91]

[86] See below, Ch. 6.

[87] See S. Mitchell, *Anatolia: Land, Men, and Gods in Asia Minor*, 2 vols. (Oxford: Clarendon, 1993), 11–51, esp. 37–43; also above at n. 29.

[88] R. Rothaus, 'Christianization and De-Paganization: The Late Antique Creation of a Conceptual Frontier', in R. W. Mathison and H. S. Sivan (eds.), *Shifting Frontiers in Late Antiquity* (Aldershot: Variorum, 1996), 299–308, 304.

[89] See above, pp. 144–5.

[90] C. Markschies, *Between Two Worlds: Structures of Earliest Christianity* (ET. London: SCM, 1999), 6.

[91] Markschies, *Between Two Worlds*, 18–24.

There is no doubt that long before then Christian texts had constructed patterns of meaning and expectation that shaped a radically distinctive self-perception. With some justification, Keith Hopkins describes the 'Christian revolution' as 'a revolution principally in symbolism and ideology', although his immediate examples are churches, prayers, sermons, and Sundays.[92] These, and much more, undoubtedly belong to the transformation of the landscape of practice and behaviour; yet behind these 'the question at whose answer we can only guess is the relation between the things Christians did and that which constituted their existence as Christians'.[93] What we have discovered in trying to discern the generative grammar of Christian practice is how the rhetoric of difference should not blind us to the threads of continuity—the ever-shifting tension between emergent deeply rooted sentiments about their place in the world, and the challenges of the ambiguities of actual living; yet neither should the threads of continuity blind us to the emergence of a new map of that world.

[92] Hopkins, *World Full of Gods*, 79.
[93] Barrett, *Acts*, i. 166, commenting on Acts 2. 42; in the context Barrett goes on to identify this as the question of 'early catholicism', namely 'the relation of the form of the church to the faith of the church', but it might also be posed as the theme of this chapter.

6

Embodiment and Gender

The notion that bodiliness is intrinsic to identity is present from the earliest development of the term: bodiliness represents individuality, while it is also the site of the contradiction inherent in personal identity as experienced continuity despite continual change.[1] In a similar fashion, when we speak of social or corporate identity, bodiliness proves to be no less ambivalent, and yet equally intrinsic. If on the individual level the body seems, but only seems, to constitute the immutable boundaries of 'this all too solid flesh', so too, socially, an identity that may claim to transcend the sum of the individual bodies of those who share it is, necessarily, inscribed on them individually. To explore this might seem to be to explore treacherous ground, as becomes self-evident if we but survey recent exploitations of the chimera: for example, in the construction of Aryan identity in Nazi Germany along with the various representations of its physical expression, or in the political power of a discovered and unifying black identity, or in the nostalgic search by some Australians for their lost Aboriginal identity.[2] The abuses of pseudo-scientific imaginings about physically determined and categorized markers of racial identities are all too well known, and counsel caution. Moreover, as is frequently pointed out, such modern notions of race are foreign to the world of antiquity.[3]

---

[1] See *OED* s.v. 2, which dates the first reference to 1638; see above, Ch. 1 n. 28.

[2] On the problem of black identity see S. Hall, 'Cultural Identity and Diaspora'; the contemporary idealizing of Australian aboriginal identity should not be confused with the justifiable search by 'the lost generation' for the roots from which they were torn.

[3] See G. de Ste Croix, *Racial Prejudice in Imperial Rome* (London: Cambridge University Press, 1967).

Equally fundamental by now should be the observations that contemporary ideas of personal identity and individuality owe much to developments in sixteenth- and seventeenth-century Europe, and that any attempt to speak of the nature of individual self-consciousness in much earlier periods is both difficult and contentious. The introspective self is a relatively modern discovery; by contrast, even if earlier ideas of corporate personality as constitutive of the ancient 'Hebrew's' self-understanding have been discredited, it has remained a truism to describe the inhabitants of the world of antiquity as aware of themselves only in relationship to the society of which they were a part.[4] However, it is, perhaps, through the concept of embodiment that these obstacles to investigating ideals of identity in antiquity may be overcome. We have already discovered the importance that Bourdieu's theory of practice gives to embodiment, seeing the body as 'the site of incorporated history', our actions as articulating the underlying generative scheme.[5] This is particularly apposite for classical sources where Greekness or Roman-ness are very much exhibited through and experienced in the body.

Yet to speak of the body in this context entails addressing questions of gender: even in the modern world ethnic stereotyping often incorporates gendered elements, while classically, the male is paradigmatic, the female is defined in relation to it as its 'other'.[6] In recent years this has become ever more evident through a vigorous exploration of constructions of gender in antiquity, the space they occupy, and the notions of self and of other implied therein. Here, as elsewhere in this study, a major focus for analysis has been the role of literary texts as the products

---

[4] On the 'introspective self' as shaping an anachronistic approach to Pauline interpretation, see the seminal article by K. Stendahl, 'The Apostle Paul and the Introspective Conscience of the West', *HTR* 56 (1963), 199–215 (which, perhaps, should be qualified by some of the insights into late antiquity in studies cited in this chapter); for a cautionary voice against the assumption that individuals saw themselves only in terms of their role in society, see D. Lowenthal, 'Identity, Heritage and History', in Gillis, *Commemorations*, 41–57, 42. For the rejection of the extreme ideas of 'corporate personality', which once shaped Old Testament scholarship, see J. Rogerson, 'The Hebrew Conception of Corporate Personality: A Re-examination', *JTS* 21 (1970), 1–16.

[5] P. Bourdieu, *Language and Symbolic Power*, 13; cf. idem, *Logic of Practice*, 56, 66.

[6] On the modern world, see Eriksen, *Ethnicity and Nationalism*, 154–5.

of a male elite and of a process of selecting, of presenting a specific point of view as the norm, and, consequently, of marginalizing those left outside. From a range of perspectives and with an array of methods, scholarship has endeavoured both to render visible those hidden or marginalized experiences of 'others', and to expose, and hence to problematize, the pervasive assumption of male normativity. While extending far beyond our concerns, and being too vast for even a survey here, this field clearly constitutes a major part of the territory for exploring the construction of identity through embodiment.

However, the void between literary construction and individual experience does require some emphasis. In so far as this male normativity is unreflective, the female is rarely accessible to us except as constructed by opposition; to move from what texts say women should do, or even do do, to their actual experience and behaviour is fraught with hazard. Studies commonly point to non-literary sources or to the anecdotal or implicit assumptions of the literary sources themselves in order to demonstrate that women's lives were often very different from their literary representation. This cannot be a significant part of our task here. At the same time, to what extent women internalized the prevalent conceptions, to what extent they reinterpreted them, or to what extent they inhabited alternative systems of meaning is largely beyond our reach.[7] Thus, how women experienced their identity not just as women but as Roman, or Jewish, and even less as Christian (women) cannot confidently be discovered, nor, for the most part, can how women might have textualized that experience.

Yet it is no less true that, since the male is conceived as norm, specifically male experience, *qua* male, is also only latent. If gender is constructed, and for antiquity constructed for us primarily through literary texts, then that means that maleness no less than femaleness is constructed.[8] An understanding of this lies at the

---

[7] This is where older-style studies of 'women in the Bible' tend to ignore the complexity of these uncertainties. It has become common to demonstrate that women did go out, appear in public, hold office, and engage in a variety of activities rejected for them by the sources, but analysis must go beyond a simplistic recovery of this nature. For a bibliography of some recent research, see above, Ch. 3 n. 13, and studies cited in what follows.

[8] Non-literary sources are also significant for classical antiquity, and offer

heart of the move from 'women's studies' to 'gender studies', and from an analysis of 'women in the ancient world' to acknowledgement also of 'making men'.[9] When our literary texts speak of Greekness, Roman-ness, barbarian-ness as articulated through bodies and bodily behaviour, they are 'writing' gender.

EMBODIMENT, GENDER, AND IDENTITY IN THE GRAECO-ROMAN WORLD . . .

This consonance between constructions of gender and constructions of social identity can be readily sketched—and here our main focus will be on the world of the later Republic and early Empire. Maleness is paradigmatic: so, properly characterized by austerity and self-control, the Roman male is supremely fitted to rule.[10] Marcus Aurelius catalogues the qualities assumed to go together when he says, 'Let the deity that is in you be the patron of a living being, male, and of due age, and engaged in city affairs, and a Roman, and a ruler' (*Med.* 3. 5). Around the male cluster a range of other congruent attributes and associations: to him belong reason and speech, but also action. Although Seneca's ultimate concern is a Stoic self-control, he represents traditional values of *male* self-understanding when he rejects as belonging to a desirable 'liberal education' both the fine arts and culinary delights, which leave the mind starved and inactive: 'do we really consider this a liberal accomplishment for our young men, whom our ancestors trained to stand up straight and throw a javelin, to toss the caber, and manage a horse, and handle weapons?' (*Epist.* 88. 19). Margaret Imber shows how, when (male!) students of oratory learned the standard, and highly unrealistic, declamations, they were in fact learning *Romanitas*; declamatory

some alternative evidence for Judaism, but for Christianity in our period literary sources are determinative.

⁹ M. Gleason, *Making Men: Sophists and Self-Presentation in Ancient Rome* (Princeton, NJ: Princeton University Press, 1995); L. Foxhall and J. Salmon (eds.), *When Men were Men: Masculinity, Power, and Identity in Classical Antiquity* (London: Routledge, 1998).

¹⁰ E. Dench, 'Austerity, Excess, Success, and Failure in Hellenistic and Early Imperial Italy', in M. Wyke (ed.), *Parchments of Gender: Deciphering the Bodies of Antiquity* (Oxford: Clarendon, 1998), 121–46.

education, followed by so many who might not use it, was an education as a *vir bonus*: '*Vir bonus* is as ideologically freighted a term as one can hope to find. The *vir bonus* is the ideal Roman who possesses and displays all the values of Roman culture, or *Romanitas*.'[11]

Here also belong constructions of space: the public sphere, the sphere where social and civic or national identity is ostensibly forged, is where the male properly belongs. Philo represents what was already a long established Greek topos: 'Market-places and council-halls and law courts and gatherings and meetings where a large number of people are assembled, and open-air life with full scope for discussion and action—all these are suitable to men both in war and peace. The women are best suited to the indoor life' (*Leg. Spec.* III. 31 (169)). So, much earlier, for Herodotus it had been a sign of the strangeness of the Egyptians that their women went to the marketplace while their men stayed at home to weave (*Hist.* II. 3. 5).[12] This association of the public with the male, and, conversely, of the private with the female, is one that has been tacitly accepted throughout a range of temporal and cultural settings extending far beyond our present concerns; more recently it has been the subject of analysis in no less wide a range of settings.[13] The initial familiarity of the pattern can be misleading, for these spheres are open to different construals in different cultures; it would be a mistake to transpose into the world of antiquity the Victorian ideal of hearth and home as valued for their privacy, and of the male as going out to his labours, no less idealized. At the same time, as we shall see, Christian ideals both emerged out of those of antiquity and generated or legitimated new forms in subsequent history, including those of more recent times. Yet for our present purpose, with its focus on the Graeco-Roman context, it is fundamental that male space, public space, is where society's sense of self is shaped; or, at least, this is how it is represented, even if we have now, after Foucault,

---

[11] M. Imber, 'Practised Speech: Oral and Written Conventions in Roman Declamations', in J. Watson (ed.), *Speaking Volumes: Orality and Literacy in the Greek and Roman World*, Mnemosyne S. 218 (Leiden: Brill, 2001), 199–216, 208.

[12] This is a sign of Egypt as 'other'; see below, pp. 274–5.

[13] J. B. Elshtain, *Public Man, Private Woman* (Princeton, NJ: Princeton University Press, 1981).

come to recognize the pervasive role of the private and of sexuality in shaping the values of the public.[14]

Within this framework, the female, however, finds her identity through maintaining her proper role vis-à-vis the male; characterized by passivity, submission, and silence, she also so establishes civic identity, although this will find different expressions in Greek and in Roman settings.[15] For a woman to exhibit manly qualities would normally be seen as a subversion of true order, as becomes clear in Xenophon's play on this topos: when Ischomachus describes his wife's voluntary compliance with his definition of their various duties, Socrates exclaims, 'You have demonstrated the manly understanding (ἀνδρικήν διάνοιαν) of [your] wife!' Here, Ischomachus's wife's submission does not serve her own needs, but is but one aspect which enables *him* to be 'noble and good', the very model of the ideal citizen, destined to serve the city and to rule others (Xenophon, *Oeconom.* 6. 16–11. 8).[16]

The Greek model cannot be directly transposed to Rome, where women could hold a public role or engage in public activity; but this too was negotiated within the framework of the family honour, and inappropriate public activity by women was readily caricatured, caricature reflecting the fear of subversion.[17] At the same time, this, as with most of what has been said so far, demonstrates that identity as encoded in texts is no less a

[14] See B. S. Strauss, *Fathers and Sons in Athens: Ideology and Society in the Era of the Peloponnesian War* (London: Routledge, 1993), 6–8, 36–41. M. Foucault, *The History of Sexuality*, i. *Introduction*; ii. *The Uses of Pleasure*; iii. *The Care of the Self* (ET. Harmondsworth: Penguin, 1979–90).

[15] Strauss, *Fathers and Sons*, 6–7, 'not only were women visible, but they were an essential part of the ideology of that supposedly all-male phenomenon, Athenian democracy'; on the Roman world, see below n. 27.

[16] Here I am following Simon Goldhill's argument that this is an exception and does not establish the acceptability of the 'manly woman': *Foucault's Virginity: Ancient Erotic Fiction and the History of Sexuality*, Stanford Memorial Lectures (Cambridge: Cambridge University Press, 1995), 139–40; however, on the 'manly' woman of 4 Maccabees, see below at nn. 56–7.

[17] On the difference between Rome and Greece see M. Skinner, 'Introduction', in J. Hallett and M. Skinner (eds.), *Roman Sexualities* (Princeton, NJ: Princeton University Press, 1997), 3–25, 8–11; on the fact of and the fear of educated women see E. A. Hemelrijk, *Matrona Docta: Educated Women in the Roman Élite from Cornelia to Julia Domna* (London: Routledge, 1999).

matter of what anachronistically might be labelled 'class'. Elite women are represented in solidarity more with elite males than with slave or plebeian women, and, no doubt, this was frequently their predominant experience.

The nuances and coherent patterns of gendered identity have become particularly clear through studies of Graeco-Roman sexuality. These have shown how the opposition within which sexual relations should be understood is not simply that of the biological gender of sexual partners, and so of heterosexuality versus homosexuality, but rather of active versus passive roles, frequently articulated as penetrator versus penetrated. Hence, for a woman to take the active role of 'penetrator' is as much a 'perversion' of proper order as for a man to take the passive role.[18] Here too, as we shall see, male dominance and a social identity that relies on and legitimates political and military control are tightly interwoven.[19] Herein lies Strabo's incredulity at the stories of the military victories of the Amazons: 'for this would be as if one were to say that the men of that time had become women, and the women men' (*Geog.* XI. 5. 3). The pervasiveness and varied uses of the model become clear when Seneca compares the relationship of Stoicism with other philosophies as that of male to female, and of the right to command to the duty to obey (*Const.* 1. 1).

Yet although characterized as genetically passive, women are also associated with the emotions, as by nature lacking the masculine virtues of reason and self-control; thus they embody unbridled lust, and so present a source of fear and a threat to male control. The ambivalence expressed here has invited an interpretation in terms of the generic anthropological model of culture, represented by the male, versus nature, represented by the female: as nature always threatens to descend into its inherent chaos, and must be restrained by culture which it nevertheless threatens—culture being the embodiment of reason and con-

---

[18] The classic text for this is Artemidorus's *Oneirokritika*, which has been exhaustively studied; see S. MacAlister, 'Gender as Sign and Symbol in Artemidorus' *ONEIROKRITIKA*: Social Aspirations and Anxieties', *Helios* 19 (1992), 140–60; H. N. Parker, 'The Teratogenic Grid', in Hallett and Skinner, *Roman Sexualities*, 47–65.

[19] Hence effeminate males in the army would be disastrous; see Livy's account of the Bacchanalia conspiracy below.

trol—so is female in relation to male.[20] The weaknesses of this model are well known: it produces too rigid and too static a dualism and it tends to reify cultural constructs, of which it itself is one; yet its suggestiveness as a template for reading the sources and for exploring notions of identity as construct—namely, as belonging to culture—are evident.

It follows from all this that the ways in which, and the degree to which, both men and women conform to their appropriate roles are not simply a matter of personal relations; they also present a measure of society and of differentiation from others. This can be articulated in a number of ways. When women of leading families in Asia Minor during the early Empire do occupy 'public' civic roles, the rhetoric of the honours paid to them locates them within the confines of their family: in contrast to their male peers, it is their modesty, submission, or moderation that is paraded. *Textually*, although here the 'texts' are epigraphic, the public representation of such women serves to reinforce models of private virtue and submissiveness as civic and social ideals. So, for example, Lalla, daughter of Timarchus, although 'priestess of the imperial cult and gymnasiarch out of her own resources', is honoured as 'chaste, cultivated, devoted to her husband', and as having 'glorified her ancestors' virtues'.[21] Civic pride and identity are reinforced by the public celebration of the 'private' feminine virtues of a 'public' woman from a leading family.

Conversely, a failure to sustain the proper order reverberates in a number of directions. The man who cannot govern his household cannot govern the state: so Pliny celebrates the fact that Trajan has no need to keep closed the doors to his privacy and home, such are the virtues of his wife and sister (Pliny, *Paneg.* 83–4). No less subversive is the man who fails to embody the role assigned to him as male: Catherine Edwards has explored how in the early Empire a rich repertoire of accusations both

---

[20] See S. B. Ortner, 'Is Female to Male as Nature is to Culture?', in M. Z. Rosaldo and L. Lamphere (eds.), *Woman, Culture and Society* (Stanford, Calif.: Stanford University Press, 1974), 67–87, repr. in J. Landes (ed.), *Feminism, the Public and the Private* (Oxford: Oxford University Press, 1998), 21–44.

[21] M. Lefkowitz and M. Fant, *Women's Life in Greece & Rome: A Source Book in Translation* (London: Duckworth, 1982), no. 159. See R. van Bremen, *The Limits of Participation: Women and Civic Life in the Greek East in the Hellenistic and Roman Periods* (Amsterdam: J. G. Gieben, 1996).

of effeminacy and of sexual promiscuity characterized political polemic.[22] Similarly, a recurring theme within historiography is one of the moral decadence of the 'bad guys' in civil conflict and war: in Tacitus's account of the events of 69 CE we grieve over the murdered Blaesus who 'possessed not only distinction of birth and the manners of a gentleman, but also unshakeable loyalty', and we anticipate the just deserts for Fabius Valens 'with a long and luxurious train of harlots and eunuchs, advancing at a pace too sluggish for a campaign' (Tacitus, *Hist.* III. 39–40).[23] The same theme is taken up by Philo in his account of Sodom where 'the men became accustomed to be treated like women, and in this way engendered among themselves the disease of women'; he goes on to comment that, if Greeks and barbarians had all followed this, 'their cities one after another would have become desolate' (*Abr.* 26 (135–6)).[24] According to Josephus, as Jerusalem descended into chaos, the zealots 'gave themselves up to effeminate practices', copying 'not merely the dress but also the passions of women' (*BJ* IV. 9. 10 (561–3)).[25]

Thus any subversion of sexual roles does not simply indicate a collapse of private or even of social morals. It betokens an attack against a corporate self-representation over against the 'other' which is played out through a gendered typology. The irrationality and emotionalism of woman, her affinity with nature and with chaos, already align her with the barbarian: as other to the male, she is de facto potentially other to the norm of Greek-, and later, Roman-ness. At the same time, the woman who does not observe the appropriate norms of female behaviour becomes 'barbarized' in the way she is represented. Conversely, it is a widespread topos both that barbarians themselves are at once effeminate and/or sexually unrestrained, and also that they characteristically fail to restrain their women: the myth of the overthrow of patriarchy is a myth of barbarism in all its threat. Already in Greek tragedy, according to Edith Hall, women who

---

[22] See C. Edwards, *The Politics of Immorality in Ancient Rome* (Cambridge: Cambridge University Press, 1993).

[23] See also S. Joshel, 'Female Desire and the Discourse of Empire: Tacitus' Messalina', in Hallett and Skinner, *Roman Sexualities*, 221–54.

[24] See below, p. 188.

[25] See M. Gleason, 'Mutilated Messengers: Body Language in Josephus', in Goldhill, *Being Greek under Rome*, 50–85.

behave in an unwomanly manner are ascribed a barbarian origin or are presented with the 'vocabulary of barbarism'.[26] From an Athenian, and also from a later Roman, point of view the right of women among the Spartans to own property is both evidence for, and also a source of, the city's decadence (Aristotle, *Rhet*. I. 5. 6).[27] Tacitus's account of the revolt of Boudicca makes much of the place of women and of emotionalism among the rebels, 'a womanly and furious troop' (*muliebre et fanaticum agmen*) (*Ann*. XIV. 30): 'the conflict is presented in terms of emotion *versus* discipline, female *versus*, by implication, male'; at the same time, since they are a conquered people, 'to be oppressed is to be feminized'.[28] We have already seen how Tacitus's comments about the Jews, that 'among them all things are profane that we hold sacred . . . they consider permissible what to us is immoral', and that they were 'most inclined to licentiousness' (*Hist*. V. 4–5), both categorize them as utterly other—and hence as justifiably warred against—and invite a reproachful comparison with what, in his eyes, Rome has become.[29]

For the Romans who inherited this typology from Greek thought, it also played a part in their own negotiation with their relationship with Greek culture. Effeminacy and incontinence become marks of Hellenism: a slave revolt under Annicetus is easily able to defeat a cohort at Trapezus which 'had been given Roman citizenship as well as Roman standards and equipment, while retaining the idle and licentious habits of the Greeks' (Tacitus, *Hist*. III. 47).[30] When Seneca contrasts the lack of discipline to be expected of a Greek orator with the self-examination and terseness of a Roman, he is thinking of bodily

[26] E. Hall, *Inventing the Barbarians*, 202–10; Y. A. Dauge, *Le Barbare: recherches sur la conception romaine de la barbarie et de la civilisation*, Coll. Latomus 176 (Brussels: Revue des Études Latins, 1981), 495–6.

[27] Cf. Dionysius of Halicarnassus, *Ant. Rom.* XX. 12. 2, who contrasts the inviolability of the private for Spartans with the Romans where the censors even oversee what goes on in the bedchamber. See also Dench, 'Austerity', 128–9.

[28] See M. Roberts, 'The Revolt of Boudicca (Tacitus, *ANNALS* 14. 29–39) and the Assertion of *LIBERTAS* in Neronian Rome', *AJPh* 109 (1988), 118–32, 121, 132, who shows how this is used to make a statement about the situation in Rome.

[29] See above, p. 123.

[30] See also Edwards, *Politics of Immorality*, 92–7.

and behavioural ideals as well (*Epist.* 40. 11–14).[31] These various themes come together when Juvenal derides women for 'doing everything Greek' (*Sat.* 6. 184–9); even more ominously, Horace contrasts the girl of the present who rejoices to learn Ionic dances, and who when married engages in adultery, with the young man of the Roman past, 'a masculine race born of rustic warriors', and so explains contemporary civic decadence and military defeat (*Odes* III. 6).[32]

In this way the vocabulary of barbarism, and of sexual licentiousness and effeminacy, can be used both against opponents and to identify 'enemies within'. According to Livy's account, the subversive threat to the Roman state posed by the Bacchanalian 'conspiracy' of 186 BCE was demonstrated both by the dominance of women within the movement, and by its corruption of young males:[33] 'a great part of them are women, and they are the source of this mischief; then there are men very like the women, debauched and debauchers, fanatical, with senses dulled'; rendered effeminate and steeped in debauchery, how could they be trusted to defend the chastity of Rome's wives and children (15)? Women and feminized men represent the threat of the 'other'; at the same time 'wives and children' embody the Rome whose purity is to be defended. Whatever the Bacchic cult's true origin and age, it is clearly represented as foreign and so as meriting exclusion from the city's confines. Apuleius's account of the devotees of the Syrian Goddess, with their ecstatic behaviour and explicit effeminacy (*'puellae'* . . . *'semiviri'*), similarly characterizes 'the other' in highly gendered terms (*Golden Ass*, VIII. 24–30).[34] In due course Christianity would be lambasted for its supposed attraction among and its exploitation of gullible women—evidence of its irrationality and of its threat to social integrity.[35]

[31] 'A way of speaking which is restrained, not bold, suits a wise man in the same way an assuming sort of walk does.'

[32] On Juvenal see de Ste Croix, *Racial Prejudice*, 75; on Horace, Dench, 'Austerity', 140–3.   [33] Livy, *Annal.* XXXIX. 8–18.

[34] Cf. also Beard, North, and Price, *Religions of Rome*, i. 164–6, on Catullus, Poem 63, on the self-castration of Attis, as representing the 'foreignness of Magna Mater'.

[35] See J. M. Lieu, 'The Attraction of Women in/to Early Judaism and Christianity: Gender and the Politics of Conversion', *Neither Jew nor Greek?*, 83–100; Beard, North, Price, *Religions of Rome*, i. 296–301.

Some have seen in the period of the early Empire a particular focusing of anxiety within the sphere of sexuality, perhaps as a response to the collapse of geographical or linguistic definitions of identity, and to the weakening of the possibilities of social self-definition and self-determination. Such a development might also be interpreted as a withdrawal into the self as the ultimate arbiter of identity at a time of social change. Symptomatic of this response would be the Hellenistic novels with their focus on the star-crossed lovers who endure separation and danger, and yet who preserve their chastity and are eventually reunited to enjoy a conjugal bliss.[36] Others have pointed out, however, that, far from signalling a retreat to the personal away from a vulnerable social or political identity, the novels ultimately reaffirm the traditional values of the elite—the city, sexual fidelity, and chastity—and reinscribe on this basis their right to rule.[37] In this way they cohere with a concern found more generally in the second century about elite male identity as definitive within the ever-widening experience of and encounters with 'others' within the Empire.[38]

Despite all that has been said about Greek and Roman identity as irreducibly embodied, it will have become clear that this contains an inherent contradiction. If the male is the norm of identity, and if maleness is paradigmatically the control by reason over the body, just as female, as 'other', is defined by the controlling forces of her bodily impulses, does not the body become problematic as the locus of identity? Here we might summon the popular Stoicism of the early Empire with its evocation of the dominance of the will and of self-control: 'It is the sign of a simple person to spend time on matters concerning the body . . . but these things are to be done in passing. Let [your] whole attention be concerning the mind (γνώμη)' (Epictetus, *Ench.* 41). For Seneca it is easier to rule over barbaric nations than to control oneself, but 'no-one is free who is a slave of the body' (*Ben.* V. 7.

---

[36] On the novels see J. Tatum (ed.), *The Search for the Ancient Novel* (Baltimore, Md.: Johns Hopkins University Press, 1994); Goldhill, *Foucault's Virginity*.

[37] See S. Swain, *Hellenism and Empire: Language, Classicism and Power in the Greek World AD 50–250* (Oxford: Clarendon, 1996), 119–28.

[38] See Gleason, *Making Men*.

5; *Epist.* 92. 33).[39] This too, popularized among the elite, was to help define the sense of self in the second century, although such views do have earlier roots in what M. Foucault has termed the 'care of the self'.[40] Such self-control need not imply celibacy, so long as procreation and not pleasure was the goal of sexual activity. None the less, it may not be surprising that the Stoic programme with its ambivalence towards public civic duty more comfortably envisaged a citizenship of the world. It is within this tradition that Philo's account of the celibate Therapeutai belongs: 'these celibate "citizens of heaven" overcome the ambiguity and division of gender, and mythically join an androgynous company of angels. Their ecstasy freed them from the limits of a social world to forge an identity that transcended the shackles of gender specificity.'[41]

. . . AND THE SCRIPTURAL CONSTRUCTION OF 'WOMAN'

As Philo demonstrates, by the late Second Temple period Jewish sources share many of the perceptions common in the Graeco-Roman world; yet these sit sometimes uneasily with an earlier tradition that presents a distinctive view of the body as the site of personal and social integrity and identity. It is often supposed that the foundational acknowledgement of Israel's God as creator, not just of the natural world, but also of human sexuality and procreativity (Gen. 1. 1–2. 3), sets the Jewish perspective apart from the potential anthropological dualism of the Greek understanding of soul and body. The created order is fundamentally good, and all human experience is embodied. While Philo's

[39] *Ben.* V. 7. 5 displays the stereotyping of the barbarian: 'Gentes facilius est barbaras impatientesque arbitrii alieni regere, quam animum suum continere et tradere sibi.'

[40] See J. Francis, *Subversive Virtue: Asceticism and Authority in the Second Century Pagan World* (University Park, Pa.: Pennsylvania State University Press, 1995); M. Foucault, *The Care of the Self.*

[41] C. Roetzel, 'Sex and the Single God: Celibacy and Social Deviancy in the Roman Period', in S. G. Wilson and M. Desjardins (eds.), *Text and Artifact in the Religions of Mediterranean Antiquity: Essays in Honour of Peter Richardson*, SCJ 9 (Waterloo, Ont.: Wilfrid Laurier University Press for the Canadian Corporation for Studies in Religion, 2000), 231–48, 240.

valorization of celibacy is certainly unusual, this assessment may be oversimplistic, not only with respect to Greek thought but also regarding the status of the body even in the Hebrew Scriptures.[42] Some of the ambiguities of the latter arise from the description of humankind as created 'in the image of God' (Gen. 1. 26–7); although this passage is often spiritualized, so as to refer to human rationality, to the ability to form relationships, or to a delegated sovereignty over creation, it has been well argued that there is here an irreducible anthropomorphism in the conception of the deity that will shape subsequent constructions of the interaction between human (male) and divine. The definition of Israel, taken up by later writers, as the one who sees God (Philo, *Leg.* 1 (4)) sharpens the dilemma. As beloved, Israel is feminized, but, in time, so too are those who gaze upon God, and express their devotion in the language of love.

A further element in the embodied construction of Judaism is the centrality of male circumcision. Already in the Hebrew Bible, 'the uncircumcised' denotes Gentiles, while such passages as Exod. 12. 48 limit religious participation to the circumcised. The significance of this, and of its gendered restriction, for Jewish identity, and specifically for the place of women within the community, has been much discussed. While undeniably an issue in the modern period, that this can be retrojected as such into antiquity has proved more contentious—a prime example of the normativity of the male rendering female knowledge ineffable.[43] The question is most easily addressed within rabbinic literature. Clearly women are not excluded from Jewish identity, since otherwise there would be no concern regarding whom they might marry; in terms of their obligations under Torah they are not approximated to the Gentiles. On the other hand, since circumcision is referred to as 'the covenant of circumcision', and since the blood shed acquires particular significance, being likened to the blood of the Passover, so the place of woman inevitably becomes anomalous; according to Sacha Stern, 'for the rabbis of

---

[42] See H. Eilberg-Schwartz (ed.), *People of the Body: Jews and Judaism from an Embodied Perspective* (Albany, NY: SUNY, 1992), especially the introductory essay by Eilberg-Schwartz, 'The Problem of the Body for the People of the Book' (pp. 17–46).

[43] See Lieu, 'Circumcision, Women, and Salvation', *Neither Jew nor Greek?*, 101–14.

the second and third centuries the covenant is purely male'.[44] So also for Howard Eilberg-Schwartz, as the symbol of Abrahamic kinship and descent, which is central to the construction of identity, 'since circumcision binds together men within and across generations, it also establishes an opposition between men and women'.[45] Sacha Stern concludes that for rabbinic writings, 'the relative exclusion of Jewish women from the experience of circumcision, *Torah* learning, and other features of Jewish identity must affect the nature of their identity as Israel'; he does, nevertheless, go on to argue that women have a different but real 'experience of Jewish identity' or *'way of "being Israel"'* which is also expressed through the body.[46] This should, of course, be qualified (as Stern would accept), as 'within the rabbinic textualized construction of Israel'. Again, it is true that non-literary and literary anecdotal or implicit evidence may point to a very different lived role for women from that asserted in the dominant texts, but it is the textual construction with which we are here concerned.[47] We are left with an ambivalence that is not simply to be ascribed to the temporally conditioned patriarchal norms of society: it is constitutive of the embodied, and hence gendered, nature of identity within this tradition, as elsewhere.

In other texts, however, circumcision does not occupy this explicit determinative role; yet gender as integral to identity may be expressed in other ways. As we have seen already, in some Second Temple sources identity is seen as safeguarded or as threatened through sexual and marital practice, inviting analysis in terms of the erection of and the vulnerability of boundaries.[48] Here, the transgression of these boundaries through sexual licence or intermarriage is described as pollution, a metaphor that signals violation, regardless of whether or not there is implied the

[44] Stern, *Jewish Identity*, 64–7; cf. L. Hoffmann, 'How Ritual Means: Ritual Circumcision in Rabbinic Culture and Today', *Stud. Lit.* 23 (1993), 78–97, 87.

[45] H. Eilberg-Schwartz, *The Savage in Judaism: An Anthropology of Israelite Religion and Ancient Judaism* (Bloomington, Ind.: Indiana University Press, 1990), 171.

[46] Stern, *Jewish Identity*, 237–47, quotations from 240 and 246–7, where he emphasizes the concept of 'modesty'.

[47] See M. Peskowitz, *Spinning Fantasies: Rabbis, Gender, and History* (Berkeley, Calif.: University of California Press, 1997).

[48] See further above, pp. 115–17; also Lieu, '"Impregnable Ramparts and Walls of Iron"', 307–9.

notion of Gentile cultic impurity; on another level, although a metaphor, 'pollution' retains its connotations of physical miasma, a bodily experience. When in Gen. 34 and its numerous retellings Dinah is described as 'defiled', it is difficult to limit this to the moral, the metaphorical, or the physical sphere: these spheres intersect, as too does Dinah as individual and as 'a daughter of Israel': '. . . they had polluted Dinah, their sister. And therefore let nothing like this be done henceforth to defile a daughter of Israel because the judgement was ordered in heaven . . . because they caused a shame in Israel' (*Jub.* 30. 4–5).[49] The fear of 'mixing' that we have also explored earlier is unreservedly embodied: 'they will be joined with harlots and adulteresses, and marry the daughters of Gentiles' (*T. Levi* 9. 9).[50] Although marriage out by either sons or daughters is feared,[51] it is, in either situation, the woman who embodies the threat to identity, 'defiled' in the case of Dinah within, unnaturally purified in the case of the rejected brides of the *Testaments*, as also earlier in the Ezra traditions: her body is the site of the spoliation of Israel.

More generally, the female body does come to represent a major source of anxiety. The *Testaments of the Twelve Patriarchs* present women as an ever-present threat to male self-control, more prone to sexual laxity, and liable to seduce, if necessary by occult means (*T. Reub.* 5. 1–5). In those traditions that reflect priestly conceptions of purity, the polluting effect of women's menstrual blood becomes a powerful image of the loss of national integrity and identity (*Ps.Sol.* 8. 10–12). Yet here we may look earlier to Hosea's representation of Israel as a woman, stripped naked in punishment for her unfaithfulness, seduced into restoration (Hos. 2), or to Ezek. 23's castigation of Samaria and Jerusalem as two prostitutes whose awful punishment will at the same time warn 'women not to commit lewdness as you have done' (Ezek. 23. 48). Here are woven inextricably together ideas of women as more liable to sexual lust and seduction, of

---

[49] Gen. 34. 5, 27 LXX μιαίνω; Judith 9.2 μίασμα (cf. 13. 16); βηλόω (cf. 9. 8); *Jos. & Asen.* 23. 14 μιαίνω; *Jub.* 30 Lat. *polluare.* However, Josephus, *Ant.* I. 21. 1 [337–8], notably does not use this language: Sychem 'ravaged' her. Cf. C. Werman, '*Jubilees* 30: Building a Paradigm for the Ban on Intermarriage', *HTR* 90 (1997), 1–22, 15–16.

[50] See above, pp. 119–21.

[51] The question of how descent is determined is not raised in this context.

their propensity for religious 'unfaithfulness', of representations of the indigenous worship in the land as directed to its fertility, and as including a female fertility god, and of the conceptualiza-tion of the land or city as woman, vulnerable and dependent. Added to this within the priestly tradition is menstruation as a source of impurity. This, too, lends itself to an interpretation in terms of the opposition between culture and nature: culture is represented by male circumcision, the sign of the covenant, but also a symbol of male self-control; nature is represented by the woman's menstrual blood, seen as polluting, dangerous, and like an uncontrollable fountain.[52]

Does the woman, then, particularly in her impurity, represent 'the Gentile within'?[53] Certainly, the narrative audience within the *Testaments* are explicitly the patriarchs' *sons*, and women appear as 'the other'. There is an unbroken continuity from gaz-ing 'upon the beauty of women' to marriage with outsiders (*T. Judah*, 17. 1); the woman whose wiles Joseph resists is given no other name than 'the Egyptian woman' (*T. Jos.* 1–3); fornication, to which women are more naturally prone and to which they then seek to seduce men, separates from God (*T. Reub.* 4. 6; 5. 1–7). In other texts more explicitly concerned with Gentiles, the latter are similarly identified by their sexual promiscuity. In the *Sibylline Oracles* the Jews are characterized by their sensibility of 'the purity of marriage' and by their rejection of the 'unholy intercourse with boys' typical of other nations, and, as we have seen, symptomatic of the collapse of 'proper' gender roles (*Sib. III*, ll. 594–9).

What we see in these texts is the adoption of the assump-tions familiar from Graeco-Roman thought of women's lack of restraint, of their propensity to licentiousness, and of the con-sequent threat they pose to male self-control, combined with scriptural traditions that equate sexual infidelity with religious apostasy. This last shows how, again, this is not a matter of private morality but of the maintenance of the identity of the people.

[52] Hoffmann, 'How Ritual Means', 91–4; Lieu, 'Circumcision, Women and Salvation', 113–14.

[53] See R. R. Ruether, 'Women's Body and Blood: The Sacred and the Impure', in A. Joseph (ed.), *Through the Devil's Gateway* (London: SPCK, 1990), 7–21, 13.

An apparently different construction appears in the Jewish counterparts to the Hellenistic novel, Esther, Judith, and *Joseph and Aseneth*, the first two of which predate the Greek types as known to us. If they are similarly engaged in exploring identity, what is striking is the way that the theme of conjugal reunion is subordinated to an emphasis on sexual continence, as well as to a concern for the preservation and separation of Jewishness even within a wider world.[54] While the details of Esther's 'marriage' with Artaxerxes are passed over in silence, Judith's fidelity to her dead husband is emphasized both at the beginning and at the end of her story, thus providing a controlling framework for her 'seduction' of Holofernes (Judith 8. 2–8; 16. 21–4). Joseph's continence is stressed, but so also is Aseneth's earlier rejection of any suitors, and her careful preservation of her virginity (*Jos. & Asen.* 2; 7. 7–8. 7). Each of the novels uses as its context the dilemma of the relationship with 'the other', with the woman playing a mediating and vulnerable role. In Esther and Judith vulnerability and threat become a mechanism by which the nation is preserved. In *Joseph and Aseneth* the woman is 'other', but through her 'conversion' she becomes a symbol whereby the true nature of Israel's separate identity is affirmed; moreover, in the later, often ignored, chapters Aseneth's preservation from the plots of Pharaoh's son which initially created division among Jacob's sons brings them back into harmony with one another: 'the Lord fights against them for us. And you spare them because they are your brothers and your father Israel's blood' (*Jos. & Asen.* 28. 11). Culturally, the woman can undergo threat and liminal experience, in a way that for a male would fundamentally undermine his essential credibility; but the ultimate goal is the reaffirmation of identity for all.[55]

Another woman who helps symbolize the threat to identity is the mother of the seven sons in 4 Maccabees, appropriately in a text that echoes the anxieties of its age about control of 'the passions of the flesh' (4 Macc. 7. 18). The brothers' nurture by their mother is inseparable from their education in the Law

[54] See L. M. Wills, *The Jewish Novel in the Ancient World* (Ithaca, NY: Cornell University Press, 1995), 226–8.

[55] Of course, Apuleius is a prime example that the male can experience the liminal, and yet the difficulty of determining the genre and intention of the *Golden Ass* probably testifies to the 'impropriety' involved.

(13. 19–27); her willingness to set fear of God ahead of parental emotion establishes her as a daughter of Abraham, and her death is the vindication of the nation (14. 20; 15. 28; 17. 9–12); indeed, she can even be celebrated as 'in steadfastness more noble than males, and in endurance more manly (braver) than men' (15. 30).[56] Yet, if reason triumphs over emotion in her, she never transgresses her proper role: rather than let her body be touched she casts herself into the fire (17. 1), and the final chapter of the story undoes its earlier recklessness by having her say that it was, after all, her husband who taught her sons the Law (18. 6–19).[57] By turning her acceptance of suffering into virtue, her own and her sons' vulnerability and pain become a testimony to the true identity of the nation in the face of tyranny. Yet, if the story is a celebration of the victory of reason over the emotions of pleasure and pain that reside in the body as well as in the soul (1. 20–7), it is axiomatic that it is won by the steadfast refusal to eat 'defiling foods' and by the endurance of physical torture of mangled bodies which is described in loving and voyeuristic detail: their delight is to 'use [their] bodies as a bulwark about the law' (13. 13).[58]

THE AMBIGUITIES OF EMBODIMENT: PAUL

Within such a context Paul's affirmation in Rom. 2. 28–9 resonates particularly starkly; here he contrasts 'the Jew in public' with 'the Jew in secret', and embodies this by a further parallel, 'circumcision *in flesh* in public' set against 'circumcision *of heart in spirit not letter*'.[59] Here, paradigmatically, construction of self and construction of 'other' are reciprocally interdependent through the body. That this is a Pauline construction is fundamental, as we have observed earlier in relation to circumcision; Jacob Neusner has protested that Jewishness is not in rabbinic

---

[56] . . . ἀνδρῶν πρὸς ὑπομονὴν ἀνδρειοτέρα.

[57] See S. Moore and J. C. Anderson, 'Taking it Like a Man: Masculinity in 4 Maccabees', *JBL* 117 (1998), 249–73; on 4 Maccabees see also B. Shaw, 'Body/Power/Identity: Passions of the Martyrs', *JECS* 4 (1996), 269–312, 276–80.

[58] χρήσωμεν τῇ περὶ τὸν νόμον φυλακῇ τὰ σώματα.

[59] The difficulty of these verses is underlined by English translations' decision to add 'true' or 'real' to 'Jew' and 'circumcision'.

literature defined by nature or birth, nor by flesh, and that it
is Paul who so identifies it, in a way that has decisively shaped
subsequent Christian constructions of Judaism.[60] This can be
overstated, and needs to be set alongside what we have seen of the
indelibly embodied character of Jewish identity.[61] Yet it serves
as an important reminder that the distinctions that Paul presents as determinative are not those that occupy centre-ground
in other Jewish texts. However, the opposing self-perception
it generates, of an identity not inscribed in flesh, becomes paradigmatic, as is shown by the development in Eph. 2. 11: 'You
once as Gentiles *in flesh*, the uncircumcision, so-called by the
so-called circumcision *in flesh, made by hands* . . .'[62]

Paul's construction is further complicated by his problematic
use of the term 'flesh', σάρξ. His mocking question, 'Are you now
completing/ending with flesh?' ('νῦν σαρκὶ ἐπιτελεῖσθε;', Gal. 3.
3), echoes contextually apposite ideas of circumcision as 'the
completion' of the body, and so sharply underlines his rejection
of those practices that were inscribed on the Jewish body; but it
also expresses the negative valency with which he invests 'flesh':
'I know that nothing good dwells in me, that is in my flesh' (Rom.
7. 18).[63] Yet the parallelism of his elliptic words in Gal. 2. 20,
'that which I now live in flesh, I live in faith' (ὃ δὲ νῦν ζῶ ἐν σαρκί,
ἐν πίστει ζῶ),[64] while sharply qualifying bodily experience, also
establishes it as the sphere of the new existence 'in faith'.

None the less, Paul will at the same time reject any construction of new identity that negates all human bodiliness.[65] The

---

[60] See above, p. 128. J. Neusner, 'Was Rabbinic Judaism Really "Ethnic"?'
CBQ 57 (1995), 281–305; note too that S. Stern, *Jewish Identity*, 223–37, also
argues that in rabbinic writings circumcision is treated as *textually* private or
implicit.

[61] So generally Stern, *Jewish Identity*; Eilberg-Schwartz, *People of the
Body*. See D. Boyarin and J. Boyarin, 'Diaspora: Generation and the Ground
of Jewish Identity', *Critical Inquiry* 19 (1993), 693–725, for an important and
finely nuanced response to the tradition of the Pauline construction of the Jew.

[62] See above, p. 129.

[63] See the whole passage to 8. 13; for discussion on the implications of this use
of 'flesh', see J. D. G. Dunn, *The Theology of Paul the Apostle* (Grand Rapids,
Mich.: Eerdmans, 1998), 62–73.

[64] NRSV 'And the life I now live in the flesh I live by faith [in (*or* of) the Son
of God]'.

[65] See A. Destro and M. Pesce, 'Self, Identity, and Body in Paul and John',

latter, expressed more often through 'body' (σῶμα) than through 'flesh', remains constitutive of the life and experience of those 'in Christ', both in the present but also in a continuing eschatological existence (1 Cor. 15. 35–50; Phil. 3. 21). The affirmation 'always carrying around in the body the death of Jesus, that the life of Jesus might also be revealed in our body' (2 Cor. 4. 10) might seem both to echo and yet to sound a more positive note than 4 Maccabees. In the present, bodiliness conditions the non-negotiability of appropriate personal and communal behaviour, eschatologically it is constituted by the body of Christ.[66] The correlates of this for 'praxis', and the multivalency for Paul of 'the body of Christ', and so of human bodily experience in relation to it, have been indicated elsewhere.[67] That interpreters of Paul contemporary with him as well as subsequently struggled to discover and to reproduce the coherence of his construction is hardly surprising.[68] How could identity be experienced as irreducibly bodily, if the body carried no marks, and if flesh belongs to the realm of 'other'?

The question need not be answered, for the point is that as a literary construction the new identity shaped by Paul is inherently unstable. That instability also emerges from a further question, namely regarding the gendered nature of this identity. This is well illustrated when Paul can famously say within a few verses, 'There is not male and female. For you are all one (*masc.*) in Christ Jesus', *and* 'God sent his son . . . that we might receive adoption as *sons*', *and* 'if you become circumcised Christ will be of no benefit to you' (Gal. 3. 28; 4. 4–5; 5. 2). Here is not the place to explore 'Paul's attitude to women', nor the by no means identical question of the roles women exercised in the 'Pauline churches'. Yet, if indeed penned by Paul, 1 Cor. 14. 33*b*–35 carefully constructs 'church' (ἐκκλησία) as public and as the place of

---

in A. Baumgarten, J. Assmann, G. Stroumsa (eds.), *Self, Soul and Body in Religious Experience*, SHR 78 (Leiden: Brill, 1998), 184–97.

[66] It should be clear here that 'eschatological' here is not limited to the future; the body of Christ is eschatological.

[67] See above, p. 170.

[68] See D. Boyarin, *A Radical Jew: Paul and the Politics of Identity* (Berkeley, Calif.: University of California Press, 1994); and the response by J. Barclay, ' "Neither Jew nor Greek": Multiculturalism and the New Perspective on Paul', in Brett, *Ethnicity*, 197–214.

women's silent invisibility; 'home' (οἶκος) as private and as the place of their submission, regardless of whether both occupied the same physical space.[69] The convoluted argument of 1 Cor. 11. 2–16 regarding the veiling of women, which continues to exercise interpreters, reflects the dilemma of determining quite what effect the introduction of Christ (mentioned only in v. 3 of that passage) has for the construction of gender within this new identity.

THE SUFFERING BODY

Another trajectory will be shaped by understandings of the human experience of Jesus. For Ignatius, 'the fleshly (σαρκικός) cannot do spiritual things (πνευματικός), nor the spiritual, fleshly' (*Eph.* 8. 2); yet as Jesus Christ is 'fleshly *and* spiritual', so this duality becomes the repeated qualifier of all individual and corporate existence: 'but that you might remain in Jesus Christ in all purity and sobriety, both fleshly and spiritually' (*Eph.* 10. 3; cf. 7. 2; *Magn.* 13. 2 etc.).[70] In particular, Ignatius's instinctive rejection of any interpretation that might undermine the fleshly integrity of Jesus's coming, future as well as past, and preeminently of Jesus's suffering (τὸ πάθειν) (*Smyrn.* 4), intersects with the impulse of his own drive to martyrdom, anticipated in vivid physical terms —'ground by the teeth of wild beasts' who must leave nothing of his body. Only in this way will Ignatius himself be proved to be a Christian (*Rom.* 4. 1–2; 3. 2).[71] This means that the body of Christ is no longer merely a metaphor of interdependency and unity, but carries the mark of suffering in which believers participate (*Trall.* 11. 2). And yet Ignatius can also say, 'When the world no longer sees my body, then I shall truly be a disciple of Jesus Christ' (*Rom.* 4. 2). In Ignatius, more than in any other Christian writer of this period, we find

[69] i.e., if the church met in a house; on the question of authenticity, see D. Horrell, *The Social Ethos of the Corinthian Correspondence: Interests and Ideology from 1 Corinthians to 1 Clement*, SNTW (Edinburgh: T&T Clark, 1996), 184–95.

[70] At *Eph.* 7. 2 the manuscript tradition of the shorter recension even reads 'he is . . . ἐν σαρκὶ γενόμενος θεός'.

[71] See further below, p. 251.

a deep concern for the self that is also a concern for authentic, and so, in a sense, for normative, identity. It is of necessity an embodied identity, and not only because of continued participation in 'what is seen': 'for this reason you are both fleshly as well as spiritual, that you may gain the favour of that which is seen and experienced; but ask that the unseen may be manifest to you so that you lack nothing but abound in every gift' (*Poly.* 2. 2). To a certain extent, also, Ignatius's highly personalized experience is not presented as paradigmatic; only in communal life, in unity with bishop, elders, and deacons, can an identity shaped by 'Jesus Christ and his flesh and blood, suffering and resurrection, fleshly and spiritual' be experienced (*Smyrn.* 12. 2).

The Acts of the Martyrs are in some ways the heirs to the Ignatian view of the body as the site of the new identity, although in their case this is not primarily ecclesially mediated. Here, the tortured but triumphant body of the martyr becomes the ultimate affirmation of the claim 'I am a Christian'.[72] At the same time, the lasting significance of the body of the martyr remains a point of conflict; the impulses towards its veneration signal an awkwardness, emphatically within the textual construction even more than within the social experience behind it:[73] the body's continued witness beyond the text is rendered superfluous, while within the text it serves as a testimony to its own contingency.[74] In the *Martyrdom of Polycarp* the martyrs even before their death are 'no longer men but already angels', while their refusal to groan shows that they were 'absent from the flesh' (2. 3). None the less, some of those not martyred longed to 'share in [Polycarp's] holy flesh', and his bones, 'more precious than valuable stones', were reverently gathered for future annual celebration. As a 'memorial of those who had contested before and a training for those to come', such celebration uses the testimony of the body to shape an identity that challenges any other construction of these events, for example, as dishonour or as defeat (17. 1; 18. 2; cf. Eusebius, *HE* V. 1. 61).

Through these narratives of trial and death, this self-conscious

---

[72] See Lieu, '"I am a Christian"'.

[73] Cf. W. Rordorf, 'Aux Origines du culte des martyrs', *Irénikon* 45 (1972), 315–31; Lieu, *Image and Reality*, 66–7.

[74] However, in *Mart. Poly.* 16. 1 the 'lawless' see that Polycarp's body could not be consumed by the fire.

use of the language of the games, with their inherent physicality, means that traditional civic values are both redefined and subverted: the body is the site of a new construction of control and triumph, its humiliation in public is an assertion of a radically defined alternative identity. Here, gender plays a distinctive role. Impaled on a stake, Blandina represents the crucified Christ to her fellows; in her final torture she is a mother of the children who have gone ahead, possibly recalling the mother of 4 Maccabees, and perhaps even embodying the church herself, already constructed as 'mother'.[75] Perpetua, famously, while never changing her gender, changes her sex: in her dream of her fight with the Egyptian she is 'smoothed down and became a male' (*Pass. Perpet.* 10. 7).[76] Yet her gender is emphasized, through the repeated vivid allusions to her and to Felicitas as recently having given birth, and through the textually inscribed concern for her modesty that simultaneously exposes her to the reader's gaze (6. 7–8; 18. 3; 20. 2–4). In contemporary thought vulnerability becomes a woman, but here a woman's embracing of submission and suffering challenges conventional structures; perhaps this reversal of values as explored through the already liminal figure of a woman authenticates the suffering and humiliation to be experienced by men.[77] Ironically, it was obvious to the bystanders that Alexander, urging others to martyrdom, was 'as one in the travail of birth', and it is hardly surprising that he is quickly condemned to martyrdom (*HE* V. 1. 49–50). Just as the heavenly voice called on Polycarp to 'play the man' as he entered the stadium (*Mart. Poly.* 9. 1), so an alternative arena for displaying the familiar yet transformed virtues of normative identity is being claimed, and for the moment it appears inclusive of women as well as of men. However, it remains ambiguous whether or how far such literary reversals, or the social reality they reflect,

---

[75] Eusebius, *HE* V. 1. 41, 55; see below, pp. 207–8.

[76] 'et expoliata sum et facta sum masculus': H. Musurillo, *The Acts of the Christian Martyrs*, OECT (Oxford: Clarendon, 1972), 119 translates 'my clothes were stripped off', presumably because she is oiled in the next sentence. On the Egyptian as 'other', see below, pp. 274–5.

[77] Yet this may not have been a Christian innovation: a number of scholars point to Achilles Tatius, *Leucippe*, where the eponymous heroine offers her body to torture to challenge the conventional exercise of power: Goldhill, *Foucault's Virginity*, 94–112; Shaw, 'Body/Power/Identity', 269–71.

impacted on an identity predicated on gendered embodiment: some have suggested that female martyrs struck a blow for female self-determination within the church, but in effect the results seem to have been marginal or soon brought under control.[78] The irony is that in the longer term the Christian rhetoric of the martyrs as soldiers or athletes could be seen as offering *for men* an alternative route to manly virtues: 'Roman men became Christians because they saw in Christian ideology a means of surmounting the gap between ancient ideals and contemporary realities.'[79]

THE ASCETIC IDEAL

Other texts address these ambiguities in more directly traditional ways. When Justin presents the elusive *sophrosune* (σωφροσύνη, sobriety?) as the heart of Jesus's teaching (*Apol.* 15), he is constructing Christian identity as the embodiment of a long tradition of classical ideals, while also continuing the Jewish denunciation of 'typical' Gentile sexual excess.[80] Yet, in Christian discourse this takes a highly distinctive form: Justin cites as evidence men and women of 60 or 70 who since childhood have remained chaste, as well as the multitudes who have turned away from licentiousness. In Athenagoras, asceticism becomes an intrinsic part of Christian self-presentation; marriage is for procreation, celibacy is an ideal adopted by many: 'The bodies of those whom we consider brothers and sisters and other family designations are treated with indifference and decorously'—an assertion contrarily illustrated by the ritual kiss

[78] See F. Klawiter, 'The Role of Martyrdom and Persecution in Developing the Priestly Role of Women in Early Christianity: A Case Study of Montanism', *Ch. Hist.* 49 (1980), 251–61. For the later development, see G. Clark, 'Bodies and Blood: Late Antique Debate on Martyrdom, Virginity and Resurrection', in D. Montserrat (ed.), *Changing Bodies, Changing Meanings: Studies on the Human Body in Antiquity* (London: Routledge, 1998), 99–115.

[79] M. Kuefler, *The Manly Eunuch: Masculinity, Gender Ambiguity, and Christian Ideology in Late Antiquity* (Chicago, Ill.: University of Chicago Press, 2001), 287.

[80] On the classical tradition of σωφροσύνη see H. North, *Sophrosyne: Self-knowledge and Self-restraint in Greek Literature*, Cornell Studies in Classical Philology 35 (Ithaca, NY: Cornell University Press, 1966).

(*Leg.* 32–3).[81] For both authors, the dominical teaching on adultery and divorce is paradigmatic; asceticism here is unreservedly sexual. 'Continence', ἐγκράτεια, acquires a distinctive meaning: '[their wives are as chaste as virgins, their daughters modest, and their men] continent, avoiding any lawless intercourse and any impurity' (Aristides, *Apology* 15. 6).[82] Yet this is not just apologetic defence against charges laid by detractors of promiscuity or of deliberate indulgence in the crime that destroys any community, incest; indeed, the fact that such charges are reported mainly by Christian authors suggests that in so doing they are simultaneously vaunting and denying the subversiveness of their claim to community (Minucius Felix, *Oct.* 9. 2). Some observers, at least, were persuaded: Galen describes men and women who refrain from cohabiting all their lives, and who are almost to be compared with philosophers in their self-control.[83]

This is, then, a conscious and determined effort at self-fashioning. In Hermas's vision of the tower it is even more clearly self-directed: the second of the seven maidens supporting the tower is girded and manly;[84] she is the daughter of Faith, and her name is Continence (ἐγκράτεια) (Hermas, *Vis.* III. 8. 4–8). There is more here than the choice of a particular ethical stance: it evidences an explicit understanding of the body as the sphere in which the new identity is played out, at the same time being both an affirmation of and a denial of the body's determinative role. This will become one of those key sites of contradiction and conflict that take us to the heart of the spectrum of Christian identities.[85]

The *Apocryphal Acts of the Apostles*, and most notably the *Acts of Paul and Thecla*, present a further literary exploration of that contradiction. Here the Gospel that Paul preaches is 'concerning

---

[81] On this, see Penn, 'Performing Family', 170–2, who sees this not as apologetic for outsiders but as self-representation.

[82] The words in brackets are only in the Syriac recension. Cf. Minucius Felix, *Oct.* 31. 5, 'Many rejoice in the perpetual virginity of an inviolate body . . .'

[83] In R. Walzer (trans. and ed.), *Galen on Jews and Christians* (London: Oxford University Press, 1949), 15.

[84] περιεζωσμένη καὶ ἀνδριζομένη—the same verb as addressed to Polycarp, above.

[85] See Eilberg-Schwartz, 'Problem of the Body', for cultural contradiction or conflict as more fundamental for understanding than the construction of a system.

continence and resurrection', and generates a new set of beatitudes: 'Blessed are they who keep their flesh holy, for they shall
be a temple of God; blessed are the continent, for God shall speak
to them . . . blessed are those who have wives as if they did not, for
they shall inherit God' (5). Yet the main focus of this narrative is
its life-transforming impact on a woman, Thecla. She rejects her
fiancé to follow Paul, and does not merely survive a panoply of
trials but survives through her bodily vulnerability, and finally
claims the right to determine her own discipleship. With their
themes of fraught relationships, separations, and journeys of
danger and threat, these apocryphal Acts also seem to belong to
the genre of Hellenistic romances, and their literary and social
backgrounds have been extensively discussed. Although they
have been hailed as evidence of circles of liberated women in
second-century Christianity, it is not clear that Thecla is seen
as a progenitrix.[86] As literary texts, however articulated in social
experience, it is probably better to see in them the manipulation
of a familiar topos in order to offer a counter-vision: 'The invention of the ascetic hero and heroine was an important element in
the formation of a Christian alternative language of power and
society.'[87] In the Hellenistic novels, chastity had been repeatedly
threatened but ultimately preserved and reserved for marriage,
which thereby sustained and protected society and the established order; here chastity is redefined in opposition to marriage
and explicitly challenges that order. The icon of embodied identity is no longer male and female in proper relationship to each
other, embodying the values and ensuring the future of society,
but the self-restrained figure, *her* gaze directed not to her husband but ultimately to God.[88]

Within this framework, Thecla's adoption of male clothing

---

[86] See Davies, *Revolt of the Widows*, and above, Ch. 4 n. 64.

[87] Cooper, *Virgin and the Bride*, 58.

[88] See E. Castelli, ' "I will make Mary male": Pieties of the Body and Gender
Transformation of Christian Women in Late Antiquity', in J. Epstein and K.
Straub (eds.), *Body Guards: The Cultural Politics of Gender Ambiguity* (London:
Routledge, 1991), 29–41, 40–3; on the woman's gaze in Tertullian, see M. R.
d'Angelo, 'Veils, Virgins and the Tongues of Men and Angels: Women's Heads
in Early Christianity', in H. Eilberg-Schwartz and W. Doniger (eds.), *Off
with her Head! The Denial of Women's Identity in Myth, Religion, and Culture*
(Berkeley, Calif.: University of California Press, 1995), 131–64, 145–7.

(*Act. Paul.* 40) is as ambiguous as is Perpetua's transformation: is it merely a convenience or does it represent something more fundamental? John Anson, for example, suggests that '[i]t signalized and effected a transformation of self, the birth of a new identity, not only in the name of Christ but in the body as well.'[89] Like many others, he links this motif with Gal. 3. 28, and with the theme of 'becoming male' that we find in a number of second-century texts: 'For every woman who will make herself male will enter the kingdom of heaven' (*Gosp. Thomas* 114).[90] Some have seen this as a symbol of the liberation of women from all that signalled their subordination elsewhere in society, and as pointing to a set of virtues no longer defined in gendered terms—the creation of an identity no longer constituted by the proper roles of the sexes in relation to each other. However, the picture seems more complex than this: Perpetua and Thecla inhabit rather different genres from the *Gospel of Thomas*, and neither of them actually become male; indeed, their failure to do so remains an offence to some viewers/readers.[91]

Others have argued that, on the contrary, such a rhetoric reinforces the feminization of the body as the site of danger and necessary submission. So, according to the *Dialogue of the Saviour* (NH III. 5), Jesus exhorted his disciples to 'pray where there is no woman', and to 'destroy the works of femaleness', an act that seems to be identified with being stripped 'from the corruption of the flesh' (143. 14–144. 22).[92]

Further, 'becoming male' could also problematize maleness, which is, as we have seen, constructed by its now dissolved

[89] J. Anson, 'The Female Transvestite in Early Monasticism: The Origin and Development of a Motif', *Viator* 5 (1974), 1–31, 11.

[90] See Castelli, '"I will make Mary male"'; also Kuefler, *Manly Eunuch*, 221–30.

[91] See above, p. 53, on Tertullian's response to the Thecla narrative; see above on the importance of Perpetua as woman in her martyrdom. However, according to Epiphanius, *Panarion*, XLIX. 2, the 'Quintillians', a Montanist (sub)group, had female bishops and elders on the grounds that 'in Christ Jesus there is neither male nor female'.

[92] Given that Mariam speaks in this text as 'a woman who knew the all' (III. 139. 12), this need not token an all-male misogynist community. Cf. *Zostrianos* (NH VIII. 1) 131. 5–8, 'Flee from the bondage of femininity, and choose for yourselves the salvation of masculinity'; however, it is not clear whether this should be labelled a 'Christian' text.

opposition: 'When you make the two one . . . the male and the female one and the same so that the male will not be male and the female not female' (*Gosp. Thom.* 22); 'For the Lord himself when asked by someone when his kingdom would come, said, "When the two shall become one, and the outside as the inside, and the male with the female, neither male nor female"' (*2 Clem.* 12. 2).[93] Any social articulation of this, perhaps eschatological, escape from multiplicity to unity remains uncertain; Richard Valantasis is surely right in arguing, with reference to the *Gospel of Thomas*, that what is happening is not to be understood in negative terms, as rejection, but in positive, as an 'intentional reformation of the self' which involves a new social location.[94] None the less, it is, on the whole, more likely to have resulted in an individualized asceticism than in new communal structures.

According to Clement of Alexandria, that is how Julius Cassianus took the dominical saying just cited;[95] Clement rejected such an ascetical reading, associating it with the teaching of Tatian and noting that the passage (as he knew it) did not come in 'the four Gospels handed down to us' but in the *Gospel of the Egyptians*. Irenaeus had already asserted that Tatian had apostasized from the church when he preached against marriage and had so introduced what was to become the heresy of the 'Continent' or 'Encratites'.[96] By associating him in this with the recognized heretics, Satorninus and Marcion, Irenaeus leaves no doubt as to where the lines are to be drawn.

However, as we have already seen, the map was far from being so clearly plotted. Renunciation of marriage lay deeply embedded within the tradition, even in the Jesus-tradition (Luke 14. 26; 18. 29), and had already been taken up by some within the Pauline churches (1 Cor. 7. 1–9); the Apocalypse's celebration of the

[93] Cf. *Gospel of Philip* (NH II. 3), 70. 12–15, 'Christ came to repair the separation which was from the beginning and again unite the two.'

[94] See R. Valantasis, 'Is the Gospel of Thomas Ascetical? Revisiting Old Problems with a New Theory', *JECS* 7 (1999), 55–81.

[95] *Strom.* III. 13. 91–3, where it takes the form, 'when you tread on the garment of shame and when the two become one and the male with the female, neither male nor female' (92. 2). See also Jerome, *Against Rufinus*, I. 28–9, for whom chastity even in marriage now begins the transformation into angels where there is neither male nor female.

[96] *Adv. Haer.* I. 28. 1, cited by Eusebius, *HE* IV. 28–9; cf. already, 1 Tim. 4. 3.

144,000 'who have not defiled themselves with women, for they are virgins', even if a metaphor drawn from the holy war tradition (Rev. 14. 3–4; Deut. 23. 9–10), still betrays an antipathy to sexuality and to women that surfaces elsewhere in that text.[97] The model of Christians as 'sojourning' that we shall explore elsewhere easily lent itself to a disregard for familial obligations and structures.[98] The origins of encratism within these dynamics remain obscure, but it does seem that in some areas this became the paradigmatic form of Christian identity.[99] The eventual rise of the paramount authority of the ascetic, while beyond our period, is not an alien growth but an expression of the simultaneous insistence on and denial of attention to the body in the formation of Christian identity, even if it also resonated with existing concerns in late antiquity.

THE PURE AND THE DEFILED DEFILERS

The valorization of the undefiled female body takes a different form when Ephesians pushes the Pauline construction in a new direction; the hierarchy of headship expressed in 1 Cor. 11. 3, God > Christ > man > woman now becomes a parallel between Christ > church//man > woman, and its goal is the unblemished purity of the woman-church (Eph. 5. 23–33). Such a feminization of the church will come to shape profoundly one dimension of the gendering of identity, intersecting with other trajectories of virginity and unsullied body, and so will produce a new language for the understanding of the self, individual and corporate.[100]

---

[97] Cf. Rev. 17. 3–8, 15–18; 2. 20–3.

[98] See below, pp. 232–3.

[99] See A. Vööbus, *History of Asceticism in the Syrian Orient: A Contribution to the History of Culture in the Near East: The Origins of Asceticism: Early Monasticism in Persia*, CSCO Subsidia 14 (Louvain: CorpusSCO, 1958), 10–30.

[100] Cf. A. Cameron, 'Virginity as Metaphor: Women and the Rhetoric of Early Christianity', in eadem (ed.), *History as Text: The Writing of Ancient History* (London: Duckworth, 1989), 181–205; Kuefler, *Manly Eunuch*, 137–40, discusses the significance for this of Origen's exegesis of the Song of Songs. S. Juster, *Disorderly Women: Sexual Politics and Evangelicalism in Revolutionary New England* (Ithaca, NY: Cornell University Press, 1994), in a discussion of the importance of women in 18th-century dissident groups, notes the significance

Fraught with a different ambiguity is Hermas's initial lust for his
fellow-servant, Rhoda, who subsequently appears in visionary
form in heaven to rebuke him, particularly when set alongside
the woman of his later visions, first old, then of increasing youth
and beauty, who is identified as the church (Hermas, *Vis.* I. 1–2;
II. 4; III. 10–13). More specifically, as bride the church will be
subordinate, as woman vulnerable. In the account of the persecutions at Lyons the church is 'Virgin Mother', an unstable and
destabilizing image that threatens illegitimacy or the anxiety of
violation—exacerbated by the description of those who failed in
confession as 'still-born' (*HE* V. 1. 45).[101] Defilement, a theme
rooted in Second Temple Judaism, can take a new turn when it
is the 'virgin church' that is corrupted, now by the appearance of
heresy (Hegesippus in Eusebius, *HE* IV. 22. 4).[102]

　　Defilement becomes more firmly attached to those in this way
ruled outside, as writers direct charges of sexual licentiousness
not only against 'the Greeks' but also against those labelled 'heretics'—often repeating the charges that had already been laid
against 'the Christians' by outsiders.[103] As reported by Eusebius,
Apollonius not only accused Montanus of 'teaching the annulment of marriage', but also claimed that the prophetesses who
accompanied him had deserted their husbands: 'How they lie
when they call Priscilla a virgin!' (Eusebius, *HE* V. 18. 2–3).
The *Kerygmata Petri* betray a similar anxiety when they portray female prophecy as deceptive and multiform (Ps.-Clement,
Hom. III. 22–3). According to Irenaeus, Marcus had a particular attraction for women, whom he also encouraged to prophesy
nonsense, while his followers entrapped gullible women and
seduced them, literally, with their physical enactment of spiritual
metaphors (Irenaeus, *adv. Haer.* I. 13). Similarly, Simon Magus
was supposedly accompanied by a former prostitute Helena
(Justin, *Apol.* 26; Irenaeus, *adv. Haer.* I. 23. 2). According to

of the view of the community as 'feminine', emphasizing 'emotionalism, sensu-
ality . . . a porous sense of the self' (p. 5).

　　[101] Cf. *HE* V. 2. 6–7, 'They did not boast over those who had stumbled, but
with their abundance supplied those that needed it with motherly compassion,
and poured out many tears for them to the father . . . they left no burden for their
mother. . .'

　　[102] See above, pp. 115–16.

　　[103] See above, p. 188.

Dionysius of Alexandria, Cerinthus taught an earthly millennial kingdom 'because he loved the body and was exceedingly carnal' (Eusebius, *HE* III. 28. 4–5). The rhetoric of distancing through the body is neatly captured by Clement of Alexandria when he asserts that the call 'to abuse the flesh' characterizes the pure in their 'continence' and yet also, through its perversion, marks 'the heretics' in their 'unrestrained licence'.[104] The discovery of an ascetic ethos in texts such as the *Gospel of Thomas* or the *Dialogue of the Saviour* cited above and often ascribed to these self-same 'gnostic' heretics has given the lie to such simplistic categories. They, too, participate in the same ambiguities of the body, and of its sexual articulation, as we have found throughout our exploration.[105]

CONSTRUCTING EARLY CHRISTIANITY, THE
BODY, AND LATE ANTIQUITY

All our texts seem agreed that Christian difference was deeply marked in and through the body. Yet how true was this? For example, it has been suggested that integral to the new identity that emerges with Christianity is a turn within: 'Christianity by eliminating the opposition between man and nature fostered a new kind of hero who, relieved of conquering his surroundings, now turned inward to conquer his inner self.'[106] Others have supposed that here the private, not the public, becomes reconceived as the sphere of self-fashioning and so determinative of identity.[107] Yet, as we have seen, these may be but part of an extensive and well-attested trend towards 'introspection, *ascesis*, philosophical self-discovery and autotherapy' that was

[104] *Strom.* II. 20. 118; III. 4. 25–6; cf. Eusebius, *HE* III. 29. 1–4.

[105] See M. A. Williams, *Rethinking 'Gnosticism': An Argument for Dismantling a Dubious Category* (Princeton, NJ: Princeton University Press, 1996), 116–38.

[106] E. G. Weltin, *Athens and Jerusalem: An Interpretative Essay on Christianity and Classical Culture*, AAR Studies in Religion 49 (Atlanta, Ga.: Scholars Press, 1987), 43 n. 28; although probably not intended, 'man' here should be taken as exclusive.

[107] See J. Elshtain, *Public Man, Private Woman*, 55–60, who suggests that Christianity gave the private the place of honour, leaving the public open to criticism.

already in train in the early Empire.[108] And how should we set them alongside Peter Brown's suggestion that the Christian revolution means that the body no longer is involved in a vertical dualism of individual and cosmos, but in a horizontal one, as the bridge between self and society?[109] Perhaps more than with any of our other explorations, when we attempt to trace the specifically Christian contours in the changing landscape of the body in late antiquity we are most faced with contradictory signals and uncertainly mapped paths. Certainly, the body as problem was deeply embedded in all forms of Christian identity, but no less was Christian identity embedded in the perplexities and the dynamics of its age. Yet what it offered, through its texts at least, was a language and a story in which both problem and solution could find their place.

[108] Whitmarsh, 'Greece is the World', 304; see above, pp. 189–90; Francis, *Subversive Virtue*.

[109] P. Brown, 'Bodies and Minds: Sexuality and Renunciation in Early Christianity', in D. Halperin, J. Winkler, F. Zeitlin (eds.), *Before Sexuality: The Construction of Erotic Experience in the Ancient Greek World* (Princeton, NJ: Princeton University Press, 1990), 479–93.

7

Space and Place

The conviction of belonging to a specific territory, whether real or imagined, as inseparable from the conviction of shared origins, is surely one of the irreducible components in a sense of identity, particularly of ethnic identity.[1] In the appeals to past history that characterize contemporary conflicts about identity, it has become evident that securing an acknowledged 'place' within space as well as within time has profoundly political implications.[2] Conversely, as has often been pointed out, it is as the 'actual geo-social boundaries of the community are undermined, blurred or otherwise weakened', that the symbolic nature and function of boundaries become more important.[3] Whereas our earlier discussion focused on the symbolic, here we shall explore the role of 'real' space in the construction of identity in antiquity, while recognizing both that the identifying and the labelling of space—for 'space' to become 'place'—are themselves acts of construction, and hence acts of power, and that it will prove difficult to maintain a distinction between metaphor and 'geo-social' actuality.[4]

[1] See above, pp. 62–6. Cf. A. D. Smith's essentialist definition of *ethnie* as 'named human populations with shared ancestry, myths, histories and cultures having an association with a specific territory and a sense of solidarity', cited above, Ch. 5 n. 2. So also Hall, *Ethnic Identity*, 25, 32, who emphasizes that such association may only be 'imagined'.

[2] See e.g. Whitelam, *Invention of Ancient Israel*, 37–70.

[3] Cohen, *Symbolic Construction*, 50; see above, pp. 98–103.

[4] So Whitelam, *Invention of Ancient Israel*, 37, 'time and space are social products which, like the construction of the past, are tied to notions of identity and authority'. See also the essays in N. Duncan (ed.), *Bodyspace: Destabilizing Geographies of Gender and Sexuality* (London: Routledge, 1996), especially G. Rose, 'As if the Mirrors Had Bled: Masculine Dwelling, Masculinist Theory and Feminist Masquerade', ibid. 56–74.

Again, contemporary studies of identity, and specifically of ethnicity, have underlined these ambiguities. They might be demonstrated, on the one hand, by the battles, often literal, over claims to territory for or by a self-defined 'people', involving the, sometimes violent, exclusion of others, when set alongside the protests from archaeologists that claims by or for particular groups to a demarcated ethnic and cultural distinctiveness are rarely recognizably replicated by artefactual and other evidences of daily life 'on the ground'.[5] On the other hand, within a multi-ethnic or multicultural context, where multiple minorities are scattered through host cultures, the diaspora model has become focal with, in the words of Michael Keith and Steve Pile, its 'imagined geography, a spatiality that draws on connections across oceans and continents'.[6] But how far such connections can be actively practised and not merely imagined will vary, and will inevitably impact on the sense of belonging to the host country. The vitality of a 'myth of return', for example, will encourage a 'sojourner mentality' and a 'tendency towards encapsulation'.[7]

ROME: FROM THE CENTRE TO THE WORLD

This ambiguity in the dynamic between fixed place and diffused 'imagined geography' has its own correlates within the world of antiquity. Here, more than Greece, it is Rome that will be our starting point, for Roman identity was in one sense defined by the sense of Rome herself. Even as the territory under her influence or control expanded, the city of Rome retained an inalienable focality in imagination as well as in practice. Within her sacred boundaries or *pomerium* a careful exercise of control, domestication, or exclusion held in check the potential infiltration by Greek and other deities.[8] Periodic bans from the city, such as that of

---

[5] See above, pp. 98–9; Jones, 'Discourses of Identity'; Wells, *The Barbarians Speak*, 109–14.

[6] Keith and Pile, 'Politics of place . . .', 17; Gilroy, 'Diaspora'; see p. 101 above.

[7] Al-Rasheed, *Iraqi Assyrian Christians*, 72–81 (quotations from p. 81); see also ibid. 186–96, for the London community's efforts to maintain contacts with other communities in Australia and the USA.

[8] See Beard, North, Price, *Religions of Rome*, i. 167–81.

'foreign rites' (*alienigena sacra*) in 19 CE by Tiberius, conveyed a clear message to those who saw themselves as Roman; it was this, for example, that persuaded Seneca to give up his youthful fascination with Pythagorean vegetarianism (Seneca, *Epist.* 108. 22). Juvenal's vivid metaphor of the Syrian Orontes flowing into the Tiber shows the imaginative power of the landscape of identity (*Sat.* 3. 60–3). From a different perspective, Catherine Edwards has explored the role of the city within literary texts, suggesting that these gave Romans 'a sense of place': 'To be at home in Rome was not to be born there . . . It was rather to be master [*sic*] of Roman knowledge. Without such knowledge Romans might be thought to imperil their own identity, while, by implication, Roman knowledge could confer *romanitas* on the foreigner.'[9]

On the other hand, as Rome's sphere of influence increased, ultimately to form an empire, she had to interpret and to justify her, characteristically centrifugal, relationships with 'the world'. Already Greek writers had described the lands and the peoples surrounding them, driven both by a scientific curiosity and by the desire to demonstrate superiority over the barbarians, yet also by a conviction that the land shapes its inhabitants. This was an ethnography by geography and vice versa, but the problems of tying peoples to land were evident from the start, particularly as writers sought to reconcile the conflicting traditions from the past. So Strabo insists both that the Phrygians and Mysians are separate tribes, and that it is difficult to mark the boundaries between them; he also admits that nothing is known of the Milesians who founded Heracleia in the territory of the Mariandyni, 'for there appears to be no dialectical or other ethnic difference' about them (*Geog.* XII. 4. 4; 3. 4).

Roman writers from the second century BCE onwards were the heirs of this ethnographical tradition, but their interests worked in tandem with the process of colonization, both interpreting and justifying it.[10] Recognition of, and the description of, peoples with their territories, practices, and myths could become the precursor to the conceptual construction of a new and unified

---

[9] C. Edwards, *Writing Rome: Textual Approaches to the City* (Cambridge: Cambridge University Press, 1996), 17; see below for a similar situation in Jewish authors.

[10] See Williams, *Beyond the Rubicon*, 22–41.

world as shaped by Rome herself.[11] Here, two poles are held in tension: on the one hand, Rome with her values and tradition, on the other, a sense that she was destined to hold universal dominion. One such confluence of newly claimed literal frontiers and of the boundaries of endowed identity is celebrated by Hadrian's building of a wall 'to separate barbarians and Romans' (*Scriptores Historiae Augustae* 11. 2).[12] A different, more universalist trend appears when Ovid, celebrating the god Terminus (23 February), recognizes that without boundaries the world would sink into disorder, but can also claim that, whereas other peoples have delimited territory, in Rome's case 'the city and world are identical'.[13] According to Pliny, Rome was chosen by the divine power to bring cohesion, culture, and co-operation to the discordant and recalcitrant peoples, 'to offer humanity to men, and, in short, that there might be a single fatherland of all the nations in the whole world' (*Nat. Hist.* III. 5. 39).[14] In his description of the world the limits of Roman control are barely noted; we merely move from the more credible to the less so. Roman power is in practice or in potential coterminous with the world.[15] A similar conclusion is reached, but from different premises, by Caecilius as presented by Minucius Felix: whereas different peoples have different religious rites and deities, the Romans worship them all; 'thus their power and authority has taken possession of the

---

[11] See Clarke, *Between History and Geography*; R. Laurence, 'Territory, Ethnonyms and Geography: The Construction of Identity in Roman Italy', in R. Laurence and J. Berry (eds.), *Cultural Identity in the Roman Empire* (London: Routledge, 1998), 95–110.

[12] 'Murumque per octoginta milia passuum primus duxit, qui barbaros Romanosque divideret'; see M. E. Jones, 'Geographical-Psychological Frontiers in Sub-Roman Britain', in R. Mathisen and H. Sivan (eds.), *Shifting Frontiers in Late Antiquity* (Aldershot: Variorum; Brookfield, Vt.: Ashgate, 1996), 45–58. On 'the barbarian' as 'the other', see pp. 104–8; 271–9.

[13] *Fasti* 659–60, 683–4, 'tu populos urbesque et regna ingentia finis | omnis erit sine te litigiosus ager . . . gentibus est aliis tellus data limite certo, | Romanae spatium est urbis et orbis idem'. On the tension between the rhetoric of universalism and the awareness of barbarians beyond the boundaries, see Whittaker, *Frontiers of the Roman Empire*, 60–79.

[14] Rome is 'omnium terrarum alumna eadem et parens . . . breviterque una cunctarum gentium in toto orbe patria fieret'.

[15] See C. Nicolet, *Space, Geography, and Politics in the Early Roman Empire* (Ann Arbor, Mich.: University of Michigan Press, 1991), 29–56; Whittaker, *Frontiers of the Roman Empire*, 10–30.

circuit of the whole earth, and has extended their rule beyond the paths of the sun and the boundaries of the ocean itself'.[16]

Such a self-perception should not be confused with Greek philosophical ideals, particularly within Stoicism and among the Cynics, of the unity of humankind or of the wise man as 'citizen of the world', ideals which relativize any particular belonging.[17] Indeed, a cosmopolitanism of that timbre could offer the philosopher-in-exile, perhaps following imperial expulsion from Rome, an alternative and incontrovertible authority—preferable, surely, to Ovid's despondent (and exaggerated) 'here I am a barbarian' (*Trist.* V. 10. 37).[18] However, similar universalist ideals could also serve a political imperialism: Aelius Aristides is often quoted as exemplifying in the second century CE the claims to the equality and extent of Empire and world; one can no longer divide the world into Greeks and barbarians, for Rome has incorporated so many more people that now it must be Romans and non-Romans—'so far have you extended the name of the city'.[19] Yet even here there remains a tensive relationship between the separateness of Rome and of a sense of Roman-ness, and the universality of her reach, presented not only as dominion but also as civilizing power.

POSSESSION AND LOSS / TEMPLE, LAND, AND THE WORLD

Separateness versus universal reach might also be said to shape the Jewish sense of space. Cassius Dio's words are often

---

[16] Minucius Felix, *Oct.* 6. 1–2; but this is a Christian presentation of the Roman position, which will shortly be challenged.

[17] e.g. Epictetus, *Diss.* III. 24; on this see H. C. Baldry, *The Unity of Mankind in Greek Thought* (Cambridge: Cambridge University Press, 1965); see further above, pp. 189–90.

[18] On the exiled philosopher as a citizen of the world see Whitmarsh, ' "Greece is the World" '.

[19] *Rom.* 63; but see J. H. Oliver, *The Ruling Power*, Transactions of the American Philosophical Society, 43 (Philadelphia, Pa.: American Philosophical Society, 1953), for how Aristides belongs to a tradition of the ideal society reaching back to Plato. That this reflects the idealism and literary conceit of the Second Sophistic is shown by his similarly adulatory language of Athens, located in the middle of the earth (*Panath.* 15).

quoted: describing 'Palestine', he acknowledges that 'the land is [also] called Judaea and the people *ioudaioi*'; although he does not know the origins of the name, it has now spread 'to other people who, although of other races, are committed to their customs' (*Hist. Rom.* XXXVII. 16–17). The point at which, or the degree to which, the geographical reference of the term ἰουδαῖοι (Judaeans/Jews) was lost is a matter of considerable debate, not least because of the difficulty of rendering the dual reference in English.[20] However, for Jewish sources themselves it is not specifically Judaea as such, which, of course, itself means different things at different times, that defines identity. Place is fundamental, but how place is identified and configured differs in different texts and different contexts—and there is not room here to review in any detail the extensive subject of the land or of sacred space in Jewish thought.

An identifying moment in literary terms is God's promise to Abraham both of offspring and of 'the land where you are now a sojourner (גר), all the land of Canaan, for an eternal possession' (Gen. 17. 1–8). The play between that promise, with its own internal tension between gift and possession, and the 'memory' of being a sojourner, canonically reinforced by the traditions of Egyptian slavery and of the Exodus (e.g. Deut. 26. 5–11), could be said to constitute the key motifs around which multiple new variations will be composed. To this should be added the identification of Jerusalem as 'the place that the LORD your God will choose to put his name there' (Deut. 12. 5 etc.), together with the Temple, once more legitimated as divinely provided (2 Sam. 7. 13); on the other hand, no less formative are the traditions of exile both in prophecy and in experience. These fundamental spatial components will shape the symbolic world within which Jewish self-identity can be fashioned and her experience interpreted, allowing both continuity and divergence in new constructions and situations.[21] That these situations in fact included not only, as we shall see, the dilemmas of exile and of diaspora, but also the realities of never being the sole inhabitants of the land—not only after the Return, even if most self-consciously then—is what

---

[20] And so its use and rendering in the New Testament is particularly contentious; see e.g. M. Lowe, 'Who were the *Ioudaioi*?', *NT* 18 (1976), 101–20.

[21] See above, pp. 153–4 for models that allow for stability of fundamentals and difference of interpretation.

drives the need for self-definition.[22] Inevitably, then, there can be no unified, coherent account of the sense of 'space' among the Jews; on the contrary, it is evident that land remains both central to identity, and yet contested, problem more than solution.[23]

On the one hand, the claim to the land becomes foundational: in *Jubilees* the 'table of nations' of Gen. 10 becomes a secret and angelically authorized division of the earth between Shem, Ham, and Japhet; it secures for Shem and his descendants for ever 'the middle of the earth', which includes the Garden of Eden, Mount Sinai, and Mount Zion, a promised land that extends far beyond any political reality.[24] Thus Canaan's settlement in the eponymous territory—which continues 'until this day'—earns the solemn curse even of his father, Ham, and of his brothers, for they recognize it as belonging by right to Shem (*Jub*. 8. 10–21; 10. 29–35). On the other hand, in the same text, while given by promise to Abraham and his descendants, the land remains problematized: it is deeply implicated in the behaviour of the people, polluted, laid waste, or rendered infertile and a source of death by their disobedience (*Jub*. 23. 18; cf. 21. 19). Behaving like the Gentiles earns exclusion from the land and enslavement among them (*Jub*. 15. 34; cf. *T. Judah* 23). Elsewhere, the continuing presence of Gentiles in the land testifies to the failure of the people (*Test. Mos.* 12. 7–13), while in 1 Maccabees the customs Antiochus instructs the cities to follow are 'alien to the land' (1 Macc. 1. 44).[25]

Within the context of the late Second Temple period, such texts both interpret recent experience and offer a barely veiled threat against other constructions of power and identity, for example against those that might affirm the present situation, or that might find positive significance in the sharing of the land: *Jubilees* emphatically rejects the biblical Isaac's hope that his

---

[22] Well emphasized by J. Neusner, 'Exile and Return in the History of Judaism', in J. M. Scott (ed.), *Exile: Old Testament, Jewish and Christian Conceptions*, S.JSJ 56 (Leiden: Brill, 1997), 221–37.

[23] See Riches, *Conflicting Mythologies*, 24–38, 58–67.

[24] On this see Mendels, *Land of Israel*, 64–9; J. M. Scott, *Geography in Early Judaism and Christianity: The Book of Jubilees*, SNTS.MS 113 (Cambridge: Cambridge University Press, 2002).

[25] On this theme in 1 Maccabees, see Lieu, 'Not Hellenes', 252, and above, p. 109.

own descendants and the Philistines might share the land and its prosperity, and has him instead anticipate eternal hostility and ultimate destruction (*Jub.* 24. 27–33; contrast Gen. 26. 22).[26]

It is not surprising, then, that the defeat of the northern kingdom (or of 'the ten tribes') by Assyria, and, more especially, that of Judah by Babylon, and the exile that followed, dominate the predictive retellings of the past that are characteristic of much of the literature of this period. This does not mean, as sometimes suggested, that in this period it was unresolved exile from, rather than possession of, the land that shaped the sense of who and where the people were.[27] For example, Baruch adopts the perspective of the people in exile in Babylon in order to proclaim their penitence and their confidence in God's promise to bring them again to their land in perpetuity (Bar. 2. 27–35). Yet if this were written in Judaea, past confidence would now carry the guarantee of future fulfilment. In this way the importance of place is both reaffirmed—hence the perplexity of exile—and destabilized—exile is not the end of the story, nor does it undermine identity. That, ultimately, confident possession of the land and its own security remain a matter of eschatological hope confirms this duality (*Jub.* 50. 5; *T. Dan.* 12–13).[28]

The relationship between the land and Jerusalem and Temple within the history of traditions seems uncertain. The late 'appearance' of the city and Temple in textual tradition and in history presents a problem that *Jubilees* solves by having Jacob prevented by God from building a sanctuary at Bethel, 'for this is not the place' (*Jub.* 32. 16–22). Locating Jerusalem in the midst of the land—as also in *Aristeas*—effects a harmony between them.[29]

---

[26] Lieu, 'Not Hellenes', 254. Mendels, *Land of Israel*, 64–9, relates this to conflicts over the coastal plain in the 2nd century BCE.

[27] For the argument and discussion see D. J. Bryan, 'Exile and Return from Jerusalem', in C. Rowland and J. Barton (eds.), *Apocalyptic in History and Tradition*, JSP.SS 43 (Sheffield: Sheffield Academic Press, 2002), 60–80.

[28] See Neusner, 'Exile and Return', 235, 'So long as memory remained, the conflicting claims of exclusivist Torah literature and universalist prophecy, of a people living in utopia, in no particular place, while framing its vision of itself in the deeply locative symbols of cult and centre—these conflicting claims would make vivid the abiding issue of self-definition.'

[29] See P. Alexander, 'Jerusalem as the *Omphalos* of the World: On the History of a Geographical Concept', in L. Levine (ed.), *Jerusalem: Its Sanctity and*

Yet, fundamentally, the Temple's function for identity does not mirror that of the land: it is not inhabited space but sacred space. However, as has been demonstrated by Seth Kunin, as such the Temple embodies a static model whereby sacred space is still determined by geography, in contrast, for example, to a dynamic model whereby sacred space is determined by activity, as in the depiction of the Tent in the wilderness.[30] This remains important: structurally, the subdivision within the Temple of space and of access, and the Temple's own place within Jerusalem, can provide the template for understanding Israel's relations with the world—as graphically argued in particular by Mary Douglas, who has shown how it replicates perceptions of purity.[31]

In a very different way, Josephus delegitimates the rebels by cataloguing their defiling acts in the Temple: there is for him a particular irony in the respect given from a distance to the Temple by the Romans, who have upheld the exclusion of foreigners from its sacred precincts, while those 'brought up in our customs and *called Jews* (ἰουδαῖοι καλούμενοι)' defile it (*BJ* IV. 3. 10 (181–4)).[32] Similarly, in a number of other texts, it is specifically the Temple or Jerusalem that embodies the failure and the judgement of the people, and that also provides the focus of the eschatological vision (*T. Levi* 15; *Sib. III*, ll. 702–30; *2 Baruch*; *Ps. Sol.* 8; 4 Ezra 10. 20–8). Again, such anticipations of the future shape of 'place' could become a means of articulating present conflicts of power and claims to authentic identity. Just as the actual control of the Jerusalem Temple had more than political implications, so claims to know the pattern of the future Temple among the Dead Sea Community seek to legitimate a contested identity (e.g. 11QT), while attacks against its present state may bespeak the sense of marginalization felt by a group for whom it none the less remains determinative. The destruction of the Temple in 70 CE and the exclusion of the Jews from

Centrality to Judaism, Christianity, and Islam (New York: Continuum, 1999), 104–19.

[30] S. Kunin, *God's Place in the World: Sacred Space and Sacred Place in Judaism* (London: Cassell, 1998), 11–27.

[31] See above, Ch. 4 at n. 21.

[32] H. StJ. Thackeray, *Josephus III: The Jewish War Books IV–VII*, LCC (Cambridge, Mass.: Harvard University Press, 1928), 57, translates as middle, 'calling themselves Jews'.

Jerusalem after the Bar Kochba revolt would provoke among the rabbis very different new constructions of that sacred space.[33]

The confession of God as the 'creator of the heaven and the earth' adds yet another dimension to the interplay of possibilities: on the one hand, this can undergird the promise of ultimate inheritance of the whole earth and of the right to judge everyone and everywhere (*Jub.* 32. 18–22); on the other, it anticipates the extension of knowledge of God to the Gentiles (*T. Levi* 18. 9). This does not mean that there is an inevitable opposition between particularism and universalism, nor that an emphasis on the land will sustain only the former.[34] As with Rome or Athens, location at the centre, and the preservation of the particular integrity of that centre, can legitimate an identity that is at once separate and universal in its claims. This is not the point at which to discuss the varied eschatological expectations of intertestamental Jewish literature, regarding both the nature and location of the eschatological kingdom, and the place of the Gentiles.[35] Yet, if the eschatological vision provides a supra-historical legitimation for an identity based on possession of the land, it also introduces a degree of provisionality about who may claim that identity, and, as we have seen, allows differentiation among groups who shared a common spatial heritage.

RECONFIGURING SPACE IN THE SECOND TEMPLE
PERIOD

The growth of the Diaspora, and its relationship with Jerusalem and Judaea, offered further challenges to relating identity to space, in experience as well as in ideology. Some have tried to argue that ideas of exile were inherent in any understanding of the Diaspora: to think of a dispersion was to recognize the one who dispersed them and the reasons for this (Deut. 28. 25

---

[33] See B. M. Bokser, 'Approaching Sacred Space', *HTR* 78 (1985), 279–99.

[34] On this and on what follows see C. J. Roetzel, '*Oikoumene* and the Limits of Pluralism in Alexandrian Judaism and Paul', in J. A. Overman and R. MacLennan, *Diaspora Jews and Judaism: Essays in Honor of, and in Dialogue with, A. Thomas Kraabel* (Atlanta, Ga.: Scholars Press, 1992), 163–82.

[35] See P. Frederiksen, 'Judaism, the Circumcision of Gentiles, and Apocalyptic Hope: Another Look at Galatians 1 and 2', *JTS* 42 (1991), 532–64.

LXX). Regardless of the actual reasons for migration—demographics, commerce, or the fortunes of war—so, it is argued, the prophetic traditions of the exile invited a sense of guilt and an abiding hope for the return of 'the dispersed of Israel' (διασπορὰ Ἰσραηλ: *Ps. Sol.* 8. 28).[36] 'Diaspora', it is suggested, indicated 'not the geographical distribution but the relationship to their God'.[37] A Jewish 'diaspora identity', we might conclude, would be an identity predicated on failure and incompleteness, spatially determined by absence.

However, the main thrust of scholarship on the Jewish Diaspora over the last forty years, particularly prompted by the archaeologically focused analysis of A. T. Kraabel and supported by Erich Gruen's reading of the literature, has been to emphasize the multilayered but largely successful integration of such communities within their social context.[38] Here, it is the interpretation of the archaeological witness that has played the most persuasive role. Unfortunately, the literary survivals—or, rather, their sparsity—are far more ambiguous in betraying how diaspora existence was interpreted internally, particularly in relation to the scriptural heritage.[39] Such conflicting clues may, indeed, betray a tension between social experience and literary reflection, and even more between Palestinian and diaspora perceptions.

There are, however, some more allusive indications that the relationship of diaspora communities to each other and to the

---

[36] Cf. *Ps. Sol.* 11. 2–6; Tobit 13. 5–13, etc.; so W. C. van Unnik, *Das Selbstverständnis der jüdischen Diaspora in der hellenistisch-römischen Zeit. Aus dem Nachlaß herausgegeben und bearbeitet von* P. W. van der Horst, AGJU 17 (Leiden: Brill, 1993).

[37] van Unnik, *Selbstverständnis*, 165.

[38] Kraabel's unpublished thesis has been highly influential ('Judaism in Western Asia Minor under the Roman Empire with a Preliminary Study of the Jewish Community at Sardis', D.Th. thesis (Harvard University, Cambridge, Mass., 1968), as has his subsequent writing, e.g. 'The Roman Diaspora: Six Questionable Assumptions'; see the various works by Gruen in the bibliography, and, most recently, *Diaspora: Jews amidst Greeks and Romans* (Cambridge, Mass.: Harvard University Press, 2002).

[39] For a positive evaluation, see Gruen, *Diaspora*; on the other side, J. M. Scott, 'Exile and the Self-Understanding of Diaspora Jews', in Scott, *Exile*, 173–218, emphasizes the hope of return in a number of texts, and raises the possibility of an eschatological motif in the Trajanic revolt.

land of Israel could pose some difficulties for self-definition. We might think, for example, of the 'letter' of Baruch, purportedly informing the nine and a half tribes of the destruction of Zion, and probably to be dated after the destruction of 70 CE: Baruch reminds them that 'all we the twelve tribes are bound by one bond inasmuch as we are born of one father', and he urges them to 'remember the law and Zion, and the holy land and your brethren, and the covenant of your fathers, and forget not the festivals and the sabbaths' (*2 Bar.* 78. 4; 84. 8).[40] Similar are the words put by Josephus into the mouth of Joshua addressing the Gilead tribes (= Josh. 22. 25): 'This kinship between us does not own any boundary. Do not regard us as others (ἑτέρους) and not as Hebrews because this river is between us; we are all Abraham's whether living here or there' (*Ant.* V. 1. 25 (97)). In Philo's account of the same moment the even greater authority of Moses is invoked: he fears that the two tribes may claim superiority and evade the need to endure the wars the others must face: 'it is for the sake of the whole that the parts are thought worthy of any inheritance at all' (*Mos.* I. 59 (324)).[41] Given that both Josephus and Philo were writing within diasporic contexts we may hear in this a response to the Diaspora and to its relation to the troubled land of promise: narratives of the past are being used to create an imagined geography where what divides is only a river. Moreover, Philo had experienced 'from the other side' the perceived tie between land and the worship of its gods during the troubles in Alexandria under Flaccus, when the Jews long established there suddenly found themselves called 'foreigners and aliens' (*Flacc.* 8 (53–4)). Josephus, too, rewriting Num. 25, has the Midianite women assert that since the young men they have seduced have come to their country, they should worship their gods, 'or seek another "*oikumene*" (οἰκουμένη), in which they could live in isolation according to their own laws' (*Ant.* IV. 6. 8 (137–8)): is this *oikumene* another 'world'—an impossibility—or another 'land to inhabit'—a recognition of what Judaea alone could provide?

A different strategy is at play when some diaspora texts en-

---

[40] This is treating the final form of the text as a unity; see further M. F. Whitters, *The Epistle of Second Baruch: A Study in Form and Message*, JSP.SS 42 (Sheffield: Sheffield Academic Press, 2003).

[41] For this episode, see the introduction to Ch. 5.

deavour to make the land, and, more specifically, Jerusalem and the Temple, familiar to those who might never directly experience it. *Aristeas* constructs for such readers a world where Eleazar, High Priest of Jerusalem, can correspond on equal terms with a Ptolemy of Egypt, while the fertility of the land and the civilization of its chief city can be readily compared with those of Alexandria (*Arist.* 105–19). Jerusalem is described as in the midst of Judaea on a high summit, with the Temple at the highest point, protected by a citadel that would ensure that no stranger or enemy force could enter it (83–91; 100–4). No doubt this is the language of hyperbole, but not so extravagant that it would fail to help Jews living at a distance and rarely—if ever—visiting to feel, if not at home there, then at least possessors of a pride of place, much as do literary accounts of Rome, as we have seen.[42] At the same time, this in no way undermines the whole thrust of *Aristeas*, which is to legitimate the distinctive character of diaspora life in Alexandria.[43]

When the language becomes more utopian, as in the *Fifth Sibylline*'s description of the 'godlike heavenly race of the blessed Jews who dwell around the city of God at the centre of the earth', and whose land alone shall bear ambrosial honey and milk (*Sib. V*, ll. 247–85), the inescapable contrast with the devastation of land and Temple in the war of 66–70 CE (ll. 394–410) spurns the implicit challenge to identity made by the latter; the certainty of eschatological hope reaffirms that 'he has destroyed every city from its foundations . . . and the city which God loved he made more radiant than the stars . . . and he set it as the jewel of the world and made a temple . . . in size of many furlongs, with a giant tower touching the very clouds and seen of all' (ll. 418–32). Here place is constitutive of identity, but it is a constructed idea of place, drawing on ancient myths and held in the face of grimmer realities.

Unsurprisingly, Philo offers a very different transformation of place: while indulging in a eulogistic representation of Jerusalem and the Temple, he never quite allows his readers to know whether their feet are firmly on the ground or are transported to the realm

---

[42] See above n. 9.
[43] So also Ps.-Hecataeus according to B. Bar-Kochva, *Pseudo-Hecataeus On the Jews: Legitimizing the Jewish Diaspora* (Berkeley, Calif.: University of California Press, 1996).

of spiritual signification; it is right that there be a Temple made by hands, yet it offers tranquillity and the test of true devotion to God for an ill-defined universal influx of worshippers (*Spec. Leg.* I. 12–14 (66–76)).[44] The eschatological hope of the return to Jerusalem and of the rebuilding of ruined cities constitutes an appeal to those who 'had forsaken their national and hereditary customs', but it is reconciliation with God that it promises more than a recovery of the people (*Praem.* 29 (165–8)).

The development of the language of race and citizenship in the Hellenistic period allows for a different construction of the tie with the land.[45] In the Maccabean literature, and also in Josephus's *Antiquities*, the appeal to possession of and the right to preserve native laws or customs draws on the privilege appropriate to possession of an ancestral land, πατρίς; such an appeal would locate the Jews, even within the Diaspora, among the recognized ethnic groups of the Hellenistic, and particularly of the Roman, world.[46] Yet the development of the language of citizenship or polity, πολιτεία or πολίτευμα, also makes possible a distancing from the land, since it is evoked even when possession of the land is no longer feasible or desirable.[47] Josephus's eulogy of the Jewish 'constitution' in his refutation of Apion is studiously careful to present a community defined not by race or land but by law and way of life; even the 'one Temple of the one God' should be 'common to all people', with never a hint of its location (*c. Apion.* II. 23 (193)).[48]

Such apologetics might offer a sense of identity not only for those in the Diaspora but also for converts. This would be even more the case when Philo interprets the patriarchs as the wise whose homeland is the heavenly regions and who are but

---

[44] On the importance of Jerusalem for Philo see Mendelson, *Philo's Jewish Identity*, 17–21.

[45] Cf. further below, Ch. 8, on race.

[46] Where 1 Maccabees appeals more to 'the fathers', 2 Maccabees, followed by 4 Maccabees, makes much of the terminology of 'native land' (πατρίς) and 'ancestral' (customs, etc.) (πάτριος); cf. Josephus, *Ant.* XIV 10. 2, 6 (194, 216); see Kippenberg, 'Die jüdischen Überlieferungen'.

[47] Again, developed by 2 and 4 Maccabees.

[48] εἰς ναὸς ἑνὸς θεοῦ . . . κοινὸς ἁπάντων κοινοῦ θεοῦ ἁπάντων. See C. Gerber, *Ein Bild des Judentums für Nichtjuden von Flavius Josephus: Untersuchungen zu seiner Schrift Contra Apionem*, AGJU 40 (Leiden: Brill, 1997), 344–52. See further below, pp. 243–5.

sojourners on the earth (*Conf.* 17 (78–82); cf. *Somn.* I. 10 (52)). Similarly, in the *Testament of Levi*, the one who knows the Law of God will never be a 'stranger', and wisdom will be their πατρίς (homeland), even in an alien land (*T. Levi* 13. 3–8). The congeniality of such views and of the vision of the whole as constituting a single city (Philo, *Deus Imm.* 36 (173–6)), in a world of Stoic sympathies and of the expanded horizons of Hellenism and of the Roman Empire, is evident; we have already seen their use to validate other exiles.[49] But not all would see it so: Tacitus describes converts to Judaism as having learned 'to cast off their native country' (*Hist.* V. 5). Here we are reminded of the swift dispatch with which Lucian also undermined the Stoic cosmopolitan idealism that had been espoused by Hermotinus but that could only be achieved by abandoning the prior commitments of native country, children, and parents.[50] Indeed, Philo himself had condemned those allegorists who behave 'as if they were living solitarily . . . and had no knowledge of any city', and who so fail in the duty to preserve their 'established customs' (*Migr. Abr.* 16 (89–90)).[51] Both impulses towards, and deep anxieties about, the dissolution of an identity based on place in the redrawn map of the contemporary world were inevitable for all implicated in that redrawing.

REWRITING THE LAND

We have already seen how the scriptural traditions of Jerusalem and the Land could be embraced in any such redrawing, retaining their focality as conceived space even for those who might never order life, or even live there. The rewritings of place that we have traced in *2 Baruch*, *4 Ezra*, or the *Testaments of the Twelve Patriarchs* were reread anew by their later Christian inheritors.[52] We may not always be able to trace such rereadings,

[49] See above, p. 215 and n. 18.

[50] Lucian, *Hermotinus*, 22–4; 84.

[51] On the tensions between a cosmopolitanism and the tendencies towards a ghetto mentality in the drawing of Jewish identity even in Philo, see Roetzel, 'Oikoumene', 174–9.

[52] The different rereadings of the historical rewritings in these texts are discussed in Ch. 3.

but we can map, as an example, the influence of *Jubilees* on the source behind Ps.-Clement, *Recognitions* 27–71.[53] That Judaea lies in the middle portion of the earth, Shem's inheritance, is reaffirmed; yet here the ultimate purpose of Moses' establishment of a place where alone they could sacrifice was in anticipation of the time when the faithful would learn that God does not require any sacrifice: devastation of the land followed whenever the people observed sacrifices, restoration when they observed the law without sacrifice—because they were in exile! (*Rec.* 30; 37). Restoration to the land thus becomes the prize for the 'new' faithful who will respond to God's final emissary.

Among other Christian writers Jerusalem and the Land retain their power as part of the transformations of eschatological hope.[54] For Justin Martyr the land recently ravaged by the Romans is identified as 'the land of the Jews', its devastation and that of Jerusalem being the just judgement of its people by God (*Apol.* 47. 1); yet the prophetic anticipations of the coming of the Gentiles to a Jerusalem 'no longer suffering war because of the lawlessnesses of the peoples' are even now being fulfilled (*Dial.* 24. 3). Beyond this, like a number of other writers, Justin also holds out an ultimate expectation of a millennial kingdom in Jerusalem for 'those who believe in our Christ'.[55]

It has been suggested that Paul's eschatological vision also includes Christ's reign as Messiah in a restored Jerusalem (1 Cor. 15. 20–8).[56] This is, at the most, implicit, and a more explicit reinterpretation of the scriptural traditions of place appears in the 'allegorical' application of Hagar to 'the present Jerusalem', and of Sarah to 'the Jerusalem above, and she is our mother' (Gal. 4. 22–7). It remains unclear whether this represents a spiritualization of the idea of Jerusalem, and so a denial of any historical reference, or whether it still anticipates

[53] On this see Jones, *Ancient Jewish Christian Source*, 138–9; Scott, *Geography*, 97–125, who argues for the mediation of Luke-Acts. For a different reuse of the tradition, see the *Apocalypse of Adam* V. 72. 15–73. 28.

[54] See W. Horbury, 'Land, Sanctuary and Worship', in J. Barclay and J. Sweet (eds.), *Early Christian Thought in its Jewish Context* (Cambridge: Cambridge University Press, 1996), 207–24, 219; R. Wilken, *The Land Called Holy: Palestine in Christian History and Thought* (New Haven, Conn.: Yale University Press, 1992), 55–62.

[55] *Dial.* 81, citing as his authority the Johannine Apocalypse (cf. Rev. 20. 4).

[56] Horbury, 'Land', 220.

a renewed Jerusalem to come.[57] Does Jerusalem still provide a defining point of reference, at least in Paul's construction of identity for his Gentile Galatian readers? In its historical context our answer might have to be shaped by some guess as to the alternative identity Galatians *de*constructs, in as much as many have supposed that Paul is throughout mounting a defence of his Gospel against opponents from, or those with a more exalted view of, a Jerusalem-based, and so, presumably, a Jerusalem-affirmative, ideology. That Paul retained a conviction about the eschatological role of Jerusalem can be supported by his concern for the collection for 'the saints' there; but there is little else in his letters to suggest that he wanted to give his communities any sense of their rooting in the city, still less in 'the Land'.[58] Indeed, although they are to see themselves as recipients not just of the promises to Abraham, but also of the 'inheritance', the Gentiles are not coming to the land, but the land to the Gentiles (Gal. 3. 14, 18; Rom. 4. 13–14); and, ultimately, it is Christ who becomes the referent of all these categories.[59]

A very different response is offered by the Letter to the Hebrews, where the scriptural theme of the Tabernacle is recast by contrastive application 'to heaven itself'; here the traditions of 'entering his rest', the promised land, are reinterpreted, and the author can assure his readers that they 'have approached the mount Zion and the city of the living God, the heavenly Jerusalem' (Heb. 3. 11–4. 11; 9. 24; 12. 22). If, as often suggested, the letter is written to those tempted to revert to a Jerusalem-focused loyalty, particularly by the calls for patriotism in the period before or after the first revolt, we could see here a radical recasting of a sense of space and so of self. An analogous situation might be reflected by the *Letter of Barnabas*'s attack against any hope for 'the city or the Temple or the people of Israel'; instead

---

[57] The latter is the argument of Horbury, 'Land', 221–2, although he does not set his interpretation within an understanding of the letter as a whole.

[58] For a recent discussion of the collection see A. J. Wedderburn, 'Paul's Collection: Chronology and History', *NTS* 48 (2002), 95–110.

[59] See P. Bilde, 'JESUS AND PAUL: A Methodological Essay in Two Cases of Religious Innovation in the Context of Centre-Periphery Relations', in P. Bilde *et al.* (eds.), *Centre and Periphery in the Hellenistic World* (Aarhus: Aarhus University Press, 1993), 316–38, who argues that Paul reinterprets the role of Jerusalem as spiritual centre by that of (the heavenly) Christ or Jerusalem.

it reapplies the language of Temple as well as the promise of 'the good land' to the readers (*Barn.* 16; 6).⁶⁰ Yet when Melito later declares that 'the Jerusalem below was precious but now is without honour because of the Jerusalem above', rhetorical antithesis seems to be more in play than any real challenge to competing claims to possession of place (*Peri Pascha*, ll. 290–300 (§45)).

This is reinforced rather than undermined by Melito's innovatory journey 'to the East', to 'the place of proclamation and event'.⁶¹ All that he gained there, and perhaps all that he hoped to gain, seems to have been knowledge of the 'books of the old covenant'. Only in the following century, beyond our timeframe, was Christian pilgrimage to develop, and only in the fourth century did, so far as our texts reveal, the 'discovery' of holy places offer 'a way of "renewing the image" of what had happened, that is re-presenting the saving events of the past in the present, of allowing believers through "memory" to "become spectators of history"'.⁶² Then, as Robert Wilken has shown, the land would offer a means of creating a continuity between biblical and Christian experience, although, as ever, this could be construed in a rich variety of ways.⁶³ A startling example of this comes from the fourth (?) century when the martyr Conon, asked where he comes from and what is his race, answers, 'I am of the city of Nazareth of Galilee, and my kinship is with Christ'.⁶⁴ Yet that lies ahead: there is little before this to suggest that believers in Jesus found in the geographical setting of his life a sense of place.

⁶⁰ *Barn.* 16. 4 refers to an expectation of the rebuilding of the Temple: Horbury, 'Land', 219, suggests that *Barnabas* seeks 'to quell Christian excitement' at this prospect.

⁶¹ Eusebius, *HE* IV. 26. 14, τοῦ τόπου γενόμενος ἔνθα ἐκηρύχθη καὶ ἐπράχθη.

⁶² Wilken, *Land*, 82–91, with the quotation from p. 91 where Wilken cites Asterius of Amasea, *Hom.* 9. 2. On memory and history in the shaping of identity see above, Ch. 3. In emphasizing the textual evidence I am not passing judgement on the question of veneration of sites by early Jewish-Christians.

⁶³ See G. Bowman, 'Christian Ideology and the Image of a Holy Land: The Place of Jerusalem in Pilgrimage in the various Christianities', in J. Eade and M. Sallnow (eds.), *Contesting the Sacred: The Anthropology of Christian Pilgrimage* (London: Routledge, 1991), 98–121, 99–100, particularly with reference to pilgrims' experience of the land.

⁶⁴ *Mart. Conon*, IV. 1, πόλεως εἰμι ἐγώ Ναζαρὲθ τῆς Γαλιλαιας, συγγένεια δὲ μοί ἐστιν προς Χριστόν. See Lieu, ' "I am a Christian" ', 215 n. 18 for the argument that this is not to be taken literally.

Certainly, place is significant for the Gospel writers, not just because the Jesus stories were inevitably geographically located, but because of the way that they use place and space to shape narrative and meaning.[65] Yet the creative impact of this for their readers' sense of their own appropriation of the story is less evident. Mark's enigmatic ending points to Galilee as the place where 'you shall see him', but interpreters are divided as to whether or not this locates for us the Markan community, and there is little sense that Galilee will continue as an irreplaceable point of reference for future generations.[66] For Matthew, Jesus is not just historically but also geographically embedded within the prophetic scriptural traditions (Matt. 2. 5–6, Bethlehem; 2. 23, Nazareth; 3. 12–17, Galilee; 11. 20–4, the cities of Galilee and their counterparts; 21. 5, Zion);[67] yet, as the closing verses of the Gospel make clear, this gives the land no privilege for the future (28. 18–19). We may begin to ask, rather, whether geography is being used to undermine an identity predicated on the land: John's anticipation of worship 'neither on this mountain nor in Jerusalem . . . but in spirit and in truth' (John 4. 21–3) could suggest this; that Jesus by his own testimony could expect no honour in his πατρίς (4. 44) counters all those exhortations to put first fidelity to one's native land and customs, even within the Jewish and Christian traditions.

To trace further such transformations of Jewish covenantal spatial categories, not just of the land and Jerusalem but also of the Temple and of the Kingdom, through spiritualization, and through Christological or ecclesiological categories, would become an exercise in mapping theological trajectories.[68] Such

[65] For a different reading in relation to the historical Jesus see H. Moxnes, 'Placing Jesus of Nazareth: Towards a Theory of Place in the Study of the Historical Jesus', in Wilson and Desjardins, *Text and Artifact*, 158–75, who lays emphasis on Jesus's relationship with non-elite space in the villages of Galilee.

[66] See H. Kee, *Community of the New Age* (London: SCM, 1977), 100–6 (locating Mark in Syria); also S. Freyne, 'Locality and Doctrine: Mark and John Revisited', in idem (ed.), *Galilee and Gospels: Collected Essays*, WUNT 125 (Tübingen: Mohr, 2000), 287–98.

[67] The last, from Zech. 9. 9, is also found in John 12. 15. On Matt. 2. 5–6 see B. Green, *Matthew, Poet of the Beatitudes*, JSNT.SS 203 (Sheffield: Sheffield Academic Press, 2001), 50–3.

[68] See W. D. Davies, *The Gospel and Land: Early Christian and Jewish Territorial Doctrine* (Berkeley, Calif.: University of California Press, 1980);

ideas, certainly, are part of the appropriation of the scriptural
themes of place, and inevitably involve a degree of disassociation
from real space. Yet they are more easily studied as theological
transformations than as providing new senses of place in ways
that would construct a cohesive identity. It is particularly difficult to discern precisely how far the scripturally inspired hope
of 'a city to come' (Heb. 13. 14), or of a restored Jerusalem, might
offer a foundational sense of place.[69]

THE CHURCH IN CORINTH / SOJOURNING IN THE WORLD

Perhaps more effective would be the appropriation of the language of sojourning (παροικία) from the pentateuchal traditions,
again echoing similar strategies in other Hellenistic Jewish
writers.[70] In Hebrews such language apparently serves to direct
the readers away from any other native land (πατρίς) than the
heavenly one, while also claiming that this was the πατρίς and
the city to which Abraham himself aspired, acknowledging that
'they were strangers and sojourners upon the earth' (Heb. 11.
13–16, quoting Gen. 23. 4; 24. 37).[71] Peter puts this tradition
to a different use: although he applies to his readers the Sinai
language of the chosen people, albeit without reference to the
promise of the gift of land (1 Pet. 2. 9–10), he addresses them as
'elect sojourners of the diaspora' and as 'transients' or 'aliens' (1.
1, 17; 2. 11). Whether such language locates their true home in
heaven, as traditionally interpreted, or whether it gives positive
value to their existing social experience of alienation, which their
Christian allegiance in turn both exacerbated yet also offered
compensation for, it still effectively problematizes their relation-

---

W. Brueggemann, *The Land*, Overtures to Biblical Theology (London: SPCK,
1978), 167–80; Horbury, 'Land', 207–8.

[69] For a positive reading see Wilken, *Land*, 52–64.

[70] See above, p. 222; on the subsequent history of this imagery see J. Roldanus,
'Références patristiques au "Chrétien-étranger" dans les trois premiers Siècles',
in *Lectures Anciennes de la Bible*, Cahiers de Biblia Patristica, 1. Centre d'analyse
et de documentation Patristiques (Strasburg: Palais Universitaire, 1987), 27–52.

[71] Heb. 11. 13 interprets γῆ = 'land' in Gen. 24. 37 (LXX) as 'the earth'.

ship with their social and political surroundings.[72] How far this would undermine any local allegiance is less patent, since 1 Peter, none the less, exhorts them to accept 'human institutions' (2. 13), illustrated through conventional codes of conduct.[73]

Yet, if in such transformations of place we find ourselves in not unfamiliar territory, Paul apparently effects a more radical reconfiguration of spatial identity. In addressing his readers at Corinth as 'the church (assembly) of God which is *in Corinth* . . . with all those who call on the name of our Lord Jesus Christ *in every place*' (1 Cor. 1. 2), he gives those gathered an inalienable significance in that particular location (ἐν Κορίνθῳ), even while tying them into a nexus that has no named geographical limits (ἐν παντὶ τόπῳ). While this need not mean that ἐκκλησία ('assembly') denotes a specific place for Paul,[74] his deep anxieties about disunity and inappropriate behaviour when they 'come together in assembly' (ἐν ἐκκλησίᾳ) does accord paramount value to their actual localized communal gathering and not just to the fact of their theoretical association (11. 17–22; 14. 33–5); moreover, it gives that communal gathering a 'public' significance that opposes it to the 'private' home in which they actually met.[75] In turn, the potentially universal reference is derivative from the local: 'those who call on the name of our Lord' will, it is assumed, be similarly located in specific places; but the local has no ultimate autonomy: 'as in all the assemblies of the saints' (14. 33; cf. 4. 17; 7. 17).[76]

However, alongside this affirmation of place we should also set the qualification implicit in the negative valency that Paul gives to 'the world' (ὁ κόσμος) as that to which believers do not,

[72] On this see Elliott, *Home for the Homeless*.

[73] ἀθρωπίνη κτίσις, itself difficult to translate; on this see pp. 168–9 above; Balch, *Let Wives be Submissive*; R. Feldmeier, 'The "Nation" of Strangers: Social Contempt and its Theological Interpretation in Ancient Judaism and Early Christianity', in Brett, *Ethnicity*, 240–70, finds in 1 Peter a basis for commitment to one's own land.

[74] The conventional translation, 'church', is misleading; we cannot here discuss whether the term has its roots in the biblical 'congregation of Israel' (= MT קהל), or in the Greek civic assembly. What is most important is that Paul is not drawing on any existing self-designation of Jewish diaspora communities.

[75] See above, pp. 198–9.

[76] Contrast Bilde, 'JESUS AND PAUL', 326–7, who gives conceptual priority to the universal.

properly, belong.[77] Strictly speaking, this does not belong to a study of place, for 'world' is for Paul a structural rather than a geographical term:[78] his acknowledgement that they cannot 'depart from the world' entirely (1 Cor. 5. 10) is a rejection of a 'ghetto-like withdrawal from the wider society', but it also draws on the apocalyptic denigration of the present age as 'this world' or 'age'.[79] Yet Paul's distancing of his readers from 'the world', a theme that will become a recurring thread in subsequent thought, can never be entirely divorced from questions of commitment to the local. When he goes on to denounce their recourse to the local courts, and when he constructs such behaviour as accepting the judgement of the unrighteous, of the world (6. 1–2), he is turning their compatriots into 'the other', and creating for those to whom he writes a new alternative 'space'.[80]

Writing to Corinth a generation or so after Paul, the author of *1 Clement* evinces a striking contesseration of some of the spatial locators we have explored so far. The local congregation is no longer 'the church of God in Corinth' but 'the church of God sojourning in Corinth' or 'in Rome'—the metaphor of sojourning is drawn from 1 Peter but here it has been recontextualized.[81] Such language fits well a repeated exhortation to 'go forth', in faith and obedience: Abraham leaves what is but 'an insignificant land ($\gamma \hat{\eta}$)' (*1 Clem.* 10. 1); but there is no challenge to patriotism here, for God, as heavenly king, gives authority to mortals (namely, to those who already hold it: 61). Exercising the 'citizenship of God' offers reassurance to those who for the sake of peace may have to leave the local community—they are bound to find a home elsewhere because 'the earth is the Lord's' (54). Even so, the readers should be proud to belong to, and to maintain, the reputation of 'the most stable and ancient church of Corinth' (47. 6).

The language of sojourning is used to very different effect in the

---

[77] The negative value given to 'the world' is particularly marked in 1 Corinthians; see E. Adams, *Constructing the World: A Study in Paul's Cosmological Language*, SNTW (Edinburgh: T&T Clark, 2000).

[78] Paul declares that 'the world has been crucified' to him, and he 'to the world' (Gal. 6. 14).

[79] Adams, *Constructing*, 126.

[80] On the world as 'other' see below, p. 294.

[81] The influence of 1 Peter is betrayed by the form of the greeting.

Martyrdom of Polycarp, written from 'the church of God sojourning at Smyrna to the church of God sojourning in Philomelium and all the sojournings (παροικίαι) in every place of the holy and catholic church'.[82] Here, any local allegiance is sharply qualified by the community itself becoming one among many temporary resting places, whose true identity is found in their totality ('all') and universality ('in every place'). In the same way, the local events—and, specifically, Polycarp's death—are located in that broader sphere by the prayers he offers for 'the churches throughout the world', among which would be the recipients of the letter.[83] This sense of detachment from a specific locality may be intensified by the contrastive description of the hostile crowd as being 'of the Gentiles and Jews *living* (κατοικούντων) in Smyrna' (12. 2).[84] A yet more explicit challenge to the mundane world is mounted by the precise dating of events by the offices held by locally based authorities—'while Philip of Tralles was chief priest and Statius Quadratus proconsul'—which is then immediately subverted by 'and while our Lord Jesus Christ was reigning for eternity' (21).

With these we should contrast Ignatius's very different construction of the significance of the local community. Echoing Paul once more, he addresses 'the church which is in Ephesus', but he describes it as 'predetermined before time for an abiding glory in every respect' (*Eph.* praef.). They are, indeed, 'Ephesian Christians' (Ἐφεσίοι οἱ χριστιανοί), yet the sense of place here is determined not by the status of Ephesus within the province of Asia, but by its heritage that stretches back to Paul and to the other apostles (11–12). It is the local community that represents the blessings of the sanctuary, so that wilful separation from it brings judgement on oneself (5. 2; compare *Magn.* 7. 2; *Trall.* 7. 2). However, the local community is itself determined by the presence of the bishop, who, as it were in microcosm, represents the unity of all local communities in Jesus: 'for where the bishop

---

[82] See also the *Letter of Polycarp*, Praef., 'Polycarp and the elders with him to the church of God sojourning at Philippi'; here, however, the theme of sojourning is not sustained. [83] *Mart. Poly.* 5. 1; 8. 1; cf. 19. 2.
[84] On this description see also above, pp. 1–2. So also, F. W. Weidmann, ' "To Sojourn" or "To Dwell"?: Scripture and Identity in the *Martyrdom of Polycarp*', in Bobertz and Brakke, *Reading in Christian Communities*, 29–40, 30–3.

is there should the congregation be, just as wherever Jesus Christ is there is the catholic church' (*Smyrn.* 8. 2). As we shall see, it is particularly through the person of the bishop that Ignatius holds together the inalienability of the local with the constitutive nature of the 'universal'. Moreover, this strong sense of the embeddedness of local identity does not lead to any sense of also belonging to the wider structures of society: of these we are given no sense. Ignatius is a prime example of a literary construction of identity that may have been sharply divorced from the experience of those to whom he wrote, but that was to become foundational for later readers. For him, the determinative place of belonging is the local community, with its sense of interconnection with the past as well as with other similarly located communities; the primary boundaries are those of the local community which, at the same time, replicate those of the 'catholic church'. Yet this does not lead to a sense of inculturation within the local society; in fact, the opposite—outside is an undifferentiated world.[85]

However, it was not only Ignatius's opponents who would have demurred at his elevation of the local; Justin dismisses his interrogator's attempt to discover where they meet: 'Do you really think we all meet together? Certainly not: the God of the Christians is not constrained by place, but, being invisible, fills heaven and earth, and is worshipped and glorified by believers everywhere' (*Mart. Just.* 3). The claim to universality is a common one, anticipated already in the mission charges of the Jesus tradition (Matt. 28. 18–19; Acts 1. 8). If it were to be more than theological aspiration it would demand acknowledging the tension between universal and local; their God might not be constrained by place, but were the Christians? How did their map correspond to the other prevalent maps of their day which dealt with a not dissimilar tension?

The *Epistle to Diognetus* charts a devious route between affirmation and denial:[86] Christians 'dwell in Greek and barbarian cities, as allotted to each, and follow the local customs . . . They live in their own native countries (ἴδιαι πατρίδες) but as sojourners'; in fact, 'every foreign land is their πατρίς (native land), and every

---

[85] This will become evident in discussion of 'the other' (Ch. 9).

[86] See J. M. Lieu, 'The Forging of Christian Identity and the *Letter to Diognetus*', in *Neither Jew nor Greek?*, 171–89; also below, p. 263.

πατρίς foreign' (*Diog.* 5. 4–5). Yet, we go on to learn, their citizenship is exercised in heaven, they are but passing time on earth (5. 9). Christians are scattered through the cities of the world, but, like the soul in the body, they are not constrained by the world (6. 2–3). This is the voice of an apologist, seeking both to deny any subversive potential in difference, and at the same time to affirm its positive value. The effectiveness of such an assertion for outside observers is not our concern here, but for 'insiders' it would surely allow them a framework within which to explore how far they might sustain their local loyalties. There is in *Diognetus* no worldwide church to claim allegiance, only others sharing the same ambivalences of daily life as they themselves.

Beyond our period, Tertullian puts it more directly, combatting the treatment of Christians by the crowds as 'outsiders', and reflecting the urban-centredness that all took for granted: 'We are your kind'; 'we are not Brahmins or Indian gymnosophists, woodland-dwellers and exiles from life' (*Apol.* 18. 4; 42. 1). In extravagant hyperbole he claims to belong to a race that covers the whole world; if Christians had withdrawn, the Romans would be stunned by the deathly silence of a deserted globe (37. 4–6).[87] Indeed, even peoples beyond Roman sway belong to the realm of Christians.[88] In a world of many such extravagant claims to a global identity, the Apologists out-claimed them all—according to Aristides the inhabited world is sustained by the prayers of Christians alone (*Apol.* 16. 6). We should not read this merely as a self-deluding assumption of numerical superiority, nor as predicated on divine omnipresence alone: in an imagined geography the world belongs to the Christians—and so, polemically, not to the Jewish diaspora communities, despite their probable numerical and social superiority (Justin, *Dial.* 117), and not even to Roman imperial might.[89] Certainly this is a theological polemic, but it also shapes an identity that refuses to be spatially marginalized, even, or perhaps especially, when they found themselves physically excluded not just from centres of civic identity,

---

[87] On the extravagance of the claim, see Hopkins, 'Christian Number', 188–92.

[88] *adv. Iud.* 7. 4–9; on this see G. Gilbert, 'The List of Nations in Acts 2: Roman Propaganda and the Lukan Response', *JBL* 121 (2002), 497–529, 508.

[89] Gilbert, 'List of Nations', traces this argument back to Acts.

'houses and baths and markets, but even from being seen in any place at all' (Eusebius, *HE* V. 1. 5).

Yet, speaking in another voice or genre, they recognize a different reality: so, Tertullian can also congratulate Christians in prison for having left the world (*Mart.* 2). Clement of Alexandria can both negotiate the exigencies of daily social integration, such as mixed bathing, and also assert that 'we have no πατρίς on the earth' (*Paed.* III. 8. 41). For Hermas it is simple: 'You . . . live in a foreign land; your city is far from this city . . . why then do you prepare fields, and costly appointments and houses and inconsequential buildings? The one who prepares such things for this city cannot return to their own' (*Sim.* I. 1–2). Here the eschatological framework is implicit; in *6 Ezra* it becomes explicit: 'Prepare for battle, and in the midst of calamities be like strangers on the earth' (16. 40);[90] there follows a long catalogue of examples—'let the one who does business be like one who will not make a profit, and let the one who builds a house be like one who will not live in it' (16. 42). Participation in society is denied even while it is acknowledged. From a very different angle but no less unequivocal in its language of spatial alienation is the *Gospel of Thomas* in its exhortation, 'Become passers-by' (42); perhaps already reflecting a contextual distance from an urban self-awareness, Jesus's disciples are like 'little children living in a field that is not theirs' (21).[91]

Would such a denial of place, perhaps like the language of sojourning, construct its own alternative place, never stable, and so produce an alternative identity—potentially in contrast to Ignatius's 'settled' community? In terms of charting a social context for such an alternative identity we might draw on the evidences of ('charismatic') itinerancy in the early church (*Did.* 11–12). How this might intersect with the ascetic impulses discussed earlier that would reject other forms of social engagement then becomes a teasing question.[92] Yet, no less teasing is the question how the suspension of a sense of settled space shaped those who were dislocated neither by ascetic lifestyle nor by the alienation

---

[90] 'advenae terrae': this is extant only in Latin but 'advena' elsewhere translates πάροικος or παρεπίδημος.

[91] i.e. the body or the world; on 'the body' for *Thomas* see above, pp. 205–6.

[92] G. Theissen, *Social Reality and the Early Christians: Theology, Ethics, and the World of the New Testament* (Minneapolis, Minn.: Fortress, 1992), 33–59.

of persecution. It would be attractive here to draw on studies
of pilgrimage as offering a model of sojourning. Pilgrimage has
been seen as encapsulating the experience of liminality, and so
as enabling a sense of community between those whose structured identities in their place of origin and return would have
been sharply divided.[93] The description of pilgrimage by Victor
and Edith Turner as characterized by 'homogenization of status;
simplicity of dress and behaviour; communitas; ordeal; reflection . . . ritualized enactment . . . emergence of the integral person
from multiple personae; movement from a mundane to a sacred
periphery . . .' sits remarkably comfortably alongside the idealism
of Acts 2. 42–7 and its account of the life of the early Jerusalem
community;[94] as such it might reinforce expectations of an egalitarian reciprocity that challenged contemporary hierarchies. Yet
the model appears to be no less idealistic than the application
suggested, whose utopianism we have more than once suspected;
field studies of pilgrimage also suggest that participants bring
to (or from) the experience their own meanings, and that exclu-
siveness may coexist with inclusiveness, something we have also
traced within early Christian self-representation.[95] We cannot
move too readily from space, or place, to style.

'Space and geography serve a powerfully metaphorical role
in the articulation of identity.'[96] What unites and what also
divides our texts lies in their attempt to construct a space to
inhabit through reference to some combination of a number
of fixed co-ordinates—the local community of believers; other
believers elsewhere, whether known in their separate localities or
imagined in their solidarity and universality; a scriptural tradition of place that was at the same time inseparable from the richly
fertile traditions of alienation and of transience; confidence in
the universal reach of God's sovereignty; yet also the immediate

---

[93] So esp. V. Turner and E. Turner, *Image and Pilgrimage in Christian Culture*
(Oxford: Blackwell, 1978), 3–9.

[94] The quotation but not the comparison comes from Turner and Turner,
Image and Pilgrimage, 34.

[95] J. Eade and M. Sallnow, 'Introduction', in Eade and Sallnow, *Contesting
the Sacred*, 1–29; also Cohen, *Symbolic Construction*, 54–6. On the deceptiveness
of utopian images of early Christian community, see the discussion in Ch. 5 on
practice.

[96] Whitmarsh, ' "Greece is the World" ', 279.

surroundings with the neighbours, family, and friends, who are so often faceless or hidden from our gaze; society at large, sometimes, but not always, conceived of as an alien space inhabited by hostile forces, human or supernatural; and articulations of hope and goal that were fixed in the spatial metaphors of Kingdom and heavenly realm. As in so much else the Christians employed the strategies that were already familiar in their world with its own dilemmas of empire, and their efforts reflected many of the ambiguities already inherent in those strategies. Their particular success lay in their ability to hide from subsequent readers the actual space(s) that they inhabited, and to persuade such readers that, 'throughout every city and village, like an over-filled threshing-floor, churches arose, filled with thousands' (Eusebius, *HE* II. 3. 2).

8

The Christian Race

Polycarp's emblematic confession with which we started, 'I am a Christian', affirms what many have assumed to be how Christians understood and presented themselves from the start—whenever that might be. Whereas most of the strategies that we have been exploring might seem to belong to the implicit and functional construction of identity, the use of 'identifying' labels or of exclusive group designators surely constitutes a claim to explicit, external recognition and 'facticity'. No sooner is this said than it can be seen to demand qualification. First, a common distinction that is often made is whether the label is given or is ascribed, whether it is imposed by others outside or is adopted from within. Further, is such labelling provoked by a particular context, perhaps situational or behavioural, or is it based on more general premises? Is it uncontested; or do some reject its ascription to or by others, whether or not they themselves also claim it?

Even these questions are not without ambiguity: groups respond to their categorization by others, particularly but not only by their apparent superiors—indeed, such labelling may generate a group where none previously existed;[1] but a label may also be assigned from outside, even in denigration, and yet be taken up and turned to positive account. Examples of this range from, in recent times, labels such as 'black', or 'dyke', to the 'Quakers' or the 'Assyrian Christians'; these last acquired their name from western Christian missionaries whose purpose was to effect a distinction from 'Nestorians', an implicitly negative label also assigned from outside, but the effect was to stimulate both the construction of a history and the sense of a national and

---

[1] Eriksen, *Ethnicity and Nationalism*, 80–1, on labelling by anthropologists and colonial powers; Wells, *The Barbarians Speak*, 114–21.

not just of a religious identity.[2] In the period with which we are
concerned something similar may have been the case with the
Pharisees, derided by others as 'separatists', but then able self-
consciously to claim the virtue of 'accuracy'.[3] Moreover, where
there is dispute over the ascription of labels, what are the criteria
for legitimacy, and as administered by whom? These further
questions disclose the exercise of power involved in all labelling, as has become particularly familiar from studies of colonial-
ism, and as may have been experienced by anyone answering
the question of origin in a census or application, who has been
faced with labels chosen not by themselves but by the anonymous authorities, and who, perhaps, has been tempted to claim
some power and to tick 'other'.[4] All this should caution us against
merely repeating assertions or acts of labelling that may silence
dissent or drown the voices of the marginalized.

JEWS, ISRAEL, AND HEBREWS

Our concern here is, more narrowly, with the designation
'Christian' (χριστιανός), and, more broadly, with other claims to a
distinct identity within the acknowledged structures of the contemporary world: thus not 'assembly (church)', ἐκκλησία, since
this did not indicate a defined unit, but 'race', 'citizen body',
and, to some extent, bearers of a particular 'piety', recognized
labels of legitimacy. These broader designations will need to be
located within the strategies for self-definition, and definition of
others, in the Graeco-Roman world, but the specific χριστιανός,
a distinctive appellation, is more problematic. For with what
sort of label should it be, or would it have been, allied? To
modern sensitivities, 'Jew' and 'Christian' are the same sort of
designation, at least to the extent that they may be coupled as in
The Council for Christians and Jews or as in Jewish–Christian
Dialogue, but whether these labels would have had the same
parity to ancient ears is much less obvious. Modern sensitivities
also assume that the labels are intrinsically reciprocally exclusive, to the extent that exceptions, those claiming both labels,

---

[2] Al-Rasheed, *Iraqi Assyrian Christians*, 37–40; see Ch. 7 at n. 7.
[3] See A. Baumgarten, 'The Names of the Pharisees', *JBL* 102 (1983), 413–28.
[4] On this see Anderson, *Imagined Communities*, 164–70.

'Jew' *and* 'Christian', present a problematic anomaly requiring special treatment. Without addressing the complex question of Jewish Christianity in the first centuries, a label that is a scholarly one rather than one claimed by the sources,[5] how and when does this exclusivity arise?

Even so, we cannot really discuss what sort of label 'Christian' might be without first asking the same of 'Jew'. To make this assertion is not to presuppose that the former is conceptually derivative from the latter; rather, since ἰουδαῖος (Jew) was already current in the first century of our era, the evident ambiguities of its reference may offer a framework for exploring 'Christian'. For the recognized fuzziness of 'Jew' we may turn again to Cassius Dio's explanation of its geographical reference and origin, and of its extension to others, even of other nations (ἀλλοεθνεῖς), who followed their customs (τὰ νόμιμα), so that the race (τὸ γένος) was even to be found among the Romans (*Hist. Rom.* XXXVII. 17. 8).[6] Similarly, in the first century Ptolemy had explained the difference between Idumaeans and Jews as: 'Jews are those by nature from the beginning (οἱ ἐξ ἀρχῆς φυσικοί); but Idumaeans originally were not Jews but Phoenicians and Syrians. Yet when defeated by them and compelled to be circumcised and to be counted in the nation,[7] and to practise the same customs they were called Jews.' Although often treated as peculiar to the Jews, this fuzziness of reference is not out of place within the ancient world: as we have seen, customs played as significant a role in Graeco-Roman ethnography as did kinship and territory; similarly, the self-appellation 'Hellenes' encompassed members of a variety of 'other nations' and, as a unifying term, functioned on a number of levels, both political and cultural.[8]

---

[5] Among the numerous discussions see A. Segal, 'Jewish Christianity', in H. Attridge and G. Hata (eds.), *Eusebius, Christianity, and Judaism*, SPB 42 (Leiden: Brill, 1992), 326–51; G. Strecker, 'Judenchristentum', *Theologische Realenzyklopädie* vol. xvii (Berlin: de Gruyter, 1988), 310–25.

[6] See above, p. 216 ; cf. also *Hist. Rom.* LXVI. 4, set during Titus's siege of Jerusalem, where the Jewish forces are described as including 'many from there and many from among those of the same practices' (πολλοὶ μὲν αὐτόθεν πολλοὶ δὲ καὶ παρὰ τῶν ὁμοήθων).

[7] συντελεῖν εἰς τὸ ἔθνος: alternatively, 'pay taxes to the nation'; however, ἔθνος is a conjectural emendation of ἔθος (*GLAJJ*, I. 356, §146; the identity of this Ptolemy is disputed).

[8] See above, pp. 105, 150. G. Bowersock, 'The Greek Moses: Confusion

Moreover, in our present discussion it is the literary function of such labels as a self-designation that concerns us more than their use by others—although we shall discover that that literary function may often be one of appropriation and of redefinition. Neither shall we decree whether they were 'really' ethnic or religious, but rather how different modes of categorization are used in the texts themselves.[9]

The use of the term 'Jew', along with the most common alternatives, 'Hebrew' and 'Israel', has been much discussed.[10] Some general conclusions are broadly agreed: 'Jew' is predominantly the outsiders' term, perceived much as Cassius Dio was neatly to encapsulate, centred in Judaea and around Jerusalem, found throughout the known world, characterized by distinctive customs, and incorporating others who adopted these.[11] This is barely challenged by those texts that claim the label for themselves: the term belongs to the post-exilic context, both in the Hebrew Bible/LXX and in Josephus's rewriting, but it is used particularly where there are dealings with outsiders. Despite its etymological association with Judaea, in both Josephus and Philo it can refer unproblematically to groups living elsewhere in the world. There is, however, little in the texts to suggest that it could be claimed by, or that it could be accorded to, converts— the Babylonians' disgusted cry that their king had 'become a Jew' in Bel and the Dragon 28 is hardly evidence to the contrary.[12]

of Ethnic and Cultural Components in Later Roman and Early Byzantine Palestine', in Lapin, *Religious and Ethnic Communities*, 31–48, illustrates well the fuzziness even though he tries to retain a distinctive ethnic identity for the Jews throughout the period, but perhaps his choice of the term 'confusion' betrays expectations alien to the subject and period; see the more nuanced discussion by Lapin, 'Introduction', 18–22; Olster, 'Classical Ethnography'.

[9] Similarly, Buell, 'Rethinking the Relevance'.

[10] A. Arazy, *The Appellations of the Jews (IOUDAIOS, HEBRAIOS, ISRAEL) in the Literature from Alexander to Justinian*, Ph.D. thesis, University Microfilms 78-3061 (New York, 1977); G. Harvey, *The True Israel: Uses of the Names Jew, Hebrew and Israel in Ancient Jewish and Christian Sources*, AGJU 35 (Leiden: Brill, 1996); P. J. Tomson, 'The Names Israel and Jew in Ancient Judaism and in the New Testament', *Bijdragen* 47 (1986), 120–40, 266–89.

[11] On the problem of 'Jew' or 'Judaean', see above Ch. 7 n. 20; for Greek and Roman views see *GLAJJ*.

[12] Ἰουδαῖος γέγονεν ὁ βασιλεύς. Esther 8.17 uses the verb ἰουδαΐζειν (MT hithpael זהד); similarly, Paul condemns Peter for compelling Gentiles to ἰουδαΐζειν, but not 'to become ἰουδαῖοι' (Gal. 2.14).

Here literary texts may well differ from social experience, for studies of epitaphs have suggested that converts did proudly declare themselves 'Jew', and, indeed, perhaps did so more frequently than did those born as Jews.[13] Did those converts find themselves comfortably incorporated into the literary histories 'of the Jews' that they might read, or did the term's use there particularly among outsiders reinforce their parvenu standing?

More interesting are both the silences and the alternatives. While the term 'Jews' is used almost exclusively by Gentiles in 1 Maccabees, it is common and apparently unproblematic in 2 Maccabees, and yet in 4 Maccabees it comes but once, a mocking slur on the oppressor's lips.[14] Although ostensibly addressing the same concerns, apparently a situation of threatened identity, each of these texts articulates that identity differently. For 4 Maccabees the term of honour is 'Hebrew', an archaism and therefore a deliberate evocation of the heroes of the past, as is fitting in a text that hearkens back to the patriarchs.[15] By contrast, for 1 Maccabees the valorific term is 'Israel', which has its own historical resonances, reinforced by the use of ἀλλόφυλοι for their opponents, 'foreigners' but also the LXX's translation for 'Philistines'.[16]

In 2 Maccabees the climax of oppression is reached when 'it was not possible to observe the sabbath or to keep the *ancestral* festivals, or simply to admit to being a Jew (ἰουδαῖον ὁμολογεῖν εἶναι)' (2 Macc. 6. 6). Here, 'to be a Jew' is contextually defined as to live by 'the ancestral laws and . . . by the laws of God' (6. 1), which, it is assumed, are alien to those of the Greeks. It implies a 'constitution', a civic way of life (πολιτεύεσθαι), that can claim both antiquity and legitimacy; if death is demanded it is death for

---

[13] R. Kraemer, 'On the Meaning of the Term "Jew" in Greco-Roman Inscriptions', *HTR* 82 (1989), 35–52, makes a good case for ἰουδαῖος in inscriptions often referring to a proselyte; this also helps explain the rarity of the term, particularly on epitaphs where there was no call to be defensive.

[14] 4 Macc. 5. 7 by Antiochus: 'you do not seem to me to be acting as a philosopher in observing the religion of the Jews'.

[15] 'Hebrew', 4. 11; 5. 2; 9. 5, 18; 12. 7; 16. 15; 17. 9; for the appeal to the patriarchs see 5. 22; 7. 11; 8. 19; 9. 21; 15. 28; 16. 20; 18. 1, 20–3; also 'children of Abraham', 6. 17, 22. In the LXX, largely followed by Josephus, 'Hebrew' is used mainly of the pre-exilic period; although it is used by outsiders with contempt in the Scriptures this does not seem to have effected its later romanticization.   [16] See Ch. 9 at n. 56, and Lieu, 'Not Hellenes', 253.

'the laws, the Temple, the city, the native land, the constitution (πολιτεία)' (13. 14).[17] When we remember that in the Graeco-Roman world to be an *ethnos* was as much a matter of customs as of place of origin, it becomes evident that this should be seen as an ethnic and not as a purely religious self-definition.[18] This is what is both assumed and reinforced by the letter that introduces the book, written from the 'Jewish brethren' (οἱ ἀδελφοί . . . ἰουδαῖοι) in Jerusalem to the 'Jewish brethren in Egypt' and urging them to observe a celebration that had been agreed as for 'the whole nation of the Jews' (1. 1; 2. 16; 10. 8: πᾶν τὸ τῶν ἰουδαίων ἔθνος). Here, in 2 Maccabees, the battle that had been fought for 'Judaism' (ἰουδαϊσμός)—a term apparently newly coined for this purpose—was a battle for maintaining a way of life that belonged to them by heritage, and to their land.[19] In this way 2 Maccabees shapes an identity that owes much to contemporary Hellenistic views of ethnicity, even while on this basis claiming the right to be different, to be an ἔθνος free 'to live according to their ancestral customs' (11. 25).[20]

It was probably outsiders, the Seleucids, who had first categorized the Jews as an ἔθνος;[21] however, 2 Maccabees appropriates that designation but uses it to challenge the consequences of Seleucid control. Other texts do something similar: the claim to be a 'people' belongs to the determination to retain separateness;

---

[17] On the idea of native land in 2 Maccabees, see above, p. 224.

[18] So rightly N. Janowitz, 'Rethinking Jewish Identity in Late Antiquity', in S. Mitchell and G. Greatrex (eds.), *Ethnicity and Culture in Late Antiquity* (London: Duckworth, 2000), 205–19, 208–9; S. Cohen, *Beginnings of Jewishness*, 109–39, speaks of the supplementation of the ethnic by the religious during the Hasmonaean period.

[19] 2 Macc. 2. 21; cf. 8. 1; 14. 38. The context does not support a religious definition of the term 'Judaism', despite the arguments of Y. Amir, 'The Term Ἰουδαισμός', *Immanuel* 14 (1982), 34–41; that it offers an outside view of the Jews as a 'separate entity in the Hellenistic world' is argued by Tomson, 'Names', 134; however, while 2 Maccabees does affirm such a separatist perspective, in 4 Maccabees the term itself does not carry the same associations: perhaps there it is implicitly the outsider's view, a label for their 'foul philosophy' (4 Macc. 4. 26; 5. 11; cf. above, n. 14).

[20] See above, p. 224; also, M. Himmelfarb, 'Judaism and Hellenism in 2 Maccabees', *Poetics Today* 19 (1998), 19–40; Kippenberg, 'Die jüdischen Überlieferungen'.

[21] So E. Bickerman, *The Jews in the Greek Age* (Cambridge, Mass.: Harvard University Press, 1988), 123–9.

in the Graeco-Roman world there was no shame in fighting for, and even in dying for, one's nation.[22] The language also belongs to the rhetoric of rights and status: against Apion's objection that those who wished to be Alexandrians should worship the gods of Alexandria, Josephus retorts that 'those who came to Alexandria from elsewhere' might be expected to remain 'within the laws established from the beginning' (*c. Apion*. II. 6 (65–7)). He reflects the same contemporary concerns for self-representation in political terms when he has Moses declare, 'I have compiled for you under God's dictation, a law and a polity (πολιτεία), and if you observe it in due fashion, you would be considered the most fortunate of people' (*Ant*. IV. 8. 3 (193)).

The term 'Ἰουδαῖος' is used by other texts, too, which seek to set 'the Jews' on the world stage, able to be compared with, if only to be differentiated from, other peoples.[23] In the *Fifth Sibylline* the 'race of the Jews' is both like the other cities and nations described—they dwell around the city of God—and different, being a 'godlike and heavenly race' (*Sib. V*, ll. 549–50). Hellenistic Jewish writers describe their earliest origins as those 'of the Jews', establishing a continuity and an antiquity in the terms recognized by their neighbours.[24] In a world of ethnographic curiosity, and of the encounter with, and the battle for, some degree of autonomy by different political units, it is hardly surprising that it should prove attractive to some to provide, or more probably to adopt, a recognized label as a means of claiming the right to preserve ancestral customs.

Yet we should not ignore how relatively limited a range of texts we can explore here, and how many use no such labels. Clearly, for some of these others the label 'Jew' carried few resonances; after all, it had little scriptural warrant and offered few etymological possibilities.[25] After the revolt of 66–70 CE its political

---

[22] So already Herodotus's account of Thermopylae in *Hist*. VII. 205–20.

[23] So it comes in *Aristeas* and in the fragments of the Hellenistic Jewish historians, Eupolemos, Artapanus, and Ps.-Hecataeus, as well as, of course, in Josephus and in Philo, *Flaccum* and *Legatio*.

[24] So, apparently, Alexander Polyhistor, Artapanus, *Aristeas*, Ps.-Hecataeus.

[25] In the LXX Ἰουδαῖος is mainly confined to 1 and 2 Ezra and to Esther besides the Maccabean books. Artapanus's obscure attempt to relate it etymologically to Ἑρμιούθ (Eusebius, *Praep. Ev*. IX. 18. 1) perhaps indicates the absence of any other tradition of exegesis; cf. below, p. 276 for Tacitus's alternative etymology (*Hist*. V. 2).

recognition by outsiders may have seemed as much a liability as a virtue.[26] It is also rare in rabbinic literature, but more, perhaps, because it did not locate the people within the tradition of God's requirements of them.[27] Non-Jewish and epigraphic evidence leave us in no doubt as to the normative currency of the term, and it is this that prompts current scholarly debate about its ethnic or religious range, but most of the literary sources exploit neither the normativity nor the ambiguity.

Neither do these sources contest ownership of the term:[28] it is, ironically, an author usually labelled 'Christian' who condemns those who 'say they are Jews but are not' (Rev. 2. 9; 3. 9), leaving interpreters perplexed as to whether or not he would prefer that label for himself.[29] It is another Christian who asserts that one would not 'accept as Jews but as self-styled Jews the Sadducees' and other sects (Justin, *Dial.* 80. 4). But this belongs to the redefining of others that we shall explore elsewhere.[30]

That 'Israel' or even 'Hebrew' should be preferred self-designations is not surprising, given their historical resonances and scriptural warrant. 'Hebrew', as we have noted, carried a heroic note taken up by 4 Maccabees, as it was also by Josephus; so, too, was it by Paul, who betrays its contested potential: 'Are they Hebrews? So am I.'[31] At about the same time outsiders were also adopting 'Hebrews' as an alternative to 'Jews' when describing the people, perhaps betraying the triumph of a burgeoning ethnographical interest over the political: for Pausanias the land of Palestine and its natural phenomena belong to the 'Hebrews';

---

[26] That Josephus is aware of this is argued by Arazy, *Appellations*, and by Tomson, 'Names', 140, both pointing to his self-designation 'Hebrew' in *BJ* I. 1 (3). See also G. Harvey, 'Synagogues of the Hebrews: "Good Jews" in the Diaspora', in Jones and Pearce, *Jewish Local Patriotism*, 132–47, 142, who notes Josephus's description in *BJ* V. 10. 5 (443) of the destruction of 'the race of the Hebrews (τὸ γένος τῶν Ἑβραίων)' by the revolutionaries in Jerusalem.

[27] For its rarity see Stern, *Jewish Identity*, 10–11.

[28] e.g. it is not used in the Dead Sea Scrolls, although Harvey, *True Israel*, 21–42, notes the different resonances of 'Judah' there.

[29] See A. Y. Collins, 'Insiders and Outsiders in the Book of Revelation', in E. S. Frerichs and J. Neusner (eds.), *'To See Ourselves as Others See Us': Christians, Jews, 'Others' in Late Antiquity* (Chico, Calif.: Scholars Press, 1985), 187–218, 206–10.

[30] See below, pp. 258, 267.

[31] Josephus, *BJ* I. 1 (3) (cf. n. 26); Paul, Phil. 3. 5; 2 Cor. 11. 22.

this offers a clear example of the different nuances the same label might carry for insiders and for outsiders.[32]

'Israel' is more common in texts from Palestine than from the Diaspora;[33] perhaps too great a dissonance with the labels used by outsiders had no positive value there. A number of studies have claimed it as an insider term, belonging in salvation-historical, and so in prayer or confessional, contexts;[34] however, to say this is to overlook the rhetorical assertiveness of the label that later emerges in its use on the coins from the Jewish revolts.[35] While the *Psalms of Solomon* agonize over the present state of *Jerusalem*, corrupt within and devastated from without, they anticipate the restoration of *Israel*, according to the promises of the 'God of Israel' (8. 4, 22, 34; 11. 1, 7–9); but the confidence of that hope, of course, simultaneously disenfranchises those, even within 'Israel', who may have rejected the ethos and programme of the *Psalms*. This contest over application becomes explicit when Paul asserts that 'for not all from Israel [by origin] *are* Israel', and possibly also in the blessing, 'peace upon them and mercy, and upon the Israel of God' (Rom. 9. 6; Gal. 6. 16).[36]

It is the Dead Sea Scrolls that most effectively illustrate the appropriation of the self-ascriptions of the past: they are simply 'the Community', or *Yahad* (יחד), but also 'the renewed covenant'.[37] Yet they can also be described as 'the majority of

---

[32] Pausanias does not use 'Jews'; see also Alexander Polyhistor, frag. 25; Plutarch, *Quaest. Con.* 6. 1; Antonius Diog. *apud* Porphyry, *Vit. Pyth.* 11 (*GLAJJ*, I. 537, §250). On the use of 'Hebrews' see further Harvey, 'Synagogues of the Hebrews', 138–43.

[33] An exception is Philo who exploits 'Israel's' putative etymology as 'those who see God' as a means of differentiation from the Jews as a sociopolitical entity: see E. Birnbaum, *The Place of Judaism in Philo's Thought: Israel, Jews, and Proselytes*, BJS 290, St. Phil. M. 2 (Atlanta, Ga.: Scholars Press, 1996).

[34] Harvey, *True Israel*, 271–2.

[35] On this see D. Goodblatt, 'From Judaeans to Israel: Names of Jewish States in Antiquity', *JSJ* 29 (1998), 1–36.

[36] See P. Richardson, *Israel in the Apostolic Church*, SNTS.MS 10 (Cambridge: Cambridge University Press, 1969), 74–84.

[37] Cf. the phrase באי הברית החדשה, CD 6. 19; 8. 21; see S. Talmon, 'The Community of the Renewed Covenant: Between Judaism and Christianity', in E. Ulrich and J. Vanderkam (eds.), *The Community of the Renewed Covenant: The Notre Dame Symposium on the Dead Sea Scrolls* (Notre Dame, Ind.: University of Notre Dame Press, 1994), 3–24, who emphasizes the communal understanding of 'covenant'.

Israel' (רב ישראל), contrary, surely, to any numerical estimates.[38]
Josephus does not know, or does not acknowledge, any of these
labels; for him these people are, if rightly identified by modern
consensus, 'Essenes', one of the schools of the Jewish philosophy;
that label, in turn, is not known by the texts probably emanat-
ing from them.[39] To complete the circle we should recall Pliny
the Elder's 'ethnographic' description of those whom he also
calls the Essenes; although he locates them in Judaea he does not
associate them with any other people there: they are a unique
and eternal people (*gens*), 'amazing compared with others in the
whole world'.[40] Both the same and different labels function differently in different contexts and from different perspectives.

The Mishnah, which uses neither 'Hebrews' nor 'Jews',[41]
similarly claims an identity from the past, but perhaps with a less
sectarian impulse: the people it addresses and so constructs is
'Israel', both singular and collective. According to Sacha Stern,
'As a monolithic entity, the people of "Israel" may serve as a
reification of the otherwise abstract notion of "Jewishness" or
Jewish identity.'[42] However, this reapplication of 'Israel' might
be said to have its roots deep within the biblical tradition where
already in the narratives of Deuteronomy it is a symbol open to
transformation (Deut. 1. 1; 4. 1; 5. 1, etc.).[43]

The archaizing resonances of 'Hebrew' or 'Israel' thus belong
together with the vogue for evoking or retelling the stories of the
past that we have seen to be characteristic of this period. Label
and narrative re-presentation are inseparable; through them

[38] 1QS 5. 22; however, 'Israel' also represents the wider body from which
volunteers might come: 1QS 1. 22–4; 6. 13–14.

[39] *BJ* II. 8. 12–13 (119–61); *Ant.* XVIII. 5. 9 (171–2). The texts and issues are
widely debated: for a survey see T. S. Beall, *Josephus' Description of the Essenes
illustrated by the Dead Sea Scrolls*, SNTS.MS 58 (Cambridge: Cambridge
University Press, 1988); G. Vermes and M. Goodman, *The Essenes according to
the Classical Sources* (Sheffield: Journal for the Study of the Old Testament for
the Oxford Centre for Postgraduate Hebrew Studies, 1989).

[40] *Nat. Hist.* V. 17. 73, 'gens sola et in tota orbe praeter ceteras mira . . . gens
aeterna est.'

[41] Except at *m. Ket.* 7. 6; *m. Ned.* 11. 12, in legal formulae about marriage.

[42] Stern, *Jewish Identity*, 11–13, quotation from 12–13; on who then belongs
to 'Israel' see ibid. 87–138.

[43] See E. T. Mullen, *Narrative History and Ethnic Boundaries*, Semeia
Studies (Atlanta, Ga.: Scholars Press, 1993), 55–85.

readers or hearers identify themselves as part of that same story, an identity that would be totally obscure to any outsider. At times the narratival echoes may even pre-empt any need for defining labels: in *Joseph and Aseneth* we know without being explicitly told that although Joseph is in Egypt he is not 'of Egypt'; but the same might equally be said of Aseneth, who 'is in no way like the virgins of the Egyptians'. Her father even assumes a certain consanguinity between them—he is 'your brother'—for both would abhor a 'foreign' (ἀλλοτρίος) partner (*Jos. & Asen.* 1. 5; 8. 1). But Joseph, who rejects this identification, has no specified alternative 'ethnic' identity, neither does Aseneth acquire one on her 'conversion'.[44] It is precisely for this reason that *Joseph and Aseneth* resists neat categorizing as 'Jewish' or 'Christian', as, too, do the *Testaments of the Twelve Patriarchs*, which similarly avoid labelling those to whom they speak; if identification and appropriation are invited by or through these texts, they abjure any exclusive epithet.

There is a similar ambiguity, through two very different genres, both in the Letter to the Hebrews and in Revelation. Both texts leave us perplexed as to what, if any, label would be claimed by those shaped by them. For 'Hebrews'—that designation was given in a later period when it could safely indicate believers of Jewish background without labelling them 'Jews'— the scriptural story addressed 'our fathers', and the epochal prophecy to Jeremiah was of a new covenant to be made 'with the house of Israel' (Heb. 1. 1; 8. 8, 10);[45] it is the covenant and not the people which is superseded.[46] For Revelation the 'twelve tribes of Israel' remain in some way determinative for the servants of God, sealed for the eschatological redemption, although their relationship with the 'great crowd from every nation, tribe, people and tongue' remains unclear (Rev. 7. 3–9; 21. 12).

---

[44] The two references to 'Hebrews' do not undermine this (1. 5; 11. 10); on the contrary, Aseneth *already* shares the beauty of 'the daughters of the Hebrews'.

[45] ἡμῶν at Heb. 1. 1 is almost certainly secondary, but perhaps it is to be understood.

[46] Contrast Ps.-Clement, *Rec.* 1. 32. 1, 'Abraham, from whom our race, the Hebrews, who are also called the Jews (Syr.; omitted from Lat.), multiplied'.

Following such patterns, *1 Clement* can claim for its readers not only Deut. 4. 9, 'Behold the Lord takes for himself a people (ἔθνος) from amongst the peoples', but also Deut. 32. 8–9, 'The portion of the Lord was his people Jacob, and Israel the share of his inheritance' (*1 Clem.* 29. 2–3). Yet the author can also use a separate set of metaphors that suggest a different focus: they belong to the 'flock of Christ'; they form the body of Christ; and the first Apostles, at least, can be called 'those in Christ' (57. 2; 38. 1; 46. 6–7; 43. 1). Pauline influence is clear, but how far does this go towards offering a defining designation? Like Paul, *1 Clement* also uses without explanation the term 'church', ἐκκλησία, as too does Revelation. It is debated whether the roots of this are septuagintal, evoking the 'congregation' of the wilderness stories, or whether they belong in the civic life of the Greek city.[47] If the former, none of our texts provides the scriptural legitimation to confirm this, and it is hard to see whether the term provides more than a functional category.

We should not be too surprised at this failure to specify. As we have seen, 'Jewish' texts do not necessarily identify themselves as such. More broadly within the Graeco-Roman world, most cults, if it is with such that we are to align 'the Christ-cult', did not have a distinct name for their devotees: there is no word for a worshipper of Mithras, and 'Isiac' is rare.[48] This makes the letters of Ignatius the more remarkable, for they are controlled by the self-conscious language of a distinct identity. First, as we have already seen, Ignatius takes *'ecclesia'* (ἐκκλησία) and fills it with significance so that it might indeed become a primary term of self-definition for his readers.[49] Even more deliberately, he takes up a far more unequivocal term, 'Christian' (χριστιανός), as the determinative term for a follower of Christ, and he weaves it into a network of related words, thus creating a new semantic field of belonging. It seems likely that in doing this he was taking up an existing term that was not only non-cultic in its associa-

---

[47] See above, Ch. 7 n. 74.

[48] So Beard, North, Price, *Religions*, i. 307–8, who also note the multivalency of 'Jew' and the infrequency of 'Christian' even into the 2nd century.

[49] See above, pp. 233–4.

tions, but that was first coined as a hostile tag by opponents of the new movement; from its earliest appearances in 1 Pet. 4. 16 and Acts 26. 28, the term 'Christian' is associated with accusation and with defence, and it is in a similar setting that it is contemporaneously used by pagan writers.[50]

Peter already encourages his readers not to be ashamed to suffer 'as a Christian', implicitly identifying this as 'being reviled for the name of Christ', perhaps a reinterpretation of a Jesus tradition (1 Pet. 4. 14, 16; Matt. 5. 11; 10. 22). Even more emphatically, and perhaps independently, Ignatius's intense desire 'not only to be named but to be proved a Christian' through his death claims that epithet, perhaps still being hurled in abuse, with pride (*Rom.* 3. 2).[51] We may also suspect that he is struggling to transform the label into something positive for his readers as well: so he assures the church at Ephesus that he longs to be found 'in the lot of the Christians of Ephesus', and he exhorts those at Magnesia that they too should not merely be called but should actually be 'Christians' (*Eph.* 11. 2; *Magn.* 4. 4). Whatever the origin of the epithet, he surrounds it with references to Christ and with other Christ-compounds, although, surprisingly, he never actually demonstrates, nor takes advantage of, its derivation from the title 'Christ' itself. He calls those at Ephesus 'Christ-bearers' (χριστοφόροι); he exhorts those at Philadelphia to behave not out of envy but from 'Christ-learning' (χριστομαθία); he praises the church at Rome as 'Christ-governed' (χριστόνομος); moreover, evidence again of the current negative valency of the term, he declares that the same church can be assured that 'Christianism' (χριστιανισμός) may not be an 'act of persuasion but it is one of greatness when it is hated by the world' (*Eph.* 9. 2; *Philad.* 8. 2; *Rom.* praef.; 3. 3).

[50] Tacitus, *Ann.* XV. 44; Suetonius, *Nero* 16, although whether these should be taken as indicative of the time of Nero or of the time of the authors is uncertain—in which case, compare also Pliny, *Epist.* X. 96; also more ambiguously, Acts 11. 26. That the term was coined by opponents is supported by the analysis that follows; it is also argued by H. Mattingley, 'The Origin of the name *Christiani*', *JTS* 9 (1958), 26–37; J. Taylor, 'Why were the Disciples first called "Christians" at Antioch? (Acts 11, 26)', *RevBib* 101 (1994), 75–94; that it was a self-designation is argued by E. Bickermann, 'The Name of Christians', *HTR* 42 (1949), 109–24; B. Lifschitz, 'L'Origine du nom des chrétiens', *VC* 16 (1962), 65–70.

[51] On this and what follows see Lieu, *Image and Reality*, 28–31.

The last of those neologisms, χριστιανισμός, also stakes a claim in a very different framework; in his letter to the church at Magnesia, like that to the Romans also written from Smyrna, Ignatius asserted that 'Christianism' did not put its faith in Judaism (ἰουδαϊσμός), but Judaism in Christianism. He was to develop a similar contrast when writing to the church at Philadelphia, suggesting that both Judaism and Christianism were things that might be 'heard' or 'interpreted' (*Magn.* 8. 1; 10. 3; *Philad.* 6. 1).[52] 'Judaism', which we, and perhaps he, have already met in 2 Maccabees, probably provided the model for his new creation, although we may wonder whether his readers also knew this.[53] It is, therefore, Ignatius who sets up the oppositional parity between the two concepts—an opposition and parity that we began by leaving open to question. However, Ignatius does not construct a similar opposition between 'Christians' and 'Jews', the latter a term he uses only once (*Smyrn.* 1. 2); further, his stress on practice, chiefly on sabbath and circumcision, in relation to Judaism suggests a concern more with conventional behaviour, perhaps gleaned from Scripture, than with organized and named groups.[54] For Ignatius, the label 'Christian' serves to define but also to exclude; it does not describe but rather produces identity, at least in his rhetoric. So, similarly, he urges the church at Tralles to seek nourishment only from *Christian* sustenance and not from alien (ἀλλοτρία) fodder 'which is heresy': here again, he anticipates a move that will be taken up by later writers (*Trall.* 6. 1).

It is its strategic use rather than its frequency that demonstrates how important 'Christian' was as a term of self-definition for Ignatius; its absence from elsewhere among the Apostolic Fathers—including from Polycarp's own letter, despite his knowledge of Ignatius—probably shows how much he was innovating.[55] Yet he sows seeds that were to be remarkably fruitful,

---

[52] The letter to Philadelphia was written later, from Troas.

[53] Ἰουδαϊσμός is also used by Paul in Gal. 1. 13–14; we have no evidence for its wider currency, and it is assumed here that 4 Maccabees, which also uses the term, may not be earlier than Ignatius. See above, n. 19.

[54] On the problem of interpreting what Ignatius means by 'Judaism' see Lieu, *Image and Reality*, 26–51.

[55] The only other use of χριστιανός in the Apostolic Fathers as such (excluding *Mart. Poly.* and *Diognetus* as later texts) is *Did.* 12. 4 where it might be read as

but only in time and in certain contexts. What sort of label would 'Christian' have been for his readers? Its novelty means that it is unlikely that it would have been heard as an equivalent alternative to 'Jew', 'Greek', 'Syrian', or even 'Gentile'; nor yet would they define it in religious terms, for the contemporary context did not recognize the category of named cult. The association with Christ, understood as a proper name, appears obvious, and this surely must have been its origin, even if coined as a term of denigration or accusation; what is surprising is how little positive benefit even Ignatius finds in that association.[56]

Something of that double-edged defensiveness and pride is also characteristic of the *Acts of the Martyrs*.[57] It is here that the success of these as literary texts in creating their own symbolic world is most evident: they both provide a means for reconceiving positively the apparent disgrace of the victims of persecution, and construct a world for those who would never experience it. Because of the way this becomes a complete and sufficient universe of meaning, they defy attempts to extract from them precise details about the charges, the numbers, and the processes involved in the early persecutions. Throughout these texts the confession 'I am a Christian', often made in public, lies at the heart of the world they write, but it becomes impossible to discover exactly how or why this confession functioned within the 'historical' events that inspire them. So, as we have seen, at the pivotal moment of the *Martyrdom of Polycarp*, its eponymous hero declares, 'You pretend not to know who I am; listen publicly, I am a Christian (χριστιανός εἰμι)' (*Mart. Poly.* 10. 1). In nearly every future account of martyrdom that confession re-echoes, one by one, in the masculine and in the feminine, in Greek and in Latin, but always in the singular: so, asked whether Justin made

a redactional addition: 'how [as a] Christian [he] may not live idly among you'; but note 'Christ-trader' (χριστεμπόρος) in the next verse.

[56] Whether that caution is further evidence for the strength of the negative associations of the term lies outside our task; see above, n. 50, and E. Paupot, 'The Anti-Roman Movement of the Christiani and the Nazorean Fragment', *VC* 54 (2000), 233–47.

[57] See further D. van Damme, '*MAPTYΣ-XPIΣTIANOC*: Überlegungen zur ursprünglichen Bedeutungen des altkirchlichen Märtyretitels', *Freiburger Zeitschrift für Philosophie und Theologie* 23 (1976), 286–303. On this and what follows see Lieu, ' "I am a Christian" ' where these themes are explored in detail; also D. Boyarin, *Dying for God.*

him a Christian, Hierax makes the simple reply, 'I was and I shall be a Christian.'[58]

Here we need not be concerned with precisely what the legal charge against 'the Christians' was, nor with what part 'the name' played, something to which we shall return. In these texts, whatever the actual origins, the epithet is not a term of abuse to be corrected nor one to be handled with care; but equally it is not optional, nor is it imposed by others. Perpetua will say to her father, 'I cannot say that I am anything but what I am, a Christian', and yet, when Tertullian writes, 'Indeed, I am a Christian—if I so choose', he denies the power that the persecutors claim.[59] 'Christian' represents an ultimate, a non-negotiable, identity that even redefines familial and other social roles: for Sanctus, 'Christian' answers for 'name, city, race, and everything else', while Hierax, when asked who his parents are, replies, 'Christ is our true father and faith in him mother.'[60] Yet the label is also inextricably tied to the martyr's death: the confession ensures the passing of the death sentence, and there are regularly those such as Alexander or Agathonice, who are moved only by another's confession and death to declare themselves also to be Christian and so to die.[61]

The consequences of this reconfiguration of identity are explored in a number of ways through the Martyr Acts. Here to be 'a Christian' is to be ranked against a host of 'others' who oppose the martyr and seek her downfall—unsurprisingly, given the genre, it is determined by opposition. These may belong to the mythological realm of the cosmic—the devil, the world—or to the immediate sociopolitical realm—Jews, Gentiles, the mob, the Roman officials.[62] How the 'Christian' martyr relates to non-martyred believers is less clear. Polycarp is identified by the crowd as 'father of the Christians', and the earlier death of a certain Germanicus had moved those watching to marvel at 'the

---

[58] *Mart. Just.* 4. 5; cf. *HE* V. 1. 19, 20, 26, 50; *Pass. Scill.* 17.

[59] *Pass. Perpet.* 3. 2; Tertullian, *Apol.* 49. 5, 'Certe, si velim, Christianus sum. Tunc ergo me damnabis, si damnari velim; cum vero quod in me potes, nisi velim, non potes, iam meae voluntatis est quod potes, non tuae potestatis.'

[60] *HE* V. 1. 20–1; *Mart. Just.* 4. 8.

[61] *HE* V. 1. 9–10, 49–51; *Mart. Carp.* A. 42; Justin, *II Apol.* 2. 15–20.

[62] On the different levels of opposition see Lieu, '"I am a Christian"', 216, 220; also below, pp. 294–5.

nobility of the God-loving and God-fearing race of Christians' (*Mart. Poly.* 12. 2; 3. 2).[63] To some extent, then, those who are not asked to confess and die—the observers, the writers, and the readers—depend on the martyrs to give meaning to their name; in practice this means that they depend on the texts, the accounts of martyrdom, which create that meaning. The letter form of the *Martyrdom of Polycarp*, with its catholic address, extends to its furthest possible extent the circle of those who will at the same time both identify themselves with Polycarp in his confession and recognize their inability to do so.[64] Yet it is notable that while the text makes us aware of and dependent on the testimony of those responsible for its production, we know little of them, and the term 'Christians' is not used more loosely or more widely within it.

The nature of the largely innovative genre, as well as numerous references within the texts, also create a distance between the martyr and 'the rest', whether witnesses within the narrative or readers of it: it is the martyr who is 'chosen' and who exercises a discipleship that is inaccessible to others, something that in time is expressed by the exclusive application of the title 'martyr', 'witness', to them.[65] On the other hand, that there were some who were arrested but whose courage failed them is readily acknowledged: yet only the faithful are allowed the confession or the epithet 'Christian'; we are even told, contrary to most other evidence, that those who denied none the less remained incarcerated, but as murderers and defilers (*HE* V. 1. 33–5).[66] An implacable polemic makes it clear that these did not have, and never had had, any claim to the label 'Christian'. Yet when some ultimately regain their courage and confess, they are then said to be 'added to the church', as if this too were constituted primarily by martyrdom.[67] Later, in a new arena, 'catholics' will assert

---

[63] See further below; Eusebius, *HE* IV. 15. 6 reads τὴν καθόλου τοῦ γένος τῶν χριστιανῶν ἀρετήν. [64] On this address see above, p. 233.

[65] See especially *HE* V. 1. 10, 23, 26, 27; 2. 2–3.

[66] This would contravene the instructions of Trajan (Pliny, *Epist.* X. 97); irregularities are not, of course, impossible, but it is more likely that the text is both warning its readers and distancing the epithet from the charges with which it was associated.

[67] *HE* V. 1. 49; the verb 'added' (προστιθέναι) is used in Acts 2. 41, 47; 5. 14; 11. 24 of the conversion of believers.

that Montanist 'martyrs' die for their criminal activities and not 'for the name', while the Montanist Tertullian will dismissively refer to a 'catholic' martyr as 'yours, not Christian'.[68] Again, the label creates boundaries, which those thus excluded would not have acknowledged.

Those who confess and die are described as 'witnesses of Christ', and their experience, both implicitly and explicitly, invites comparison with the story of Jesus himself.[69] But the label 'Christian' is not interpreted in relation to this imitation, and indeed it is assumed to require no interpretation at all. Pothinus shrugs off the question, 'Who is the God of the Christians?' as if confession does not demand explanatory content (*HE* V. 1. 31). Admittedly, when Polycarp made his public confession he did offer to teach the interrogating proconsul 'the argument of *Christianism*' (τὸν τοῦ χριστιανισμοῦ λόγον) (*Mart. Poly.* 10. 1). While that term is, presumably, drawn from Ignatius, the nuance has changed: here, 'Christianism' is a *logos* that might be learned, at least by one of the proconsul's status, but, since he refuses, we discover nothing more. We cannot help but recall the coinage of 'Judaism' in a similar martyrological text, but, whatever the historical and literary links between the two traditions, 'Christian' and 'Christianism' here are not being constructed on the model of the embattled Jews and Judaism of the Maccabean literature, defending a way of life and political survival.[70] Although there may be other echoes of the Jewish tradition—as we have already heard, the Christians form a 'race' (γένος), and Polycarp will be characterized by his citizenship (πολιτεία) (3. 2; 17. 1)—there is nothing here of the legitimacy of national existence nor of ancestral laws and customs, neither are the martyrs 'saviours of the Christian people'; conversely, there is no cry 'I am a Jew' in those other traditions.[71] The Martyr Acts do seem to draw on

---

[68] *HE* V. 18. 5–10; Tertullian, *de Ieiun.* 12.

[69] *Mart. Poly.* 2. 2, οἱ μάρτυρες τοῦ Χριστοῦ; *HE* V. 1. 41 where Blandina's spreadeagled body becomes a re-presentation of 'him who was crucified for them'.

[70] On the differences between the two traditions see T. Rajak, 'Dying for the Law: The Martyr's Portrait in Jewish-Greek Literature', in M. J. Edwards and S. Swain (eds.), *Portraits: Biographical Representation in the Greek and Latin Literature of the Roman Empire* (Oxford: Clarendon, 1997), 39–67.

[71] The former draws from the title of J. W. van Henten, *The Maccabean*

the political concepts of the Jewish tradition as well as on the imagery of the Greek city and its institutions,[72] but they do not do so in order to invest the label 'Christian' with a politico-ethnic content.

The extent to which the Martyr Acts of the second century construct an identity around the label 'Christian' cannot be underestimated, and the influence of the topos of confession is evidenced by its continuing centrality in the developing genre. Yet quite how those who are not martyred are to appropriate that identity is less clear. Given the harsh polemic against denial, they are presumably to make that confession their own; but they are not invited to follow to death, for it is clear that the opportunity is not given to all. By maintaining this sense of distance between reader and narrative, the texts remove the title from the ordinary discourse of meaning and debate: it provides a measure for self-understanding while refusing to supply the measurements. There are no alternatives to this title, and it itself brooks of no alternative application.

Just how creative this was, and potentially how contested, becomes apparent when we turn to the very different construction of the Apologists. They, too, know that χριστιανός belongs to the vocabulary of opposition and denigration, and they, too, seek both to neutralize its negative associations and to invest it with positive ones. Theophilus complains, 'you call me Christian as if bearing a name that is evil' (*Autolyc.* I. 1); and the illogicality of 'the name' itself being criminal, even where no crimes can be demonstrated, is a repeated complaint (Octavius, *Min. Felix* 28. 1–6; Athenagoras, *Leg.* 2. 2–4).

However, things appear less straightforward when Justin asserts that Christians who are also felons should be punished for their crimes but not as Christians—an admission that the epithet itself was no safeguard of virtue.[73] The problem in the title that these writers are compelled to admit to is that it is simply too promiscuous—at least in their eyes; for it was borne not only by

Martyrs as Saviours of the Jewish People: A Study of 2 and 4 Maccabees, S.JSJ 57 (Leiden: Brill, 1997); for the latter see also Boyarin, *Dying for God*, 121–2. On 2 Macc. 6. 6, 'to confess being a Jew', see above, p. 243; but this does not imply a formal affirmation.

[72] e.g. in the use of the imagery of the stadium and the games.

[73] *Apol.* 4. 7; 7; cf. Athenagoras, *Leg.* 2. 1–4.

those whose reprehensible behaviour belies their claim, but also by others, most notably by a long catalogue of teachers—Simon, Menander, Marcion—and their followers, whom Justin sets aside as heretics but whose differences may have been of little concern to outsiders (*Apol.* 16. 8, 14; 26). There is a difficulty here: Justin claims that all these 'are called Christians', but he also states that they are not persecuted by the Romans despite their pernicious teachings (26. 6–7); he thus contradicts the complaint that the name itself earned persecution, or, more probably, falsifies his own denial of their suffering. By whom, we may wonder, were they 'called Christians'? By themselves—and so giving evidence of the currency and value of the term—or by the Romans? However we answer this, the texts strive to control possession or application of the label 'Christian', even while admitting the impossibility of securing any ultimate means of control.

Justin seeks both to disenfranchise any other claimants, and to redefine the term. First, he assimilates it to a philosophical model, giving it the same timbre as 'Stoics', and acknowledging that philosophical schools have a similar problem of recreant adherents.[74] Indeed, it is this model that enables him to identify as 'Christians' those heroes of the past, such as Socrates as well as Abraham, 'who lived with the word' (*Apol.* 46. 3). Within this framework he can also trace the name to that of 'our teacher . . . Jesus Christ' (12. 9). Even so, what he finds more effective is its assonance with *chrestos* (χρηστός), 'useful': 'We are charged with being *Christians*, but it is not right to hate what is *chrestos*'; similarly, all those in the past who lived without the word were *achrestoi* (ἄχρηστοι), 'not useful' (4. 5; 46. 4).[75] This is a favour-

---

[74] *Apol.* 26. 6; *II Apol.* 7. 3; 13. 1–4. For the influence on Justin of traditional accounts of philosophical schools, see A. Le Boulluec, *La Notion d'hérésie dans la littérature grecque, IIe–IIIe siècles*, i. *De Justin à Irénée* (Paris: Études Augustiniennes, 1985), 40.

[75] Hermas, who does not use the word 'Christian', can still see 'conversion' in terms of becoming 'useful' to God: *Vis.* III. 6. 7. It is not easy to trace the development of this etymology, since '*chrest-*' frequently appears as an alternative spelling to '*christ-*', as already in Tacitus, *Ann.* XV. 44. 2. Since the root '*chrest-*' was also common in the names of slaves and freedmen, both the confusion and the multiple possibilities for mockery and reinterpretation are evident. See O. Montevecchi, 'Nomen Christianorum', in R. Cantalamessa and L. Pizzolato

ite etymology among the Apologists: Theophilus of Antioch is proud to confess to being a Christian because he hopes to be very useful (εὔχρηστος) to God, while those whom he addresses are useless; he even manages a double etymology—just as anointing (*christon*: τὸ χριστόν) is sweet and useful, Christians are thus named because they are anointed with the oil of God (*Autolyc*. I. 1; 12).[76] Here, in this attempt to mediate between the term and contemporary values, we are a long way from the world of the Martyr Acts. Embarrassment with the label remains and there is no driving urgency to redeem it: so Athenagoras still speaks of 'us' as 'those called Christians' (οἱ λεγόμενοι χριστιανοί), while other contemporaries avoid the term altogether; it has its uses but it does not appear to be a primary form of self-definition.[77] By the early third century, this has changed: Clement of Alexandria, for example, considers it natural to speak of 'the life called Christian'.[78]

THE RACE OF THE CHRISTIANS

This initial caution perhaps reflects the genre of the Apologies as texts directed to outsiders, in contrast to the 'internal' Martyr Acts; yet, in so far as they were in practice read more by insiders than by outsiders, the Apologies would construct for such readers a very different sense of the significance of the label χριστιανός.[79] However, despite this caution, the Apologists do find ways of developing the tradition of claimed ethnic privilege that we found in the Jewish sources. Athenagoras himself starts by reminding the Emperors Marcus Aurelius and Lucius Aurelius that the world they rule allows different peoples to follow their own different customs, and that no one is prohibited by law or by fear of punishment from 'loving their ancestral

---

(eds.), *Paradoxus Politeia: Studi Patristici in onore di Guiseppe Lazzati*, Studia Patristica Mediolanensia 10 (Milan: Vita e Pensiero, 1979), 485–500.

[76] For the continuity of this etymology see Clement, *Strom*. II. 4. 4.

[77] Athenagoras, *Leg*. 1. 3; Theophilus of Antioch qualifies it with καλούμενοι in *Autolyc*. II. 33; III. 4; it is not used by Tatian; see E. Peterson, '*Christianus*', in *Frühkirche, Judentum und Gnosis* (Freiburg: Herder, 1958), 64–87. For the equal rarity of 'Christ', see above, pp. 88–9.　　　　　[78] *Paed*. II. 1. 1.

[79] On the problem of audience see above, pp. 57–8.

customs', however unsavoury; 'we who are called Christians', who do no one harm, therefore, at least deserve a hearing (*Leg.* 1. 1). Admittedly, much of his argument then shifts into philosophical mode to demonstrate the irrationality of other views of the gods and the rationality of their own, but it closes with a political appeal and assurance that 'we pray for your rule' (37; cf. 1. 3): this is an attempt to position themselves between the rights due an ethnic group and the respect accorded a philosophical tradition.

More assertively, Aristides reconfigures the traditional division of humanity into different 'races' (γένος; Syr.: ܓܢܣܐ). According to the Syriac tradition of his *Apology*, these are 'barbarians and Greeks, Jews and Christians';[80] the barbarians can trace the 'origin of their race' from Cronos and Rhea, the Greeks from Hellen, the Jews from Abraham, while the Christians trace 'the beginning of their religion' (*dḥlta*: ܕܚܠܬܐ) from Jesus the Messiah (*Apol.* 2. 3–6 Syr.).[81] The change from 'race' to 'religion' is notable but not to be over-stressed since Aristides is clear that all four, including the Christians, are 'races'.[82] Since the terms 'Christians' (*krstina*: ܟܪܣܛܝܢܐ) and '(Jesus) the Messiah' (*mšiḥa*: ܡܫܝܚܐ) are not etymologically related in Syriac as they are in Greek, it is also difficult to know whether Aristides drew attention to that relationship in his Greek original; instead he explains the name as deriving from the word for 'preaching' (*kruzuta*: ܟܪܘܙܘܬܐ), an explanation that works only in Syriac but is retained in the Greek version.[83]

---

[80] On the problem of the Greek and Syriac versions see Lieu, *Image and Reality*, 165–9. In what follows both Greek and Syriac are cited according to the chapter division of E. Goodspeed, *Die ältesten Apologeten: Texte mit kurzen Einleitungen* (Göttingen: Vandenhoeck & Ruprecht, 1984 (1914)), 2–23; Goodspeed gives a Latin translation of the Syriac, the text of which here is taken from J. Rendel Harris (ed.), *The Apology of Aristides on behalf of the Christians* (Cambridge: Cambridge University Press, 1891).

[81] In the Syriac the barbarians trace the 'origin of their race of religion', but 'religion' is not read by the Armenian, which generally follows the Syriac, and so may be secondary.

[82] The difference is emphasized by J. Siker, *Disinheriting the Jews: Abraham in early Christian Controversy* (Louisville, Ky.: Westminster/John Knox Press, 1991), 152; but in 17. 5 Aristides speaks of the 'race of the Christians'; see also n. 81 on the text regarding the barbarians.

[83] Syr. 2. 8; Gk. 15. 2, ὅθεν οἱ εἰσέτι διακονοῦντες τῇ δικαιοσύνῃ τοῦ κηρύγματος αὐτῶν καλοῦνται χριστιανοί.

According to the alternative Greek version, Aristides spoke not of four but of three races, 'the worshippers of those called by you gods, Jews, and Christians'; the first of these is further divided into three races, 'Chaldaeans, Greeks, and Egyptians'. He gives that first group no ancestry, describes the Jews as descendants (ἀπόγονοι) of Abraham, Isaac, and Jacob, and says that the Christians 'have a genealogy (γενεαλογοῦνται) from the Lord Jesus Christ'. In his account of the races, however, Aristides does little more than follow, in both recensions, the traditional denunciation of pagan polytheism and, in the Greek version, of Jewish unbelief.[84] This is not inconsistent with an 'ethnic' defence, for worship belonged firmly within the parameters of ethnic identity, and Josephus, too, had responded to Apion by exposing Egyptian disputes about the gods.[85] Moreover, in the Syriac version at least, Aristides' extended account of 'the Christians' focuses rather more on ethics than on belief, and so could be seen as presenting them as a people with a distinct and admirable pattern of custom and practice: 'This, O King is the authority of the law and the customs of the Christians' (15. 12 Syr.).[86]

This is a bold attempt to position the Christians alongside the other acknowledged divisions of humanity; it gives them a place within the Empire that can expect legitimacy, but also one within the wider world. It is unlikely that Aristides was totally innovating here. The description of the Christians as a third 'kind' or 'race' is usually traced earlier to the *Kerygma Petri* as cited by Clement of Alexandria, where they are sharply differentiated from the Greeks and the Jews: 'worship this God not according to the Greeks . . . nor according to the Jews . . . but worshipping God in a new way (καινῶς) through Christ . . . [Jer. 31. 31–2]. For the ways of Greeks and Jews are old, but we Christians are those who worship him in a new way in a third race/kind (τρίτῳ γένει).'[87]

---

[84] On the more sympathetic account of the Syriac see Lieu, *Image and Reality*, 169–77.

[85] On worship as part of an ethnic identity see above, pp. 106, 244; for Josephus's response to Apion (*c. Apion*. II. 6 (65–7)) see above, p. 245.

[86] The Greek is more 'evangelical'.

[87] In Clement of Alexandria, *Strom.* VI. 5. 41; see H. Paulsen, 'Das Kerygma Petri und die urchristlichen Apologetik', in *Zur Literatur und Geschichte des frühen Christentum: Gesammelte Aufsätze*, WUNT 99 (Tübingen: Mohr, 1997), 173–209.

It is, however, not impossible that the final sentence following the Jeremiah quotation is, in fact, Clement's comment; further, in either case, γένος is ambiguous and could be translated 'kind'— although the subversive implications of 'new kinds of worship' were well known.[88] Nevertheless, as a derogatory term of abuse used from outside, the epithet does appear to have earlier roots; Tertullian knows the mocking cry of the 'pagans', 'whence the third race (*tertium genus*)?', and Suetonius had already described the Christians as 'a *genus* of men holding a new and mischievous superstition'.[89] It is tempting to recall Livy's account of the Bacchic conspiracy, which grew so large as 'almost to make up an alternative race (*paene alterum genus*)'.[90] Yet, if both novelty and claiming to be an alien people within the bounds of the Empire conventionally implied subversion, Christian writers were again boldly redefining the charge as they claimed newness as a virtue, and peoplehood as a source of credit. We have already heard how the *Martyrdom of Polycarp* makes the crowds acknowledge the 'god-loving and god-fearing race of the Christians', and this becomes a recurring epithet in apologetic and other writings.[91] Yet for the apologetic writers it is not so much the label 'Christians' that matters as the sense of having a place in history and in the world, and this not in their individuality, as the Martyr Acts might suggest, nor as organized within local communities, of which there is no mention, but in their corporate mutuality.[92]

---

[88] E. von Dobschütz, *Das Kerygma Petri kritisch Untersucht*, TU 11. 1 (Leipzig: Hinrichs, 1893), 21–2, acknowledges that some take the quotation as ending with the Jeremiah citation; there is no parallel to the sentence in Origen's citation of the *Kerygma Petri*. The recent edition by P. Descourtiez (introd., transl., and notes), *Clément d'Alexandrie Les Stromates: Stromate VI*, SC 446 (Paris: Éditions du Cerf, 1999), 144, does retain the last sentence for the *Kerygma*. On the subversiveness of new ways of worshipping, see above, pp. 212–13.

[89] Tertullian, *ad Nat.* I. 8. 1; 20. 4; *Scorp.* 10. 10; Suetonius, *Nero* 16. 2.

[90] Livy, *Hist.* XXXIX. 13; cf. W. Schäfke, 'Frühchristliche Widerstand', *ANRW* II. 23. 1 (1979), 460–723, 615–19.

[91] So Melito's Apology bewailed the unprecedented persecution of 'the race of the god-fearing' (τὸ τῶν θεοσεβῶν γένος) (Eusebius, *HE* IV. 26. 5); see J. M. Lieu, 'The Race of the Godfearers', in *Neither Jew nor Greek?*, 49–68.

[92] So Paulsen, 'Das Kerygma Petri', 209, on that text: 'eine Gemeinde, die sich als herausgehobenes Glied der Geschichte begreift und diese Geschichte auf die Zeit μετὰ τὴν ἀνάστασιν gründet, eine neue Art von Selbstverständnis entwickelt; ein kleiner Schritt ist es dann nur noch, wenn solches Selbstverständnis als Selbstbewußtsein nach außen sich kehrt'.

Yet if Aristides could seem to suggest that 'the Christians' were a race just as were Greeks or Jews, the *Letter to Diognetus* again treads a more nuanced path. It, too, envisages its addressee wondering why the Christians worship neither like the Greeks, nor like the Jews, 'and why indeed this new race or practice (γένος ἢ ἐπιτήδευμα) entered life now and not earlier' (*Diog.* 1). Yet, as we have seen, the author denies that they have separate territory or language, cities, customs, or way of life, all the hallmarks of a people in the contemporary world. They may choose in one sense to be foreigners (ξένοι), and may exercise their own 'citizenship' (πολιτεία), but this is emphatically not an alternative to obedience to Roman law.[93] Although the author does not make the point, his argument would also distance the Christians from the rhetoric of Jewish claims to the right to observe their own ancestral customs. Instead he claims for the Christians a peculiar piety ('fear of God', θεοσέβεια), one which is a mystery and invisible (4. 6; 6. 4); if their presence in the world is as the soul in the body, then their citizenship in heaven can hardly offer any threat to the Empire (6. 1–4; 5. 8). *Diognetus* finds no awkwardness in using the epithet 'Christians', yet neither it nor the contrast with Greeks and Jews produces a strong model of their cohesive identity; its epicentre lies elsewhere, but how this would function for specific readers, individually or in groups, is less clear.

The inherent tension within *Diognetus* only exposes a deeper problem in the apologetic model of identity. Its purpose is, as we have seen, to claim the right to a place within the sociopolitical world of the time, to claim for differentness a virtue. Yet to claim to be on a par not with the Germans or Britons, nor even with the Romans, but with the barbarians or the Greeks, was to claim a universal domain, coextensive with Roman rule: so, Melito explicitly asserted that 'our philosophy came to full flower among your peoples . . . and became a good omen for your empire'.[94] The claim was made more ambiguous where the Jews were included within the equation, evidence of the Jewish roots of the strategy; it was a Jewish perspective, not a Greek one, that could set the Jews alongside the barbarians and Greeks, and not just as a prime example of the former. From a Jewish point

[93] *Diog.* 5. 1–5, 10; see above, pp. 234–5.
[94] *HE* IV. 26. 7; see Lieu, *Image and Reality*, 182–4.

of view at least, and to some extent from outside, the Graeco-Roman understanding of being an *ethnos* could accommodate the primacy of Jewish religious distinctiveness; the apologetic programme wanted Christians to be both the same and different—in that sense the pagan rejection of a third *genus* was justified.[95]

Looking to the future we might find new formulations of the self-presentation as a third race. Clement of Alexandria, continuing his commentary on the *Kerygma Petri*, holds together the unity of God replicated by the 'one race of the saved people' (τὸ ἕν γένος τοῦ σωζομένου λαοῦ), which itself holds together God's prior revelation both to Greeks and to Jews (*Strom*. VI. 5. 42. 2).[96] By contrast, the *Gospel of Philip*, although later than our period, engages in a similar discourse but to a different purpose: just as no Jew was ever born of a Greek, so, adamantly, Christians do not descend from the Jews; their name is derived from 'chrism' and they alone are the 'true race' (γενος αληθεινος).[97] The theme will be transformed by the *Tripartite Tractate* (NH I. 5) into three types or races (ουσια or γενος), the spiritual, the psychic, and the material, rooted in 'the triple disposition of the Logos' but each destined to a different experience of salvation (I. 118. 14–119. 34). In each case, a similar rhetoric is reshaped to construct a new identity through textual rewriting.

It seems likely from what we have seen that the Christian apologetic defence of being 'a race' was developed by taking over and inverting pagan denigration. Yet it also drew on deeper roots, on struggles to understand the continuing identity of the people of God. We have already seen how those struggles could be articulated through manipulation of the biblical epithet 'Israel'; a parallel move was through claims to be the (new) 'people' (*laos*: λαός), using the distinctive term of the biblical tradition: 'Let us see whether this people is the heir, or the first' (*Barn*. 13. 1). If, as here, the claim involved the potential disenfranchisement of others, how were both continuity and discontinuity to be

---

[95] See D. van Damme, 'Gottesvolk und Gottesreich in der christlichen Antike', *Theologische Berichte*, iii. *Judentum und Kirche: Volk Gottes* (Zurich: Benziger Verlag, 1974), 157–68.

[96] On this see now Buell, 'Race and Universalism'.

[97] *NH* II. 74. 13–15; 75. 30–76. 4: the state of the text makes the argument partly conjectural. On the derivation of 'Christian' from 'chrism', see above, p. 259.

retained? We have explored elsewhere how appropriating Israel's history shaped what was to become Christian identity.[98] More significant here is the awareness of discontinuity. The synoptic Parable of the Vineyard takes up the familiar scriptural image of Israel as a vine (Mark 12. 1–12); in the Matthaean version, however, at its end Jesus adds the chilling words, 'Therefore I tell you that the Kingdom of God will be taken from you and given to a nation which produces its fruit' (Matt. 21. 43).[99] The language of 'nation' (ἔθνος) is, in the light of future developments, striking; so, too, when Paul urges the community at Corinth 'Be blameless before both Jews and Greeks and the church of God' (1 Cor. 10. 32), the threefold division hints at what is to come. But in these cases 'the Kingdom of God' postpones any sociopolitical form of that 'nation', and 'the church of God' is different in kind from both Jews and Greeks.[100] What we have seen in the Apologists is a concern for sociopolitical legitimacy, and an awareness, perhaps, that too much difference becomes incommunicable to others and also to self.[101]

Justin's *Dialogue with Trypho* shows how these dynamics of ambiguity would operate in a very different literary setting. There, too, he assumes the association of the name 'Christians' with persecution, here blaming the Jews for initially spreading rumours about 'the godless sect (αἵρεσις) of Christians' (*Dial.* 17. 1). He also has to admit that the epithet 'Christian' is actively claimed by those from whom he would wish to distance himself, whether because of their laxity about food offered to idols or because of their varying eschatological beliefs: not all who call themselves Christians are Christians, he asserts (35. 3–6; 80. 2–5).[102] With some caution he seeks to capitalize on the term's

---

[98] On this in Christian sources see Richardson, *Israel in the Apostolic Church*.

[99] Stanton, *Gospel for a New People*, 11–12, sees here 'in effect a "third race" (*tertium genus*) over against Jews and Gentiles'.

[100] Compare Ignatius, *Smyrn.* 1. 2, 'whether among Jews or among Gentiles, in the one body of his church'.

[101] Origen cites Deut. 32. 21, 'I will make them jealous of a non-nation (ἐπ' οὐκ ἔθνει)', and says, 'We are a non-nation (*non gens*)', but he immediately goes on to claim to be a *gens* but not like the Jews or Egyptians because of their diverse origin (*Hom. in Ps.* 36 (*PG* XX, 1321c, extant only in Latin)).

[102] See above, p. 000, and, for a similar situation among the Jews, 000.

derivation from the name of Christ, and this allows him to appropriate scriptural references to 'my name' (63. 5; 117. 3). However, this move exposes a problem that emerges in one of those moments when we feel that perhaps a Jewish voice really is speaking: 'that's fine for you Gentiles', says Trypho, 'who, as the Scriptures indicate, have come to know the Lord and Christ and God; but *we* worship the God who made him and so we do not need to acknowledge or worship him' (64. 1). To be named after Christ implies newness, and the epithet 'Christian' may separate its bearers from the scriptural tradition they claim, a possibility that Justin is determined to exclude: 'we Christians who flee to the God of Jacob and the God of Israel, having come to knowledge of the fear of God from "the law" and "the word which proceeded from Jerusalem" [Mic. 4. 2] through the apostles of Jesus' (110. 2).

It is this that leads him to say, 'We are not an ignominious populace (δῆμος) nor a barbarian tribe (φῦλον), nor like the nations (ἔθνη) of the Carians or Phrygians'; taking up Isa. 65. 1, 'Behold I am [God] for a nation (ἔθνος) who did not call my name', he denies that the promise to Abraham to be father of many nations could refer to 'the Arabs or Egyptians or Idumaeans', since different nations have different progenitors—a commonplace in the ethnography of the time; instead, he argues, it must anticipate 'us', 'the nation which is both god-fearing and righteous' (*Dial.* 119. 4–5).[103] Yet it is no less important to Justin also to claim that Christians 'are Israel' (123).[104] That, as we have seen, was a label that had only internal resonances, and, even so, we may suspect that it worked better in exegesis than in supplying a majority Gentile group with an identity that they would take into their daily lives; where Justin could expect greater success was in enabling them to be both a 'nation' and the heir to the promises of Scripture.

---

[103] Justin's quotation from Isa. 65. 1 is not identical to the LXX.
[104] On this see Lieu, *Image and Reality*, 136–40.

THE POWER OF LABELLING

The adoption of the label 'Christians' engendered a degree of differentiation. It did not, of course, determine the content of that label nor decide who could claim it. Outsiders had their own criteria for definition for when they needed it: as a literary type, for a Galen 'Christian' might be a byword of blind faith or of obstinate commitment to a way of life or to death; for a Lucian no less a byword, but of gullibility and of a misguided conviction about their own immortality.[105] More practically, Pliny required those who denied that they were Christians to do obeisance to the gods, supplicate the image of the Emperor, and curse Christ, 'none of which things those who are truly Christians can be compelled to do'.[106]

Our texts, as we have seen, reject the power of others to determine the meaning of the name: they seize the label given by others and both reshape it and allow it to shape their own self-presentation. Yet to do so was to claim control over it, and to deny it to others. This we have seen already in Ignatius, while we are left to wonder who was excluded from the *Gospel of Philip*'s 'true race' of Christians, or, indeed, who would have challenged their possession of the label. Justin finds himself forced to treat the Christians as 'the same sort of thing' as the Jews, or as a philosophical school, determined by a set of doctrines and practices, and unfortunately susceptible to attracting those with unacceptable deviations.[107] But this will mean that labelling generates more labelling: Justin's refusal to others of the epithet 'Christian' is maintained through the imposition of an alternative label, Marcionians, Valentinians, Basilidians, Satornilians; in these the shared ending, '-ians' (-ιανοί), attached to the name of their putative founder, parodies 'Christians' and so serves to underline their fraudulent character (*Dial*. 35. 6).[108] The success of the

---

[105] Galen in Walzer, *Galen*, 15 §6; Lucian, *Mort. Pereg.* 11–13.

[106] Pliny, *Epist*. X. 96; *Mart. Poly*. 10. 1, accepts that definition in that Polycarp makes his confession in direct opposition to the proconsul's invitation to him to swear by Caesar's Fortune.

[107] *Apol*. 16. 8, 14; 26; *Dial*. 35. 1–6; 80. 2–5; see above at n. 74.

[108] Reading Μαρκιωνιανοί against the Μαρκιανοί (Marcians) of the manuscript: so Le Boulluec, *La Notion d'hérésie*, 62 n. 117.

venture is demonstrated both by the alacrity with which such naming was taken up, and multiplied, by Justin's heresiological successors, and by the way it has continued to persuade more recent scholars, even when the texts they endeavour to assign to such groups fail to oblige by acknowledging their labels.[109] Similarly, Serapion of Antioch dismissively attributed the *Gospel of Peter*, which had until then earned a ready audience, to those 'whom we call Docetists/Appearancers';[110] again, the epithet has stuck, and scholars labour to define it, and the doctrine of 'appearance' that it denotes, ignoring the irony and the power of denying existence inherent in the very giving of the label.

If to name is 'to other', so, perhaps also, to accept naming is to reproduce that process. The multiformity of 'Christianities' is implicit in its own attempt to claim definition.

[109] On the former see Le Boulluec, *La Notion d'hérésie*. However, note the self-styled 4th-century 'Synagogue of the Marcionites' (*OGIS* 608. 1).

[110] Eusebius, *HE* VI. 12. 5, οὓς δοκητὰς καλοῦμεν.

9

'The Other'

Wherever we look for the emergence of 'the self' there looms the spectre of 'the other'. This has been true in the explorations of the preceding chapters: tracing the boundaries demands peering over to see what lies beyond, and asking why it (or 'they') must be excluded; stereotypes of the paradigmatic masculinity of the self assimilate the threat of woman to that of 'the other'; naming and being named involves being named as, or naming, those who are not 'us'. So, also, it is a commonplace throughout the literature on the construction of identity that the discovery of the self is inseparable from that of 'the other'. Certainly, further questions follow: it can be asked which comes first—does the recognition of that which is 'not-us' make it then possible to speak of 'us', or is our articulation of who 'we' already are achieved by the subsequent description of the doppelgänger of otherness? It is difficult to suppose that the question could be answered in absolute terms, both because in practice what we find is a dialectic between the two, and because once we decide that identity is constructed, then clearly both the sense of self and that of the other are constructed in mutual interaction. However, to recognize this is to recognize that the other is no more other absolutely and in essence than is the self primordially given, even though the senses of givenness and of unchangeability always are a potential, and frequently become a rhetorically asserted truth in the discourse of identity. Acknowledging this acts as a reminder that there can be other relationships with difference and alterity than the oppositional, although it is the latter that has tended to dominate studies of identity and otherness in antiquity as well as in the present. It forces the question as to whether 'the other' as other, negatively stereotyped if not demonized, may, after all, not be necessary for any stable and secure identity.[1]

Paul Gilroy has suggested that

'[o]therness' can only be a threat when identity refers to an indelible mark or code which is conceived as somehow written into the bodies of its carriers. Here, identity is latent destiny. Seen or unseen, on the surface of the body or buried deep in its cells, identity forever sets one group apart from others, who lack the particular, chosen traits which become the basis of a classifying typology and comparative evaluation.[2]

Although written about the modern world, this quotation could readily be transferred to the ancient world, Jewish and Graeco-Roman as well as Christian. Supposed physical characteristics were not, indeed, a primary part of the discourse of identity in antiquity—although Pliny could describe very distant peoples as having no heads, but ears and eyes on their chest, and Tacitus both assumes a match between the physique, the character, and the land of the Britons, and also reports that peoples far distant from Rome (and civilization) 'have human faces and features but limbs and bodies of beasts'.[3] However, we have already had ample evidence that even in antiquity embodiment was inextricably implicated in being 'Roman', 'Jew', or 'Christian'. Gilroy's observation also draws attention to the selectivity, to 'the particular, chosen traits', that we have already discovered in the drawing of boundaries: difference is never absolute, even if it is represented as such; rather, the invention of 'the other' involves the selection of some—the boundary-markers—while ignoring similarities.

Most important, Gilroy shows that otherness becomes a threat in particular circumstances and in relation to a particular understanding of the self, although, again, we might ask just how far we are able to assign priority to one or the other. Rather, recognition of one is implicated in the other: as we have already seen in thinking of naming, to speak of 'the other' is to claim the

---

[1] See R. Schwartz, *Curse of Cain*, 5, 'acts of identity formation are themselves acts of violence', quoted above Ch. 1 at n. 36; however, Schwartz's own analysis uncovers alternative models even within her paradigm text, the Hebrew Bible.

[2] Gilroy, 'Diaspora', 308.

[3] Pliny, *Nat. Hist.* V. 8. 45–6; Tacitus, *Agric.* 11–12; *Germ.* 46, 'so it is said'.

power to define the other, denying them their own voice and self-description. This makes it all the more important to recognize, even if it is perhaps less susceptible to easy analysis in antiquity, that difference is frequently an element within the self, individual or corporate, and is projected outwards as otherness.[4] To explore the delineation of the other is not just to discover the construction of identity by opposition; it is also to be invited to search for traces of such otherness within, and to ask why these cannot be integrated—whether those questions are asked from within or from without.[5]

Given the way that the presence of the other pervades almost any question about identity, some overlap with our previous explorations is unavoidable. Here we are most concerned, first, with the broader binary pattern of thinking by which the negation of collective others serves simultaneously to assert the self; of more specific interest are the motifs used in the delineation of the other, the continuities and the discontinuities as well as the different uses to which these can be put.

'BARBARIANS'

As we have already seen, a pivotal moment was the creation of the barbarian as 'the other' within the Greek construction of identity at least from the Persian crisis of the fifth century BCE; Plato acknowledges, even while he criticizes, the division of humanity that separates the Greek from the barbarian, described under a single label.[6] Here, the barbarians were the 'anti-Greeks against whom Hellenic culture and character were defined'.[7] As many have stressed, this function means that from this point, and through the centuries to follow, the barbarian is very largely

---

[4] See Gilroy, 'Diaspora', 315. This leads into that other form of 'otherness' that is rooted in the ultimate unknowability of 'the other', and also of the self.

[5] See J. Rutherford, 'A Place Called Home: Identity and the Cultural Politics of Difference', in Rutherford, *Identity*, 9–27, who speaks of 'the recognition of the otherness of ourselves' (26).

[6] Plato, *Politicus* 262D, βάρβαρον μιᾷ κλήσει προσειπόντες.

[7] Hall, *Inventing the Barbarians*, 51; see the discussion in Ch. 4. On the history of the idea of 'the barbarian' see W. Speyer and I. Opelt, 'Barbar', *JAC* 10 (1967), 251–90 (= 'Barbar I', *Reallexikon für Antike und Christentum*, Suppl. vol. I. 5/6, 811–98).

characterized negatively—by tyranny, by the lack of social institutions, by luxury, and by moral and sexual degeneracy; that
means, not merely by the absence of, but by the mirror-opposite
of, the virtues claimed by the Greeks (and their successors) for
themselves.[8] Yet Edith Hall has also described the contradictory
mix of 'inferiority and utopia' in the description of the barbarians, which she traces to the ambivalent suspicion that the growth
of civilization is in some sense also 'a fall'.[9] Here the stereotype
of the other acts yet again as a mirror, but one upon which the
tension between ideal and experience in awareness of the self can
be traced. On yet another level, the language of 'mixing' that we
have marked earlier, expressed in the term μιξοβάρβαρος, evinces
the abhorrence of the ever-possible impossibility.[10]

The continuity of such stereotypes of otherness, together with
their susceptibility to the incorporation of new nuances and to
an application to new contexts, becomes clear in the appropriation of the 'barbarian' by the Romans. The Romans came into
contact, did battle, and traded with, and even incorporated into
their Empire, many of those barbarians with whom they also
had become familiar from the Greek ethnographical tradition.[11]
Yet, as they themselves acknowledged, the Romans were barbarians within the Greek model: so, Cato complains to his son that
the Greeks call them, the Romans, 'barbarians' and 'blacken us
more disgracefully than others with the label "Simpleton"'; at
the same time he asserts that the Greeks are a most wicked and
intractable people whose writings corrupt and whose doctors are
to be avoided because they have a secret oath to kill all barbarians (us!).[12] Such apparent xenophobia, we should note, did not,
however, bar him from contact with all things Greek;[13] we again
need to make a careful distinction between literary constructions

---

[8] For the image see also Hartog, *The Mirror*.

[9] *Inventing the Barbarians*, 149.

[10] See Ch. 4 at n. 34; Dubuisson, 'Remarques sur le vocabulaire grec
d'acculturation'.   [11] See also above, pp. 213–15.

[12] *apud* Pliny, *Nat. Hist.* XXIX. 14, 'vincam nequissimum et indocile esse
genus illorum . . . nos quoque dictitant barbaros et spurcius nos quam alios
Opicon appellatione foedant'.

[13] E. Gruen, *Culture and National Identity*, 52–83, warns that the most negative comments about the Greeks come in this advice to his son, and that a
broader, more nuanced, picture of Cato's attitudes emerges from the sources
as a whole.

of alienation and the multiple layers of actual, criss-crossing, social relations.

This counter-offensive reflected the ambivalence felt from the standpoint of traditional Roman values towards Greek culture, even while inevitably embracing it: Cicero claims that Rome's superiority in virtue is achieved by nature, not by 'literature' —seen as an art excelled in by the Greeks—and that it cannot be matched by Greece or by any other nation: those virtues include *gravitas, constantia, probitas, fides*.[14] 'Part of the attraction of Greece for the Romans is that it can be a screen against which to project all that is un-Roman.'[15] So, the labels of 'being Greek' became slurs signifying the vices and laxity that the Romans did not recognize as part of their own identity.[16] We have seen how Roman writers bewail, and yet assume, the attraction of women to things Greek, and vice versa: the attraction of forms of otherness to each other and their insidious presence 'within'.[17] Yet all this also means that 'the most radical hellenophobe finds that he cannot escape from the Greek, who is indispensable to his self-fashioning'.[18]

Given such dynamics it is perhaps not surprising that under Roman rule Greek perceptions of the barbarian also change; now, not all non-Greeks, particularly not the Romans, may count as barbarians or as inferior. Moreover, for the Greek self-understanding, questions of manners and of culture, sustainable in the new political situation, can further dominate the construction of self, and so will also serve a vision of self that may often have harked back to an idealized earlier age.[19] Even amidst the apparent rigidity of constructions of the other, we must expect to find both adaptation and negotiation.

[14] Cicero, *Tusc. Disp.* I. 1. 2.

[15] D. Feeney, *Literature and Religion at Rome: Cultures, Contexts and Beliefs* (Cambridge: Cambridge University Press, 1998), 68–9.

[16] M. Dubuisson, '*Graecus, graeculus, graecari*: l'emploi péjoratif du nom des Grecs en latin', in Said, Ἑλληνισμος, 315–35.

[17] See above, p. 188.

[18] Feeney, *Literature and Religion*, 68–9, continuing the quotation at n. 15 above.

[19] See S. Said, 'The Discourse of Identity in Greek Rhetoric from Isocrates to Aristides', in Malkin, *Ancient Perceptions*, 275–99; E. L. Bowie, 'Hellenes and Hellenism in Writers of the early Second Sophistic', in Said, Ἑλληνισμος, 183–204.

Yet from the Roman perspective such claims, not just over against otherness but even more for the superiority of the self, also served a political purpose, as they earlier had for the Greeks: it was on such superiority over all others that could be founded the right to rule the world.[20] Conversely, a high degree of self-awareness both generated and necessitated a sustained and coherent sense of the uncivilized barbarians who might actually be encountered in various manifestations, not least through conquest. Yet such real encounters, and the military requirement of reliable practical information, did little, it would appear, to supplant the received stereotyped traditions that could serve so useful a purpose. Numerous studies of the descriptions by Romans of other peoples who we might expect them to have known from direct experience have confirmed that 'the filtering agents of tradition, ideology and Roman moral outlook create a cultural construction from an observed reality'.[21]

Although, theoretically, the stereotype of the other moves towards a lack of any differentiation, in practice the interaction with the ethnographical tradition that we have already explored does enable the recognition of differences between various 'others': so it is possible to isolate Roman views of Egypt, or of Parthia, or of the Germans. Yet frequently these differences are but manifestations that confirm and contribute to the overall picture, while, conversely, they also generate a cross-fertilization of the vocabulary and of the imagery of vilification. Cicero had asked, 'Who does not know the practice of the Egyptians? Their minds steeped in depraved errors would sooner face execution than harm ibis, asp . . .', and Juvenal duly recounts a tale to prove that that depravity extends to cannibalism, something to which not even the savage Cimbri or Britons, although known for their fierce inhospitality, would sink.[22] During this period the Romans had come to know Egypt well and had themselves absorbed the

---

[20] Dubuisson, '*Graecus*', 316, 'La vision romaine de l'étranger présente cette particularité d'être, plus que d'autres, organisée en un système cohérent fondé sur la prétension de Rome à gouverner le monde.' See also the seminal study by Y. A. Dauge, *Le Barbare*, who suggests some of the references cited in this discussion. See above, pp. 212–15.

[21] S. P. Mattern, *Rome and the Enemy: Imperial Strategy in the Principate* (Berkeley, Calif.: University of California Press, 1999), 77.

[22] Cicero, *Tusc. Disp.* V. 78; Juvenal, *Sat.* 15. 1–32.

worship of Isis; but they also now relied on that land's prosperity and had learned from experience the threat it offered through anyone who claimed it as a power base.[23] The fascination of the exotic that Egypt embodied already in Greek thought had proved its danger. This, however, only encouraged the stereotyping of the Egyptian barbarism rather than modifying it: Pomponius Mela can repeat in the first century what Herodotus had said four hundred years earlier, that the Egyptians behave differently from the rest of humankind.[24] In a new transformation, Philo would blend such views with the biblical tradition of Egypt as the place of Israel's oppression, so that it becomes the symbol of the corporeal and of the passions, as well as of archetypal impiety.[25]

Tacitus's description of 'the Germans', which draws on a tradition going back to include Caesar's own campaign records, moves in a different direction: as we have seen, he creates out of them a unified people that was in fact not to come into being for another millennium (*Germ.* 4). For him the land of the Germans matches their character, rugged, harsh, and miserable (2); yet despite his description of their near inhumanity, he also praises them as a 'race unmixed by intermarriage, peculiar and pure', asserting that their monogamy and their chastity set them apart from all other barbarians.[26] His celebration of their lack of arenas, dinner tables, secret letters, and adulteries, and his approval of their lifelong marriage and their refusal to limit their children (19) also serve a further agenda. All this makes it clear that they were an enemy to be taken seriously, but also uses their barbarism to establish what Rome is not, and their virtue to show what Rome should be.[27]

---

[23] e.g. through Anthony's liaison with Cleopatra: see H. Sonnabend, *Fremdenbild und Politik: Vorstellungen der Römer von Ägypten und dem Partherreich in der späten Republik und frühen Kaiserzeit*, EH III. 3. 286 (Frankfurt am Main: P. Lang, 1986), who suggests some of the references used in this discussion.

[24] Pomponius Mela, *Chron.* I. 57, 'cultores regionum multo aliter a ceteris agunt'; Herodotus, *Hist.* II. 3. 5.

[25] Philo, *Migr.* 27 (151); *Somn.* II. 42 (279–81); *Mos.* II. 36 (194).

[26] Cf. above Ch. 4 at n. 83; they have 'human faces and features, but the limbs and bodies of beasts', *Germ.* 46; 4; 18–19. On the tradition see also J. B. Rives (trans., introd., and commentary), *Tacitus* Germania, Clarendon Ancient History Series (Oxford: Clarendon, 1999), 1–75.

[27] For the former see F. Dupont, ' "En Germanie c'est-à-dire nulle part". Rhétorique de l'alterité et rhétorique de l'identité: l'aporie descriptive d'un

It is within this framework that we may understand better Tacitus's description of the Jews. Cicero had already described the Jews' religion as abhorrent to everything of which Rome could be proud, while Seneca had spoken of them as a most wicked of races (*sceleratissima gens*), and that before the revolt of 66 CE.[28] Now describing that revolt, Tacitus claims that the Jews, following Moses' guidance, observed 'new rites contrary to those of all other mortals': they are 'other' to humanity, as indeed they show by their 'hatred of all others'.[29] Even their name is formed by a barbarian (*in barbarum*) corruption of an originally Greek term, *Iudaei* from *Idaei* (*Hist.* V. 2). Further, 'among them everything is profane which among us is sacred; again, what to us is defiled among them is allowed'. He fails to illustrate this claim but nevertheless continues, 'the other practices of the Jews are sinister and revolting': in short, they are utterly other. Consequently, in contrast to his praise of the Germans, their separate beds and their refusal to marry foreigners become a vice only reinforced by their excessive promiscuity (V. 5). Tacitus's explicit fear is for those who are attracted by them and who will 'learn to revile the gods, repudiate their native land, and despise parents, children and brothers'. Here, the Jews are the barbarian within, a threat because, contrary to how it should be, they do in fact attract those who will then—in Tacitus's eyes—surrender their Roman-ness.

Yet there also is a further irony: the defeat of Jerusalem marks a significant stage in the Flavian establishment of power (*Hist.* II. 78. 2); the story of that period that Tacitus traces in the *Histories* is a story of civil war and violence, of barbarity, betrayal, and self-interest, and of individuals who portray a galaxy of vices. The Jews, perhaps, provide a mocking mirror-image of what Rome, in Tacitus's estimation, had become, as well as a fitting

territoire barbare dans la *Germanie* de Tacite', in Rousselle, *Frontières terrestres*, 189–219, 201, 'Ils ne viennent à l'existence que par la confrontation avec l'Autre. Ils n'ont d'autre identité que leur barbarie même, semblables à la terre qu'ils habitent, terre barbare et par conséquent informe, et innommée.'

[28] Cicero, *in Flacc.* 69, 'istorum religio sacrorum a splendore huius imperii, gravitate nominis nostri, maiorum institutis abhorrebat'; Seneca, *de Sup. apud* Augustine, *de Civ. Dei* VI. 10.

[29] Tacitus, *Hist.* V. 4–5, 'novos ritus contrariosque ceteris mortalibus . . . adversus omnes alios hostile odium'.

enemy to be destroyed in the war that he is describing. It is true that Tacitus, like other Roman authors, does not explicitly call the Jews 'barbarians', but there could be no more cogent depiction of an inverted or anti-world.[30] The threat they represent is the greater because they lie not beyond the boundaries of the Empire but within, the ultimate threat 'the other' may pose: so, elsewhere Tacitus laments the fear in which Romans now live, that in the person of their slaves they have 'the nations in our families . . . who have alien rites (*externa sacra*) or none'. In the first century, as Y. Dauge commented, 'le barbare se trouve partout'.[31]

Before long, the Christians would be depicted in a similar fashion: insidiously within and yet representing the reversal of all that was normal and civilized, they engage in 'unnatural repasts'; they 'despise the gods and mock at our sacred rites', whilst their own celebrations are marked by incest and all manner of sexual sacrilege; on every level of belief and behaviour they reverse the proper order of things.[32] When Christians turned the same accusations against their accusers, this was not merely a contest over morality and piety, but one over the right to belong 'within', and over the power to name and so to exclude the other. But this is to anticipate . . .

All such accounts exploit a vocabulary of 'otherness'; the charge of being 'alien' (*externus*; *alienigenus*) justified Tiberius's prohibition of Egyptian and Jewish rites, as it had earlier that of the Bacchic cult.[33] 'Foreign' influence is characterized by the language of corruption and infection, while their character is defined by descriptions of warlikeness, ferocity, and inhumanity, but also of weakness and vacillation.[34] We have noted elsewhere, and seen examples above, how the representation of

---

[30] See the thorough analysis of R. Bloch, *Antike Vorstellungen vom Judentum: Der Judenexkurs des Tacitus im Rahmen der griechisch-römischen Ethnographie*, Historia Einzelschriften 160 (Stuttgart: Franz Steiner, 2002), who overemphasizes this as having a primarily literary function for Tacitus.

[31] Tacitus, *Ann.* XIV. 44. 5, 'nationes in familiis habemus, quobus diversi ritus, externa sacra aut nulla sunt'; Dauge, *Le Barbare*, 148.

[32] See Minucius Felix, *Oct.* 9–11, but note that this is a Christian's account.

[33] Suetonius, *Tib.* 36; Livy, *Hist.* XXXIX. 15. 3, 'pravi et externi religiones'; for *alienigenus* see Livy, *Hist.* XXXI. 29. 15, above, p. 104.

[34] On all this see Dauge, *Le Barbare*, 466–510, esp. 500–3, and above, pp. 185–8.

sexuality, both sexual practice and sexual stereotypes, occupies a significant place within this rhetoric. Religion, too, belongs here despite the supposed tolerance of Rome towards religious diversity—as witnessed by the examples just cited of the suppression of the Bacchic cult and of Tiberius's expulsions. Here, the tensions between literary rhetoric and social practice become apparent: Rome did absorb other religious traditions, and exercised various techniques of translation to do so, yet the language of superstition and of its danger remains powerful. Beard, North, and Price suggest that 'it was partly in this contest with enemies real and imaginary that true *religio* found its definition—and the Roman élite, as religion's most active defenders, displayed (to themselves as much as to anyone else) their own indispensability to the religious, political and social order they, and their ancestors, had created'.[35] Again, the spectre of 'the other' is a powerful weapon in the maintenance of the power-holders as well as of the cohesive identity of the many.

Yet the image of the barbarians can also have a powerful force for its utopian potential: we have already noted Tacitus's archaizing ideals about the marital fidelity of the Germans. Pliny, following a tradition that reaches back to Herodotus, describes the Hyperboreans who live in the distant regions of the north in woods and groves; there, there is no discord or sorrow, and they choose their death when the right moment comes.[36] Quintus Curtius is amazed at the wisdom to be found among the Scythians, who are not crude and undisciplined like the other barbarians, and in India 'among such vices'.[37] The ideal of the 'noble savage' has a long history, but so too does the hankering after the 'wisdom of the barbarians'.[38] Here, too, the image of the other offers opportunities for reflecting on the realities and the limitations of the self, of exploring other possibilities without taking on the challenges and the dangers that that might involve if put into practice.

Thus, although much of this account has emphasized the exclusionary use of the divide, other strategies were also possible. Otherness may be ritually explored and so may be allowed expres-

---

[35] Beard, North, Price, *Religions of Rome*, i. 244.
[36] Pliny, *Nat. Hist.* IV. 12. 82; Herodotus, *Hist.* IV.
[37] Quintus Curtius, *Hist.* VII. 8. 10; VIII. 9. 31; IX. 1. 24.
[38] Dauge, *Le Barbare*, 179–90; Speyer and Opelt, 'Barbar', 258–9.

sion and yet be contained.[39] A more dialogical analysis would also suggest that, even in some of the texts we have adduced, exploring images of the other can become a means of testing alternative possibilities in the definition of the self.[40] Erich Gruen has emphasized how, by adopting Aeneas of Troy as founder, Rome effectively took over, and so neutralized the threat of, the symbols through which the Greeks vaunted their own antiquity and triumph: 'Ancient societies defined themselves by reference to "the other", but did so most effectively by expropriating "the other".'[41] Shadowing Graeco-Roman models, even 1 Maccabees ameliorates any potential absolutism by claiming a common ancestry with Sparta (1 Macc. 12. 5–23). Similarly, Hellenistic Jewish texts represent Abraham as the originator of all that was best about Greek culture, although this need not result in any diminution of difference—it is merely another way of dealing with the threat, here of claimed superiority.[42]

THE OTHERNESS OF THE 'NATIONS'

So it may be that such expropriation is most effective when it appears to retain the other as other, but now divested of threat. The Hebrew Bible is, of course, an exemplar of such expropriation, for example claiming for the LORD the imagery and epithets of the indigenous deities of Palestine who elsewhere are denounced (Psalm 29). Yet the Hebrew Bible has also been seen as archetypal in its construction of otherness as utterly alien and beyond negotiation, for it assumes that all other ways are false, alien to Israel's understanding of the true God and to her unique covenantal role in God's purposes.[43] That 'the LORD your God has chosen you out of all the peoples on earth to be his people, his treasured possession' can become a licence to utterly destroy 'the

---

[39] For this, see H. Kenner, *Das Phänomen der verkehrten Welt in der griechisch-römischen Antike* (Bonn: Habelt, 1970).

[40] See Dench, *From Barbarians to New Men*, 22.

[41] Gruen, 'Cultural Fictions', 1–14, 14.

[42] On these, see Gruen, 'Cultural Fictions'; also above, pp. 72–4.

[43] See J. Assmann, 'The Mosaic Distinction: Israel, Egypt, and the Invention of Paganism', *Representations* 56 (1996), 48–67; Schwartz, *The Curse of Cain*, esp. pp. 15–38.

many nations' (גוים רבים; ἔθνη μεγάλα) who threaten the integrity
of the people (Deut. 7. 1–6). By the time of Deuteronomy these
nations, the 'Hittites and the Amorites, the Canaanites and the
Perizzites, the Hivites and the Jebusites' (20. 17) were long gone;
they represent a rhetorical other, which, like the narrative of
which they are part, represses the actual origins of Israel within
the mix of movements and peoples of the region.[44]

None the less, 'the ways of the Amorite' will retain their
symbolic otherness for centuries to come (t. Sabb. 6–7).[45] By
contrast, Edom, in Deuteronomy still 'your kin' (as 'Esau') and
not to be rooted out (Deut. 2. 4, 5; 23. 7), becomes progressively
excoriated in Second Temple literature (compare Jub. 26. 33–
5), 'the exemplification of a nation and a people opposed to the
Jews'.[46] The people behind that mask of otherness will change,
from Idumaea to the Roman Empire in rabbinic writings, to its
Christian successors, but the mask remains, with all its sibling
ambiguity.

As other, the 'nations' in Deuteronomy are defined as a single
entity, characterized by their 'altars, their pillars, their Asherim,
and their idols' (Deut. 7. 3–6), as well as by the threat of intermarriage that they represented. We have already traced the continuity of these boundary markers of idolatry and intermarriage
throughout our period, and noted how, again, the same mask
is worn by other 'others' in new and different circumstances.
Here already in Deuteronomy their naming as 'the nations', 'the
Gentiles' (גוים; ἔθνη), pre-empts the need for any differentiation or
for the recognition of change. There is no ethnographic curiosity
within the scriptural tradition, and no grounds on which there
could be any. In fact, the only acknowledgement of multiplicity
among 'the Gentiles' seems to be in the Psalms of Solomon's
description of them as 'the mixed nations' (ἔθνη συμμίκτα) (Ps.
Sol. 17. 17), or in 2 Baruch's description of those 'who withdrew
and mingled (ܘܠܛ) with the seed of the mixed peoples (ܡܘ)'
(42. 4); the image of 'mixed nations' may come from Jer. 25.
20, 24, but its force seems to effect a contrast with Israel who

---

[44] See Sparks, Ethnicity and Identity, 12, 258–9. On Deuteronomy and the
creation of a history see Mullen, Narrative History, and above, pp. 63–4.

[45] See Stern, Jewish Identity, 181–5.

[46] See Cresson, 'Condemnation of Edom', 147, and above, Ch. 3 at n. 26.

are to be pure and who are not themselves to 'mingle'.[47] In this way, as we have repeatedly seen already, the label 'Gentiles' can come to act as the signifier of anything that is alien and rejected; that it denotes licentious or incestuous practice, or polytheistic identification of images (idols) with deities, is an accepted part of the image, and so can be assumed to require no further demonstration.[48] Within such a rhetoric there is no room for hearing how these others might define their own sexual mores or articulate their own understanding of the gods—and the power of the rhetoric is seen in the continuing vitality of the construct as fact in subsequent (and modern) popular imagination.

As we have also already seen, *Jubilees* acts as a paradigm of such a construction: it warns against walking 'after the Gentiles, and after their uncleanness, and after their shame' (*Jub.* 1. 9), knowing that no more needs to be said. 'Not as the Gentiles' becomes a catch-phrase (3. 31) that relies on an unquestioning acceptance of the premise.[49] It is because the construct of the abhorrent Gentile is presumed to be shared and not to be questioned that it can be turned against others 'within': *Jubilees* fulminates against those who certainly saw themselves as Jews, and redefines them as other, labelling not only their apparent responses to Hellenism but also their internal calendrical disagreements as 'walking according to the Gentiles' (6. 36). The uniform mask of Gentile otherness denies their own voice not only to actual Gentiles but also to any within Israel subsumed within the rhetoric, making any recovery of them a matter only of conjecture. Similarly, for example, when among the Dead Sea Community the *Halakhic Letter* rejects the wheat and the sacrifice 'of the Gentiles' (4QMMT 6–11), we can no longer be certain who it is that hides behind that epithet.[50]

At the same time, the uniform mask also serves the particular concerns of the text and its authors, and so invariably fails to replicate accurately the complexities of actual daily life. As we have seen, within rabbinic literature the 'Gentile as idolater' is utterly other; according to Gary Porton this is an otherness

---

[47] Jer. 25. 20, 24, MT הערב, whose meaning is uncertain, but see above Ch. 4 at n. 48 on this root; LXX (ch. 32), οἱ σύμμικτοι; see above, Ch. 4 at n. 69.

[48] See above, pp. 112–22.

[49] Cf. Eph. 4. 17 and the further discussion below.

[50] See above pp. 113–14.

that is not just a consequence of Israel's chosenness but which is built into the structure of the universe.[51] As the 'not-Israelite' the Gentile, identified by idolatry and religious practice, thus defines who the Israelite is; conversely, it is almost inevitable that 'the *Mishna* considers the nations as a amorphous "melting-pot", an undifferentiated, homogenous collectivity'.[52] Yet outside this framework it is assumed that Jews and Gentiles will interact on a number of levels: otherness is selective in time and place.[53]

A different meeting of scriptural and then-contemporary models of otherness surfaces in the Maccabean literature. Again, we have seen in more than one context that, despite the common construction of the Maccabean tradition as one of conflict between the Jewish tradition and the 'other' of Hellenism, this antinomy, which was to prove so cardinal to later Jewish self-understanding, is not primary in the texts themselves.[54] In 1 Maccabees, where the word 'Greek' comes but three times (1. 10; 6. 2; 18. 18), the vocabulary of otherness is just that: ἀλλογενής ('of other race'), ἀλλότριος ('alien'), and ἀλλόφυλος ('foreign').[55] The last of these generates a neologism in 2 Maccabees, ἀλλοφυλισμός, 'foreignness' (2 Macc. 4. 13; 6. 24), and in 4 Maccabees, the verb ἀλλοφυλεῖν, 'to become foreign' (4 Macc. 18. 5). All these terms belong within the familiar register of otherness in Greek thought, and rejection of the presence in the land of those thus described, or of dealing with them, would surprise no contemporary Greek reader. Yet for insiders, 1 Maccabees also constructs a further layer of alienation, for in the Septuagint ἀλλόφυλος ('foreigner') is the primary translation for 'Philistine'. We need not trace here either the reasons for this translation choice nor its wider ramifications in other literature; what matters is that 1 Maccabees thus evokes the scriptural account of the battles

[51] Porton, *Goyim*, 221–39; cf. Stern, *Jewish Identity*, 195–7.

[52] Stern, *Jewish Identity*, 14.

[53] See above, pp. 121–2.

[54] On this topos see Y. Shavit, *Athens in Jerusalem: Classical Antiquity and Hellenism in the Making of the Modern Secular Jew*, ET. Littman Library of Jewish Civilization (London: Valentine Mitchell, 1997), and above, Ch. 4 at n. 36.

[55] ἀλλογενής: 3 times, ἀλλότριος: 8 times, and ἀλλόφυλος: 10 times; on this and what follows see Lieu, 'Not Hellenes', 248–55.

with the Philistines (cf. also 4. 30), who, as the 'uncircumcised', are themselves the archetypal others of Israel's story.[56] Thus, for those who accept the identity being constructed by the pro-Hasmonaean propaganda of 1 Maccabees, they themselves are the heirs of Saul and David, while the enemy is their same enemy, even if under a different guise.

The adoption by 2 Maccabees of this root works within a very different strategy. Although it does speak of 'Hellenism' (ἑλληνισμός) as the enemy, it redefines what was an existing term by further qualifying it with what for a Greek would evoke its antithesis, 'foreignness' (ἀλλοφυλισμός) (2 Macc. 4. 13; cf. 6. 24); it further inverts the conventional polarities of the time by iden-tifying the Jewish campaign against 'Greek customs' as a pursuit of 'the barbaric hordes' (τὰ βάρβαρα πλήθη) (2. 21). The battle is, as we have seen, a battle for 'Judaism' (ἰουδαϊσμός), another neologism, but one that would have represented what for many Greeks belonged firmly alongside the barbarian.[57] Here, the contemporary rhetoric of otherness is being skilfully redeployed to legitimate, both internally and externally, a particular agenda of self-definition that has little to do with what more recent scholars might label 'Hebraism' and 'Hellenism'.

From the Maccabean perspective the danger that threatened was as much from within as from without. For this an additional vocabulary of distancing was needed, one that was provided by the scriptural tradition: the enemy are 'sinners' (ἁμαρτωλοί), 'lawless' (ἀνόμοι), 'impious' (ἀσεβεῖς), 'unholy' (ἀνόσιοι): 'and there came to him (Demetrius) all the lawless and impious of Israel . . .' (1 Macc. 7. 5).[58] Such epithets pre-empt the need for more precise description or for justification, and they continue to obfuscate any attempt to find an alternative identity for those so identified; instead, they justify whatever action is meted against them and define them as outside any divine purpose, while equal-ly defining those who oppose them. The same rhetoric appears elsewhere, and, because it denies 'the other' any self-description,

---

[56] On the importance of 'Israel' in 1 Maccabees, see above, Ch. 8 at n. 16.

[57] On 'Judaism' see above, Ch. 8 at n. 19.

[58] ἁμαρτωλ-: 1 Macc. 5 times; ἀνόμ-: 1 Macc. 12 times; 2 Macc. once; 3 Macc. 5 times; ἀσεβ-: 1 Macc. 7 times; 2 Macc. 6 times; 4 Macc. 6 times; ἀνόσ-: 2 Macc. twice; 3 Macc. 3 times; 4 Macc. once.

it may cover actual variety.[59] In the *Psalms of Solomon* Pompey is not named, for it is enough that he is 'the sinner'; yet 'the sinner' is also the archetypal other to the righteous for whom the Psalmist speaks: God will distinguish between the righteous and the sinner (*Ps. Sol.* 2. 1, 34). For these *Psalms*, sinners are to be found within as well as without. They are characterized only in stereotypical terms that may do little more than tell us that behind the label stood opponents of the authors' party: the accusations of profligate adultery and of menstrual defilement of the sacrifices (8. 11–14) are unlikely to be merely descriptive; although it is possible that they reflect differing interpretations of Torah, it is more probable that they simply draw on traditional conceptions of the utterly abhorrent. 'The sinners' serve to define and so to reassure 'the righteous', but the terminology belongs to the rhetoric of reprobation and does not invite historical reconstruction: 'The portion and inheritance of God is Israel. The sinners and lawless are not so, those who love the day in liaison with their sin. Their desire is in the transitoriness of corruption and they have not remembered God' (14. 5–6).

It is but a short step from here to the 'men of the lot of Belial' in the *Manual of Discipline* (1QS 2. 4–5 etc.). In this text the rhetoric of otherness is subsumed into a cosmic construction: the sons of deceit belong not only to darkness but to the dominion of the Angel of Darkness (3. 20–2). It is difficult to know whether we should pursue our exploration of the other further into this dualistic and apocalyptic world-view. Such a move on the one hand, we might suppose, is only an extension of the homogenization and demonization implicit in many a (if not in any) construction; the lists of vices that belong to the spirit of darkness, despite their scriptural resonances, are not so very different from those that a Greek or Roman rhetoric would ascribe to the barbarian—greed, dishonesty, trickery, 'appalling acts in a spirit of sexual profligacy' (4. 9–10).[60] Yet it also reifies the refusal to acknowledge the ambiguities inherent in the encounter with the other, and makes not just a cultural but a cosmic judgement on any attempt

---

[59] This means that we cannot rediscover 'the sinners' of the Jesus tradition through these other texts: it is a blanket label of reprobation.

[60] מעשי תועבה ברוח זנות: the terms are scriptural but the translation given deliberately renders in a classical voice.

to confuse the categories: 'In these consist the generations of all humankind, and in their divisions share all their hosts by their generations . . . for God has placed them in equal parts until the very end, and has caused an eternal hostility (עולם איבת) between their divisions' (4. 15–17).[61] It is, then, ironic that it is this text that makes the most nuanced 'theological' effort to mediate between the incommensurability of the spirits of light and darkness and of their characteristics, and the ultimate indeterminacy of where any human being may belong, by setting them within the constraints of the transcendence of God and of God's ultimate purposes (3. 17–4. 20).

We should recall here again how powerful a weapon of otherness in much of this literature is provided by the vocabulary of impurity, pollution, uncleanness, abomination, and infection. The roots of such language are deeply scriptural, but in the literature of this period it becomes both much more prolific and more polysemous.[62] Yet there is a similar vocabulary of infection in Roman sources. Judah can fear being 'mixed with the abominations of the Gentiles (βδελύγματα ἐθνῶν)' (T. Jud. 23. 2), just as Tacitus can envisage the Parthians' sense of shame at accepting a king who had been brought up in Rome, 'from another world . . . infected with enemy arts [alium orbem . . . hostibus artibus infectum]' (Ann. II. 2).[63] It is a rhetoric that reinforces the alienness of the other, while simultaneously recognizing a susceptibility to the threat it carries.

Yet if all this might seem to confirm the picture of Judaism in this period as operating with a very powerful and uniform image of the other, there are, as generally in the Graeco-Roman world, also other currents in motion. Eschatology, with its uncertainties about the ultimate place of 'the Gentiles', might potentially recognize an element of contingency about their otherness; such a contingency was, moreover, already embedded in the scriptural

---

[61] For the 'eternal hostility' compare Livy's 'aeternum bellum' between Greeks and barbarians (Hist. XXXI. 29. 15).

[62] On this see Lieu, ' "Impregnable Ramparts" ', 309–10, and above, pp. 119–21.

[63] Cf. Ann. XI. 16, where the Germans in a similar situation are anxious about one who would be 'infectum alimonio servitio cultu omnibus externis'; in Ann. II. 85, describing the expulsion of Jews and Egyptians from Rome, he speaks of those 'infected by that superstition'.

stories of Gen. 1–11, and particularly in the genealogies that ultimately integrated the people of Israel into all the peoples of the world. It is in the spirit of the former of these dynamics that Revelation can both say that 'all the Gentiles have been led astray', and still anticipate the final 'healing of the Gentiles' (Rev. 18. 23; 22. 2). Further, as we have already discovered, there are those who textually as well as in social practice mediate across, or actually cross, the boundaries, archetypically the 'alien' (גר).[64] The alien might be seen as 'the other within', but as such s/he represents not threat but one in need of protection; yet equally, as we have seen, Israel's own experience of being the alien, the other, may constrain the instinct for excoriation: 'You shall not abhor any of the Egyptians, because you were an alien residing in their land' (Deut. 23. 7).[65] And throughout the Scriptures there are those who undermine the model of the obduracy of the Gentile other, Ruth, the Ninevites in Jonah, Cyrus in Second Isaiah. It may be, as is often argued, that these texts represent a different construction of identity from that of the 'exclusivist' trajectory that runs from Ezra to *Jubilees*. Yet both remained, and remain, within the resources of later generations.

Grey areas continue to challenge the assumed starkness of the rhetoric of the other. In rabbinic literature, Sacha Stern has traced the place of the 'people of the land' (*am ha-aretz*), of 'sinners', and of apostates, noting that, demographically, they may have been in the majority. On one level, the dichotomy of Israel/ non-Israel is sustained; on another, the texts both recognize and ignore the shifting and ambiguous inhabitants of the margins.[66]

(NEITHER) GENTILES, JEWS NOR GREEKS?

When Paul writes to the Galatians that 'we ourselves . . . are Jews by nature and not sinners from the Gentiles' he affirms the binary division that is familiar from the texts that we have explored above.[67] Yet his next emphatic 'we' (ἡμεῖς) goes on to

[64] See above Ch. 4 at n. 68.

[65] See J. Ramírez Kidd, *Alterity and Identity in Israel*, BZAW 283 (Berlin: de Gruyter, 1999), 92–8. See above, Ch. 7 at n. 70, for the alien and place.

[66] Stern, *Jewish Identity*, 105–38.

[67] Thus, whatever its social articulation, his antithesis between Peter, as a

problematize this: 'And *we* believed in Christ Jesus in order that we might be justified by faith of Christ' (Gal. 2. 15–16); this becomes clear when he continues in parallel terms, and as scripturally founded, that 'God justifies the Gentiles by faith' (3. 8).[68] Paul continues to work with and to transform the Jew versus Gentile polarity, as he also does with that between Jew and Greek, to the extent that he rarely mentions the first, Jew, without adding (τε καί) one or other of the latter.[69] 'Greek' he uses mainly inclusively, affirming an abolition of the distinctions that the label once represented, and for many still did represent, through the more familiar 'Greek versus barbarian' (Rom. 1. 16; Gal. 3. 28).[70] 'Gentile', however, remains ambiguous for Paul: the label, betraying, as we have seen, a Jewish and not a natural self-perception, represents their standing before God, which has now entered a new stage focused in Paul's own activity amongst them: they *were* Gentiles and have as such received the Gospel (1 Cor. 12. 2). Paul can, it is true, address the Romans as 'you Gentiles' (Rom. 11. 13), but it seems that the term cannot totally shake off its legacy of moral and religious perfidy: he is horrified to find in the Corinthian community sexual immorality 'such as is not even found among the Gentiles' (1 Cor. 5. 1).[71]

The ambiguity of 'Gentile', and its consequent inutility in a rhetoric of distinction, is widespread. Many of our texts address those who had never been Jews, but at the same time identify 'Gentile' as 'the other who does not know God'. For *1 Clement*,

---

Jew, living 'in Gentile fashion (ἐθνικῶς)', and the impossibility of compelling Gentiles 'to become Jewish (ἰουδαΐζειν)' (Gal. 2. 14) does not just refer to the 'boundary markers of national identity' but operates within the dichotomies of otherness and the tensions regarding its dissolution that we have noted above. On these grounds we should assign this phrasing to the Paul who is writing Galatians and not to the Paul at the time of the Antioch incident.

[68] I am using the traditional translation of δικαίοω and πίστις Χριστοῦ without entering the debate into the precise meaning of either of these.

[69] 'Jew' appears without 'Greek' or 'Gentile' in close proximity only in Rom. 2. 17, 28; 3. 1; 1 Cor. 9. 20.

[70] Also Rom. 2. 9–10; 3. 9; 10. 12; 1 Cor. 1. 22, 24; 10. 32; 12. 13; Col. 3. 11; only in Rom. 1. 14 ('to Greeks and to barbarians') and Gal. 2. 3 is 'Greek' not accompanied by 'Jew'.

[71] Perhaps also 1 Cor. 10. 20 where there is significant evidence for 'the sacrifices the Gentiles offer': the omission of 'Gentiles' by BDFG, although a strong combination, could be occasioned by the ambiguity that we are here exploring.

'Gentiles' is used only of outsiders, and even in the prayer that 'all the Gentiles might know that you alone are God' there is no hint that the readers once belonged among them (*1 Clem.* 55. 1; 59. 3–4).[72] Hermas sees the fundamental division as between 'the righteous and the Gentiles and apostates', and he fears for those who at the end will 'live with the Gentiles and be carried away by the empty opinions of the Gentiles and turn away from God and do the deeds of the Gentiles' (Hermas, *Vis.* I. 4. 2; *Sim.* VIII. 9. 1–3; cf. IV. 4); 'as do the Gentiles', with its evocation of idolatry and sexual immorality, and its echo of texts such as *Jubilees*, continues as a castigation of those who fail to sustain the difference that the text demands (Hermas, *Mand.* IV. 1. 9; XI. 4). Although Ephesians can remind its readers that they 'were Gentiles in the flesh', the author still urges them not to 'walk as do the Gentiles in the foolishness of their understanding' (Eph. 2. 11; 4. 17). Matthew can both promise that the disciples will 'be hated by all the Gentiles', and instruct them to 'make disciples of all the Gentiles'; his use of an alternative term, *ethnicos* (ἐθνικός)—'do not babble like the *ethnicoi*'—does not really resolve the tension, even if it is an attempt to do so (Matt. 24. 9; 28. 19; 6. 7; cf. 5. 47; 18. 17). Even in the middle of the second century in Gaul the persecution is described as 'the wrath of the Gentiles against the saints', while elsewhere, 'Gentiles' combine with 'Jews' as outsiders: like the apostles before him, Polycarp is opposed by a crowd of 'lawless Gentiles', although also, as we shall see, by both Jews and Gentiles in concert.[73]

However, although Justin does refer neutrally to '*other* nations' (ἄλλα ἔθνη), meaning neither the Jews nor 'us' (*Dial.* 16. 2; 17. 1), the term does not maintain its pejorative 'outsider' status. He alone among the Apologists takes up its rich possibilities from scriptural prophecy and gives it a positive tone;[74] he explains to an outside audience that 'all the other human races (γένη) are called "Gentiles" (ἔθνη) by the prophetic spirit', and asserts that 'Christians from the Gentiles are more in number and truer than those from Jews or Samaritans' (*Apol.* 53. 2–5; cf. 31. 7). Even more polemically in the *Dialogue*, he emphasizes believers 'from

---

[72] *1 Clement* does not use 'Greek'.

[73] *HE* V. 1. 4; *Mart. Poly.* 9. 2, 12. 2; cf. Acts 14. 5.

[74] The few occurrences in Aristides and Athenagoras can be translated 'nations'.

the Gentiles' as those who do not practise idolatry, in contrast to the Jews who now, through the language of Scripture, are constructed as so doing (*Dial*. 34. 7–8; 130. 4); it is to the former that are given the epithets claimed by the Jews through their texts, 'Godfearing and righteous' (52. 4). It is, then, unsurprising that Justin does not hesitate to speak of 'we Gentiles' (*Dial*. 41. 3).

The ambiguous reconfiguration of 'Gentile' as other inevitably rebounds on 'Jew' as self. The language of 'we [Jews]' is rare apart from Paul's anguished wrestling with the dilemma that he perceives; even he approaches the term with some care, but despite the antithetical rhetoric of his defence of justification by faith, there is not even here any stable other in Paul's letters.[75] Whether the Apocalypse's denunciation of 'those who say they are Jews and are not' (Rev. 2. 9; 3. 9) should be seen as an implicit claim to the label remains unclear.[76] More important is the way that 'Jew' becomes 'other'. It is in John's Gospel where this undeniably but controversially emerges. The issue here is not whether either the Gospel or the Jesus it presents are Jewish: both undoubtedly are. It is rather that those labelled 'the Jews' (οἱ ἰουδαῖοι), whoever might be intended by that label on the stage of the narrative, are repeatedly presented as over against Jesus and his own: they persecute him, murmur against him, seek to kill him (John 5. 16, 18; 6. 41; 10. 31). The label itself blankets the different characters involved—the Pharisees, scribes, Sadducees, or elders of the Synoptics—and in this way it effects a degree of homogenizing.[77] The antithesis is, however, not yet absolute: there are those among the Jews who do believe (8. 31; cf. 12. 42), and even among the rest there is as much division as consensus (10. 19; 9. 22)—although in a text that so urges unity it may be that dissension itself belongs to the characterization of 'otherness'. Adopting and transforming the tradition

---

[75] On Paul's caution towards 'Jew', see J. D. G. Dunn, 'Who Did Paul Think That He Was? A Study of Jewish Christian Identity', *NTS* 45 (1999), 174–93, esp. 179–85. See above, Ch. 4 at n. 95, on 'unbelievers' in 1 Corinthians, but these are not sufficiently characterized to function as 'other'.

[76] See above, Ch. 8 at n. 29.

[77] John does also use 'Pharisees'. There is a substantial literature on the issue; on this and what follows see R. Bieringer, D. Pollefeyt, F. Vandecasteele-Vanneuville (eds.), *Anti-Judaism and the Fourth Gospel: Papers of the Leuven Colloquium, 2000* (Assen: Van Gorcum, 2001).

of apocalyptic dualism, John will also oppose light to darkness, truth to falsehood, and being not of the world to being of the world (3. 19–21; 17. 9–16); but the Jews do not fully belong to this schema: salvation is 'of the Jews' (4. 22).

It has become conventional to explain that the community for which John speaks identified itself over against the Jews, who represent those from whom they had separated and who continued to represent a real or imagined threat, and who, presumably, were so labelled by outsiders and insiders alike. This may be so, and it is undeniable that the Gospel is constructing an understanding of what it is to be a believer or a disciple of Jesus, an understanding in which 'the Jews' as such belong outside. However, Jesus's story is carried out 'among them' (11. 54), and not as a stranger visiting barbarians with whom he cannot communicate; the Jews are defined by an unbelief that for some may not be irrevocable (8. 31)—although whether, if they sustained belief, they would still be Jews remains unasked and so unanswerable. Yet, for all this ameliorating potential, the Fourth Gospel still makes possible a self-understanding by which 'the Jews' are not 'us', and whose anticipated hostility only confirms that neither are they 'of God' (8. 47).

Within subsequent literature 'the Jews' are used in a variety of ways and to serve a range of purposes, although we may not always want to categorize these as species of otherness.[78] Certainly, Ignatius fashions his neologism *christianism* by opposition to the more familiar *ioudaism*, itself, as we have seen, already generated within the rhetoric of otherness of the Maccabean tradition.[79] There can, for him, be no contact between the two (*Philad.* 6. 1; *Magn.* 10. 2), and, in his refusal to define 'Judaism', or perhaps in his assumption that it requires no definition because it is excluded merely by being named, he contributes to the undifferentiated mask of otherness that the Jews will come to wear in Christian discourse. Ignatius, of course, deals in oppositions: in the same letter in which he abhors Judaism, he speaks of there being two coinages, God's and the world's (*Magn.* 5. 2); his exhortation to the church at Philadelphia to avoid Judaism is

---

[78] Lieu, *Image and Reality*. For a later period see also D. M. Olster, *Roman Defeat, Christian Response, and the Literary Construction of the Jew* (Philadelphia: University of Pennsylvania Press, 1994).

[79] See above, Ch. 8 at n. 19.

followed by one to 'flee the wiles and snares of the prince of this world' (*Philad*. 6. 2). The incipient absorption of the Jews into that most fundamental of oppositions, by definition built into the very structure of the universe, the opposition against the world and the devil, will ensure that in later writers at least they lose any more human features.

Here again we encounter the intersection between the identity-sustaining rhetoric of otherness and an apocalyptic dualism, which is no less constitutive of identity-formation. However, it is the explicit naming of 'the Jews' rather than their implicit positioning within this schema that is most constructive. The latter, an implicit positioning, certainly, is not ineffective, and to it would belong *Barnabas*'s repeated warnings against the Evil One in a letter that systematically rewrites the significance of the scriptural institutions, and so rewrites Jewishness for its own purposes (*Barn*. 2. 10; 4. 10, 13): 'an evil angel beguiled them', a charge that has particular force in the current form of the text with its dualism of the light-giving angels of God who rule over the way of light, and the angels of Satan who rule over the way of darkness (9. 4; 18. 1).[80] More explicit is Revelation's renaming of those 'who are not' Jews as the 'synagogue of Satan' (Rev. 2. 9; 3. 9). Yet more explicit still is Justin's assertion that the Jews sacrificed to demons, a charge that earlier had been associated with idolatrous Gentiles (1 Cor. 10. 2), together with his declaration that they were agents of demons in the persecution of Christians (*Dial*. 19; 131).[81] The topos is well established when, in the *Acts of John*, Jesus is arrested by 'the lawless Jews whose lawgiver is the lawless serpent' (*Act. Joh*. 94). That the demons are not the sole prerogative of the Jews—for Justin they are also responsible both for heresy and for pagan imitations of the Christian story—only confirms the triumph of an undifferentiated opposition over the variegated world of experience.

Yet with this we have left the confines of the apocalyptic world-view, or perhaps that world-view has helped provide for these

[80] The relationship of the 'two way' chapters (18–20) to the rest of *Barnabas* is disputed, and it is notable that the characterization of the way of darkness in these chapters is conventional and is not directly related to the earlier polemic.

[81] For this see J. M. Lieu, 'Accusations of Jewish Persecution in Early Christian Sources', in *Neither Jew nor Greek?*, 135–50; cf. also *Mart. Poly*. 17. 1–2.

texts the lens for viewing the present. Scripture, too, adds its voice: for Justin, as we have just seen, the Jews are pre-eminently defined by their unbelief; but, through an appeal to the prophetic tradition, they can also be defined by precisely the same behaviour that traditionally marked the Gentiles, by idolatry, magical arts, godlessness, and even by adulterous polygamy (*Dial.* 34. 8; 85. 3; 120. 2; 130. 4; 141. 4). Beyond Justin, the Jews will increasingly become the means against which, and therefore the means by which, the faithful behaviour of and the proper interpretation of the Scriptures by the Christians can be defined—a trajectory traced by numerous studies of Christian anti-Judaism or anti-Semitism.[82]

If, in these ways, 'Christians' emerge out of the existing opposition between Jew and Gentile, they could be positioned differently in relation to those other categories of opposition, barbarian and Greek. Despite Paul's vision of inclusiveness, in other writers 'Greek' retains some of its effectiveness for polemic. This is particularly true for the Apologists in whose works it is 'the Greeks' that represent the rejected religious and social practices of the world in which they found themselves, practices described not from experience but from within the traditions of mockery and polemic inherited from the Jews. This means that 'Greeks' become 'others', almost exclusively religiously defined; on the other hand, outside the apologetic tradition this never becomes fixed, and the positive values of Greekness could not totally be forgotten.[83]

Something rather different happens with 'barbarians'; Jewish writers had been ambivalent as to whether or not to include themselves among barbarians.[84] Tatian, the Syrian, has no qualms about so identifying himself, and draws readily on the tradition of the 'wisdom of the barbarians': 'Do not be so utterly hostile to the barbarians, O Greeks, nor despise their doctrines. For what

---

[82] e.g. R. R. Ruether, *Faith and Fratricide: The Theological Roots of Anti-Semitism* (New York: Seabury, 1974), 117–82.

[83] The move of 'Greek' to 'non-Christian' is particularly associated with Origen: see I. Opelt, 'Griechische und lateinische Bezeichungen der Nicht-christen', *VC* 19 (1965), 1–22, 5–6; but note the caution of M. Vinzent, 'Das "heidnische" Ägypten im 5. Jahrhundert', in J. van Oort and D. Wyrwa (eds.), *Heiden und Christen im 5. Jahrhundert* (Leuven: Peeters, 1998), 32–65, 34–7.

[84] See Lieu, *Image and Reality*, 166–7.

practice is there among you which did not acquire its substance from the barbarians?' (Tatian, *Orat.* 1. 1). Other writers were more cautious: Justin acknowledges that Abraham and others who experienced the Logos belonged to the barbarians, but elsewhere denies that 'we are a barbarian tribe', perhaps because the epithet could be used as a term of repudiation, as it was to be by Celsus.[85] When Melito tells Marcus Aurelius that 'our philosophy first grew up among the barbarians, but flourished among your people', he is distancing himself from any Jewish origins, and the Jews from a place in the world in which he claims to belong.[86] The transformation that would eventually firmly locate the barbarians outside the Empire is perhaps already being felt: however, still in the distant future lay the assumption that the barbarians belonged outside a now Christian Empire and were by definition pagan.[87]

ALONE AGAINST ALL OTHERS?

One trajectory from this would be the one we have already traced, towards the Christians as 'a third race', neither Jews nor Greeks.[88] Potentially this could domesticate 'the other', allowing them to be described not as a threat but as inadequate alternatives. There is something of this in Aristides' *Apology*, particularly in the Syriac recension with its fourfold division and more nuanced understanding of the Jews, who here may belong on the same side of the divide as the Christians, over against barbarians and Greeks.[89] Yet even here the effect is, nevertheless, to further 'desacralize' the Jews, who no longer have a role in God's divine purposes in the world. For the most part, moreover, the more

---

[85] Justin, *Apol.* 5. 4; *Dial.* 119. 4; Origen, *c. Cels.* I. 2.

[86] *HE* IV. 26. 7.

[87] See R. Browning, 'Greeks and Others: From Antiquity to the Renaissance', in E. Harrison (ed.), *Greeks and Barbarians*, Edinburgh Readings in the Ancient World (Edinburgh: Edinburgh University Press, 2002), 257–77; P. Heather, 'The Barbarian in Late Antiquity: Image, Reality, and Transformation', in Miles, *Constructing Identities*, 234–58. Initially, of course, 'paganism' lies within.

[88] See the discussion of this theme in Ch. 8.

[89] See above, pp. 260–1.

common tripartite division does not clash with a binary one: Jews and Greeks combine as 'the other'; they manifest but different faces of the same error. Polycarp is opposed by 'the whole mass of Gentiles and Jews living in Smyrna', while in *Diognetus* Christians 'are warred against by the Jews as foreigners and persecuted by the Greeks', but this opposition then dissolves into hatred exhibited by the world towards the Christians (*Mart. Poly.* 12. 2; *Diog.* 5. 16; 6. 5).

Here *Diognetus* moves the opposition onto a different plane: he turns the Christians into 'the other'—their citizenship is self-evidently strange (παραδοξός) (*Diog.* 5. 4)—but he claims for that otherness, virtue. Opponents of Christianity, such as Celsus, had directed against Christians the same rhetoric as against the Jews: they are 'a people who . . . wall themselves off and break away from the rest of humankind' (Origen, *c. Cels.* VIII. 2).[90] *Diognetus* translates that separation into a positive marker, and to do so he takes up the language of 'the world': 'the world hates the Christians although it has not been wronged by them' (*Diog.* 6. 5). The roots of such an opposition reach out widely in the tradition: we have noted the opposition between God and those who belong to God, and 'the world' and its own, both in the Gospel of John and in Ignatius. In exploring the construction of space we have found it in Paul, especially in 1 Corinthians, while for Hermas Christians are those 'who have fled this world' (*Vis.* IV. 3. 4). However, the Apologists once again avoid any negative use of the term 'world', which, perhaps, makes the 'apologetic' *Diognetus*'s construction of it the more surprising. Here, 'the world' is not abstract, representing the fount of temptation, 'the vain world's golden store'; the world's hatred is, presumably, experienced in persecution. Yet 'the world' is always threatening to slip into a mythopoetic other, perhaps reflecting the apocalyptic roots of the idea: Christianity's greatness is when it is 'hated by the world' (Ignatius, *Rom.* 3. 3).

The assumption of hatred is widespread: to call it an assumption need not prejudge the extent of actual persecution or harassment. Later, Tertullian will make explicit what is implicit

---

[90] For this as a charge against the Jews, see *c. Cels.* V. 41; Tacitus, *Hist.* V, discussed above; against the Christians, Tacitus, *Ann.* XV. 44, 'odium humani generis'.

elsewhere: that 'there are as many enemies as outsiders (*extranei*); the Jews, appropriately, out of envy, soldiers for extortion, and even our own slaves out of their nature' (*Apol.* 7. 3)—the echo of Tacitus in this last betrays the longevity of that topos.[91] Certainly this shapes the perception of 'outside', but perhaps more important is the way that it serves to define the Christians. The oft-repeated dominical injunction to 'pray for those who hate you' presupposes a fundamental fissure between 'they', who hate, and 'we', who pray and love.[92] Ignatius urges prayer for 'all other people' and continues with an exhortation to 'be meek in the face of their fury, humble in the face of their boasting, prayers in the face of their slanders . . . do not be quick to imitate them' (*Eph.* 10. 1–2).

That the texts associated with martyrdom should particularly build such a world shaped by opposition is hardly surprising.[93] Here 'the other' both takes a number of forms and still represents a uniform face. On the 'human' level the watching crowd can be characterized as 'lawless', 'godless', 'inhuman', 'maddened'; indeed, they are 'wild and barbarous tribes incited by a wild beast'.[94] Yet a deeper opposition is at work: positively, martyrdom establishes 'the distinction between the unbelievers and the elect'; on the other hand, it is also the point at which, in the words of the *Letter of the Churches of Vienne and Lyons*, 'the one who opposes the race of the elect', the Evil One himself, repeatedly exerts his greatest endeavours.[95] Similarly, in the *Passion of Perpetua* the eponymous heroine sees herself in a vision doing battle with an Egyptian (10): the Egyptian as 'other' has, as we have seen, roots deep within the Graeco-Roman world, and also within the scriptural story, but here her opponent represents the Devil, her true adversary.

We have already met the explicit demonization of opposition in relation to the Jews. But it is also used to exclude those who think 'otherwise'. Ignatius responds to any opposition by ascribing it to 'the ruler of this age' (*Eph.* 17; *Trall.* 4); those who assert that Jesus's suffering was but a semblance are not just 'godless,

---

[91] See above at n. 31.
[92] *1 Clem.* 60. 3; Polycarp, *Phil.* 12. 3; cf. *Diog.* 5. 17.
[93] See Lieu, ' "I am a Christian" ', 215–16, 219–21.
[94] *Mart. Poly.* 9. 2; Eusebius, *HE* V. 1. 37–8, 57.
[95] *Mart. Poly.* 16. 1–17. 1; Eusebius, *HE* V. 1. 4, 27, 42.

unbelievers', they are 'bodiless and demonic' (*Trall.* 10; *Smyrn.* 2). 1 John spoke of those who rejected the author's view of Christ as 'antichrists'; Polycarp picks up the epithet and adds to it that they are 'from the devil' (1 John 2. 18; 4. 2; Polycarp, *Phil.* 7. 1); the apocryphal 'Paul' warns the Corinthians of those who 'have the accursed belief of the serpent' (*3 Cor.* 20); Dionysius of Corinth, according to Eusebius, blamed the falsification of his own correspondence on 'the apostles of the devil' (*HE* IV. 23. 12). Such polemic absolutely mystifies 'the other', creating unity from variety, and denying it its right to be heard; such silencing bears witness to the threat were their voices to be heard. Most of all, as ever, the creation of a unitary 'heresy' is what enables the perhaps no less mystified and mythologized 'orthodoxy' to claim existence.[96]

Mystification of alternative voices within an actual diversity so as to render them a unitary 'other' is achieved through a variety of means. The Letter to Titus appeals to a proverbial caricature of the Cretans to silence potential opponents, while its words, 'to the defiled and unbelieving nothing is pure' recalls the polemic of inversion of values used against the Jews (Titus 1. 10–12, 15). We have already seen how, through caricature and stereotyped polemic, the traditional invective against the barbarians is beginning to be redirected in order to identify and reject what comes to be known as 'heresy'.[97] The language of 'outsiders', 'unbelieving' (ἄπιστος), 'impious' (ἀσεβής), 'godless' (ἄθεος), and 'lawless' (ἄνομος), achieves much the same as it did in the Maccabean literature or as did that of 'as the Gentiles' in *Jubilees*. Justin can direct it not only against the Jews but also against those whom he wishes to label heretics: for the former, God establishes sabbath, sacrifice, and temple 'so, as it says, you might not be idolators and forgetful of God, impious and godless, as you always seem to have been'; of the latter, 'I have already shown you that there are those who are called Christians but who are godless and impious

---

[96] Le Boulluec, *La Notion d'hérésie*, i. 11, 'est-il possible de préciser la date et les circonstances où apparaissent et s'imposent largement parmis les chrétiens des représentations d'altérité assez claires et uniformisées pour autoriser à leur sujet l'emploi de la notion d'hérésie?' See also D. Boyarin, 'Borderlines'; I am grateful to the author for access to his unpublished manuscript.

[97] See A. le Boulluec, 'Clement d'Alexandrie et la conversion du "parler grec"', in Said, Ἑλληνισμός, 233–50, 234.

heretics, for they teach according to all that is slanderous, god-less, and mindless' (*Dial.* 92. 4; 80. 3; cf. 35. 5; 123. 3). Casting them as wild beasts both denies their humanity and echoes the biblical tradition of the psalmist's opponents (Ignatius, *Smyrn.* 4. 1). Eschatological dualism locates them beyond the possibili-ties of negotiation (Jude 8–19). Exhortations to avoidance follow naturally (2 John 10–11; Ignatius, *Smyrn.* 4. 1; *3 Cor.* 21, etc.), and bode ill for when such rhetoric will be accompanied by real political power.

Such a rhetoric seeks to persuade that 'heretics', like 'Jews', are plainly identifiable and as incontrovertibly 'other' as the most inveterate of 'Gentile idolaters'; in so doing it also seeks to persuade that 'we' are no less identifiable, and ever have been. Its success as rhetoric is written clear in subsequent rewritings of 'the history of the early church' which confidently retell the triumph of orthodoxy and the many battles won against evi-dent heresy or paganism. More than once we have suggested that Christians may not have been so sharply distinguished, or have always distinguished themselves, from their neighbours. Similarly, once we set aside the assertions of the heresiologists it becomes difficult to label early Christian texts as clearly either 'orthodox' or 'heretical'. Again, the creation of otherness is a literary enterprise, reproduced no doubt in worship and homily. The tools used are those provided by both Jewish and Graeco-Roman experience; but the vigour with which they are used was to become ingrained within Christian discourse, and was, per-haps, to provide the most compelling challenge to how she was to respond to further encounters with new 'others'.

Made Not Born: Conclusions

'We are from among you: Christians are made, not born.'[1] So, famously, Tertullian, in words that, in the context of the previous chapters, have a surprisingly modern ring. Not just what it meant to claim, but even the possibility of claiming, to be 'Christian', as we have traced it, was 'made', constructed, through texts. And what marks that making has been the continuities that set 'Christian' 'among' other currents of identity-making in the ancient world, both in the modes of shaping identity—which have provided the subject of each of the preceding chapters—but also in the formative patterns of that shape: similar co-ordinates in plotting boundaries, similar concerns about the body, similar characterizations of 'the other'. Yet continuity is not Tertullian's concern here: once, indeed, they would have shared in the mockery that he anticipates towards his message of coming judgement, but no longer so—for him, being 'from among you' lies in the past, separated by a gulf. That gulf at first appears to be filled with a new mode of continuity, for Tertullian immediately goes on to authenticate his message by appeal to the messengers or prophets, and to the story of the translation into Greek of the Jewish Scriptures: 'the treasury of the whole Jewish religion, and so now of ours'.[2] Yet, no sooner claimed than is that continuity also proved illusory, for the Jews have forfeited their rights, and wander, exiles, without man or God as king, forbid-

---

[1] Tertullian, *Apol.* 18. 4, 'De vestris sumus. Fiunt, non nascuntur Christiani'. Picking up this theme, but without reference to Tertullian, see Denise Buell's study of Clement of Alexandria's language, *Making Christians: Clement of Alexandria and the Rhetoric of Legitimacy* (Princeton, NJ: Princeton University Press, 1999).

[2] *Apol.* 19. 2, ' . . . in quo videtur thesaurus collocatus totius Iudaici sacramenti et inde iam nostri'.

den any access to their native land (*Apol.* 21. 5). So, as again we have discovered more than once, continuity is transformed into discontinuity, and discontinuity into continuity, in the effort to forge a place where difference can be acknowledged.

We should not be surprised that the overwhelming thrust of the majority of the texts that we have surveyed has been their determination to create and to sustain a sense of differentiation, and so of self; to evoke identity. Were it not so they would not have survived, and perhaps some of the texts that did not survive failed precisely on this score—although others did not survive because the differentiation that they sought to effect eventually failed to make possible ever new ways of self-understanding within an imagined continuity. Moreover, the remarkable literary creativity and shared activity of the nascent movement that was to become Christianity itself testifies to this sense of being involved in the shaping of a new world. It is of the nature of that process as we have explored it here that this last assertion has demanded immediate qualification. We began by recognizing that to understand the Roman Empire we must endeavour to hold together low levels of literacy with the power of the written word: here the early Christians were children of their time. And the question of for whom the texts speak, and for whom they do not, has repeatedly had to acknowledge the evidences of alternative voices or resistant patterns of life.

Most important, if there is a strong thrust towards the formation of an 'identity', that identity does not follow a single prescriptive shape. Between the texts themselves we have found both continuities and sharp discontinuities, and these no doubt would become yet more marked if we could also plot on our map the social groupings behind them. Moreover, despite the tendency of the texts to erect boundaries, we have discovered actual fluidity and negotiation, both amongst themselves and with the excluded others. To the by-now commonplace that early Christianity was marked by its heterodoxy, its pluralism, should be added that this pluralism is not to be set alongside the equally pluralistic Judaism and paganism but that it intersects with them. Yet all such fluidity, as has also been recognized in recent study, is inherent in the construction of all identities. Thus the discovery of pluralism cannot undermine recognition of a drive towards coherent self-definition, while affirmations of non-negotiable identity-controls, whether policed by creeds or by martyrdom, cannot nullify evidence of weak boundaries being crossed both by individuals and by ideas.

All this has important consequences for how we understand a number of the conundrums with which we started, and so for helping us speak about the making of Christians or of Christianity.

TEXTS AND COMMUNITIES

How may we negotiate between the texts and the social realities to which they surely bear witness? The path to be trodden has proved to be a precarious one. On the one hand, those social realities are, in our period, for the most part accessible to us only as mediated through the texts that survive; even so, they are never mediated directly. We have discovered how rarely we can read the texts as descriptive; we have endeavoured to ask what they are 'doing', without always being sure what level of success they may have even expected. Yet, if it would be naive to assume that exhortation or apologetic gives an account of what people believed or did, it would be no less naive to believe that they inevitably bear witness to the complete opposite, which they try to correct. Setting the texts within their broader contemporary context may offer some guidance; so, social historians of early Christianity have learned to project a dialogue between the concerns of the texts and the dynamics of life in the Graeco-Roman world, its structures and its value systems, and within this framework to imagine the often conflicting impulses at work within communities of faith and practice.[3] Yet this can never be more than an exercise in imaginative recreation, subject to challenge.

On the other hand, the texts should not be seen as merely secondary to the lived experience of actual communities. If it is with the texts and not with the people that we must deal, this is because it is the former that survive; yet we must suppose that they survive because so also did those who valued them, and who found their own self-understanding affirmed and shaped by them. So, we have already described the early Christian communities as to a high degree 'textual communities', centred around and shaped

---

[3] So e.g. Theissen, *Social Setting.*

by the interpretation of particular texts.[4] We have also caught glimpses of how the texts might become embodied in the lives of individuals, part of their 'knowledge'—for example, when Ignatius encourages the Christians of Ephesus as fellow-initiates of Paul, when Polycarp's martyrdom is described as 'according to the Gospel', when the celebration of the anniversary of that event, perhaps to be marked by the reading of the account, is anticipated, or in the attempts by some to live out through ascetic practice the declaration of the annulment of a differentiated gendered existence.[5]

However, as that last example reminds us, any primacy we may give to the texts is articulated through a number of different voices, and not only through those of author, of implied opponents, or of those silenced. No doubt, in the intention of their authors, they will shape the recipients' perception and their interpretation of present experience, while also directing future hope and behaviour. However, the texts may both be resisted by and resist the constructions of those who will receive them, both immediately and in subsequent receptions; it is this openness to resistance that makes possible any continuing interpretation, and particularly those that 'read against the grain'.[6]

On the other hand, it is possible that some of these texts may be as much, if not more, a literary than a social phenomenon, at least in their immediate context.[7] We would do wrong to assume differently self-identifying communities behind or around each of the different texts we have explored. It has been the constructions of identity by the texts with which we have been concerned, regardless of whether there were those whose self-understanding was produced or reproduced through them, yet also with the conviction that it was through its texts that early Christianity, as we know it, took shape.

Recognizing the necessary albeit unstable relationship between text and community warns against seeing texts merely as the

---

[4] See above, Ch. 2.

[5] Ignatius, *Eph.* 2. 2; *Mart. Poly.* 1. 1; 18; on the ascetic response to 'neither male nor female', see pp. 205–7 above.

[6] See above, pp. 24–5.

[7] See F. Wisse, 'Use of Early Christian Literature' on gnostic texts; but, arguing that finding a communal context is possible, see M. A. Williams, *The Immovable Race: A Gnostic Designation and the Theme of Stability in Late Antiquity*, NHS 29 (Leiden: Brill, 1985), 190–209.

vessels for an individualized self-understanding of faith that, if not intrinsically atemporal, can be so rendered, for example through a programme of demythologizing. Here we must agree with Leander Keck's criticism of 'Bultmann's magisterial *New Testament Theology* [which] regards the dialectic of eschatological existence as having reached its purest form in John, and treats Paul as a decisive moment on the way to this apex—*the achievement of the existential "essence" of Christianity*', and particularly Keck's charge that this enterprise fails to relate these theologies 'to the social realities of the early Christian communities'.[8] To focus on the texts as we have done is not to suppose that ideas function and develop independently of those who hold them, or of those who reject them—it does not offer a short-cut to the question of essence.

An obvious response, however, may still be that this has been *our* reading of the texts, conditioned by a twenty-first-century agenda. It may not be how anyone in the first three centuries understood what they heard, read, or wrote. The distinction between the earliest readers of the texts and ourselves as their present readers has, it might be protested, become vicariously annulled. That is, of course, always the historiographical dilemma. But in showing how early Christian texts share the same dynamics and many of the same strategies with other Jewish and Graeco-Roman texts we have sought to neutralize this objection. It does not matter that we have supplied the agenda and the framework for our reading of the texts; what matters is that by so doing we can conceive a coherent social world that encompassed and enabled differentiation among the actual lives of those whom we cannot otherwise know.

THE ORIGINS OF CHRISTIANITY

From all that has been said so far it should be obvious that we have not described or explained 'the origins of Christianity'. This was not our task. An exploration of the construction of identity is by

---

[8] L. E. Keck, 'On the Ethos of Early Christians', 439, with reference to R. Bultmann, *New Testament Theology*, 2 vols. (ET. London: SCM, 1952); italics mine.

nature more likely to discover processes; it can neither replace nor duplicate the historian's other tasks which may also require the assemblage of dates, numbers, and places. More specifically, in focusing on texts it might also be objected that we have said nothing about the conversion of individuals, about the impact on their lives of the Christian message, and about the eventual impact of those lives on the shape of the ancient world.[9] The dynamics of conversion to early Christianity are extraordinarily difficult to trace, for even in our earliest texts the topos of dramatic reversal overshadows the perhaps more mundane experiences of the majority. Contemporary studies of conversion have also tended to stress not reversal or repudiation but process, often rooted in continuities as much as in discontinuities: 'an intersubjective, transitional, and transactional mode of negotiation between two otherwise irreconcilable world-views'.[10] Negotiation, transaction, and transition could well be seen as characterizing the emergence of Christian identity as we have traced it.

Often hidden from us, too, but surely of decisive significance, is the way that the new movement seized the imagination of particular individuals, such as Tertullian, Justin Martyr, or Clement of Alexandria, but also like the more shadowy Aristides or Athenagoras, or the unknown authors of the *Martyrdom of Polycarp* or the *Letter of the Churches of Vienne and Lugdunum*, individuals who brought to their new convictions the rhetorical skills and literary heritage of the world to which they already belonged (*de vestris sumus*), as well as of the world that they embraced, that of the 'treasury of the whole Jewish religion, which is also ours'.[11] These, too, force us to search, not for the either/or of identity but for hierarchies, for how the claim 'I am a Christian' need not exclude all other forms of being, but might be situated within them, as individuals relocated themselves or redefined the structure of their allegiances.

---

[9] But see above, pp. 164–9.

[10] G. Viswanathan, *Outside the Fold: Conversion, Modernity, and Belief* (Princeton, NJ: Princeton University Press, 1998), 175–6. On some of the problems in the study of early Christianity see Lieu, ' "Attraction of Women" '.

[11] Justin gives us an account of his 'conversion' (*Dial.* 1–9), but so stylized is it that we can perhaps treat it only as a literary construct. Perhaps at the head of this list should have been placed Paul, except that that 'treasury' was already his.

None the less, awareness of how discontinuities may only be possible within a framework of continuity should not lead us to ignore the moments of radical disruption. Peter Brown has described the emergence of Christianity as a new landscape shaped by the movements of major tectonic plates.[12] This may not be a *creatio ex nihilo*—those plates had already shaped the earlier landscape—but it is the transformation that is most inescapable. Others have used the models of revolution or of crisis.[13] Such models may variously locate the dynamic driving force within or outside the new movement, and clearly there must be a balance between the two, but what is remarkable is that they tend to view it all not from the first or second century but from the fourth, when Christian constructions of time, space, and of the individual's place within the world displaced those that had gone before, for the world was no longer 'full of gods'.[14] How far had such transformations already been embodied in the lives of individuals and communities in the preceding centuries? To answer this would take us into another exercise, the relationship between pre- and post-Nicene or -Constantinian Christianity: Robert Markus entitles his analysis 'The End of Ancient Christianity', but he never fully tells us what that end entailed or whether there was a radical difference about the ancient.[15]

Yet where these different estimations agree, and what we have also discovered, is that 'origins' cannot just be described in terms of the growth of structures, or of the innovatory and successful attempts at 'worldwide' proselytizing. The existence of the latter may be questioned, while the former, although properly directing our attention to questions of power, cannot really help us fathom Tertullian's words with which we started. Rather, at the heart of the question of origins must lie the persuasive construction through discourse of a coherent world, whose contours

[12] Brown, 'Bodies and Minds'.
[13] Hopkins, *World Full of Gods*, 78–83, describes the Christian revolution as in some ways parallel to the Chinese revolution of the 20th century; R. Markus, *The End of Ancient Christianity* (Cambridge: Cambridge University Press, 1990), 362, describes Christianity as a response to an epistemological crisis in the Roman Empire.
[14] See also Markschies, *Between Two Worlds*, Ch. 5 at n. 90.
[15] Although see *End of Ancient Christianity*, 17, 'That ascetic take-over signals the end of ancient Christianity.'

could be evoked by the simple statement, 'I am a Christian', forged by the mysterious and largely unmappable interplay between the creative imaginations of individuals and their reception and transmission by their audiences.

JUDAISM AND CHRISTIANITY

Evidently the relationship between Christianity and Judaism is not simply *an* issue but *the* issue in our quest. Recent debate has largely failed to achieve a consensus as to how, when, and why Christianity separated from Judaism. There are two key reasons for this failure: first, because it is never clear whether the objects of that question are ideas, or people, or systems; and, secondly, because much depends on whether the respondent is a hypothetical Jew, Christian, or pagan of the time, or is the contemporary scholar, or even the believer, both the latter having the benefits (if such they are) of hindsight and of subsequent history. So, for example, that people often did not separate socially has long been evident, however unacceptable an Origen or a John Chrysostom might have found this.[16] How widespread such patterns were we can have little idea, and in most cases we cannot know whether those involved would have adopted the label 'Jew' and/or 'Christian', or would have felt constrained to choose between them, while the labels that they may have been ascribed by others might be different again.[17] We should probably expect that answers to this would have varied, not only between the *minim* of the Land of Israel and the 'worshippers of the most high God' of Asia Minor, but also among them, whilst the authorities who surveyed them within either tradition would find new labels designed to marginalize.[18]

To the extent that people are driven by ideas, such patterns of social experience may point to *perceived* conceptual continuities. The affirmation of such continuities was indeed an important element in the attempts of many of our texts to construct a distinct identity: claims to the scriptural history, to Abrahamic

[16] See above, Ch. 4 at n. 130.
[17] See Jerome, *Epist.* 112. 13.
[18] On the Land of Israel, see Segal, 'Jewish Christianity'; on the situation in Asia Minor, see above, Ch. 4 n. 125.

descent, to an ethos based on Scripture, to true maintenance of the boundaries against idolatry and sexual profligacy, suggest a community of ideas that in the past has prompted talk of 'the Judaeo-Christian tradition'. Yet, whether we should anticipate a community of persons in every case where we find such a community of ideas is another question. Quite clearly, often the opposite is true, certainly textually, as the *Letter of Barnabas* graphically testifies; in other cases, however, as with the *Testaments of the Twelve Patriarchs*, or, in a very different way, with the *Apocalypse of Adam*, we are at a loss as to whether to conceive of community or of symbolic annihilation. Here, the application of labels, *either* 'Jewish' *or* 'Christian', *or* even 'Jewish-Christian', may be either to demand a self-conscious exclusivity of self-definition that the texts themselves forbid, or to fix in a moment of time texts that were fluid in their reception and in the identities they produced. It is for this reason that the language of 'Judaeo-Christian' is deceptive with its assumption that each element can at the same time be isolated from the other and then be combined: the hyphen that intersects the terms measures both sameness and difference, while sameness feeds on difference, and difference on sameness.

Thus, while it is possible, it is not particularly productive to debate whether the ways have really parted either when we encounter in supposedly Christian texts ideas that could have been held by Jewish writers, or when we hear of Christians apparently at home in Jewish social contexts, or of Jews, however and by whomsoever defined, in Christian social contexts. That the ways parted at different places, at different times, and in different ways is now obvious, but equally unproductive of greater understanding. The dividing of paths does not determine who will choose to walk along them, nor who will journey without regard to their different destinations.

Yet even more problematic is whether, when we have read the individual texts, or when we have considered the practice of a variety of individuals, we can then properly speak of the systems, 'Judaism', 'Christianity'. As we have seen, although rooted in the language of (a very small minority of) our texts, the conceptual baggage these terms carry belongs rather more to our contemporary agenda. Far too frequently recent scholarly discussion has forgotten this, and slips without noticing from speaking of 'Jews' and 'Christians', to conceptualizing and fixing 'Judaism' and 'Christianity' as if these, at least, required no further definition.

Here there becomes explicit the troubling binary mode of thinking that is perhaps implicit throughout. Certainly crucial in much, although not in all, identity-making is the role of 'the other'. It is precisely because of the continuities that we have already traced that the vigorous construction of the Jews as others was so important in many of our Christian texts; this does not mean merely treating the Jews as other, but so constructing them that they might function as other. Yet this must lead us to ask, then, on the one hand, if Judaism and Christianity (if not already Christians and Jews) are implicated in the construction of each other, then how can we speak of a parting between them? *Conceptually*, the existence of the one is predicated upon that of the other.[19] Which does not mean, of course, that there were not those who understood themselves as Christians without reference to the Jews, and, even more so, those who understood themselves as Jews without reference to the Christians. For, on the other hand, the actual dynamics of relationship with real 'others' are always fluid and unpredictable. Indeed, if we recognize the possibility of other patterns of relationship with 'the other', or of other ways of maintaining multiple identities, whether or not hierarchically structured, we may find ourselves challenging the binary construction of Jew v. Christian.

It is for all these reasons that we not only can but must say that in many situations Jews and Christians behaved as if there were no rigid boundaries to separate them, *and* that 'Jews' and 'Christians' shared a common culture, *and* that Judaism and Christianity are reciprocally exclusive—so long as reciprocal exclusivity is not taken to mean a necessary reciprocal antagonism, and so long as this opposition is as open to negotiation and mediation as all others. Yet if all three of these statements could have been true simultaneously at various times and places, we still have to explain how both insiders and outsiders, at least in their discourse, came to give priority to the reciprocal exclusivity of systems. This was not socially driven, at least to the extent

[19] My thinking about this has been stimulated by Daniel Boyarin, both in conversation and in *Dying for God*. Compare the problem of 'male' and 'female', for example in readings of the formation of 'woman' from *adam* and the emergence thence of 'man' in Gen. 2.

that there is little firm evidence for Jews formally excluding from their social life Christians, or at least Christian Jews who may have expected to belong, and still less for the Jewish persecution of Christians, while actual Christian exclusion of Jews self-evidently belongs to a time after the Christianization of the Empire.[20] There were increasingly, of course, communities predominately or entirely constituted of those who had not come to belief in Jesus from an ethnic Jewish background; they might have expected little contact with non-Jesus-believing Jews, but neither need they have assumed a distancing as great as that from their polytheistic past and peers. The systemic 'othering' was, then, a textual achievement. As such, we can only understand it as part of the multidimensional construction of Christian identity through the texts, as we have traced it here.

A RELIGIOUS IDENTITY?

To adopt the language of 'Judaism' and 'Christianity', or to speak about a 'systemic othering', may appear to imply that these two -isms, or, indeed, that Jews and Christians, were the same sort of thing.[21] Yet to what extent were they? We have challenged elsewhere claims that Christians did not form an ethnic entity and consequently had to construct a new paradigm.[22] Yet this claim has been particularly important in understanding Christianity's self-distancing from its Jewish origins, not least in terms of Gal. 3. 28 as mapped at our starting-point. In particular, a supposed Jewish ethnic identity has often been set over against a supposed Christian denial of ethnic privilege.[23] It is Paul who apparently invites such an analysis through his contrast of 'the Jew who is one in public and the circumcision in public in flesh' with the 'circumcision of heart in spirit not letter' (Rom. 2. 28): 'It was the tension between "Jew" as an ethnic label and "Jew" as a religious label, we might say, which undermined Paul's efforts as

---

[20] See Lieu, 'Accusations of Jewish Persecution'.
[21] See above, pp. 240–1.
[22] See Ch. 1 at n. 52 and Ch. 4 at n. 134.
[23] So Dunn, *Partings*, 143–9; Neusner, 'Was Rabbinic Judaism Really "Ethnic"?' denies the proposition.

apostle of Israel'[24] —and, it is implied, the intractability of the former turned tension into division. Yet, although this diagnosis offers a superficially attractive understanding of the continuities and the discontinuities, it should be treated with caution, and not only because of the note of superiority implied.[25] Identity as defined from outside—in so far as Paul is, or is here positioning himself, 'outside'—bears an unstable relationship with identity as self-perceived; it is Paul who so defines 'the Jew'.[26] Moreover, the question of difference, while inherent in most identity-formation, is liable to invite answers couched in its own terms: if Paul is here engaged in constructing a unifying identity for a mixed community of Jesus-believers, he does so by constructing a deliberately oppositional 'Jew'.

As we have noted more than once, 'ethnicity' is not an objective measurement; it may be constructed in a variety of ways. True in the modern world, this is even more the case in the ancient. There, 'ethnic identity' has proved a heuristically useful model, but not one that can be readily contrasted with either the religious or the cultural.[27] Jewish self-definition was carried out in the encounter with the others of the Graeco-Roman world, where all were engaged in the same process, and it was characterized by the same ambiguities. Yet the same must also be said of Christian self-definition; even while denying ethnic particularism, Christians were also adopting many of the same categories and strategies of ethnic identity as were their Jewish and Greek or Roman peers, among which religion and practice played a central role. Like each one of these groups, the Christians claimed both difference and comparability, and, like each of them, those claims could be both challenged and acknowledged, then and now. 'Christian', 'Jewish', 'Greek', 'Roman', may not be 'the same

---

[24] J. D. G. Dunn, 'Paul: Apostate or Apostle of Israel', *ZNW* 89 (1998), 256–71, 271; so, already, Justin, *Dial.* 102. 6, τετυφωμένοι διὰ τὸ γένος; Tertullian, *Apol.* 21. 5, 'fiducia patrum inflati', which demonstrate the longevity and rhetorical power of the *topos* but not its veracity. For Rom. 2. 28, see above, p. 196.

[25] The dangers of claims to 'ethnic privilege' and the force of warnings against them will be evident to any who reflect on the last century.

[26] See above, p. 128, and Neusner, 'Was Rabbinic Judaism Really Ethnic?'.

[27] See also Hall, *Hellenicity*, who both defends a distinctive category of 'ethnic identity' (pp. 9–12) and demonstrates the difficulty of sustaining it in the later period.

sort of thing'; indeed, none of them is only one sort of thing.[28]
They are not necessarily mutually incompatible, although they
may on occasion be so constructed. There were, no doubt, those
who would claim more than one of these labels—again suggesting a hierarchy of identities—and those who would refuse such
a claim. Yet neither are any of them intrinsically oppositional,
although this, too, is how they could be constructed. We shall not
get at the heart of a 'Christian' identity by according it a privi-
leged label, 'religious'.

THE PROBLEM OF ESSENCE

If all this seems to put the emphasis on contingency and pluriformity, the question of essence will not leave us. It has proved
a pressing historical as well as an urgent theological question,
prompted both by a growing sensitivity to the multiple manifestations of self-styled 'Christian' experience throughout history, even in the earliest period, and by an equal and perhaps
greater multiplicity of contemporary manifestations, in an age
when claims to normativity by any one of these are increasingly
discredited, yet when the search for some principle of unity has
become a driving force. Here, merely to answer that all constructions of identity work by disguising themselves as displaying an
essence, or as demonstrating continuity, will hardly satisfy. Even
a modicum of realism, ill at ease with a rampant constructionism,
is bound to ask what, if anything, is the referent of these texts.
Focusing on texts, we have been (rightly) unable to silence the
voices of those who provoked and received them, of whom we
have already spoken, and so we are bound to ask what, if anything, is the referent of their experience and how may it be articulated.

Here the answers we would most expect fail us. In the modern
world it is central affirmations of faith that are offered as criteria of unity: 'The World Council of Churches is a fellowship
of churches which confess the Lord Jesus Christ as God and
Saviour according to the scriptures and therefore seek to fulfil
together their common calling to one God, Father, Son and Holy

---

[28] See above, Ch. 1 at n. 55.

Spirit.'[29] The lack of attention to such core doctrinal formulae in the preceding chapters has not only been because doctrine does not so easily fit into the sociological models with which we have worked. Of course, the rejection of a polytheistic worship of the images of the gods, and a concern for a proper understanding of the created order, and particularly of humankind, in their relationship to the divine, are implicit if not explicit throughout. Already within our period, and increasingly thereafter, the further working out of these certainties would provide the raw material for the construction of new boundaries around the notion of right belief and towards the exclusion of heresy.[30] Yet, in as much as those on both sides of the boundaries claimed the epithet 'Christian', this cannot help us except (perhaps) in retrospect. Similarly, implicitly or explicitly, the figure of Jesus, however conceived, must have featured as an inalienable point of reference; so, already for Ignatius a proper estimation of the person of Jesus and his human experience was cardinal. But this has to be balanced not only by the multiplicity of such estimations but also by the lack of interest in Jesus shown by many of the texts we have studied. Although duly claimed as continuous with the faith of the Apostles, credal formulations do not yet form the defining core of a Christian identity across time and place. We are reminded that a confession such as that of the World Council of Churches, and its location as a defining core, are themselves products of particular historical and geo-social conditions.

What explorations into the nature of identity may be able to teach us is that the only real continuity lies in the *experienced* continuity of 'essence'. That essence is only accessible, and to that extent only real, in so far as it is experienced but also communicated as a continuity. Yet because it is experienced, which means because it is tied to historical variables, it will, and indeed must, always be contested. This affirmation might be worked through in dialogue with each of the approaches to identity that we have adopted. Instead we shall take two perspectives that have continually re-emerged, the sense of continuity through time, belonging to and being able to tell a story, and the sense of separateness or otherness.

[29] The Basis of the Constitution of the World Council of Churches: see http://www.wcc-coe.org, last accessed 14 October 2003.

[30] See Le Boulluec, *La Notion d'hérésie.*

Identity through Narrative

We can explore the possibilities and the limitations of the focality of belonging to, and being able to tell, a story, by a comparison with two theological applications of this idea. The first is the once popular narrative theology that drew on the rediscovery of the biblical 'theology of recital',[31] and of the powerful and empowering function, within the continuing tradition, of 'remembering' a common faith-narrative, not least when the community was threatened with fragmentation (Isa. 43. 1, 15–21)—the point at which we started our analysis of 'history and remembering'. Particularly within the context of the contemporary exploration of the dynamics of identity, Christian narrative, it has been argued, could provide an answer to the current perceived sense of the foreignness of metaphysics, and to the loss of a common theological language, as also to the contemporary dilemmas over the nature of revelation and over the status of '(salvation) history'. Encompassing both Scripture and 'the history of the diverse ways in which Scripture has been read', this (theology as) narrative never achieves closure, although there are moments of *dis*closure 'when Christian narrative ceases to be merely an object for historical curiosity', and 'when its horizon collides with that of reader and hearer'.[32] The dialectic between continuity and the retelling and reinterpretation intrinsic to narrative might also be seen to provide a framework for understanding the tensions between unity and diversity, and between relativity and finality, that are just as intrinsic to all Christian theological reflection. Similarly, the individual's conversion and continuing experience could be accommodated as 'the lengthy, difficult process of reinterpreting his or her personal history in the light of the narratives and symbols that give the Christian community its identity'.[33]

In some ways, such a narrative theology does both recognize the role of, and offer a form of, shaping identity through remembering. Moreover, it allows problematic questions of 'historicity' to be treated with rather less dogmatism than in some other inter-

---

[31] It lies at the heart of G. von Rad, *Old Testament Theology*, 2 vols. (ET. London: SCM, 1962/75); see esp. i. 121–6, 296–305.

[32] G. W. Stroup, *The Promise of Narrative Theology* (London: SCM, 1981), 241.   [33] Ibid. 171.

pretations of the link between revelation and 'history'; diversity of interpretation is acknowledged, although constrained at least by the 'shared symbols and narratives'.[34] Yet the weakness of such an approach lies in its inability to affirm that interpretations may serve a variety of ends, or even conflicting ends; it still assumes a single story where we have found multiple stories or a variety of alternative claims to the same story. No less troublesome is its disinclination to ask about who is excluded both by the narratives and by their uses in the formation of identity: such a complicity in the exercise of power may no longer be possible.

In a key article more directly concerned with our period, Rowan Williams has also suggested that it is hearing a story, and being brought into a relationship with it, namely the story of Jesus, that lies at the heart of 'what is mysterious in Christian beginnings'.[35] In pointing to such a conclusion, the New Testament Gospels, and particularly the differences between them, play a crucial role—for in this way the fact of difference, of cultural variability, becomes part of normativity and not a regrettable obstacle to it. This is a valuable insight, and one frequently echoed by those with sympathies with a postmodern age. Yet—for Williams' essay is a theological reflection—for him the possibility of difference demands 'that for that hearing to go on being a hearing of the *same* story, canons of authorization are necessary for those who tell or enact it'.[36] Historically, we may object to this assessment by referring again to the apparent lack of widespread use of the Jesus story in this period and beyond.[37] Logically, too, in practice such canons cannot guarantee that it is the same story

---

[34] Ibid. 165; on pp. 233–7 he emphasizes that 'the historical referent in Christian faith' is indispensable; in this framework he considers necessary the crucifixion of Jesus but not the empty tomb, but seems to assume the Exodus and Settlement as unproblematic.

[35] R. Williams, 'Does It Make Sense to Speak of Pre-Nicene Orthodoxy?', in idem (ed.), *The Making of Orthodoxy: Essays in Honour of Henry Chadwick* (Cambridge: Cambridge University Press, 1989), 1–23, 17.

[36] Williams, 'Does It Make Sense', 16.

[37] Although this does not determine whether Williams is right in supposing that early preaching was focused more on bringing people in relationship to this story than in inculcating ideas and practices. In conversation, J. Leslie Houlden has also pointed out the continuing uncertainty among Christian writers, even commentators, throughout the early centuries as to what 'to do with' the Gospels.

unless this is assumed a priori to be the case; the possibility of
sameness or of identifying it is precisely the problem with which
we have to deal—some would say, is the contradiction that lies
at the heart of all claims to identity. Moreover, once again, there
are inevitably implicated in any such judgement issues of power
and of exclusion that cannot be ignored, either historically or
theologically.

Separateness and the 'Other'

Such issues belong to any construction of identity; they become
most explicit in the sense of separateness. As we have seen
repeatedly, identity develops only in social interaction; the sense
of those outside the boundaries, whose claims to the same history and Scriptures are denied, whose practice is excoriated,
who embody the 'other' over against whom 'we' are defined,
who represent a way of being that 'we' have left behind, has per-
vaded every chapter. So encountered, the 'other' is herself or
himself constructed by opposition, so that even where we may
catch authentic glimpses of their shadows these serve only the
purposes of the self being so shaped. More frequently, the contrastive necessity produces only a chimera, whose essential character, marked, for example, by sexual excess, can admit of no
change or challenge: 'pagans', 'Jews', or 'heretics' are produced
by the rhetoric of antithesis that they exist only to make possible.
Despite this, the dilemma with which our texts struggle has been
how to claim the right to determine the parameters of alienation
while also celebrating the denial of initiating hostility.

Yet there are some constraints, and alongside the pressures
to the creation of a monolithic 'other' it remains true that in our
period there is no single term for what more recent accounts are
often driven to call, anachronistically, 'paganism'.[38] Similarly,
for all the loss of any real sensitivity to contemporary diaspora
experience, the Jews are only beginning to emerge as those
whose own story can be told through stereotypes whose veracity
requires no justification, and whose existence, theologically,
serves only to bear witness to the truth of Christ.[39] Neither can

---

[38] So Vinzent, 'Das "heidnische" Ägypten', 36.
[39] As influentially formulated by Augustine, *Civ. Dei* XVIII. 46–7.

we ignore those other 'others' who, at times within the texts and perhaps more frequently behind them, are also engaged in more conciliatory dialogue, in an exchange of shared values and heroes. Whispers of other lives lived according to the divine *logos*, the assumption of common values of virtue and self-sacrifice, or the acknowledgement of the need to defend a shared story, point to alternative patterns of relationship.

Also disturbing the conventional dynamics of exclusion are the recurring efforts towards the creation of a sense of being themselves 'other'; of being strangers in the world. This did not, of course, entail identifying with those other 'others'—although the time could come when it might do so. Moreover, it could be put to different and contrasting uses, as compatible with affirming contemporary political realities as with challenging them.[40] Here, too, otherness required its own antithesis: Celsus remarked that 'If all men wanted to be Christians, the Christians would no longer want them', and, although Origen vehemently denies the charge, we may wonder at what provoked the insight (*c. Cels.* III. 9).

TOWARDS A NARRATIVE OF IDENTITY

So, if we are to speak of 'experienced essence' perhaps we should see this in terms of a narrative of otherness, a story of separation, albeit taking different forms in different texts. To that extent the declaration of Gal. 3. 28 with which we started may indeed offer a clue, not in its obliteration of distinctions so much as in its affirmation of distinction, 'neither . . . nor . . .'. The models of sustaining this narrative of difference are inevitably various; and it is as narrative that it exercises its power, independently of, and sometimes challenging, the ambiguities of social experience.[41] Moreover, it is also sustained by being projected within, creating new 'others' who must needs be excluded. In these ways

---

[40] See Feldmeier, ' "Nation" of Strangers'.

[41] So also R. Doran, *Birth of a Worldview: Early Christianity in its Jewish and Pagan Context* (Lanham, Md.: Rowman & Littlefield, 1999), 65, 'This sense of marginality, of being aliens in this world, strangers within it, would remain entrenched in the Christian self-definition throughout this period.'

the memories of being excluded and of excluding become themselves the apparently indispensable ingredients of continuing 'Christian' identity/ies.[42]

This suggests that the most fundamental contemporary challenge offered by and to Christian remembering may indeed be whether diversity can be affirmed without the denial of that history; or, rather, whether the memory of other patterns of relationship, other meetings with the 'other', can be given a place without fear of dissolution. Here, again, the fashioning of Christian identity finds itself within the broader dynamics of the—this time our—contemporary search for identity, where we are being urged to discover and to honour the value of difference and diversity, to give ear to the voices from the margins, to acknowledge the integrity of the 'other', and our need for them, and, only so, to affirm our own as well as their integrity.[43]

For such an endeavour there are rich resources from the past: the moments of discontinuity and disruption that, despite the common constructed discourse of 'essential' homogeneity, are integral to the shaping of Christian identity from the very beginning; the unexpected continuities with various 'others'; the voices long silenced that now demand a hearing. Through all these the exposure of rupture and the undermining of stability, which perhaps lies at the heart of any searched-for 'essence', forbids any form of fundamentalism, whether textual or institutional. If Christianity was 'made not born' within the dynamics of the society of which it was a part, so it will continue to be.

[42] Hence, labels such as 'Jew', 'Arian', or 'Manichaean' continue to be applied in order to exclude those who have no historical or theological right to the terms.

[43] Assmann, 'Mosaic Distinction', 63, calls for 'the development of new techniques of intercultural translation, not in order to appropriate the "other", but to overcome the stereotyping of otherness that we have projected on to the other by drawing distinctions'; cf. Bhabha, 'Introduction', 4, 'The "other" is never outside or beyond us; it emerges forcefully within cultural discourse, when we *think* we speak most intimately and indigenously "between ourselves".' On the value of 'difference', see also Rutherford, 'A Place called Home', 26. It is being argued here that to do so is not to conform with a contemporary fad, but to acknowledge and continue the search for identity which never transcends the specificities of time and space.

BIBLIOGRAPHY

ADAMS, E., *Constructing the World: A Study in Paul's Cosmological Language*, SNTW (Edinburgh: T&T Clark, 2000).

AL-RASHEED, M., *Iraqi Assyrian Christians in London: The Construction of Ethnicity*, Mellen Studies in Sociology 21 (Lewiston, NY: Edward Mellen, 1998).

ALEXANDER, L., 'The Acts of the Apostles as an Apologetic Text', in Edwards, Goodman, Price, Rowland, *Apologetics*, 15–44.

ALEXANDER, P., 'Jerusalem as the *Omphalos* of the World: On the History of a Geographical Concept', in L. Levine (ed.), *Jerusalem: Its Sanctity and Centrality to Judaism, Christianity, and Islam* (New York: Continuum, 1999), 104–19.

AMIR, Y., 'The Term Ἰουδαϊσμός', *Immanuel* 14 (1982), 34–41.

ANDERSON, B., *Imagined Communities: Reflections on the Origins and Spread of Nationalism*, rev. edn. (London: Verso, 1991 (1983)).

ANSON, J., 'The Female Transvestite in Early Monasticism: The Origin and Development of a Motif', *Viator* 5 (1974), 1–31.

ARAZY, A., *The Appellations of the Jews (IOUDAIOS, HEBRAIOS, ISRAEL) in the Literature from Alexander to Justinian*, Ph.D. thesis, University Microfilms 78-3061 (New York, 1977).

ASSMANN, J., 'The Mosaic Distinction: Israel, Egypt, and the Invention of Paganism', *Representations* 56 (1996), 48–67.

AUNE, D., 'Orthodoxy in First Century Judaism? A Response to N. J. McEleney', *JSJ* 7 (1976), 1–10.

BALCH, D., *Let Wives be Submissive: The Domestic Code in 1 Peter*, SBL. MS 26 (Atlanta, Ga.: Scholars Press, 1981).

BALDRY, H. C., *The Unity of Mankind in Greek Thought* (Cambridge: Cambridge University Press, 1965).

BAR-KOCHVA, B., *Pseudo-Hecataeus On the Jews: Legitimizing the Jewish Diaspora* (Berkeley, Calif.: University of California Press, 1996).

BARCLAY, J., ' "Do We Undermine the Law?": A Study of Romans 14.1–15.6', in J. D. G. Dunn (ed.), *Paul and the Mosaic Law: The Third Durham–Tübingen Research Symposium on Earliest Christianity and Judaism (Durham, September, 1994)*, WUNT 89 (Tübingen: Mohr, 1996), 287–308.

——– ' "Neither Jew nor Greek": Multiculturalism and the New Perspective on Paul', in Brett, *Ethnicity*, 197–214.

BARCLAY, J., *The Jews in the Mediterranean Diaspora* (Edinburgh: T&T Clark, 1996).

BARRETT, C. K., *A Critical and Exegetical Commentary on the Acts of the Apostles*, ICC, 2 vols. (Edinburgh: T&T Clark, 1994–9).

BARTH, F. (ed.), *Ethnic Groups and Boundaries: The Organization of Cultural Difference* (Oslo: Universitet Forlaget Bergen; London: G. Allen & Unwin, 1969).

BARTLETT, J. R., 'Edomites and Idumaeans', *PEQ* 131 (1999), 102–14.

BARTON, S., 'Early Christianity and the Sociology of the Sect', in F. Watson (ed.), *The Open Text: New Directions for Biblical Studies* (London: SCM, 1993), 140–62.

——*Discipleship and Family Ties in Mark and Matthew*, SNTS.MS 80 (Cambridge: Cambridge University Press, 1994).

BAUCKHAM, R. (ed.), *The Gospels for All Christians: Rethinking the Gospel Audiences* (Grand Rapids, Mich.: Eerdmans, 1998).

——'Jews and Jewish Christians in the Land of Israel at the Time of the Bar Kochba War, with Special Reference to the *Apocalypse of Peter*', in Stanton and Stroumsa, *Tolerance and Intolerance*, 228–38.

BAUER, W., *Orthodoxy and Heresy in Earliest Christianity* (ET. Philadelphia, Pa.: Fortress, 1971) = *Rechtglaubigkeit und Ketzerei im altesten Christentum* (Tübingen: Mohr, 1934 (1965)).

BAUMGARTEN, A., 'The Names of the Pharisees', *JBL* 102 (1983), 413–28.

——'Invented Traditions of the Maccabean Era', in Cancik, Lichtenberger, Schäfer (eds.), *Geschichte, Tradition, Reflexion*, i. 197–210.

——*The Flourishing of Jewish Sects in the Maccabean Era: An Interpretation*, S.JSJ 55 (Leiden: Brill, 1997).

——'Graeco-Roman Voluntary Associations and Ancient Jewish Sects', in Goodman, *Jews in a Graeco-Roman World*, 93–111.

BEALL, T. S., *Josephus' Description of the Essenes Illustrated by the Dead Sea Scrolls*, SNTS.MS 58 (Cambridge: Cambridge University Press, 1988).

BEARD, M., '*Ancient Literacy* and the Function of the Written Word in Roman Religion', in Beard *et al.*, *Literacy in the Roman World*, 35–58.

BEARD, M., NORTH, J., PRICE, S. (eds.), *Religions of Rome*, i. *A History* (Cambridge: Cambridge University Press, 1998).

BEARD, M. *et al.* (eds.), *Literacy in the Roman World*, JRA.SS 3 (Ann Arbor, Mich.: University of Michigan Press, 1991).

BECKWITH, R., *The Old Testament Canon of the New Testament Church and its Background in Early Judaism* (London: SPCK, 1985).

BENTLEY, G. C., 'Ethnicity and Practice', *Comparative Studies in Society and History* 29 (1987), 24–51.

BERGEN, T., *Fifth Ezra: The Text, Origin and Early History*, Septuagint and Cognate Studies 25 (Atlanta, Ga.: Scholars Press, 1990).

BERGER, P., and LUCKMAN, T., *The Social Construction of Reality: A Treatise in the Sociology of Knowledge* (Harmondsworth: Penguin, 1967).

BERNAL, M., *Black Athena: The Afroasiatic Roots of Classical Civilisation*, i. *The Fabrication of Ancient Greece 1785–1985* (London: Free Association Books, 1987).

BERTHELOT, K., 'La Notion de ר׳ dans les Textes de Qumrân', *RevQ* 19 (1999), 171–216.

BETZ, H. D., *Galatians: A Commentary on Paul's Letter to the Churches in Galatia*, Hermeneia (Philadelphia, Pa.: Fortress, 1979).

BHABHA, H., 'Introduction: Narrating the Nation', in idem (ed.), *Nation and Narration* (London: Routledge, 1990), 1–7.

BICKERMAN[N], E., 'The Name of Christians', *HTR* 42 (1949), 109–24.

——'Origines Gentium', *Classical Philology* 47 (1952), 65–81.

——*The Jews in the Greek Age* (Cambridge, Mass.: Harvard University Press, 1988).

BIERINGER, R., POLLEFEYT, D., VANDECASTEELE-VANNEUVILLE, F. (eds.), *Anti-Judaism and the Fourth Gospel: Papers of the Leuven Colloquium, 2000* (Assen: Van Gorcum, 2001).

BILDE, P., 'JESUS AND PAUL: A Methodological Essay in Two Cases of Religious Innovation in the Context of Centre-Periphery Relations', in P. Bilde *et al.* (eds.), *Centre and Periphery in the Hellenistic World* (Aarhus: Aarhus University Press, 1993), 316–38.

——*et al.* (eds.), *Religion and Religious Practice in the Seleucid Kingdom* (Aarhus: Aarhus University Press, 1990).

—— (eds.), *Ethnicity in Hellenistic Egypt* (Aarhus: Aarhus University Press, 1992).

BIRNBAUM, E., *The Place of Judaism in Philo's Thought: Israel, Jews, and Proselytes*, BJS 290. St. Phil. M. 2 (Atlanta, Ga.: Scholars Press, 1996).

BLOCH, R., *Antike Vorstellungen vom Judentum: Der Judenexkurs des Tacitus im Rahmen der griechisch-römischen Ethnographie*, Historia Einzelschriften 160 (Stuttgart: Franz Steiner, 2002).

BLOMQUIST, L. G., BONNEAU, N., COYLE, J. K., 'Prolegomena to a Sociological Study of Early Christianity', *Social Compass* 39 (1992), 221–39.

BOBERTZ, C. A., and BRAKKE, D., *Reading in Christian Communities: Essays on Interpretation in the Early Church* (Notre Dame, Ind.: University of Notre Dame Press, 2002).

BOCCACCINI, G., 'History of Judaism: Its Periods in Antiquity', in

J. Neusner (ed.), *Judaism in Late Antiquity*, ii. *Historical Syntheses*, HdO I.17 (Leiden: Brill, 1995), 285–308.

BOHAK, G., *Joseph and Aseneth and the Jewish Temple in Heliopolis*, Early Judaism and its Literature 10 (Atlanta, Ga.: Scholars Press, 1996).

BOKSER, B. M., 'Approaching Sacred Space', *HTR* 78 (1985), 279–99.

BOND, G., and GILLIAM, A., *Social Construction of the Past: Representation as Power* (London: Routledge, 1994).

BONZ, M. P., *The Past as Legacy: Luke-Acts and Ancient Epic* (Minneapolis, Minn.: Fortress, 2000).

BOURDIEU, P., *The Logic of Practice* (ET. Cambridge: Polity Press, 1990).

——*Language and Symbolic Power*, ed. and introd. J. B. Thompson (ET. Cambridge: Polity, 1991).

BOWERSOCK, G., *Fiction as History: Nero to Julian*, Sather Classical Lectures 58 (Berkeley, Calif.: University of California Press, 1994).

——'The Greek Moses: Confusion of Ethnic and Cultural Components in Later Roman and Early Byzantine Palestine', in Lapin, *Religious and Ethnic Communities*, 31–48.

BOWIE, E. L., 'Hellenes and Hellenism in Writers of the early Second Sophistic', in S. Said, Ἑλληνισμος, 183–204.

BOWMAN, A. K., 'Literacy in the Roman Empire: Mass and Mode', in Beard *et al.*, *Literacy*, 119–31.

——and WOOLF, G. (eds.), *Literacy and Power in the Ancient World* (Cambridge: Cambridge University Press, 1994).

——'Literacy and Power in the Ancient World', in Bowman and Woolf, *Literacy and Power*, 1–16.

BOWMAN, G., 'Christian Ideology and the Image of a Holy Land: The Place of Jerusalem in Pilgrimage in the Various Christianities', in Eade and Sallnow (eds.), *Contesting the Sacred*, 98–121.

BOYARIN, D., *A Radical Jew: Paul and the Politics of Identity* (Berkeley, Calif.: University of California Press, 1994).

——'Martyrdom and the Making of Christianity and Judaism', *JECS* 6 (1998), 577–627.

——*Dying for God: Martyrdom and the Making of Christianity and Judaism* (Stanford, Calif.: Stanford University Press, 1999).

——and BOYARIN, J., 'Diaspora: Generation and the Ground of Jewish Identity', *Critical Inquiry* 19 (1993), 693–725.

BRAKKE, D., 'Canon Formation and Social Conflict in Fourth Century Egypt', *HTR* 87 (1994), 395–419.

——*Athanasius and the Politics of Asceticism*, OECS (Oxford: Clarendon, 1995).

BRETT, M. (ed.), *Ethnicity and the Bible*, BIS 19 (Leiden: Brill, 1996).

BROWN, P., 'Bodies and Minds: Sexuality and Renunciation in Early Christianity', in D. Halperin, J. Winkler, F. Zeitlin (eds.), *Before Sexuality: The Construction of Erotic Experience in the Ancient Greek World* (Princeton, NJ: Princeton University Press, 1990), 479–93.

BROWN, R. E., *The Community of the Beloved Disciple* (London: Chapman, 1979).

BROWNING, R., 'Greeks and Others: From Antiquity to the Renaissance', in E. Harrison (ed.), *Greeks and Barbarians*, Edinburgh Readings in the Ancient World (Edinburgh: Edinburgh University Press, 2002), 257–77.

BRUEGGEMANN, W., *The Land*, Overtures to Biblical Theology (London: SPCK, 1978).

BRYAN, D. J., 'Exile and Return from Jerusalem', in C. Rowland and J. Barton (eds.), *Apocalyptic in History and Tradition*, JSP.SS 43 (Sheffield: Sheffield Academic Press, 2002), 60–80.

BUELL, D. K., *Making Christians: Clement of Alexandria and the Rhetoric of Legitimacy* (Princeton, NJ: Princeton University Press, 1999).

——'Race and Universalism in Early Christianity', *JECS* 10 (2002), 429–68.

——'Rethinking the Relevance of Race for Early Christian Self-Definition', *HTR* 94 (2001), 449–76.

BURRIDGE, R., *What are the Gospels?*, SNTS.MS 70 (Cambridge: Cambridge University Press, 1992).

BUSCHMANN, G., *Martyrium Polycarpi: Eine formkritische Studie*, BZNW 70 (Berlin: de Gruyter, 1994).

CAMERON, A., 'Virginity as Metaphor: Women and the Rhetoric of Early Christianity', in eadem (ed.), *History as Text: The Writing of Ancient History* (London: Duckworth, 1989), 181–205.

——*Christianity and the Rhetoric of Empire: The Development of Christian Discourse*, Sather Classical Lectures 45 (Berkeley, Calif.: University of California Press, 1991).

——and KUHRT, A., *Images of Women in Antiquity*, 2nd edn. (London: Routledge, 1993 [1983]).

CAMERON, R., 'Alternative Beginnings—Different Ends: Eusebius, Thomas, and the Construction of Christian Origins', in L. Bormann, K. del Tredici, A. Standhartinger (eds.), *Religious Propaganda and Missionary Competition in the New Testament World: Essays Honoring D. Georgi*, NT.S 74 (Leiden: Brill, 1994), 501–25.

CANCIK, H., 'The History of Culture, Religion and Institutions in Ancient Historiography: Philological Observations Concerning Luke's History', *JBL* 116 (1997), 673–95.

CANCIK, H., LICHTENBERGER, H., SCHÄFER, P. (eds.), *Geschichte, Tradi-*

tion, Reflexion: Festschrift für Martin Hengel zum 70. Geburtstag: i. *Judentum;* ii. *Griecheische und Römische Religion;* iii. *Frühes Christentum* (Tübingen: Mohr, 1996).

CASEWITZ, M., '*Hellenismos*: Formation et function des verbes en ΙΖΩ et de leurs dérivés', in S. Said, Ἑλληνισμός, 9–16.

——'Le Vocabulaire du mélange démographique: Mixobarbares et Mixhellènes', in V. Fromentin and S. Gotteland (eds.), *Origenes Gentium*, Ausonius Publications 7 (Paris: de Boccard, 2001), 41–7.

CASTELLI, E., ' "I Will Make Mary Male": Pieties of the Body and Gender Transformation of Christian Women in Late Antiquity', in J. Epstein and K. Straub (eds.), *Body Guards: The Cultural Politics of Gender Ambiguity* (London: Routledge, 1991), 29–49.

CHADWICK, H., *Origen* Contra Celsum (Cambridge: Cambridge University Press, 1953).

CHAPMAN, S., *The Law and the Prophets: A Study in Old Testament Canon Formation*, FAT 27 (Tübingen: Mohr, 2000).

CHESNUT, G. F., *The First Christian Histories*, 2nd edn. (Macon, Ga.: Mercer University Press, 1986).

CHRISTIANSEN, E. J., *The Covenant in Judaism and Paul: A Study of Ritual Boundaries as Identity Markers*, AGJU 27 (Leiden: Brill, 1995).

——'The Consciousness of Belonging to God's Covenant and what it entails according to the Damascus Document and the Community Rule', in F. H. Cryer and T. L. Thompson (eds.), *Qumran between the Old and New Testaments*, JSOT.SS 290 (Sheffield: Sheffield Academic Press, 1998), 69–97.

CLARK, G., 'Bodies and Blood: Late Antique Debate on Martyrdom, Virginity and Resurrection', in D. Montserrat (ed.), *Changing Bodies, Changing Meanings: Studies on the Human Body in Antiquity* (London: Routledge, 1998), 99–115.

CLARKE, K., *Between History and Geography: Hellenistic Constructions of the Roman World* (Oxford: Clarendon, 1999).

COHEN, A. P., *The Symbolic Construction of Community* (Chichester: Ellis Horwood, 1985).

COHEN, D., *Law, Sexuality, and Society: The Enforcement of Morals in Classical Athens* (Cambridge: Cambridge University Press, 1991).

COHEN, S., 'Religion, Ethnicity and "Hellenism" in the Emergence of Jewish Identity in Maccabean Palestine', in Bilde *et al.*, *Religion and Religious Practice*, 204–23.

——*The Beginnings of Jewishness: Boundaries, Varieties, Uncertainties* (Berkeley, Calif.: University of California Press, 1999).

COLLINS, A. Y., *Crisis and Catharsis: The Power of the Apocalypse* (Philadelphia, Pa.: Westminster, 1984).

——'Insiders and Outsiders in the Book of Revelation', in E. S. Frerichs and J. Neusner (eds.), *To See Ourselves as Others see us': Christians, Jews, 'Others' in Late Antiquity* (Chico, Calif.: Scholars Press, 1985), 187–218.

COLLINS, J., *Between Athens and Jerusalem: Jewish Identity in the Hellenistic Diaspora* (New York: Crossroad, 1983).

COMAROFF, J. and J., *Ethnography and the Historical Imagination* (Boulder, Colo.: Westview, 1992).

COOPER, K., *The Virgin and the Bride: Idealized Womanhood in Late Antiquity* (Cambridge, Mass.: Harvard University Press, 1996).

COYLE, K., 'Empire and Eschaton: The Early Church and the Question of Domestic Relationships', *Église et Théologie* 12 (1981), 35–94.

CRESSON, B., 'The Condemnation of Edom in Postexilic Judaism', in J. Efird (ed.), *The Use of the Old Testament in the New and Other Essays: Studies in Honor of William F. Stinespring* (Durham, NC: Duke University Press, 1972), 125–48.

CULLMANN, O., *The Johannine Circle* (ET. London: SCM, 1975).

D'ANGELO, M. R., 'Veils, Virgins and the Tongues of Men and Angels: Women's Heads in Early Christianity', in H. Eilberg-Schwartz and W. Doniger (eds.), *Off with her Head! The Denial of Women's Identity in Myth, Religion, and Culture* (Berkeley, Calif.: University of California Press, 1995), 131–64.

DAIM, F., 'Archaeology, Ethnicity and the Structures of Identification: The Example of the Arars, Carantanians and Moravians in the Eighth Century', in Pohl with Reimitz, *Strategies of Distinction*, 71–93.

DAUGE, Y. A., *Le Barbare: recherches sur la conception romaine de la barbarie et de la civilisation*, Coll. Latomus 176 (Brussels: Revue des Études Latins, 1981).

DAVIES, P. R., *Scribes and Schools: The Canonization of the Hebrew Scriptures* (London: SPCK, 1998).

DAVIES, S. L., *The Revolt of the Widows: The Social World of the Apocryphal Acts* (Carbondale, Ill.: South Illinois University Press, 1980).

DAVIES, W. D., *The Gospel and Land: Early Christian and Jewish Territorial Doctrine* (Berkeley, Calif.: University of California Press, 1980).

DE JONGE, M., 'The Pre-Mosaic Servants of God in the Testaments of the Twelve Patriarchs and in the Writings of Justin and Irenaeus', *VC* 39 (1985), 157–70.

——and TROMPF, J., *The Life of Adam and Eve and Related Literature*, Guides to the Apocrypha and Pseudepigrapha (Sheffield: Sheffield Academic Press, 1997).

DE STE CROIX, G., *Racial Prejudice in Imperial Rome* (London: Cambridge University Press, 1967).

324 *Bibliography*

DE VOS, G., 'Ethnic Pluralism: Conflict and Accommodation', in de Vos and Romanucci-Ross, *Ethnic Identity*, 5–41.

——and ROMANUCCI-ROSS, L., *Ethnic Identity, Cultural Continuities and Change* (Chicago, Ill.: University of Chicago, 1982 [1975]).

DENCH, E., *From Barbarians to New Men: Greek, Roman and Modern Perceptions of Peoples of the Central Appennines* (Oxford: Clarendon, 1995).

——'Austerity, Excess, Success, and Failure in Hellenistic and Early Imperial Italy', in M. Wyke (ed.), *Parchments of Gender: Deciphering the Bodies of Antiquity* (Oxford: Clarendon, 1998), 121–46.

DESCOURTIEZ, P. (introd., transl., and notes), *Clément d'Alexandrie Les Stromates: Stromate VI*, SC 446 (Paris: Éditions du Cerf, 1999).

DESTRO, A., and PESCE, M., 'Self, Identity, and Body in Paul and John', in A. Baumgarten, J. Assmann, G. Stroumsa (eds.), *Self, Soul and Body in Religious Experience*, SHR 78 (Leiden: Brill, 1998), 184–97.

DEVER, W., 'Archaeology and the Emergence of Israel', in J. Bartlett (ed.), *Archaeology and Biblical Interpretation* (London: Routledge, 1997), 20–50.

DÍAZ-ANDREU, M., 'Constructing Identities through Culture: The Past in the Forging of Europe', in Graves-Brown, Jones, Gamble (eds.), *Cultural Identity and Archaeology*, 48–61.

DIHLE, A., 'The Gospels and Greek Biography', in P. Stühlmacher (ed.), *The Gospel and the Gospels* (ET. Grand Rapids, Mich.: Eerdmans, 1991), 361–86.

DONALDSON, L. (ed.), *Postcolonialism and Scriptural Reading*, Semeia 75 (Atlanta, Ga.: Scholars Press, 1996).

DORAN, R., *Birth of a Worldview: Early Christianity in its Jewish and Pagan Context* (Lanham, Md.: Rowman & Littlefield, 1999).

DOUGLAS, M., 'The Abominations of Leviticus', in *Purity and Danger*, 2nd edn. (London: Routledge, 1978), 41–57.

DROGE, A., *Homer or Moses? Early Christian Interpretation of the History of Culture*, HUT 26 (Tübingen: Mohr, 1989).

——'Josephus between Greeks and Barbarians', in L. Feldman and J. Levison (eds.), *Josephus' Contra Apionem: Studies in its Character and Context with a Latin Concordance to the Portion Missing in Greek*, AGJU 34 (Leiden: Brill, 1996), 115–42.

——and TABOR, J., *A Noble Death: Suicide and Martyrdom among Christians and Jews in Antiquity* (San Francisco: Harper, 1992).

DUBUISSON, M., 'Remarques sur le vocabulaire grec d'acculturation', *Revue belge de philologie et d'histoire* 60 (1982), 5–32.

——'*Graecus, graeculus, graecari*: L'emploi péjoratif du nom des Grecs en latin', in Said, Ἑλληνισμος, 315–35.

DUNCAN, N. (ed.), *Bodyspace: Destabilizing Geographies of Gender and Sexuality* (London: Routledge, 1996).

DUNN, J. D. G., 'Works of the Law and the Curse of the Law (Galatians 3.10–14)', *NTS* 31 (1985), 523–42.

—— *The Partings of the Ways* (London: SCM; Philadelphia: Trinity, 1991).

—— (ed.), *Jews and Christians: The Parting of the Ways AD 70 to 135*, WUNT 66 (Tübingen: Mohr, 1992).

—— 'Paul: Apostate or Apostle of Israel', *ZNW* 89 (1998), 256–71.

—— *The Theology of Paul the Apostle* (Grand Rapids, Mich.: Eerdmans, 1998).

—— 'Who Did Paul Think He Was? A Study of Jewish Christian Identity', *NTS* 45 (1999), 174–93.

DUPONT, F., ' "En Germanie c'est-à-dire nulle part". Rhétorique de l'alterité et rhétorique de l'identité: l'aporie descriptive d'un territoire barbare dans la *Germanie* de Tacite', in Rousselle, *Frontières terrestres*, 189–219.

EADE, J., and SALLNOW, M. (eds.), *Contesting the Sacred: The Anthropology of Christian Pilgrimage* (London: Routledge, 1991).

—— 'Introduction', in Eade and Sallnow, *Contesting the Sacred*, 1–29.

EDWARDS, C., *The Politics of Immorality in Ancient Rome* (Cambridge: Cambridge University Press, 1993).

—— *Writing Rome: Textual Approaches to the City* (Cambridge: Cambridge University Press, 1996).

EDWARDS, M., GOODMAN, M., PRICE, S. in assoc. with ROWLAND, C. (eds.), *Apologetics in the Roman Empire: Pagans, Jews, and Christians* (Oxford: Oxford University Press, 1999).

EFROYMSON, D. P., 'The Patristic Connection', in A. T. Davies (ed.), *Antisemitism and the Foundations of Christianity* (New York: Paulist Press, 1979), 98–117.

EHRMAN, B., *The Orthodox Corruption of Scripture: The Effect of Early Controversies on the Text of the New Testament* (New York: Oxford University Press, 1993).

—— *Jesus: Apocalyptic Prophet of the New Millennium* (New York: Oxford University Press, 1999).

EILBERG-SCHWARTZ, H., *The Savage in Judaism: An Anthropology of Israelite Religion and Ancient Judaism* (Bloomington, Ind.: Indiana University Press, 1990).

—— 'The Problem of the Body for the People of the Book', in idem (ed.), *People of the Body: Jews and Judaism from an Embodied Perspective* (Albany, NY: SUNY, 1992), 17–46.

ELDRIDGE, M., *Dying Adam with his Multiethnic Family: Understanding the* Greek Life of Adam and Eve, SVTP 16 (Leiden: Brill, 2001).

ELLIOTT, J. H., *The Elect and the Holy*, NT.S 12 (Leiden: Brill, 1966).
—— *A Home for the Homeless: A Sociological Exegesis of 1 PETER: Its Situation and Strategy* (London: SCM, 1981).
ELLIOTT, J. K., *Essays and Studies in New Testament Textual Criticism*, Estudios de Filologia Neotestamentaria 3 (Cordoba: Ed. el Almendro, 1992).
—— (ed.), *The Apocryphal New Testament: A Collection of Apocryphal Christian Literature in English Translation* (Oxford: Clarendon, 1993).
ELLIS, E., 'Biblical Interpretation in the New Testament Church', in Mulder, *Mikra*, 691–725.
ELSHTAIN, J. B., *Public Man, Private Woman* (Princeton, NJ: Princeton University Press, 1981).
ELSNER, J., *Imperial Rome and Christian Triumph: The Art of the Roman Empire AD 100–450*, Oxford History of Art (Oxford: Oxford University Press, 1998).
EMMEL, S., 'Religious Tradition, Textual Transmission and the Nag Hammadi Codices', in J. D. Turner and A. McGuire (eds.), *The Nag Hammadi Library after Fifty Years: Proceedings of the 1995 Society of Biblical Literature Commemoration*, NHMS 44 (Leiden: Brill, 1997), 34–43.
ERIKSEN, T. H., *Ethnicity and Nationalism: Anthropological Perspectives* (London: Philo, 1993).
ESBENSHADE, R., 'Remembering to Forget: Memory, History, National Identity in Postwar East-Central Europe', *Representations* 49 (1995), 72–96.
EVANS, G. R., 'Ecumenical Historical Method', *JES* 31 (1994), 93–110.
FATUM, L., 'Image of God and Glory of Man: Women in the Pauline Congregation', in K. Börreson (ed.), *Image of God and Gender Models in the Judaeo-Christian Tradition* (Oslo: Solum, 1991), 56–135.
FEENEY, D., *Literature and Religion at Rome: Cultures, Contexts and Beliefs* (Cambridge: Cambridge University Press, 1998).
FELDMEIER, R., 'The "Nation" of Strangers: Social Contempt and its Theological Interpretation in Ancient Judaism and Early Christianity', in Brett, *Ethnicity*, 240–70.
FISHMAN, J., 'Language, Ethnicity and Racism', in idem, *Language and Ethnicity in Minority Sociolinguistic Perspective* (Clevedon: Multilingual Matters, 1989), 9–65.
FOUCAULT, M., *The History of Sexuality*, i. *Introduction*; ii. *The Uses of Pleasure*; iii. *The Care of the Self* (ET. Harmondsworth: Penguin, 1979–91).
FOX, R. L., 'Literacy and Power in Early Christianity', in Bowman and Woolf, *Literacy and Power*, 126–48.

FOXHALL, L., and SALMON, J. (eds.), *When Men were Men: Masculinity, Power, and Identity in Classical Antiquity* (London: Routledge, 1998).

FRANCIS, J., *Subversive Virtue: Asceticism and Authority in the Second Century Pagan World* (University Park, Pa.: Pennsylvania State University Press, 1995).

FREDERIKSEN, P., 'Judaism, the Circumcision of Gentiles, and Apocalyptic Hope: Another Look at Galatians 1 and 2', *JTS* 42 (1991), 532–64.

FREYNE, S., 'Locality and Doctrine: Mark and John Revisited', in idem, *Galilee and Gospel: Collected Essays*, WUNT 125 (Tübingen: Mohr, 2000), 287–95.

FRIEDMAN, J., 'Notes on Culture and Identity in Imperial Worlds', in Bilde *et al.*, *Religion and Religious Practice*, 14–39.

GAGER, J., *Kingdom and Community: The Social World of Early Christianity* (Englewood Cliffs, NJ: Prentice-Hall, 1975).

GERBER, C., *Ein Bild des Judentums für Nichtjuden von Flavius Josephus. Untersuchungen zu seiner Schrift* Contra Apionem, AGJU 40 (Leiden: Brill, 1997).

GERGEN, K. J., 'Social Constructionist Inquiry: Context and Implications', in K. Gergen and K. Davis (eds.), *The Social Construction of the Person* (New York: Springer, 1985), 3–17.

—— 'Social Understanding and the Inscription of the Self', in J. Stigler, R. Shweder, G. Herdt (eds.), *Cultural Psychology: Essays on Comparative Human Development* (Cambridge: Cambridge University Press, 1990), 569–606.

GIDDENS, A., *The Consequences of Modernity* (Cambridge: Polity, 1990).

GILBERT, G., 'The List of Nations in Acts 2: Roman Propaganda and the Lukan Response', *JBL* 121 (2002), 497–529.

GILLIS, J. (ed.), *Commemorations: The Politics of National Identity* (Princeton, NJ: Princeton University Press, 1994).

—— 'Memory and Identity: The History of a Relationship', in Gillis, *Commemorations*, 3–24.

GILROY, P., 'Diaspora and the Detours of Identity', in Woodward, *Identity and Difference*, 299–343.

GLEASON, M., *Making Men: Sophists and Self-Presentation in Ancient Rome* (Princeton, NJ: Princeton University Press, 1995).

—— 'Mutilated Messengers: Body Language in Josephus', in Goldhill, *Being Greek under Rome*, 50–85.

GOLDHILL, S., *Foucault's Virginity: Ancient Erotic Fiction and the History of Sexuality*, Stanford Memorial Lectures (Cambridge: Cambridge University Press, 1995).

GOLDHILL, S. (ed.), *Being Greek under Rome: Cultural Identity, the Second Sophistic and the Development of Empire* (Cambridge: Cambridge University Press, 2001).

GOODBLATT, D., 'From Judaeans to Israel: Names of Jewish States in Antiquity', *JSJ* 29 (1998), 1–36.

GOODMAN, M., 'Identity and Authority in Ancient Judaism', *Judaism* 39 (1990), 192–201.

—— 'Kosher Olive Oil in Antiquity', in P. R. Davies and R. T. White (eds.), *A Tribute to Geza Vermes: Essays on Jewish and Christian Literature and History*, JSOT.SS 100 (Sheffield: Sheffield Academic Press, 1990), 227–45.

—— 'Texts, Scribes and Power in Roman Judaea', in Bowman and Woolf, *Literacy and Power*, 99–100.

—— (ed.), *Jews in a Graeco-Roman World* (Oxford: Clarendon, 1998).

GOODSPEED, E., *Die ältesten Apologeten: Texte mit kurzen Einleitungen* (Göttingen: Vandenhoeck & Ruprecht, 1984 (1914)).

GOUDRIAAN, K., *Ethnicity in Ptolemaic Egypt* (Amsterdam: Gieben, 1988).

—— 'Ethnical Strategies in Graeco-Roman Egypt', in Bilde *et al.*, *Ethnicity in Hellenistic Egypt*, 74–99.

GRABBE, L. L., 'Orthodoxy in First Century Judaism?', *JSJ* 8 (1977), 149–53.

—— 'The Social Setting of Jewish Apocalypticism', *JSP* 4 (1989), 27–47.

GRAHAM, W. A., *Beyond the Written Word: Oral Aspects of Scripture in the History of Religion* (Cambridge: Cambridge University Press, 1987).

GRANT, R. M., *Theophilus of Antioch* Ad Autolycum, OECT (Oxford: Clarendon, 1970).

—— *Greek Apologists of the Second Century* (Philadelphia, Pa.: Westminster, 1988).

GRAVES-BROWN, P., JONES, S., GAMBLE, C. (eds.), *Cultural Identity and Archaeology: The Construction of European Communities* (London: Routledge, 1996).

GREEN, B., *Matthew, Poet of the Beatitudes*, JSNT.SS 203 (Sheffield: Sheffield Academic Press, 2001).

GRUEN, E., *Culture and National Identity in Republican Rome* (Ithaca, NY: Cornell University Press, 1992).

—— 'Cultural Fictions and Cultural Identity', *TAPA* 123 (1993), 1–14.

—— 'Fact and Fiction: Jewish Legends in a Hellenistic Context', in P. Cartledge, P. Garnsey, E. Gruen (eds.), *Hellenistic Constructs: Essays in Culture, History and Historiography* (Berkeley, Calif.: University of California Press, 1997), 72–88.

——*Heritage and Hellenism: The Reinvention of Jewish Tradition* (Berkeley, Calif.: University of California Press, 1998).

—— 'Jewish Perspectives on Greek Culture and Ethnicity', in Malkin, *Ancient Perceptions*, 347–73.

——*Diaspora: Jews amidst Greeks and Romans* (Cambridge, Mass.: Harvard University Press, 2002).

GUILLAUMIN, M. L., 'En Marge du "Martyre de Polycarpe": le discernement des allusions scripturaires', in *Forma Futuri: Studi in honore del Cardinale Michele Pellegrino* (Turin: Bottega d'Erasmo, 1975), 462–9.

HABINEK, T., *The Politics of Latin Literature: Writing, Identity, and Empire in Ancient Rome* (Princeton, NJ: Princeton University Press, 1998).

HAINES-EITZEN, K., *Guardians of Letters: Literacy, Power, and the Transmitters of Early Christian Literature* (New York: Oxford University Press, 2000).

HALBERTAL, M., *People of the Book: Canon, Meaning, and Authority* (Cambridge, Mass.: Harvard University Press, 1997).

—— 'Co-existing with the Enemy: Jews and Pagans in the Mishnah', in Stanton and Stroumsa, *Tolerance and Intolerance*, 159–72.

HALL, E., *Inventing the Barbarians: Greek Self-Definition through Tragedy* (Oxford: Clarendon, 1989).

HALL, J., *Ethnic Identity in Greek Antiquity* (Cambridge: Cambridge University Press, 1997).

——*Hellenicity: Between Ethnicity and Culture* (Chicago, Ill.: University of Chicago Press, 2002).

HALL, S., 'Cultural Identity and Diaspora', in Rutherford, *Identity*, 222–37.

HALL, S. G. (ed.), *Melito of Sardis* On Pascha *and Fragments*, OECT (Oxford: Clarendon, 1979).

HALLETT, J., and SKINNER, M. (eds.), *Roman Sexualities* (Princeton, NJ: Princeton University Press, 1997).

HALPERN-AMARU, B., *Rewriting the Bible: Land and Covenant in Post-biblical Jewish Literature* (Valley Forge, Pa.: Trinity, 1994).

—— *The Empowerment of Women in the* Book of Jubilees, S.JSJ 60 (Leiden: Brill, 1999).

HANDLER, R., 'Is "Identity" a Useful Cross-cultural Concept?', in Gillis, *Commemorations*, 27–40.

HARGIS, J. W., *Against the Christians: The Rise of Early Anti-Christian Polemic* (New York: P. Lang, 1999).

HARLOW, D. C., *The Greek Apocalypse of Baruch (3 Baruch) in Hellenistic Judaism and Early Christianity*, SVTP 12 (Leiden: Brill, 1996).

HARLOW, D. C., 'The Christianization of Early Jewish Pseudepigrapha: The Case of 3 Baruch', *JSJ* 32 (2001), 416–44.

HARRIS, W. V., *Ancient Literacy* (Cambridge, Mass.: Harvard University Press, 1989).

HARTOG, F., *The Mirror of Herodotus: The Representation of the Other in the Writing of History* (ET. Berkeley, Calif.: University of California Press, 1988).

HARVEY, G., *The True Israel: Uses of the Names Jew, Hebrew and Israel in Ancient Jewish and Christian Literature*, AGJU 25 (Leiden: Brill, 1996).

—— 'Synagogues of the Hebrews: "Good Jews" in the Diaspora', in Jones and Pearce, *Jewish Local Patriotism*, 132–47.

HASTINGS, A., *The Construction of Nationhood: Ethnicity, Religion and Nationalism* (Cambridge: Cambridge University Press, 1997).

HAWLEY, R., and LEVICK, B. (eds.), *Women in Antiquity: New Assessments* (London: Routledge, 1995).

HAYES, C., 'Intermarriage and Impurity in Ancient Jewish Sources', *HTR* 92 (1999), 3–36.

HAYES, J. H., and MILLER, J. M. (eds.), *Israelite and Judaean History*, Old Testament Library (London: SCM, 1977).

HEATHER, P., 'The Barbarian in Late Antiquity: Image, Reality, and Transformation', in Miles, *Constructing Identities*, 234–58.

'Hellenism and Hebraism Reconsidered: The Poetics of Cultural Influence and Exchange I–II', *Poetics Today* 19/1–2 (1998).

HEMELRIJK, E. A., *Matrona Docta: Educated Women in the Roman Élite from Cornelia to Julia Domna* (London: Routledge, 1999).

HERZ, P., 'Einleitung', in P. Herz and J. Kobes (eds.), *Ethnische und religiöse Minderheiten in Kleinasien von der hellenistischen Antike bis in das byzantinische Mittelalter* (Wiesbaden: Harassowitz, 1998), pp. xiii–xx.

HEZSER, C., *Jewish Literacy in Roman Palestine*, TSAJ 81 (Tübingen: Mohr, 2001).

HIMMELFARB, M., 'Judaism and Hellenism in 2 Maccabees', *Poetics Today* 19 (1998), 19–40.

HOBSBAWM, E., 'Introduction: Inventing Traditions', in Hobsbawm and Ranger, *Invention of Tradition*, 1–14.

—— and RANGER, T. (eds.), *The Invention of Tradition* (Cambridge: Cambridge University Press, 1983).

HOFFMANN, L., 'How Ritual Means: Ritual Circumcision in Rabbinic Culture and Today', *Stud. Lit.* 23 (1993), 78–97.

HOLLADAY, C. R., *Fragments from Hellenistic Jewish Authors*, i. *Historians* (Chico, Calif.: Scholars Press, 1983).

HOLLANDER, B. W., and DE JONGE, M., *The Testaments of the Twelve*

Patriarchs: A Commentary, SVTP 8 (Leiden: Brill, 1985).

HOPKINS, K., 'Christian Number and Its Implications', *JECS* 6 (1998), 185–226.

——*A World Full of Gods: Pagans, Jews and Christians in the Roman Empire* (London: Orion, 2000 (1999)).

HORBURY, W., 'Old Testament Interpretation in the Writings of the Church Fathers', in Mulder, *Mikra*, 727–89.

——'Jews and Christians on the Bible: Demarcation and Convergence (325–451)', in J. van Oort and U. Wickert (eds.), *Christliche Exegese zwischen Nicaea und Chalcedon* (Kampen: Kok Pharos, 1992), 72–103.

——'Land, Sanctuary and Worship', in J. Barclay and J. Sweet (eds.), *Early Christian Thought in its Jewish Context* (Cambridge: Cambridge University Press, 1996), 207–24.

HORRELL, D., *The Social Ethos of the Corinthian Correspondence: Interests and Ideology from 1 Corinthians to 1 Clement*, SNTW (Edinburgh: T&T Clark, 1996).

http://www.wcc-coe.org (The World Council of Churches), accessed 14 October 2003.

(HUTTON, M.) *Tacitus* Dialogus, trans. W. Peterson, Agricola, Germania, trans. M. Hutton, LCC (London: Heinemann, 1970 [1914]).

IMBER, M., 'Practised Speech: Oral and Written Conventions in Roman Declamations', in J. Watson (ed.), *Speaking Volumes: Orality and Literacy in the Greek and Roman World*, Mnemosyne Suppl. 218 (Leiden: Brill, 2001), 199–216.

IRVIN, D. T., 'From One Story to Many: An Ecumenical Reappraisal of Church History', *JES* 28 (1991), 537–54.

ISAJIW, W., 'Definitions of Identity', *Ethnicity* 1 (1974), 111–24.

JANOWITZ, N., 'Rethinking Jewish Identity in Late Antiquity', in S. Mitchell and G. Greatrex (eds.), *Ethnicity and Culture in Late Antiquity* (London: Duckworth, 2000), 205–19.

JEFFORD, C. N., *The Sayings of Jesus in the Teachings of the Twelve Apostles*, VC.S 11 (Leiden: Brill, 1989).

JENKINS, R., *Social Identity* (London: Routledge, 1996).

JERVELL, J., *Luke and the People of God* (Minneapolis, Minn.: Augsburg, 1972).

JOHNSON, M. D., *The Purpose of the Biblical Genealogies*, SNTS.MS 8, 2nd edn. (Cambridge: Cambridge University Press, 1988).

JONES, F. S., *An Ancient Jewish Christian Source on the History of Christianity. PSEUDO-CLEMENTINE RECOGNITIONS 1.27–71*, SBL Texts and Translations: Christian Apocrypha Series (Atlanta, Ga.: Scholars Press, 1995).

JONES, M. E., 'Geographical-Psychological Frontiers in Sub-Roman

Britain', in Mathisen and Sivan, *Shifting Frontiers*, 45–58.

JONES, S., 'Discourses of Identity in the Interpretation of the Past', in Graves-Brown, Jones, Gamble, *Cultural Identity and Archaeology*, 62–80.

—— *The Archaeology of Ethnicity: Constructing Identities in the Past and Present* (London: Routledge, 1997).

—— 'Identities in Practice: Towards an Archaeological Perspective on Jewish Identity in Antiquity', in Jones and Pearce, *Jewish Local Patriotism*, 29–49.

—— and GRAVES-BROWN, P., 'Introduction: Archaeology and Cultural Identity in Europe', in Graves-Brown, Jones, Gamble, *Cultural Identity and Archaeology*, 1–24.

—— and PEARCE, S. (eds.), *Jewish Local Patriotism and Self-Identification in the Graeco-Roman Period*, JSP.SS 31 (Sheffield: Sheffield Academic Press, 1998).

JOSHEL, S., 'Female Desire and the Discourse of Empire: Tacitus' Messalina', in Hallett and Skinner, *Roman Sexualities*, 221–54.

JUSTER, S., *Disorderly Women: Sexual Politics and Evangelicalism in Revolutionary New England* (Ithaca, NY: Cornell University Press, 1994).

KECK, L. E., 'On the Ethos of Early Christians', *JAAR* 42 (1974), 435–52.

KEE, H., *Community of the New Age* (London: SCM, 1977).

KEITH, M., and PILE, S., 'Introduction: Part 1, The Politics of Place . . .', in *Place and the Politics of Identity*, 1–21.

—— 'Introduction: Part 2, The Place of Politics . . .', in *Place and the Politics of Identity*, 22–40.

—— *Place and the Politics of Identity* (London: Routledge, 1993).

KENNER, H., *Das Phänomen der verkehrten Welt in der griechisch-römischen Antike* (Bonn: Habelt, 1970).

KIPPENBERG, H., 'Die jüdischen Überlieferungen als "patrioi nomoi"', in R. Faber and R. Schlesier (eds.), *Die Restauration der Götter. Antike Religion und Neo-Paganismus* (Würzburg: Königshausen & Neumann, 1988), 45–60.

KLAUCK, H.-J., *Hausgemeinde und Hauskirche im frühen Christentum*, Stuttgarter Bibelstudien 103 (Stuttgart: Katholisches Bibelwerk, 1981).

KLAWITER, F., 'The Role of Martyrdom and Persecution in Developing the Priestly Role of Women in Early Christianity: A Case Study of Montanism', *Ch. Hist.* 49 (1980), 251–61.

KLOPPENBERG, J., 'The Transformation of Moral Exhortation in *Didache* 1–5', in C. N. Jefford (ed.), *The Didache in Context*, NT.S 77 (Leiden: Brill, 1995), 88–109.

——and WILSON, S. G. (eds.), *Voluntary Associations in the Graeco-Roman World* (London: Routledge, 1996).

KNIBB, M., 'The Martyrdom of Isaiah', in M. de Jonge (ed.), *Outside the Old Testament*, Cambridge Commentaries on Writings of the Jewish and Christian World 200 BC to AD 200, 4 (Cambridge: Cambridge University Press, 1985), 178–92.

——'Christian Adoption and Transmission of Jewish Pseudepigrapha: The Case of *1 Enoch*', *JSJ* 32 (2001), 396–415.

KNIGHT, J., *The Ascension of Isaiah*, Guides to the Apocrypha and Pseudepigrapha (Sheffield: Sheffield Academic Press, 1995).

KOESTER, H., 'Writings and the Spirit: Authority and Politics in Ancient Christianity', *HTR* 84 (1991), 353–72.

KRAABEL, A. T., 'Judaism in Western Asia Minor under the Roman Empire with a Preliminary Study of the Jewish Community at Sardis', D.Th. thesis (Harvard University, Cambridge, Mass., 1968).

——'The Roman Diaspora: Six Questionable Assumptions', *JJS* 33 (1982), 445–64.

KRAEMER, R., 'On the Meaning of the Term "Jew" in Greco-Roman Inscriptions', *HTR* 82 (1989), 35–52.

——*When Aseneth met Joseph: A Late Antique Tale of the Biblical Patriarch and His Wife, Reconsidered* (New York: Oxford University Press, 1998).

KRAFT, R. A., 'Setting the Stage and Framing Some Questions', *JSJ* 32 (2001), 371–95.

KRETSCHMAR, G., 'Die Kirche aus Juden und Heiden', in van Amersfoort and van Oort, *Juden und Christen*, 9–43.

KUEFLER, M., *The Manly Eunuch: Masculinity, Gender Ambiguity, and Christian Ideology in Late Antiquity* (Chicago, Ill.: University of Chicago Press, 2001).

KUNIN, S., *God's Place in the World: Sacred Space and Sacred Place in Judaism* (London: Cassell, 1998).

LAPIN, H. (ed.), *Religious and Ethnic Communities in Later Roman Palestine*, Studies and Texts in Jewish History and Culture V (Bethesda, Md.: University Press of Maryland, 1998).

——'Introduction: Locating Ethnicity and Religious Community in Later Roman Palestine', in Lapin, *Religious and Ethnic Communities*, 1–28.

LAURENCE, R., 'Territory, Ethnonyms and Geography: The Construction of Identity in Roman Italy', in Laurence and Berry, *Cultural Identity*, 95–110.

——and BERRY, J. (eds.), *Cultural Identity in the Roman Empire* (London: Routledge, 1998).

Le Boulluec, A., *La Notion d'hérésie dans la littérature grecque, IIe–IIIe siècles*, i. *De Justin à Irénée* (Paris: Études Augustiniennes, 1985).

—— 'Clement d'Alexandrie et la conversion du "parler grec" ', in Said, Ἑλληνισμος, 233–50.

le Déaut, R., 'Le Thème de la circoncision du cœur (Dt. XXX 6; Jér. IV 4) dans les versions anciennes (LXX et Targum) et à Qumran', in J. Emerton (ed.), *Congress Volume Vienna 1980*, VT.S 32 (Leiden: Brill, 1981), 178–205.

Lefkowitz, M., and Fant, M., *Women's Life in Greece & Rome: A Source Book in Translation* (London: Duckworth, 1982).

LeMarquand, G., 'The Historical Jesus and African New Testament Scholarship', in W. Arnal and M. Desjardins (eds.), *Whose Historical Jesus?*, Studies in Christianity & Judaism 7 (Waterloo, Ont.: W. Laurier University Press, 1997), 161–80.

Levenson, J. D., *The Death and Resurrection of the Beloved Son: The Transformation of Child Sacrifice in Judaism and Christianity* (New Haven, Conn.: Yale University Press, 1993).

Levi, I., 'La Dispute entre les Égyptiens et les Juifs', *REJ* 63 (1912), 211–16.

Lieu, J. M., *The Second and Third Epistles of John: History and Background*, SNTW (Edinburgh: T&T Clark, 1986).

—— *Image and Reality: The Jews in the World of the Christians in the Second Century* (Edinburgh: T&T Clark, 1996).

—— 'Narrative Analysis and Scripture in John', in S. Moyise (ed.), *The Old Testament in the New Testament: Essays in Honour of J. L. North*, JSNT.SS 189 (Sheffield: Sheffield Academic Press, 2000), 144–63.

—— ' "Impregnable Ramparts and Walls of Iron": Boundary and Identity in Early "Judaism" and "Christianity" ', *NTS* 48 (2002), 297–313.

—— 'Not Hellenes but Philistines? The Maccabees and Josephus Defining the "Other" ', *JJS* 53 (2002), 243–63.

—— *Neither Jew nor Greek? Constructing Early Christianity* (Edinburgh: T&T Clark, 2002).

—— 'Accusations of Jewish Persecution in Early Christian Sources', in *Neither Jew nor Greek?*, 135–50.

—— 'The "Attraction of Women" in/to early Judaism and Christianity: Gender and the Politics of Conversion', in *Neither Jew nor Greek?*, 83–100.

—— 'Circumcision, Women, and Salvation', in *Neither Jew nor Greek?*, 101–14.

—— 'The Forging of Christian Identity and the *Letter to Diognetus*', in *Neither Jew nor Greek?*, 171–89.

—— ' "I am a Christian": Martyrdom and the Beginning of "Christian" Identity', in *Neither Jew nor Greek?*, 211–31.

—— 'The New Testament and Early Christian Identity', in *Neither Jew nor Greek?*, 191–209.

—— ' "The Parting of the Ways": Theological Construct or Historical Reality?', in *Neither Jew nor Greek?*, 11–29.

—— 'The Race of the Godfearers', in *Neither Jew nor Greek?*, 49–68.

LIFSCHITZ, B., 'L'Origine du Nom des Chrétiens', *VC* 16 (1962), 65–70.

LIGHTSTONE, J., *Society, the Sacred and Scripture in Ancient Judaism*, Studies in Christianity and Judaism, 3 (Waterloo, Ont.: Wilfred Laurier University Press, 1988).

LINCOLN, B., *Discourse and the Construction of Society: Comparative Studies in Myth, Ritual, and Classification* (New York: Oxford University Press, 1989).

LOWE, M., 'Who Were the *Ioudaioi*?', *NT* 18 (1976), 101–20.

LOWENTHAL, D., 'Identity, Heritage and History', in Gillis, *Commemorations*, 41–57.

MACALISTER, S., 'Gender as Sign and Symbol in Artemidorus' *ONEIRO-KRITIKA*: Social Aspirations and Anxieties', *Helios* 19 (1992), 140–60.

McDONALD, J. I. H., *The Crucible of Christian Morality* (London: Routledge, 1998).

McELENEY, N., 'Orthodoxy in Judaism of the First Christian Century', *JSJ* 4 (1973), 19–42.

—— 'Orthodoxy in Judaism of the First Christian Century', *JSJ* 9 (1978), 83–8.

McGINN, S., 'The Acts of Thecla', in Schüssler Fiorenza, *Searching the Scriptures*, ii. *A Commentary*, 800–28.

McGOWAN, A., *Ascetic Eucharists: Food and Drink in Early Christian Ritual Meals*, OECS (Oxford: Clarendon, 1999).

MacMULLEN, R., 'Two Types of Conversion to Early Christianity', *VC* 37 (1983), 174–92.

—— *Enemies of the Roman Order: Treason, Unrest, and Alienation in the Empire* (London: Routledge, 1992).

McRAE, G. (ed.), 'The Apocalypse of Adam, V,5: 64.1–85.32', in D. Parrott (ed.), *Nag Hammadi Codices V,2–5 and VI with Papyrus Berolinensis 8502, 1 and 4*, NHS 11 (Leiden: Brill, 1979), 151–95.

MALKIN, I. (ed.), *Ancient Perceptions of Greek Ethnicity* (Center for Hellenic Studies, Trustees for Harvard University. Cambridge, Mass.: Harvard University Press, 2001).

—— 'Introduction', in Malkin, *Ancient Perceptions*, 1–28.

MARCUS, J., 'The Circumcision and the Uncircumcision in Rome', *NTS* 35 (1989), 67–81.

MARKSCHIES, C., *Between Two Worlds: Structures of Earliest Christianity* (ET. London: SCM, 1999).

336   *Bibliography*

MARKUS, R., *The End of Ancient Christianity* (Cambridge: Cambridge University Press, 1990).

MARTIN, D. B., *The Corinthian Body* (New Haven, Conn.: Yale University Press, 1995).

MARTINEZ, F. G., 'The Problem of Purity: The Qumran Solution', in F. G. Martinez and J. T. Barrera (eds.), *The People of the Dead Sea Scrolls: Their Writings, Beliefs and Practices* (ET. Leiden: Brill, 1995), 139–57.

MARTYN, J. L., *History and Theology in the Fourth Gospel*, 2nd edn. (New York: Abingdon, 1979).

MATHISEN, R., and SIVAN, H. (eds.), *Shifting Frontiers in Late Antiquity* (Aldershot: Variorum; Brookfield, Vt.: Ashgate, 1996).

MATTERN, S. P., *Rome and the Enemy: Imperial Strategy in the Principate* (Berkeley, Calif.: University of California Press, 1999).

MATTINGLEY, H., 'The Origin of the Name *Christiani*', *JTS* 9 (1958), 26–37.

MBITI, J. S. (ed.), *Confessing Christ in Different Cultures* (Bossey: Ecumenical Institute, 1977).

MEADE, D., *Pseudonymity and Canon: An Investigation into the Relationship of Authorship and Authority in Jewish and Earliest Christian Tradition* (Grand Rapids, Mich.: Eerdmans, 1987).

MEEKS, W., 'The Image of the Androgyne: Some Uses of a Symbol in Earliest Christianity', *HR* 13 (1974), 165–208.

—— *The First Urban Christians: The Social World of the Apostle Paul* (New Haven, Conn.: Yale University Press, 1983).

MENDELS, D., *The Land of Israel as a Political Concept in Hasmonean Literature: Recourse to History in Second Century B.C. Claims to the Holy Land*, TSAJ 15 (Tübingen: Mohr, 1987).

MENDELSON, A., *Philo's Jewish Identity*, BJS 161 (Atlanta, Ga.: Scholars Press, 1988).

MENKEN, M., *Old Testament Quotations in the Fourth Gospel: Studies in Textual Form*, Contributions to Biblical Exegesis and Theology 15 (Kampen: Kok, 1996).

METZGER, B. M., *The Canon of the New Testament: Its Origin, Development and Significance* (Oxford: Clarendon, 1987).

MEYER, B., *The Early Christians: Their World Mission and Self-Discovery* (Wilmington, Del.: Michael Glazier, 1986).

—— *Christus Faber: The Master Builder and the House of God* (Allison Park, Pa.: Pickwick, 1992).

MILES, R. (ed.), *Constructing Identities in Late Antiquity* (London: Routledge, 1999).

—— 'Introduction: Constructing Identities in Late Antiquity', in Miles, *Constructing Identities*, 1–15.

MILLAR, F., 'Hagar, Ishmael, Josephus and the Origins of Islam', *JJS* 44 (1993), 23–45.

—— *The Roman Near East, 31 BC–AD337* (Cambridge, Mass.: Harvard University Press, 1993).

MILLER, P. C., *Dreams in Late Antiquity: Studies in the Imaginations of a Culture* (Princeton, NJ: Princeton University Press, 1994).

MITCHELL, S., *Anatolia: Land, Men, and Gods in Asia Minor*, 2 vols. (Oxford: Clarendon, 1993).

MONTEVECCHI, O., 'Nomen Christianorum', in R. Cantalamessa and L. Pizzolato (eds.), *Paradoxus Politeia: Studi Patristici in onore di Guiseppe Lazzati*, Studia Patristica Mediolanensia 10 (Milan: Vita e Pensiero, 1979), 485–500.

MOORE, S., and ANDERSON, J. C., 'Taking it Like a Man: Masculinity in 4 Maccabees', *JBL* 117 (1998), 249–73.

MORARD, F. (ed. and introd.), *L'Apocalypse d'Adam (NH V,5)*, BCNH 15 (Quebec: Presses de l'Université Laval, 1985).

MORTLEY, R., 'The Hellenistic Foundation of Ecclesiastical Historiography', in G. Clarke with B. Croke, R. Mortley, A. Emmett Nobbs (eds.), *Reading the Past in Late Antiquity* (Ruschcutters Bay: Australian National University Press, 1990), 225–50.

MOXNES, H., 'What is Family? Problems in Constructing Early Christian Families', in idem (ed.), *Early Christian Families: Family as Social Reality and Metaphor* (London: Routledge, 1997), 13–41.

—— 'Placing Jesus of Nazareth: Towards a Theory of Place in the Study of the Historical Jesus', in Wilson and Desjardins, *Text and Artifact*, 158–75.

MULDER, M. J. (ed.), *Mikra: Text, Translation, Reading and Interpretation of the Hebrew Bible in Ancient Judaism and Early Christianity*, CRINT (Assen: Van Gorcum; Philadelphia, Pa.: Fortress, 1988).

MULLEN, E. T., *Narrative History and Ethnic Boundaries*, Semeia (Atlanta, Ga.: Scholars Press, 1993).

MÜLLER, M., 'Graeca sive Hebraica Veritas? The Defence of the Septuagint in the Early Church', *SJOT* 1989/1 (1989), 103–24.

—— *The First Bible of the Church: A Plea for the Septuagint*, JSOT.SS 206 (Sheffield: Sheffield Academic Press, 1996).

MURRAY, O. (ed.), *Sympotica: A Symposium on the* Symposium (Oxford: Clarendon, 1990).

MUSURILLO, H., *The Acts of the Christian Martyrs*, OECT (Oxford: Clarendon, 1972).

NEUSNER, J., *The Idea of Purity in Ancient Judaism*, SJLA 1 (Leiden: Brill, 1973).

—— *A History of the Mishnaic Law of Purities*, Part 22, *The Mishnaic*

System of Uncleanness: Its Context and History, SJLA 6 (Leiden: Brill, 1977).

—— 'Was Rabbinic Judaism Really "Ethnic"?', *CBQ* 57 (1995), 281–305.

—— 'Exile and Return in the History of Judaism', in Scott, *Exile*, 221–37.

—— GREEN, W. S., FRERICHS, E. (eds.), *Judaisms and their Messiahs at the Turn of the Christian Era* (Cambridge: Cambridge University Press, 1987).

NICOLET, C., *Space, Geography, and Politics in the Early Roman Empire* (Ann Arbor, Mich.: University of Michigan Press, 1991).

NIEHOFF, M., 'Philo's Views on Paganism', in Stanton and Stroumsa, *Tolerance and Intolerance*, 135–58.

NORTH, H., *Sophrosyne: Self-knowledge and Self-restraint in Greek Literature*, Cornell Studies in Classical Philology 35 (Ithaca, NY: Cornell University Press, 1966).

NOVAK, D., *The Election of Israel: The Idea of the Chosen People* (Cambridge: Cambridge University Press, 1995).

OLIVER, J. H., *The Ruling Power*, Transactions of the American Philological Society, 43 (Philadelphia, Pa.: American Philological Society, 1953).

OLSSON, B., *Structure and Meaning in the Fourth Gospel: A Text-Linguistic Analysis of John 2:1–11 and 4:1–42*, CBNT 6 (Lund: Gleerup, 1974).

OLSTER, D. M., *Roman Defeat, Christian Response, and the Literary Construction of the Jew* (Philadelphia, Pa.: University of Pennsylvania Press, 1994).

—— 'Classical Ethnography and Early Christianity', in K. B. Free (ed.), *The Formulation of Christianity by Conflict through the Ages* (Lewiston, NY: Edward Mellen Press, 1995), 9–31.

OPELT, I., 'Griechische und lateinische Bezeichnungen der Nichtchristen', *VC* 19 (1965), 1–22.

ORTNER, S. B., 'Is Female to Male as Nature is to Culture?', in M. Z. Rosaldo and L. Lamphere (eds.), *Woman, Culture and Society* (Stanford, Calif.: Stanford University Press, 1974), 67–87, repr. in J. Landes (ed.), *Feminism, the Public and the Private* (Oxford: Oxford University Press, 1998), 21–44.

OSBORN, E., *Justin Martyr*, BHT 47 (Tübingen: Mohr, 1973).

ØSTERGÅRD, U., 'What is National and Ethnic Identity?', in Bilde *et al.*, *Ethnicity in Hellenistic Egypt*, 16–38.

PARKER, H. N., 'The Teratogenic Grid', in Hallett and Skinner, *Roman Sexualities*, 47–65.

PAULSEN, H., 'Das Kerygma Petri und die urchristlichen Apologetik', in *Zur Literatur und Geschichte des frühen Christentum: Gesammelte Aufsätze*, WUNT 99 (Tübingen: Mohr, 1997), 173–209.

PAUPOT, E., 'The Anti-Roman Movement of the Christiani and the Nazorean Fragment', *VC* 54 (2000), 233–47.

PENN, M., 'Performing Family: Ritual Kissing and the Construction of Early Christian Kinship', *JECS* 10 (2002), 151–74.

PERKINS, J., *The Suffering Self: Pain and Narrative Representation in the Early Christian Era* (London: Routledge, 1995).

PESKOWITZ, M., *Spinning Fantasies: Rabbis, Gender, and History* (Berkeley, Calif.: University of California Press, 1997).

PETERMAN, G. W., *Paul's Gift from Philippi: Conventions of Gift-Exchange and Christian Giving*, SNTS.MS 92 (Cambridge: Cambridge University Press, 1997).

PETERSEN, W., *Tatian's Diatesseron: Its Creation, Dissemination, Significance and History in Scholarship*, VC.S 25 (Leiden: Brill, 1994).

PETERSON, E., '*Christianus*', in *Frühkirche, Judentum und Gnosis* (Freiburg: Herder, 1958), 64–87.

PLASKOW, J., *Standing again at Sinai: Judaism from a Feminist Perspective* (San Francisco: HarperCollins, 1990).

POHL, W., 'Telling the Difference: Signs of Ethnic Identity', in Pohl with Reimitz, *Strategies of Distinction*, 17–69.

——with REIMITZ, H. (eds.), *Strategies of Distinction: The Construction of Ethnic Communities, 300–800*, The Transformation of the Roman World 2 (Leiden: Brill, 1998).

PORTON, G., *GOYIM: Gentiles and Israelites in Mishnah–Tosefta*, BJS 155 (Atlanta, Ga.: Scholars Press, 1988).

POTTER, D., *Prophets and Emperors: Divine Authority from Augustus to Theodosius* (Cambridge, Mass.: Harvard University Press, 1994).

——*Literary Texts and the Roman Historian* (London: Routledge, 1999).

RAJAK, T., 'Dying for the Law: The Martyr's Portrait in Jewish-Greek Literature', in M. J. Edwards and S. Swain (eds.), *Portraits: Biographical Representation in the Greek and Latin Literature of the Roman Empire* (Oxford: Clarendon, 1997), 39–67.

——'Jews and Greeks: The Invention and Exploitation of Polarities in the Nineteenth Century', in M. Wyke and M. Biddiss (eds.), *The Uses and Abuses of Antiquity* (Berne: P. Lang, 1999), 57–77.

RAMÍREZ KIDD, J., *Alterity and Identity in Israel*, BZAW 283 (Berlin: de Gruyter, 1999).

RENDEL HARRIS, J. (ed.), *The Apology of Aristides on Behalf of the Christians* (Cambridge: Cambridge University Press, 1891).

RESNICK, I. M., 'The Codex in Early Jewish and Christian Communities', *JRH* 17 (1992), 1–17.

340 *Bibliography*

RICHARDSON, P., *Israel in the Apostolic Church*, SNTS.MS 10 (Cambridge: Cambridge University Press, 1969).

RICHES, J. K., *Conflicting Mythologies: Identity Formation in the Gospels of Mark and Matthew*, SNTW (Edinburgh: T&T Clark, 2000).

RIVES, J. B. (trans., introd., and commentary), *Tacitus Germania*, Clarendon Ancient History Series (Oxford: Clarendon, 1999).

ROBERTS, M., 'The Revolt of Boudicca (Tacitus, *ANNALS* 14. 29–39) and the Assertion of *LIBERTAS* in Neronian Rome', *AJPh* 109 (1988), 118–32.

ROBINSON, J. (ed.), *The Nag Hammadi Library in English* (Leiden: Brill, 1977).

ROETZEL, C. J., '*Oikoumene* and the Limits of Pluralism in Alexandrian Judaism and Paul', in J. A. Overman and R. MacLennan, *Diaspora Jews and Judaism: Essays in Honor of, and in Dialogue with, A. Thomas Kraabel* (Atlanta, Ga.: Scholars Press, 1992), 163–82.

—— 'Sex and the Single God: Celibacy and Social Deviancy in the Roman Period', in Wilson and Desjardins, *Text and Artifact*, 231–48.

ROGERSON, J., 'The Hebrew Conception of Corporate Personality: A Re-examination', *JTS* 21 (1970), 1–16.

ROLDANUS, J., 'Références patristiques au "chrétien-étranger" dans les trois premiers siècles', in *Lectures anciennes de la Bible*, Cahiers de Biblia Patristica I (Centre d'analyse et de documentation Patristiques. Strasbourg: Palais Universitaire, 1987), 27–52.

RORDORF, W., 'Aux origines du culte des martyrs', *Irénikon* 45 (1972), 315–31.

ROSE, G., 'As if the Mirrors Had Bled: Masculine Dwelling, Masculinist Theory and Feminist Masquerade', in Duncan, *Bodyspace*, 56–74.

ROTHAUS, R., 'Christianization and De-Paganization: The Late Antique Creation of a Conceptual Frontier', in Mathisen and Sivan, *Shifting Frontiers*, 299–308.

ROULEAU, D., *L'Épître apocryphe de Jacques (NH 1,2)*, BCNH 18 (Quebec: Presses de l'Université Laval, 1987).

ROUSELLE, A. (ed.), *Frontières terrestres, Frontières célestes dans l'antiquité* (Paris: Presses Université de Perpignan, 1995).

—— 'Présentation', in *Frontières terrestres, Frontières célestes*, 7–16.

RUETHER, R. R., *Faith and Fratricide: The Theological Roots of Anti-Semitism* (New York: Seabury, 1974).

—— 'Women's Body and Blood: The Sacred and the Impure', in A. Joseph (ed.), *Through the Devil's Gateway* (London: SPCK, 1990), 7–21.

RUTHERFORD, J. (ed.), *Identity: Community, Culture, Difference* (London: Lawrence & Wishart, 1990).

—— 'A Place called Home: Identity and the Cultural Politics of Difference', in Rutherford, *Identity*, 9–27.

SAID, S. (ed.), Ἑλληνισμος. *Quelques Jalons pour une Histoire de l'Identité Grecque*, Actes du Colloque de Strasbourg 25–27 octobre 1989 (Leiden: Brill, 1991).

—— 'The Discourse of Identity in Greek Rhetoric from Isocrates to Aristides', in Malkin, *Ancient Perceptions*, 275–99.

SALDARINI, A., *Matthew's Christian-Jewish Community* (Chicago, Ill.: University of Chicago Press, 1994).

SALVESEN, A., *Symmachus on the Pentateuch*, JSS.M 15 (Manchester: University of Manchester Press, 1991).

SANDERS, E. P., *Paul and Palestinian Judaism: A Comparison of Patterns of Religion* (London: SCM, 1977).

—— *Judaism: Practice and Belief 63 BCE–66CE* (London: SCM, 1992).

SANDERS, J. T., *The Jews in Luke-Acts* (London: SCM, 1987).

SATRAN, D., *Biblical Prophets in Byzantine Palestine. Reassessing the Lives of the Prophets*, SVTP 11 (Leiden: Brill, 1995).

SAWYER, J., *Sacred Languages and Sacred Texts* (London: Routledge, 1999).

SCHÄFER, P., *Judeophobia: Attitudes towards the Jews in the Ancient World* (Cambridge, Mass.: Harvard University Press, 1997).

SCHÄFKE, W., 'Frühchristliche Widerstand', *ANRW* II. 23. 1 (1979), 460–723.

SCHIFMAN, L., *Who was a Jew? Rabbinic and Halakhic Perspectives on the Jewish–Christian Schism* (Hoboken, NJ: KTAV, 1985).

SCHÖPFLIN, G., *Nations, Identity, Power: The New Politics of Europe* (London: Hurst, 2000).

SCHRAGE, W., *The Ethics of the New Testament* (ET. Edinburgh: T&T Clark, 1988).

—— 'Skizze eine Auslegungs- und Wirkungsgeschichte von Gal 3,28', in D. Aschenbrenner (ed.), *Der Dienst der ganzen Gemeinde Jesu Christi und das Problem der Herrschaft* (Gütersloh: Gütersloher Verlaghaus, 1999), 63–92.

SCHÜSSLER FIORENZA, E., *In Memory of Her: A Feminist Theological Reconstruction of Christian Origins* (London: SCM, 1983).

—— (ed.), *Searching the Scriptures*, i. *A Feminist Introduction*; ii. *A Feminist Commentary* (New York: Crossroad, 1993–4).

SCHUTTER, W. L., *Hermeneutic and Composition in 1 Peter*, WUNT 2. 30 (Tübingen: Mohr, 1989).

SCHWARTZ, R., *The Curse of Cain: The Violent Legacy of Monotheism* (Chicago, Ill.: University of Chicago Press, 1997).

SCHWARTZ, S., 'Language, Power and Identity in Ancient Palestine', *Past and Present* 148 (1995), 3–47.

SCHWARTZ, S., *Imperialism and Jewish Society, 200 B.C.E. to 640 C.E.* (Princeton, NJ: Princeton University Press, 2001).

SCHWARZ, E., *Identität durch Abgrenzung: Abgrenzungsprozesse in Israel im 2. vorchristlichen Jahrhundert und ihre traditionsgeschichtlichen Voraussetzungen*, EH XXIII/162 (Frankfurt am Main: P. Lang, 1982).

SCOTT, J. M., 'Exile and the Self-Understanding of Diaspora Jews', in Scott, *Exile*, 173–218.

——*Exile: Old Testament, Jewish and Christian Conceptions*, S.JSJ 56 (Leiden: Brill, 1997).

——*Geography in Early Judaism and Christianity: The Book of Jubilees*, SNTS.MS 113 (Cambridge: Cambridge University Press, 2002).

SCROGGS, R., 'The Earliest Christian Communities as Sectarian Movement', in J. Neusner (ed.), *Christianity, Judaism, and Other Greco-Roman Cults: Studies for Morton Smith at Sixty*, 4 vols., SJLA 12 (Leiden: Brill, 1975), ii. 1–23.

SEGAL, A., 'Jewish Christianity', in H. Attridge and G. Hata (eds.), *Eusebius, Christianity, and Judaism*, SPB 42 (Leiden: Brill, 1992), 326–51.

SHAVIT, Y., *Athens in Jerusalem: Classical Antiquity and Hellenism in the Making of the Modern Secular Jew*, ET. Littman Library of Jewish Civilization (London: Valentine Mitchell, 1997).

SHAW, B., 'Body/Power/Identity: Passions of the Martyrs', *JECS* 4 (1996), 269–312.

SHELLRUDE, G. M., 'The Apocalypse of Adam: Evidence for a Christian Gnostic Provenance', in M. Krause (ed.), *Gnosis and Gnosticism: Papers Read at the Eighth International Conference on Patristic Studies*, NHS 17 (Leiden: Brill, 1981), 82–91.

SIKER, J., *Disinheriting the Jews: Abraham in Early Christian Controversy* (Louisville, Ky.: Westminster/John Knox, 1991).

SILBERMAN, N. A., and SMALL, D. (eds.), *The Archaeology of Israel: Constructing the Past, Interpreting the Present*, JSOT.SS 237 (Sheffield: Sheffield Academic Press, 1997).

SILBERSTEIN, L. J., 'Others Within and Others Without: Rethinking Jewish Identity and Culture', in Silberstein and Cohn, *The Other in Jewish Thought and History*, 1–34.

——and COHN, R. L. (eds.), *The Other in Jewish Thought and History* (New York: New York University Press, 1994).

SIM, D., *The Gospel of Matthew and Christian Judaism*, SNTW (Edinburgh: T&T Clark, 1998).

SKARSAUNE, O., 'From Books to Testimonies: Remarks on the Transmission of the Old Testament in the Early Church', *Immanuel* 24/5 (1990), 207–19.

SLUGOWSKI, B. R., and GINSBURG, G. P., 'Ego Identity and Explanatory Speech', in J. Shotter and K. Gergen (eds.), *Texts of Identity* (London: Sage, 1989), 36–55.

SMITH, A. D., 'Structure and Persistence of *Ethnie*' (extract), in M. Guibernau and J. Rex (eds.), *The Ethnicity Reader: Nationalism. Multiculturalism. Migration* (Cambridge: Polity, 1997), 27–33 (originally published in *The Ethnic Origin of Nations* (Oxford: Blackwell, 1986)).

SMITH, D. L., 'Between Ezra and Isaiah: Exclusion, Transformation, and Inclusion of the "Foreigner" in Post-exilic Biblical Theology', in Brett, *Ethnicity and the Bible*, 116–42.

SMITH, J. D., 'The Ignatian Long Recension and Christian Communities in Fourth Century Syrian Antioch', Th.D. thesis (Harvard, 1986).

SMITH, J. Z., 'Fences and Neighbours: Some Contours of Early Judaism', in W. S. Green (ed.), *Approaches to Ancient Judaism II*, BJS 9 (Chico, Calif.: Scholars Press, 1980), 1–26.

SNODGRASS, K., '1 Peter ii. 1–10: Its Formation and Literary Affinities', *NTS* 24 (1977–8), 97–106.

SNYDER, G. F., *Ante Pacem: Archaeological Evidence of Church Life before Constantine* (Macon, Ga.: Mercer University Press, 1985).

SONNABEND, H., *Fremdenbild und Politik: Vorstellungen der Römer von Ägypten und dem Partherreich in der späten Republik und frühen Kaiserzeit*, EH III.3.286 (Frankfurt am Main: P. Lang, 1986).

SPARKS, K. L., *Ethnicity and Identity in Ancient Israel: Prolegomena to the Study of Ethnic Sentiments and their Expression in the Hebrew Bible* (Winona Lake, Ind.: Eisenbrauns, 1998).

SPEYER, W., and OPELT, I., 'Barbar', *JAC* 10 (1967), 251–90 (= 'Barbar I', *Reallexikon für Antike und Christentum: Suppl. vol. I. 5/6*, 811–98).

STANLEY, C., *Paul and the Language of Scripture: Citation Technique in the Pauline Epistles and Contemporary Literature*, SNTS.MS 74 (Cambridge: Cambridge University Press, 1992).

STANTON, G. N., *A Gospel for a New People: Studies in Matthew* (Edinburgh: T&T Clark, 1992).

——and STROUMSA, G. (eds.), *Tolerance and Intolerance in Early Judaism and Christianity* (Cambridge: Cambridge University Press, 1998).

STENDAHL, K., 'The Apostle Paul and the Introspective Conscience of the West', *HTR* 56 (1963), 199–215.

STERLING, G., *Historiography and Self-Definition: Josephus, Luke-Acts and Apologetic Historiography*, NT.S 64 (Leiden: Brill, 1992).

STERN, D., 'Introduction', *Poetics Today* 19 (1998), 1–17.

STERN, S., *Jewish Identity in Early Rabbinic Writings*, AGJU 23 (Leiden: Brill, 1994).

STOCK, B., *The Implications of Literacy: Written Language and Models of Interpretation in the Eleventh and Twelfth Centuries* (Princeton, NJ: Princeton University Press, 1983).

——*Listening for the Text: On the Uses of the Past* (Baltimore, Md.: Johns Hopkins University Press, 1990).

STÖTZEL, A., 'Warum Christus so spät erschien—das apologetische Argumentation des frühen Christentums', *ZKG* 92 (1981), 147–60.

STOWERS, S., *Letter Writing in Greco-Roman Antiquity* (Philadelphia, Pa.: Westminster/John Knox, 1986).

STRAUSS, B. S., *Fathers and Sons in Athens: Ideology and Society in the Era of the Peloponnesian War* (London: Routledge, 1993).

STRECKER, G., 'Judenchristentum', *Theologische Realenzyklopädie* 17 (Berlin: de Gruyter, 1988), 310–25.

STROUMSA, G., 'Herméneutique biblique et identité: l'exemple d'Isaac', *RevBib* 99 (1992), 529–43.

——'Philosophy of the Barbarians: On Early Christian Ethnological Representations', in Cancik, Lichtenberger, Schäfer, *Geschichte, Tradition, Reflexion*, ii. 339–68.

—— 'The Christian Hermeneutical Revolution and its Double Helix', in L. V. Rutgers *et al.* (eds.), *The Use of Sacred Books in the Ancient World* (Leuven: Peeters, 1998), 9–28.

STROUP, G. W., *The Promise of Narrative Theology* (London: SCM, 1981).

SUTER, D., 'Fallen Angel, Fallen Priest: The Problem of Family Purity in 1 Enoch', *HUCA* 50 (1979), 115–35.

SWAIN, S., *Hellenism and Empire: Language, Classicism and Power in the Greek World AD 50–250* (Oxford: Clarendon, 1996).

TACITUS *Dialogus*, trans. W. Peterson, *Agricola. Germania*, trans. M. Hutton, LCC (London: Heinemann, 1970 (1914)).

TALMON, S., 'The Community of the Renewed Covenant: Between Judaism and Christianity', in E. Ulrich and J. Vanderkam (eds.), *The Community of the Renewed Covenant: The Notre Dame Symposium on the Dead Sea Scrolls* (Notre Dame, Ind.: University of Notre Dame Press, 1994), 3–24.

TATUM, J. (ed.), *The Search for the Ancient Novel* (Baltimore, Md.: Johns Hopkins University Press, 1994).

TAYLOR, J., 'Why Were the Disciples First Called "Christians" at Antioch? (Acts 11,26)', *RevBib* 101 (1994), 75–94.

TCHERIKOVER, V., 'The Ideology of the Letter of Aristeas', *HTR* 51 (1958), 59–85.

THACKERAY, H. StJ., *Josephus III: The Jewish War Books IV–VII*,

LCC (Cambridge, Mass.: Harvard University Press, 1928).

THATCHER, T., 'Literacy, Textual Communities and Josephus' *Jewish War*', *JSJ* 19 (1998), 123–42.

THEISSEN, G., *The Social Setting of Pauline Christianity* (ET. Edinburgh: T&T Clark, 1982).

——*Social Reality and the Early Christians: Theology, Ethics, and the World of the New Testament* (Minneapolis, Minn.: Fortress, 1992).

——*The Religion of the Earliest Churches: Creating a Symbolic World* (Minneapolis, Minn.: Fortress, 1999).

THOMPSON, T., *The Bible in History: How Writers Create a Past* (London: J. Cape, 1999).

TOMSON, P. J., 'The Names Israel and Jew in Ancient Judaism and in the New Testament', *Bijdragen* 47 (1986), 120–40.

TONKIN, E., *Narrating Our Pasts: The Social Construction of Oral History* (Cambridge: Cambridge University Press, 1992).

——MCDONALD, M., CHAPMAN, M. (eds.), *History and Ethnicity* (London: Routledge, 1989).

TREU, K., 'Die Bedeutung des Griechischen für die Juden im Römischen Reich', *Kairos* 15 (1973), 123–44.

TREVETT, C., *Montanism: Gender, Authority and the New Prophecy* (Cambridge: Cambridge University Press, 1996).

TRIANDIS, H. C., *et al.*, 'Allocentric versus Idiocentric Tendencies: Convergent and Discriminant Validation', *Journal of Research in Personality* 19 (1985), 395–415.

TURNER, V., and TURNER, E., *Image and Pilgrimage in Christian Culture* (Oxford: Blackwell, 1978).

ULRICH, E., 'The Community of Israel and the Composition of the Scripture', in C. Evans and S. Talmon (eds.), *The Quest for Context and Meaning: Studies in Biblical Intertextuality in Honor of James A. Sanders*, BIS 28 (Leiden: Brill, 1997), 327–42.

——*The Dead Sea Scrolls and the Origins of the Bible* (Grand Rapids, Mich.: Eerdmans, 1999).

VALANTASIS, R., 'Is the Gospel of Thomas Ascetical? Revisiting Old Problems with a New Theory', *JECS* 7 (1999), 55–81.

VAN AMERSFOORT, J., and VAN OORT, J. (eds.), *Juden und Christen in der Antike* (Kampen: Kok, 1990).

VAN BREMEN, R., *The Limits of Participation: Women and Civic Life in the Greek East in the Hellenistic and Roman Periods* (Amsterdam: J. G. Gieben, 1996).

VAN DAMME, D., 'Gottesvolk und Gottesreich in der christlichen Antike', *Theologische Berichte*, iii. *Judentum und Kirche: Volk Gottes* (Zurich: Benziger, 1974), 157–68.

——*'ΜΑΡΤΥΣ-ΧΡΙΣΤΙΑΝΟС*: Überlegungen zur ursprünglichen

Bedeutungen des altkirchlichen Märtyretitels', *Freiburger Zeitschrift für Philosophie und Theologie* 23 (1976), 286–303.

VAN DER HORST, P. W., *Ancient Jewish Epitaphs: An Introductory Survey of a Millennium of Jewish Funerary Epigraphy (300 BCE–700 CE)* (Kampen: Kok Pharos, 1991).

VAN HENTEN, J. W., *The Maccabean Martyrs as Saviours of the Jewish People: A Study of 2 and 4 Maccabees*, S.JSJ 57 (Leiden: Brill, 1997).

VAN HOUTEN, C., *The Alien in Israelite Law*, JSOT.SS 107 (Sheffield: Sheffield Academic Press, 1991).

VAN UNNIK, W. C., *Das Selbstverständnis der jüdischen Diaspora in der hellenistisch-römischen Zeit*. Aus dem Nachlaß herausgegeben und bearbeitet von P. W. van der Horst, AGJU 17 (Leiden: Brill, 1993).

VANDERKAM, J. C. (trans.), *The Book of Jubilees*, CSCO 511. Script. Aeth. 88 (Louvain: Peeters, 1989).

VASTA, E., 'Multiculturalism and Ethnic Identity: The Relationship between Racism and Resistance', *ANZJS* 29 (1993), 209–25.

VERMES, G., and GOODMAN, M., *The Essenes according to the Classical Sources* (Sheffield: Journal for the Study of the Old Testament for the Oxford Centre for Postgraduate Hebrew Studies, 1989).

VEYNE, P., *Bread and Circuses: Historical Sociology and Political Pluralism*, abridged and introduced by O. Murray (ET. London: Allen Lane, 1990).

VINZENT, M., 'Das "heidnische" Ägypten im 5. Jahrhundert', in J. van Oort and D. Wyrwa (eds.), *Heiden und Christen im 5. Jahrhundert* (Leuven: Peeters, 1998), 32–65.

VISWANATHAN, G., *Outside the Fold. Conversion, Modernity, and Belief* (Princeton, NJ: Princeton University Press, 1998).

VON CAMPENHAUSEN, H., 'Die Enstehung der Heilsgeschichte: Der Aufbau des christlichen Geschichtsbildes in der Theologie des ersten und zweiten Jahrhunderts', *Saeculum* 21 (1970), 189–212.

VON DOBSCHÜTZ, E., *Das Kerygma Petri kritisch Untersucht*, TU 11. 1 (Leipzig: Hinrichs, 1893).

VON HARNACK, A., *What is Christianity?*, 3rd rev. edn. (ET. London: Williams & Norgate, 1904) = *Das Wesen des Christentums* (Leipzig: Hinrichs, 1900).

VON RAD, G., *Old Testament Theology*, 2 vols. (ET. London: SCM, 1962/75).

VÖÖBUS, A., *History of Asceticism in the Syrian Orient: A Contribution to the History of Culture in the Near East: The Origins of Asceticism: Early Monasticism in Persia*, CSCO Subsidia 14 (Louvain: CSCO, 1958).

VOS, J. S., 'Legem statuimus: Rhetorische Aspeckte der Gesetzesdebatte zwischen Juden und Christen', in van Amersfoort and van Oort, *Juden und Christen*, 44–60.

VOSS, B., *Der Dialog in der frühchristlichen Literatur* (Munich: W. Funk, 1970).

WALZER, R. (trans. and ed.), *Galen on Jews and Christians* (London: Oxford University Press, 1949).

WANDER, B., *Gottesfürchtige und Sympathisanten*, WUNT 104 (Tübingen: Mohr, 1998).

WEDDERBURN, A. J., *Baptism and Resurrection*, WUNT 44 (Tübingen: Mohr, 1987).

—— 'Paul's Collection: Chronology and History', *NTS* 48 (2002), 95–110.

WEIDMANN, F. W., ' "To Sojourn" or "To Dwell"?: Scripture and Identity in the *Martyrdom of Polycarp*', in Boertz and Brakke, *Reading in Christian Communities*, 29–40.

WELLS, P. S., *The Barbarians Speak: How the Conquered Peoples Shaped Roman Europe* (Princeton, NJ: Princeton University Press, 1999).

WELTIN, E. G., *Athens and Jerusalem: An Interpretative Essay on Christianity and Classical Culture*, AAR Studies in Religion 49 (Atlanta, Ga.: Scholars Press, 1987).

WERMAN, C., '*Jubilees* 30: Building a Paradigm for the Ban on Intermarriage', *HTR* 90 (1997), 1–22.

WESTCOTT, B. F., *A General Survey of the History of the Canon of the New Testament*, 7th edn. (London: Macmillan, 1896).

WHITE, L. M., 'The Delos Synagogue Revisited: Recent Fieldwork in the Graeco-Roman Diaspora', *HTR* 80 (1987), 133–60.

WHITELAM, K., *The Invention of Ancient Israel: The Silencing of Palestinian History* (London: Routledge, 1996).

WHITMARSH, T., ' "Greece is the World": Exile and Identity in the Second Sophistic', in Goldhill, *Being Greek under Rome*, 269–305.

WHITTAKER, C. R., *Frontiers of the Roman Empire: A Social and Economic Study* (Baltimore, Md.: Johns Hopkins University Press, 1994).

WHITTERS, M. F., *The Epistle of Second Baruch: A Study in Form and Message*, JSP.SS 42 (Sheffield: Sheffield Academic Press, 2003).

WILKEN, R., 'The Jews and Christian Polemics after Theodosius I *Cunctos Populos*', *HTR* 73 (1980), 451–71.

—— *The Myth of Christian Beginnings: History's Impact on Belief* (Garden City, NY: Doubleday, 1971).

—— *The Land Called Holy: Palestine in Christian History and Thought* (New Haven, Conn.: Yale University Press, 1992).

WILLIAMS, J. H. C., *Beyond the Rubicon. Romans and Gauls in Republican Italy* (Oxford: Oxford University Press, 2001).

WILLIAMS, M. A., *The Immovable Race: A Gnostic Designation and the Theme of Stability in Late Antiquity*, NHS 29 (Leiden: Brill, 1985).

—— 'Interpreting the Nag Hammadi Library as "Collection(s)" in the History of "Gnosticism(s)" ', in L. Painchaud and A. Pasquier (eds.), *Les Textes de Nag Hammadi et le problème de leur classification: Actes du Colloque tenu à Quebec des 15 au 19 septembre 1993*, BCNH Études 3 (Quebec: Presses de l'Université Laval; Louvain: Peeters, 1995), 3–50.

—— *Rethinking 'Gnosticism': An Argument for Dismantling a Dubious Category* (Princeton, NJ: Princeton University Press, 1996).

WILLIAMS, M., 'The Meaning of *Ioudaios* in Graeco-Roman Inscriptions', *ZPE* 116 (1997), 249–63.

WILLIAMS, R., 'Does It Make Sense to Speak of Pre-Nicene Orthodoxy', in idem (ed.), *The Making of Orthodoxy: Essays in Honour of Henry Chadwick* (Cambridge: Cambridge University Press, 1989), 1–23.

WILLS, L. M., *The Jewish Novel in the Ancient World* (Ithaca, NY: Cornell University Press, 1995).

—— *The Quest of the Historical Gospel: Mark, John and the Origins of the Gospel Genre* (New York: Routledge, 1997).

WILSON, B., *Patterns of Sectarianism* (London: Heinemann, 1967).

WILSON, S. G., *Related Strangers: Jews and Christians 70–170 C.E.* (Minneapolis, Minn.: Fortress, 1995).

—— and DESJARDINS, M. (eds.), *Text and Artifact in the Religions of Mediterranean Antiquity: Essays in Honour of Peter Richardson*, Studies in Christianity and Judaism 9 (Waterloo, Ont.: Wilfrid Laurier University Press for the Canadian Corporation for Studies in Religion, 2000).

WISCHMEYER, W., 'A Christian? What's That? On the Difficulty of Managing Christian Diversity in Late Antiquity', in M. F. Wiles and E. Y. Yarnold, with the assistance of P. M. Parvis (eds.), *Studia Patristica 34: Papers Presented at the 13th International Conference of Patristic Studies held in Oxford 1999* (Leuven: Peeters, 2001), 270–81.

WISSE, F., 'The Use of Early Christian Literature as Evidence for Inner Diversity and Conflict', in C. Hedrick and R. Hodgson (eds.), *Nag Hammadi, Gnosticism and Early Christianity* (Peabody: Hendrickson, 1986), 177–90.

WITHERINGTON, B., *Women in the Earliest Churches*, SNTS.MS 58 (Cambridge: Cambridge University Press, 1988).

WOLFF, E., *Europe and the People without History* (Berkeley, Calif.: University of California Press, 1982).

WOODWARD, K. (ed.), *Identity and Difference* (Milton Keynes: Open University, 1997).

WOOLF, G., 'Becoming Roman, Staying Greek: Culture, Identity and the Civilizing Process in the Roman East', *Proceedings of the Cambridge Philological Society* 40 (1994), 116–43.

YOUNG, F. M., *Biblical Exegesis and the Formation of Christian Culture* (Cambridge: Cambridge University Press, 1997).

ZLOTNICK-SIVAN, H., 'The Silent Women of Yehud: Notes on Ezra 9–10', *JJS* 51 (2000), 3–18.

INDEX OF ANCIENT AUTHORS
AND SOURCES

Authors and sources of whatever provenance are listed alphabetically. The following 'collections' of texts are grouped in their appropriate location with constituent texts listed alphabetically: Dead Sea Scrolls; Mishnah; Nag Hammadi Codices; New Testament; Old Testament and Apocrypha (as included in the NRSV). Since sequences of passages are often given to illustrate an argument, these are not all listed separately; only a selection of passages from footnotes are given.

INDEX OF SUBJECTS